Spencer E. Roberts is Professor in the Russian Department at Brooklyn College of The City University of New York. He has served with American embassies in Moscow and Vienna and was Chairman of the Russian Area Program at Rutgers — The State University. His latest book is *Essays in Russian Literature: The Conservative View.*

THE TRIBES OF ISRAEL

STUDIA SEMITICA NEERLANDICA

edited by

Prof. Dr. M. A. Beek, Prof. Dr. J. H. Hospers, Prof. Dr. Th. C. Vriezen and
Prof. Dr. R. Frankena †

C. H. J. DE GEUS

THE TRIBES OF ISRAEL

AN INVESTIGATION
INTO SOME OF THE PRESUPPOSITIONS
OF MARTIN NOTH'S
AMPHICTYONY HYPOTHESIS

1976

VAN GORCUM, ASSEN/AMSTERDAM, THE NETHERLANDS

ISBN 90 232 1337 8

Printed in The Netherlands by Van Gorcum, Assen

PREFACE

The present work is the in many parts revised and expanded version of a doctoral dissertation submitted to the Faculty of Theology of the State University at Groningen. *Promotores* were professors Dr J. H. Hospers and Dr A. S. van der Woude.

Although from my first days as a student a great admirer of the work of Martin Noth, I have also been critical of his amphictyony hypothesis for many years. But as I found it very difficult to prove that something never existed, I concentrated on what in my opinion are his most fundamental presuppositions: the twelve-tribes system(s) and the supposed process of sedentarization which is also used by Noth as a model to explain Israel's earliest history.

Of course those presuppositions are not the only ones, one could add critical questions as to Noth's literary methods or his understanding of the early development of Yahwism. I do hope that for an investigation of the latter my third chapter will prove to be useful. I am myself fully aware of the limitations of this book. To stimulate further research in this field I included the lengthy bibliography.

The quotations of biblical passages in the English language are all taken from the *New English Bible*, as are the spellings of biblical names and the abbreviations of the books of the Bible. On the other hand, references without translation refer solely to the Hebrew Bible and follow the division into verses of the Masoretic Text.

It goes without saying that I am greatly indebted to Mrs G. F. van Baaren-Pape who translated the manuscript of this rather dull book into English and so made possible its publication in print!

In conclusion I want to thank all who have given me their comments on the typewritten Dutch edition. Their remarks have been very useful!

Groningen, october 1974.

CONTENTS

ABBREVIATIONS

For the abbreviations the system was choosen of the encyclopedia *Die Religion in Geschichte und Gegenwart*, third edition ed. by Kurt Galling, and in particular those of the VIth volume, Tübingen 1962. Current dictionaries, encyclopedia's and text-editions are not included in the bibliography.

List of abbreviations which deviate or are absent from the VIth volume of the *RGG*:

AAS	Annales Archéologiques Arabes Syriennes
ADPV	Abhandlungen des Deutschen Palästina-Vereins
AES	The American Ethnological Society
AHL	Kathleen Kenyon, Archaeology in the Holy Land London 1965[2]
AJTh	American Journal of Theology
AOAT	Alter Orient und Altes Testament
AS	Assyriological Studies
BANE	"The Bible and the Ancient Near East", Albright-*Festschrift*. New York 1962
BAR	The Biblical Archaeologist Reader
BCH	Bulletin de Correspondence Hellénique
CP	Classical Philology
CR	Classical Review
DISO	Jean-Hoftijzer, Dictionaire des Inscriptions Sémitiques de l'Ouest
Dtr	Deuteronomistic History (Noth: *Das deuteronomistische Geschichtswerk*)
EAZ	Ethnographische Archäologische Zeitschrift
EI	Erets Israel
GI	Geschichte Israels
GVI	Geschichte des Volkes Israel

GSAT	Gesammelte Studien zum Alten Testament
IAE	Internationales Archiv für Etnographie
ISSJ	International Social Sciences Journal
JESHO	Journal of Economic and Social History of the Orient
KS	A. Alt, Kleine Schriften zur Geschichte Israels
MDP	Mémoires de la Délégation en Perse
MSL	Materialen zur Sumerischen Lexikon
NBG	Dutch Bible Society
NThT	Nederlands Theologisch Tijdschrift
POTT	"Peoples of Old Testament Times". Ed. by J. D. Wiseman for the Society for Old Testament Study. Oxford 1973
RAI	Rencontre Assyriologique Internationale
RSO	Rivista degli Studi Orientali
SThU	Schweizerische Theologische Umschau
SVT	Supplements to Vetus Testamentum
ThT	Theologisch Tijdschrift
TTh	Tijdschrift voor Theologie (Nijmegen)
ThZBs	Theologische Zeitschrift (Basel)
Ueb.Stud.	M. Noth, Ueberlieferungsgeschichtliche Studien. Tübingen 1957^2
UF	Ugarit Forschungen
UP	M. Noth, Ueberlieferungsgeschichte des Pentateuch. Stuttgart 1948^2
VBVHS	"Das Verhältnis von Bodenbauern und Viehzüchtern in historischer Sicht." Deutsche Akk. d. Wiss. zu Berlin, Inst. f. Orientforschung, Veröffentlichung Nr. 69, Berlin 1968

CHAPTER I

EARLIEST ISRAEL
IN MODERN HISTORIOGRAPHY

Modern research into the earliest and original meaning of the term *yiśrā'ēl* began in the eighties of the previous century. Only then did the literary historical method as developed and applied by Wellhausen come to afford a serviceable instrument for seeking out the earliest references to Israel in the Old Testament. Hence Eduard Mcyer's essay based on this method '*Kritik der Berichte über der Eroberung Palaestinas*'[1] may be regarded as the beginning of an entirely new phase in the search for Israel's most ancient history. The last two decades of that century also saw two important discoveries, which brought additional data and problems. These were the discovery of the Amarna letters in 1887, and that of the Merenptah stela in 1895.

1. From B. Stade to C. Steuernagel

Older literature on the subject of Israel's origins always took its departure from the genealogies in Gen. 10 and 11. There the descendants of Shem and Eber are contrasted with those of Ham and Canaan. The Hebrews are strictly set apart from the Canaanite original population of Canaan. Included with the Hebrews were also the Edomites, Moabites and Ammonites, who according to Genesis were closely related to the Israelites. An original tribe or people, the Hebrews, was supposed to have split up into four smaller tribes, each of which again grew into a nation: Israel, Edom, Moab and Ammon. Before the discovery of the Amarna letters, the name 'Hebrews' was generally explained as 'those on the other side', that is to say as a name given by the Canaanite population to the west of the Jordan. Later on this 'other side' was sometimes taken to be the other side of the Euphrates. A good example of this old approach is often still to be seen in the '*Geschichte des Volkes Israel*' by B. Stade.[2]

---

[1] *ZAW* I (1881) S. 117-146.
[2] Band I, Berlin 1887.

A work still entirely founded on the tradition that flourished until about 1880 is that of E. Renan.[3]

According to Stade the people of Israel originated when a tribe called Israel – one of the Hebrew tribes – was forced to leave its original habitat to the east of the Jordan around the centres Penuel and Mahanaim. The tribe was driven away there by the intrusion of the Amorites, and moved to the west, crossing the Jordan. On the other side of this river the tribe of Israel intermingled with the tribe of Jacob living there, whose centre was in Bethel. Moreover, there was a strong admixture of Canaanite elements. The tribe of Israel had already taken Yahweh as their tribal god while living east of the Jordan. Yahweh is of Arabian, Midianite origin and became the tribal god of this Hebrew tribe through the man Moses. That the tribe Israel was not entirely absorbed into the West-Jordanian population was due to its religion. Moving across the Jordan from east to west was an extremely gradual process, the last phase of which took place in the time of Saul and David. The division into exactly twelve tribes Stade regards as a late fiction on the part of the priesthood, the Israelite tribes never having actually functioned. Their origin may be sufficiently explained from the geographical situation west of the Jordan. The Hebrew tribes, including Ammon, Moab and Edom, took over almost their entire culture, even the language, from Canaan. Yet they retained their identity to a great extent. While this was so in the case of the Moabites, who always remained east of the Jordan, it was naturally still more strongly marked in the case of the Israelites. It was their superior religion, Stade thinks, which enabled them to remain themselves.[4] The difference between Israel and Canaan is first of all their religion. The difference between the Israelites and the closely related peoples east of the Jordan, is first of all the far greater intermingling of Canaanite elements.[5] Mainly under influence of Ed. Meyer, Stade later also considered the question how that first 'tribe of

---

[3] *Histoire du peuple d'Israël*. Tome I, Paris 1887[2]. The well-known books by A. H. Sayce: *The early history of the Hebrews*, London 1897 and *Early Israel and the surrounding nations*, London 1899, must also be mentioned here, as the author does not accept the historio-critical method as it was developed by Wellhausen.

[4] At that time, Canaanite culture was generally regarded as quite degenerate. Renan, *o.c.* p. 231: 'En réalité, ce monde chananéen représentait une forme de société humaine assez médiocre.'

[5] 'Da aber die vom Sinai stammende Religion Jahwes der Kanaans ebenso überlegen war, wie Israel Kanaan an sittlicher Kraft, so kam es, dass das aus der Mischung israelitischer und kananäischer Bestandteile entstehende neue Produkt in allen geistigen Dingen nach Israel schlug ... So eroberte Israel wesentlich auf friedlichem Wege Kanaan'. Stade, *o.c.* S. 140.

2

Israel' had originated.[6] He was of opinion that the later Rachel tribes developed from Semites living in Egypt. Other tribes who had migrated to Midian, there became the Leah tribes and became acquainted with the god Yahweh there in Midian. After the Exodus, the two groups formed a league that was primarily of a military nature and directed against Egypt. The centre of this confederation was the sanctuary Sinai or Kades; Yahweh became its protector. The fact that it was a *military* confederation explains the intolerance of later Yahwism.[7] This confederation was already 'Israel'. The people were still nomads, but the settled, civilized country tempted them. Their first conquest was Gilead. However, the real, historic Israel only developed after this 'Israel' had penetrated into Palestine proper and settled into a sedentary, agrarian way of life. These new conditions caused the speedy decline of the confederation. In time of war, though, 'Israel' was always formed anew around their war-god Yahweh.[8]

Although Julius Wellhausen is justly called the father of modern Israelitic historiography, he himself paid comparatively little attention to the origin and earliest history of Israel. His merit lies mainly in the literary field, not in a detailed reconstruction of Israel's history. Others were to do that after him, thanks to the historio-critical method he developed. Wellhausen himself gave only 'Prolegomena' and an 'Abriss'.[9]

An actual history of Israel cannot begin until David, according to Wellhausen, since it was only in his reign that the $m^e nuh\bar{a}$ was instituted,[10] as we hear in II Sam. 7:11 and I Kings 5:18. In his Prolegomena Wellhausen argues at length that the picture of Israel before David as organized in twelve tribes and ruled by the priesthood was created by P: it is a post-exilic fiction. 'Davids geschichtliche Bedeutung kann man nicht leicht zu hoch anschlagen. Juda und Jerusalem waren lediglich seine Schöpfungen, und wenn auch das gesammt-israelitische Reich dass er zusammen mit Saul gegründet hatte, bald zerfiel, so blieb doch die Erinnerung daran allezeit der Stolz des ganzen Volkes.'[11] David first made Israel into a political power. Yet 'Israel' itself had long existed,

[6] B. Stade, Die Entstehung des Volkes Israel. In: *Ausgewählte akademische Reden und Abhandlungen.* Giessen 1907[2].

[7] Entstehung, S. 107 seq. Influence of Wellhausen? Stade denies all connection between Chabiri and Hebrews. Hebrews is a name of honour, 'those of the other side', of the later Israelites, p. 110-113.

[8] Entstehung, S. 118.

[9] J. Wellhausen: Abriss der Geschichte Israel's und Juda's. *Skizzen und Vorarbeiten I,* Berlin 1884. *Israelitische und Jüdische Geschichte.* Berlin 1894. *Prolegomena zur Geschichte Israels.* Berlin 1905[6], Neudruck 1927.

[10] *Prolegomena,* S. 20 n. 1.

[11] Abriss, S. 26.

that is the presupposition of the action taken by David and Saul. Wellhausen saw this very clearly. But what was that Israel like? The traditional picture of Israel before David is based entirely on the fiction of P, and therefore does not conform to the facts. It would indeed be altogether improbable for the hierocratically organized Israel of P, so suddenly appearing out of the void in the desert, to have disappeared just as suddenly when the people came into a settled country. For in Judges we hear nothing of such an organization.[12] Yet development towards a unified state would not have been possible if the Israelites had not been kept together in some way or another. 'Eine gewisse innerliche Einheit bestand also, lange ehe sie in einem politischen Gemeinwesen zum Ausdruck kam; sie geht bis in die Zeit Moses zurück und Moses wird als ihr Begründer anzusehen sein.' 'Israel ist nur eine Idee. Und Israel als Idee ist gleichbedeutend mit Jahve.'[13]

According to Wellhausen, then, Moses is the creator of the concept Israel, and David gave it political shape. Thus the 'Gemeingefühl der Stämme' only came into being when a number of tribes joined together under Moses.[14]

Wellhausen considers it very doubtful whether those tribes already had any common bond before.[15] The centre of this Moses-league lay at Kades. The exact number of twelve tribes belongs to P's fiction. Earliest Israel consisted of the six Leah tribes with the addition of Joseph. These tribes were linked by Moses through belief in Yahweh.[16] An important point is that Moses institutionalized this belief in Yahweh in two separate ways. First there was the jurisdiction he directed in Kades. Wellhausen is of opinion that originally Yahwism functioned more in law than in the cult. Thus Moses did indeed become the founder of the Torah.[17] Secondly, the league of the tribes was given a military purpose. The name Israel is a programme: God fights. 'Das Kriegslager war die Wiege der Nation, es

---

[12] *Prolegomena* S. 122; on the contrary, in the period of the Judges 'sehen wir nicht die traurigen Reste einer einst unter Moses und Josua vorhandenen, dann aber zerfallenen kirchlich-politischen Ordnung, sondern die ersten Anfänge staatlicher Autorität, die sich weiter und weiter entwickelnd schliesslich zum Königtum geführt haben.'

[13] *Israelitische und Jüdische Geschichte*, S. 21. *Cf.* also S. 13 and 9: 'Das Fundament, auf dem zu allen Zeiten das Gemeinbewusstsein Israels ruhte war der Glaube: Jahve der Gott Israels und Israel das Volk Jahve's'.

[14] Abriss, S. 8.

[15] These tribes are Hebrew tribes, by which Wellhausen means: tribes from north-west Arabia and the Sinai peninsula. No relation to the Aramaeans! *Israelitische und Jüdische Geschichte*, S. 8.

[16] Abriss, S. 10.

[17] *Ibid.*

war auch das älteste Heiligtum. Da war Israel und da war Jahve'.[18] War and justice were religious matters before they became institutions of profane life. Beside these two main supports of the new covenant Israel, the old tribal organizations long remained in existence, and the old tribal gods were also long-lived. This war-like league of tribes named 'Israel' then speedily fell apart after entering into the agricultural country, owing to the new, peaceful circumstances.[19]

In 1881, Eduard Meyer rather abruptly gave a new turn to research after the origins of Israel by his decided statement 'dass von historisch verwerthbaren Nachrichten über die Eroberung Palaestinas, geschweige denn über die älteren Zustände des Landes, nicht die Rede sein kann.'[20] In his view, the Old Testament contains no traditions giving us a histori- cally reliable picture of the period of the entry into Palestine, nor of any earlier period. Israel's earliest history remains nebulous. That is the period of their transition from a nomadic people to a people of farmers. On the one hand, this transition was accompanied by the gradual breaking up of the organization patterns of the nomadic period. The tribes fall apart into smaller groups which are inclined to become independent, while other groups are assimilated, etc. On the other hand, new political units are formed in the settled country: the town, the city-state and finally the national state. This is a general process, inherent in sed- entarization.[21] Like Stade, Meyer assumes that there was originally a tribe 'Israel'. This tribe was already settled in Palestine in the thirteenth century B.C.E., since it is mentioned on the stela of Merenptah, and mainly resided on the mountain-slopes either side of the Jordan. The tribe, of a strict military organization, enters as part of the host of the 'Chabiri',[22] who swept over Syria and Palestine in the fourteenth century. Although entering the region of its subsequent residence from the east, the tribe Israel itself hailed from the northwest-Arabian desert area, as is apparent from a comparison of the name Israel with *y^erahm^e'ēl*

---

[18] *Ibid.*
[19] *Ibid.* S. 12, Wellhausen even speaks of an 'unorganisiertes Conglomerat gleich- artiger Elemente'.
[20] Ed. Meyer, Kritik der Berichte über die Eroberung Palaestinas. *ZAW* I (1881) S. 145. *Cf. Geschichte des Altertums* II, 2, S. 203.
[21] *Geschichte des Altertums* I, 1, S. 13 *seq.*
[22] Chabiri = 'Leute von Jenseits' *sc.* from the other side of the Jordan. According to Meyer this is the Canaanite name for those parts of the population of Aramaean descent from the Syro-Arabian desert. It was always spelt 'Chabiri' in the older literature. At first Meyer identified the 'Chabiri' with the Israelites, *Cf.* Der Stamm Jakob und die Entstehung der israelitischen Stämme, *ZAW* VI (1886) S. 11, after- wards he changed his mind.

or *yišmāʿēl*.[23] Their belief in the god Yahweh the Israelites brought with them from the south. While still living as Hebrews (= 'Chabiri') and as nomads in the desert, they had already known him as the El of Sinai. Thus, says Meyer, Yahweh and Israel belong together of old.[24] However, once this strong tribe Israel had given up nomadic life, it quickly crumbled and fell apart into a number of smaller units. The nucleus remained the Ephraimite mountain country. What we now call the Israelite tribes, are in fact later, secondary developments.[25] Ephraim, Benjamin, Issachar, Gilead are names which only originated in the settled country, from which they can be explained. The genealogical system of the twelve tribes supposed to derive from a single ancestor through their eponyms is entirely without historical value; it simply renders the situation at a particular moment of time and seeks to explain it.[26] The number twelve is artificial, a sacred number. Not only did the great tribal league of Israel fall apart into smaller groups, there was also a process of assimilation. In the settled country a number of groups were assimilated which are now usually called the southern tribes: Judah, Levi, Simeon; these tribes had a completely different background. Meyer speaks of 'edomitische und halbedomitische Südstämme'.[27] This negative attitude towards Judah is typical of Meyer, and had considerable influence after him.[28] Of these tribes, Simeon and Levi were entirely absorbed into Israel, but not so Judah. Judah always kept up a close bond with the Edomite-Ishmaelite group.[29] It is of importance that Meyer considers II Sam. 19:44 as part of an earlier genealogical system in which Israel

[23] *Geschichte des Altertums*, II, 2, S. 214.
[24] *Die Israeliten und ihre Nachbarstämme*, S. 213, espec. note 3.
[25] *Ibid.* S. 506.
[26] *Geschichte des Altertums*, I, 2, S. 362.
[27] *Die Israeliten und ihre Nachbarstämme*, Ss. 248 and 446. Meyer would keep open the possibility that we have to do with an earlier phase of the westward migration of the Aramaeans, since Ja'udi and Jahu are also found in northern Syria. To this group also belong Jerahme'el, Kenan/Caleb, Korah, Cain/Amalek. Originally the southern tribes inhabited the northern Sinai desert with Kades Barnea as their religious centre. Here the tribe of Levi lived. Annual markets were held there, and lawsuits decided for the surrounding tribes. Here Meyer even refers to the classical amphictyonies! (*Cf. o.c.* p. 80).
[28] Thus in his *Prolegomena* Wellhausen takes a much more negative view of Judah's inclusion in Israel than he did in the earlier Abriss, no doubt under influence of Meyer.
[29] 'Ueberhaupt ist es nur eine Fiktion, dass der Stamm Juda zu Israel gehöre. Im theologischen Sprachgebrauch der Propheten und Gesetzbücher wird sie festgehalten, aber im realen Leben ist bis auf die im 19. Jahrhundert aufgekommene Prüderie niemals ein Jude als Israelit bezeichnet worden!' *Geschichte des Altertums II*, 2, S. 215.

and Judah are called brothers, as Moab and Ammon were regarded as brothers.[30] The later system of the twelve tribes reflects conditions in the reign of David and Solomon.

Thus in the twelfth and thirteenth century the various groups of Israelites in Palestine lived without much contact with one another, 'eine durch irgend eine reale Institution vertretene Einheit Israels gab es nicht mehr, nich einmal, soweit wir sehen können, in der Form einer lockeren Konföderation oder eines gemeinsamen Heiligtums mit Bundesversammlungen.'[31]

Bernard Luther closely follows Ed. Meyer, continuing on the same lines and working out some ideas in further detail.[32] He places the original Israel in Ephraim and Gilead. A later addition was the Jacob group coming from the south and closely related to Edom. Only after entry into the cultivated lands did the actual tribes come into being. They really only functioned as geographical areas, at least in historical times. Some tribal and many family names are obvious geographical names: Ephraim, Manasseh, Machir, Zebulon, Issachar. In the O.T. a person's tribe is very rarely mentioned, 'im grossen und ganzen sind aber die das geschichtliche Leben bestimmenden Faktoren nicht die Stämme, sondern der Gegensatz zwischen Israel und Juda!'[33] Israel and Judah were originally fraternal peoples, Luther deduces from II Sam. 19:44. We saw above that Meyer took over this thesis from Luther. It was David who joined these peoples together into a single kingdom. In the time of the Judges Luther only acknowledges an ideal unity of Israel, consisting of Yahwism.[34] The system of statute-labour under Solomon, divided over the twelve months of the year, gave rise to the later theory of exactly twelve tribes (1 Kings 4). Judah was only incorporated into the system when it had actually become a son of Jacob or Israel, that is in the ninth century under Ahab.[35] In the older parts of the Old Testament Israel always means the Northern Realm!

The first phase of research into Israel's origins was rounded off by C. Steuernagel. His monograph on the Entry of the Israelite tribes may still be regarded as one of the most important contributions towards the

[30] *Die Israeliten und ihre Nachbarstämme*, S. 230 *seq.*; *Geschichte des Altertums* S 258, 283.

[31] *Die Israeliten und ihre Nachbarstämme*, S. 507. But see *ad.* S. 80 and here note 38 for the southern tribes, who must have had something of the kind at Kades!

[32] B. Luther, Die israelitische Stämme. *ZAW* XXI (1901) S. 1-77. *Cf.* also his contribution to Meyer's *Die Israeliten und ihre Nachbarstämme*.

[33] Die israelitische Stämme, S. 22.

[34] S. 20 *seq.*

[35] Ss. 32 a. 49.

solution of this problem.[36] In a changed form, Steuernagel takes up the thesis of Stade that the classification of the tribes (and also the tribes themselves!) goes back to original female figures. Behind the later tribal systems an earlier classification is still visible going back to the wives of the tribal ancestor: the groups of Rachel (with Bilhah) and Leah (with Zilpah). These two groups each had a separate Conquest and only coalesced in Canaan. The Leah group, which was afterwards to split into quite a number of tribes, was part of the movement of the 'Chabiri'. Their arrival in Palestine took place towards the end of the fifteenth century, and for Palestine this group may be identified with the 'Chabiri' of the Amarna letters. The Leah group first settled in the central mountain country. Steuernagel thinks he can show that most tribes first lived on or near Mount Ephraim. An exception is the tribe of Judah. Between Judah and Ephraim there was originally Reuben. Transjordan was colonized from the west (see the example of Reuben)! From the vicissitudes of the ark one can still see that the centre was the Ephraimite mountain country. The direction of the Entry by the Leah groups was south-east to north-west. The Rachel group came almost a century later. This group goes back to a tribe of Jacob also belonging to the 'Chabiri', but who halted before the Jordan and in Transjordan remained living for a considerable time in the region of Gilead.[37] The Rachel group, with the old Jacob tribe as nucleus, crossed the Jordan at the Jabbok and then penetrated into the country conquered by the Leah group (Genesis 35!). Thus the Conquest of the Rachel group followed the direction north to south. This group was also much more militant than the Leah group. Their leader was Joshua. The name Israel was perhaps originally the battle-cry and watch-word of the Rachel group. The meaning is: 'El fights'. It is also possible, though, that the name Israel preserves the memory of the amalgamation of a Jacob tribe and a Rachel tribe. Then the name Israel would be a corruption of 'īš rāḥēl. In either case, however, the name turned from a battle-cry into the name of a people.[38] The elder Leah group coalesced with the Rachel group into Israel as we meet with it in the time of the Judges. In Canaan the Rachel group

[36] C. Steuernagel, *Die Einwanderung der Israelitischen Stämme in Kanaan*. Berlin 1901.
[37] Steuernagel strongly contests the accepted view of the time that Jacob was a Canaanite hero. S. 61. He thinks it wrong to follow Luther and then Meyer in shifting Jacob's change of name to Israel from Gilead to Bethel. S. 62.
[38] It must be emphasized that Steuernagel only suggests the derivation from 'īš rāḥēl on S. 62 as a possibility. This derivation has mistakenly been represented in the literature as Steuernagel's preference. Actually, he always bases his argument on the translation given on S. 61: 'El kämpft, *scil.* für ihn/uns'.

divided almost at once into Ephraim, Manasseh and Benjamin. Only Judah, through its isolated position, remained outside Israel. That is the reason why in the time of the Judges Israel and Judah exist independently side by side. The genealogical systems only originated much later. Steuernagel distinguishes three of them: the oldest has Levi, Joseph and Dinah as ordinary tribes, but does not yet include Benjamin (Gen. 29). The second no longer has Dinah, but does include Benjamin. In the youngest Levi is missing, and Joseph has split up into Ephraim and Manasseh. In the time of the Judges there was a rather loose bond between these tribes, only based on the fact that they had the same religion and belonged to the same God.[39] The conviction carried by this reconstruction is largely due to the way Steuernagel regards the tales of the patriarchs and tribal ancestors as primarily old legends of the Entry. In the legend Jacob, Abraham, Joseph etc. appear as persons, but actually they are personifications of tribes and tribal groups.

Thus for Steuernagel every marriage becomes an amalgamation of tribes, and every journey the migration of a tribe.[40] There is no question, therefore, of a backward projection from the time of the Kings, as Wellhausen and to some extent Stade view the traditions of Genesis. Yet also the view of Luther and Meyer is rejected, who looked upon the traditions as historicized myths, the patriarchs and others having originally been gods. The stories did contain historically reliable memories, but their origin was not historical; the material was of mythological origin. Steuernagel on the contrary, while acknowledging that mythology may have helped to determine the outward form of the legends, denies that they originated in mythology.

Obviously a historical reconstruction after this fashion is more convincing than reconstructions which have no other support than material which the authors themselves consider to be of doubtful historical reliability. Such can never be satisfactory in the long run.

2. H. Winckler

Yet the general tendency around the turn of the century was towards a mythological explanation. Only later was Steuernagel to be appreciated

---

[39] 'Die Einheit is also schon zur Zeit der Debora vorhanden, aber sie ist lediglich eine ideale, die Einheit der Religion.' S. 8. This theme always returns in Steuernagel's later studies, cf. Jahwe, der Gott Israels. *BZAW 27 (Wellhausen Festschrift)* (1914) S. 329-349. And: Jahwe und die Vätergötter, *Festschrift G. Beer.* Stuttgart 1935, S. 62-71.
[40] Although Steuernagel has the reputation of having introduced this tribe-historical exegesis of the tales of the patriarchs, honesty bids us state that we already also found this view in *Geschichte des Volkes Israel* by C. H. Cornill, 1898.

as he deserved. Scholars at that time were carried away, to a greater or lesser extent, by 'pan–Babylonism'. H. Winckler especially must be noticed here.[41] Winckler begins by assuming that the Old Testament does not contain historically reliable information regarding the origin and the earliest history of Israel. What we have are historicized myths. These were originally astral myths. The identification of Jacob and Israel, for instance, was possible because both were originally moon-gods. Joseph is a sun-god. Sometimes the myth had difficulty with the astral interpretation of certain data. Thus the dividing of Joseph into Ephraim and Manasseh is an artifice in order to arrive at the number of twelve tribes after the twelve months, the sons of the moon-god.[42]

Just like Stade, Winckler takes it that the $b^e n\bar{e}$ $yi\acute{s}r\bar{a}'\bar{e}l$ were only a small part of a much greater wandering people, the Hebrews. These Hebrews are the Ḥabiri of the Amarna letters. Ḥabiri is the collective name given by the sedentary Canaanite population to the nomads who were penetrating into the country since the beginning of the second millennium. This Entry was very gradual. Winckler will not hear of a big military campaign, centrally directed. On this point he quite agrees with Meyer's judgement as to the reliability of the biblical information. That the various groups (hordes) of Hebrews coalesced into tribes and then into a tribal league was the result of a different process, of sedentarization.[43] Before coming into Palestine the Hebrew groups who were to become the Israelites had no contact with one another, any more than they made contact after arriving with the groups in the region of the later kingdom of Judah. All other Hebrew groups were equally strange to them. Their happening to be neighbours, and the necessity of defending common interests against a common enemy, were the factors which both brought and kept them together.[44] From this reconstruction, Winckler

---

[41] H. Winckler, *Geschichte Israels in Einzeldarstellungen*. 2 Tle, Leipzig 1895 and 1900. The great work of this school is P. Jensen, *Das Gilgameschepos in der Weltliteratur*. Strassburg 1906. *Cf.* also his *Moses, Jesus, Paulus. Drei Sagenvarianten des babylonischen Gottmenschen Gilgamesch*. Frankfurt a. Main 1909. D. Völter followed the identical method in *Ägypten und die Bibel*. Leiden 1903, only starting from the culture of Egypt.

[42] *Geschichte Israels in Einzeldarstellungen*, II, S. 55 *seq.*; S. 67 *seq.* The derivation of the number twelve from the Zodiac or the twelve months is an obvious idea and has often been borrowed, also by H. Gunkel in his Genesis commentary (*HK I, 1* Göttingen 1902² S. 293; 1922⁵ S. 332).

[43] The definitive union of the tribes only took place under Saul and David. Yet Winckler distils from Judg. 3 that then there already lived a tribal league 'Israel' in the Ephraimite mountain country. Benjamin did not yet belong to it, being added to Israel by Saul. *I*, S. 50.

[44] Especially *I*, S. 156 and 20 *seq.*

draws an interesting and logical conclusion: it is inconsistent to call up a picture on the one hand of a very gradual penetration into Palestine and a long period of growing into one coherent people, and on the other hand to attempt to explain the later process from a unity of the Israelite tribes supposed to have existed before the Conquest. In the first place Winckler thinks it extremely unlikely that an existing whole should as it were dissolve into very little groups, intrude into a country, and after great difficulties again become a single people there.[45] Secondly, if the expression of the unity of the Israelites was always their joint belief in Yahweh, it is very strange indeed that the 'Sitz des Kultes'of this Yahweh was not in their country of origin, but by the Sinai or Horeb in the Midianite country.[46] In other words, if one assumes that David was the first to unite the twelve tribes, as Winckler explicitly does, then it must be considered methodically wrong to postulate this unity as a 'spiritual unity' in preceding times, expressed in Yahwism. In that case one would certainly expect the 'Sitz des Kultes' to lie in the Transjordan. On the other hand, if one does not assume a 'spiritual unity' in the time before David, then one would expect to find the 'Sitz des Kultes' in Palestine itself. In this perplexity, Winckler broaches a somewhat modified 'Kenite theory': Yahweh is the god of the groups who afterwards were to form the kingdom of Judah under Caleb. This god was of Midianite or Edomite origin.[47] This is the 'Jahve des ewigen Seins'.[48] Besides this new god, the Canaanite pantheon had long known a god Yahu. This Yahu was of old worshipped on Mount Sinai. David identified his god Yahweh[49] with Yahu who was worshipped by some Israelite tribes and known to the others.[50]

Winckler was followed along this path by his pupil W. Erbt, who devoted a monograph to the subject.[51] Erbt also identifies the Hebrews

---

[45] Ed. Sachsse, *Die Bedeutung des Namens Israel II*, S. 90 *seq.* (see below) shows that the penetration of the Germanic tribes into the Roman empire did indeed take place after this fashion. The process is therefore less improbable than it would seem at first sight.

[46] Here Winckler is polemizing with Stade (on whom he very strongly depends) and assumes an original Israel east of the Jordan. *Cf.* also the 'Sittimstaat' of C. Niebuhr, *Geschichte des Ebräischen Zeitalters*, I Band. Berlin 1894.

[47] Winckler supposes a confusion in the O T between *Miṣraim* = Egypt and *Muṣri* = Midian/Edom. *I*, S. 29.

[48] *I*, S. 38.

[49] David was a Calebite chief from Hebron, for Winckler takes the expression *roš kālẹb* in II Sam. 3:8 literally. *I*, S. 25.

[50] *I*, S. 35 *seq.*

[51] W. Erbt, *Die Hebräer. Kanaan im Zeitalter der hebräischen Wanderung und hebräischer Staatengründungen*. Leipzig 1906.

as the Ḥabiri, and lets them form a kingdom 'Israel' east of the Jordan,[52] existing from about 1500 to 1220, and finally destroyed by Merenptah.[53] This Israel was essentially identical with what was afterwards to be known as the tribe of Gad.[54] The capital of this kingdom was Peniel. The Jacob traditions recount the prehistory of this kingdom 'Israel'. Survivors of this kingdom fled across the Jordan, where they formed tribes and set up a tribal league under a priestly ruler, with Shechem as its centre. Erbt then reverses Steuernagel's famous sequence, and only lets the four 'real Leah tribes' migrate northward at a much later date. These tribes are accepted into a new tribal league. Moses and Joseph were the leaders of the Leah tribes, and it was only with them that Yahwism came to Israel.

In the early time of the Kings, Saul and David consciously went back to the traditions of that old kingdom Israel east of the Jordan, 'melek jisra'el ist nun derjenige, der über Pənu'el-Maḥanaim verfügt'.[55]

3. B. D. Eerdmans and F. M. Th. Böhl

We see, then, how in the course of research two particular problems come to the fore. Firstly: in what way and to what extent can the traditions

[52] *Cf.* note 46. For this, support is sought in the puzzling text of Judg. 11:26.
[53] The initial enthusiasm at the finding of the stela of Merenptah in 1895 soon cooled down, when its mention of Israel soon proved to make the problem of the Conquest more difficult rather than easier of solution. (W. Spiegelberg, Die erste Erwähnung Israels in einem ägyptischen Texte. *Sitzungsberichte der Berliner Akademie der Wissenschaften*, Jahrgang 1896, S. 593-598. G. Steindorf, Israel in einer altägyptischen Inschrift. *ZAW* XVI (1896) S. 330-334). The stela was found in the pharaoh's temple and its date is well attested; even if the text may be composed of some separate songs, the chance that all or one of them might be much older than the time of Merenptah, who ruled from 1224-1216, is considered practically nil. This means that around 1220 the pharaoh already found a people named Israel in Palestine. The determinative following the name Israel shows that this Israel is not regarded as a long-established inhabitant. Many would have preferred it, if this mention of Israel could have been dated two centuries earlier, in the Amarna period and well before the events around the Exodus and Entry. Erbt's solution, then, is really a compromise: the Israel of the stela is not yet the later true Israel. This is seen even more plainly in C. F. Lehman-Haupt, *Israel. Seine Entwicklung im Rahmen der Weltgeschichte*. Tübingen 1911. The Israel of the stela is here identified with the Israel that wandered in the desert and came to Kades (S. 29). It is, indeed, impossible to tell where the stela would place the habitat of the people or tribe 'Israel'. See for this problem *e.g.* B. D. Eerdmans, *Alttestamentliche Studien* II, S. 57 *seq.* and F. Böhl, *Kanaanäer und Hebräer*, S. 78 *seq.* see note 67.
[54] Erbt already points out the indeed rather common connexion ḥabiru-ḥabattu (= robber). Gad also means robber according to Erbt, being a derivation of *gᵉdud*, *o.c.* S. 40 *seq.*
[55] S. 23.

about the patriarchs and their sons be used by the historian as source material for the origins of Israel and its earliest history? Secondly: what is the relationship between the Israelites and the Hebrews or Ḥabiru?

Both problems are central in the fairly sharp criticism Eerdmans brings to bear on the Old Testament scholars of his day.[56] It is not permissible, he says, to approach all the Genesis traditions from the same angle, either viewing them all as projections into the past from the time of the Kings (Wellhausen) or as material that was originally mythological (Meyer) or possibly astral (Winckler), or interpreting too much material as tribal history (Steuernagel).[57] The content of Genesis is far too varied for such treatment! Eerdmans is convinced, however, that there is a historically reliable nucleus, even though it is plain that the various legends were read and worked over until far later times.

Eerdmans then strongly criticizes the great presupposition underlying all these theories, viz. that the Hebrews, the ancestors of the later Israelites, were nomads and lived as Beduin, so that the Conquest comes to coincide with *sedentarization*.[58]

Once one has formed a picture of the patriarchs on the analogy of the modern Beduin, the travels of Abraham and Jacob can naturally be fitted in splendidly with the far greater migration of the Ḥabiru, who were then generally regarded as a people thrusting into settled country from the desert. The Ḥabiru formed one of the many waves of nomads, accustomed at set times to make an attack upon the settled, civilized

---

[56] B. D. Eerdmans, *Alttestamentliche Studien, Band II, Die Vorgeschichte Israels*. Giessen 1908.

[57] 'Die Patriarchen sind ursprunglich keine Götter. Die Patriarchensagen sind keine mythologischen Erzählungen. Die Patriarchensagen sind keine Abspiegelungen der ethnologischen Verhältnisse und Kultuseinrichtungen der Königzeit.' S. 5. *Cf.* espec. p. 48-51. The nucleus of the legends is formed by the persons. This view was also defended by H. Gressmann, Sage und Geschichte in den Patriarchenerzählungen, *ZAW* XXX (1910) S. 1-35. For this interpretation of the Genesis traditions, one should particularly consult the famous introduction in the Genesis commentary of Gunkel (see note 42).

[58] Eerdmans, *o.c.* S. 38-48. The much read travel books of Burckhardt, Burton, Doughty and others gave rise in Europe to a far too romantic conception of the Beduin and the Arabs in general. (It is by no means fortuitous that the works of Karl May treat both of Indians and of Arabs!). The consequences for Old Testament studies show up clearly in the afterwards famous essay of K. Budde, Das nomadische Ideal im Alten Testament. *Preussische Jahrbücher*, Band 85 (1896) S. 57-79. Eerdmans justly points out that the Beduin are not the only Arabs, even if they consider themselves so. The world of the great majority of the Syro-Palestine Arabs looks entirely different. Eerdmans points to the researches of A. Jaussen, *Coutumes des Arabes au pays de Moab*. Paris 1908.

country (a decadent civilization, of course!). Eerdmans most strongly denies that the patriarchs, and thus the earliest known ancestors of the Israelites, are depicted as nomads. Certainly Meyer and Wellhausen always spoke of *semi-nomads*, but then they went on to argue as if they had to do with full nomads. It is Abraham who has the most resemblance to a Beduin: 'die meisten Züge, welche an das Nomadenleben erinnern, finden wir in den Abrahamsagen. Er zieht von Haran nach Mamre, dort wohnt er in einem Zelte und bewirtet seine Gäste mit Milch und Butter (18, 1 ff.). Er besitzt Herden und seine Knechte sind Hirten 13, 2, 7. Ein echter Nomade ist er aber nicht. Er wohnt während längerer Zeit an einem Orte und bricht nur auf, um sich für längere Zeit an einem andern Orte anzusiedeln. Er lebt nicht, wie ein Nomade, von den Milch der Herden, sondern ist für seinen Lebensunterhalt hauptsächlich auf die Produkte des Ackerbaus angewiesen (12, 10). Wenn Hungersnot da ist, zieht er in das Kulturland Aegypten. Genesis 13 setzt voraus, dass Abraham und Lot sich ansiedeln wollen. Darum wählt jeder eine bestimmte Gegend zum Wohnen (*yšb*). Von Lot wird sogar berichtet, dass er in Städten wohnt (13, 12; 18; 19). Auch Abraham wohnt bei den Terebinthen von Mamre als ein sesshafter Mann und kann darum (23, 4) sagen, dass er ein 'Ger und Tošab' bei den Stadtbewohnern Hebrons ist. Vielleicht würde man bei 23, 4 einwenden, dass hier keine alte Sage vorliegt, weil man Genesis 23 P zuteilt. Dem gegenüber verweise ich auf 'Die Komposition der Genesis' S. 20 f., wo gezeigt wurde, dass Genesis 23 alter ist als P und in die vorexilische Zeit zurückgehen muss. Es lässt sich nicht denken, dass P eine Erzählung erfinden würde, welche den Heroenkult und die Ahnenverehrung förderte. Aber auch, wenn wir Genesis 23 bei Seite lassen, bleibt es dabei, dass Abraham ein Halbnomade ist, der den Bauern näher steht als den Beduinen.'[59]

Eerdmans demonstrates in detail that cattle-breeding does not *necessarily* entail living as a semi-nomad. Even if one must join the herds for a time, one's permanent dwelling remains in one of the many townlets of the period. Cf. the way of life of Laban, Judah (Genesis 3) and Nabal (I Sam. 25).

In chapter III we hope to show how much Eerdmans was ahead of his time with this insight. Nevertheless, he certainly went too far in also maintaining that the Kenites were not nomads, and that the 'seed' on the stela of Merenptah must be taken literally, so that 'Israel' would already be represented there as an agrarian people.[60] Eerdmans again

[59] S. 40.
[60] S. 45 a. 55. For the text of the stela in an English translation, see *ANET* p. 375-378.

disconnects the origin of the people of Israel from the Exodus and the Entry. The Merenptah stela shows that Israel was already in Palestine around 1230. The Exodus of a small group of Hebrews from Egypt and their Entry into Palestine only took place a century later.[61] The real Israelites were in no way connected with these Hebrews, but were descended from Aramaean groups who settled in the wadis of Palestine as semi-nomads.[62] Eerdmans also rejects the identification of Hebrews and Ḥabiru. However, his suggestion Ḥabiru // Ḥawiru // Horites is philologically untenable.[63] In his rejection of nomadism for the patriarchs and his emphasis upon the agrarian background of the stories in Genesis, Eerdmans was only followed by H. Gressmann[64] and by H. Weinheimer.[65] A. H. Sayce, indeed, had already pointed out earlier that it is quite mistaken to represent the patriarchs as Beduin. It is just the true Beduin, like the Amalekites, who are the arch-enemies of the Israelites! 'The fact is important, and the forgetfulness of it has led more than one historian astray!'[66]

[61] Eerdmans, o.c. S. 77 seq.

[62] S. 82.

[63] Cf. already H. Th. Obbink, Het Exodus Vraagstuk, ThT XLIII (1909) p. 238-258 and ThT XLIV (1910) p. 127-161.

[64] In spite of the promising title, Gressmann in 'Die Anfänge Israels'. Göttingen 1914, 1922², has hardly anything historical to tell us of Israel's origin. He too regards the intruding Hebrews (= Ḥabiri) as intruding Aramaeans (S. 8-14). The culture of the earliest Israelites and of Genesis was that of semi-nomads There were three stages: 1) agriculture (original Cain); 2) semi-nomads (Abel); nomads (Cain after the curse). Sage und Geschichte, S. 25 seq. espec. also S. 27³. The semi-nomad is far closer to the farmer than to the Beduin! (S. 28). Also B. Stade rightly stressed in his famous essay Das Kainszeichen, ZAW XIV (1894), S. 259 seq., that the life of the Beduin was seen as a curse! The patriarchs lived in the northern Negeb. The transition from Hebrews to Israelites coincides with the appearance of Moses. Israel's origin goes back to the single tremendous personality of Moses, who founded Yahwism as a religion and called Israel into being as a separate people by his juridical and political prescripts. Mose und seine Zeit. Ein Kommentar zu den Mose-Sage. Göttingen 1913. See further below.

[65] In two articles, Hebräer und Israeliten, ZAW XXIX (1909) S. 275 seq. and Die Einwanderung der Hebräer und der Israeliten in Kanaan, ZDMG LXXVI (1912) S. 365-389, H. Weinheimer attempted to ascribe all data concerning Hebrews and the long journeys of the patriarchs and all excessive territorial claims (such as e.g. in Josh. 1) to a Ḥabiru source. This would have preserved all kinds of traditions which did not originally concern Israel, but the migration of the Ḥabiru in general. Everything in the O.T. recalling nomads etc. belongs to Ḥabiru tradition. Abraham was originally one of the leaders of the Ḥabiru. The patriarchs of Israel, on the contrary, were not nomads. One might at most term them semi-nomads, but certainly settled and agrarian. 'Die Knechte ziehen mit den Herden durch die Steppe. Der Herr aber bleibt zu Hause und wohnt bei seinen Äckern als sesshafter Mann!' (Die Einwanderung, S. 386).

[66] Early Israel and the Surrounding Nations, p. 51.

The Hebrew-Ḥabiru problem was provisionally elucidated by F. Böhl.[67] His famous conclusions are: 1) 'Alle Israeliten sind Hebräer, aber nicht alle Hebräer sind Israeliten. 2) Die Israeliten heissen Hebräer hauptsächlich gegenüber und im Munde von Ausländer'.[68] Böhl summarizes the matter as follows: 'Hebräer ist die Bezeichnung einer ganzen Völkergruppe, zu der neben anderen auch die Israelstämme gehören. Sich selbst bezeichnet der Israelit mit dem Ehrennamen seines eigenen Stammes und Volkes; der weiteren Perspektive des Auslandes dagegen gilt er – doch nicht konsequent – als Angehöriger der grossen Volksgruppe.'[69] That which separated some Hebrews from the rest of the Hebrews/ Ḥabiru and made them into Israelites, were the events at Kades and Sinai. The difference was primarily of a religious nature, and that explains why it was seen much more clearly by the Israelites themselves than by outsiders. It must be remarked that the fact that the determinative following the name 'Israel' on the stela of Merenptah is the determinative for foreign peoples, may not lead to the conclusion that Israel was then not yet sedentary. In Egyptian, there are only two ordinary names for Palestine: Canaan and Ḥaru; every other name *had* to be followed by the determinative for foreign peoples.[70] Exodus and Entry would have taken place long before Merenptah, in the Amarna period.[71]

In judging Böhl's work one must take account of the fact that he disposed of the new data and texts regarding the Ḥabiru which had come to light during Winckler's excavations at Boghazköy. These set the whole Ḥabiru problem in a much wider perspective, so that from a specific Old Testament problem, it became a problem touching the ancient history of the whole Near East.

The discovery of the state and the culture of the Hittites – which had been postulated more than a decade before by A. H. Sayce and others[72] – not only made it quite clear that the Hebrews could at most have been a branch of the far greater Ḥabiru migration, but also that their entrance upon the scene was of comparatively recent date. This swept away all earlier notions of the Hebrews/Ḥabiru as one of the oldest peoples in the world. The Israelites proved to be a *young* people and new-comers in Hither Asia. The direct genealogical descent of the Israelites from the

---

[67] F. (M. Th.) Böhl, *Kanaanäer und Hebräer. Untersuchungen zur Vorgeschichte des Volkstums und der Religion Israels auf dem Boden Kanaans.* BWAT 9, Leipzig 1911.
[68] *o.c.* S. 67.
[69] S. 73.
[70] S. 78.
[71] Here Böhl follows Obbink, *cf.* note 63.
[72] In his *Early Israel and the Surrounding Nations.*

ancestors of all the Semites, as set forth in Gen. 10, thus really became impossible. As we have seen, it was early recognized that the determinant element in Israel's national character was its religion. It was Yahweh, through whom Israel became Israel. This was repeated again and again. Yet at the same time Yahwism was seen to develop from a primitive monolatry into the much praised 'ethical monotheism' just as gradually, as the later people of Israel was seen to emerge from its Hebrew background. The opening of the Hittite and Mesopotamian archives made it more and more plain that Israel is a new-comer and that it is very hard to explain the phenomenon of 'Israel' by way of evolution.

Though in a lesser degree than by the discovery of the archives of Boghazköy, a somewhat similar effect was evoked by the publication of the stela found at Susa in 1902, with the since famous Codex of Ḥammurapi.[73] Ancient Babylon now also proved to have had a legal code of high level, so that Israel's claim to be first in the field was destroyed at a blow. Moreover, the great resemblance between laws of the Code of Ḥammurapi and e.g. laws of the Book of the Covenant compelled one to conclude that either the Old Testament had borrowed certain laws from the Mesopotamian legislation, or that both derived from still older prototypes, but that in any case such legislation could not have originated in Israel. The discovery of this stela just while the pan-Babylonian school was in full flower, naturally afforded strong support to those scholars who opined that Mesopotamia was the source of nearly all the traditions in the Old Testament, and confirmed their view that Israel constituted but one aspect of a far larger culture in Hither Asia, of which Mesopotamia was the centre.

4. The school of 'Religionsgeschichte'. Ed. Sachsse and W. Caspari

For the great majority of the Old Testament scholars, however, there was an alternative: if Israel as a people and Yahwism as an ethical religion are not extremely ancient but comparatively young, then it is very likely that the Old Testament traditions of the *founding* of a religion by Moses are based on truth. And indeed, around 1900 one suddenly sees that a good deal of interest comes to be taken in the man Moses and his work. The central question here, put forward especially by the 'religionsgeschichtliche Schule', is that of the relationship between the history of Yahwism and the history of the people of Israel. How does 'Israel' as a religious entity stand to 'Israel' as a people? This question was centred upon the person of Moses. In the nineteenth century, as

[73] V. Scheil, *MDP 4*, Paris 1902, p. 11-162 + pl. 3-15.

17

we have seen, the history of the religion and of the people were taken to be largely parallel. Just as Israel preserved the language of Paradise, so it also remained faithful to the creator god, from whom the other peoples, one by one, fell away. The idea of an Israelite primordial monotheism as we find it in the work of E. Renan became widely known.[74] Yet also a scholar such as Ed. Meyer always stressed that, to whatever date Israel might go back as a people – and he certainly did not take it so far back as Renan – Yahweh and Israel belonged together of old.[75] A clearly evolutionist conception of Israel's religion is presented by R. Smend in his renowned 'Alttestamentliche Religionsgeschichte'. According to Smend also, in the final instance Yahwism developed from the Semitic primordial religion, and Yahweh too was originally a nature-god.[76] The significance of Moses, then, was primarily in the politico-historical field. He caused a number of Hebrew tribes to join together in a league of Yahweh, on the basis of a history that had been their common experience. Moses did not bring a strange god to these tribes, no, one or more of them already worshipped this god.

Similar views were also held by O. Procksch, for whom Moses was also primarily the 'founder of a people' and not the 'founder of a religion'. The god Moses proclaimed was truly the 'God of their Fathers'.[77] In general, however, the trend of Stade and Wellhausen is continued and the significance of Moses is seen in his introduction of a new god, who may or may not be of Midianite or Kenite origin. That Israel became a separate people is then regarded as the result of this founding of a religion. We already saw that Wellhausen conceived Israel as first of all an 'idea', which came into being when Moses brought together some tribes on the basis of belief in Yahweh.[78] This role of Moses was discussed in a number of studies, of which we can only mention here[79] those of G. Beer,[80] H. Gressmann[81] and P. Volz.[82]

[74] *Histoire du peuple d'Israel*, p. 108 *seq.* he already develops a remainder theology: the pure religion passed from the Semites to the Hebrews and subsequently to the 'Beni-Israel, un rendez-vous de purs'.
[75] See above p. 6.
[76] Freiburg und Leipzig, 1893; S. 19 *seq.*
[77] *Das nordhebräische Sagenbuch; die Elohimquelle*. Leipzig 1906, S. 368 *seq.*
[78] See above p. 4.
[79] It is impossible to attempt completeness here. Fortunately, we have two monographs on the history of the 'Mose-Forschung', namely a historical one by Eva Osswald, *Das Bild des Mose in der kritischen alttestamentlichen Wissenschaft seit Julius Wellhausen*, Berlin 1960, and a systematic one by R. Smend, *Das Mosebild von Heinrich Ewald bis Martin Noth*, Tübingen 1959. The book of Eva Osswald in particular has a most useful and extensive bibliography.
[80] *Mose und sein Werk*. Giessen 1912. *Cf.* espec. *Welches war die älteste Religion Israels?* Ein Vortrag, Giessen 1927.

We have seen that Gressmann regarded Moses as the 'author' of the new political and juridical form of organization which was the starting-point of Israel as an independent nation.[83] In this he stands close to Wellhausen, who also strongly emphasized that it was Moses who created and instituted the law of Israel, and that this law was a prominent factor in the origin of Israel. Gressmann explicitly puts it that Yahweh was unknown to the Israelites before Moses. Nor was it the case that Yahweh was already the god of one of the later Israelite tribes before the time of Moses, for instance of a continually re-suggested tribe of Israel, that of Joseph or of Levi. The stupendous event at the Sea of Reeds (= the gulf of Akabah!) revealed the god of Midian to the Israelites. This god was the god of the Sinai, which Gressmann locates in Midian. The eternal significance of Moses lies in his having accepted the consequence that this god must obviously have a very special intention concerning this people, which after all was a stranger to him, and that in future the two would belong together![84] Afterwards, in Kades (Sinai), this was worked out in organizational form. For that matter, the connexion with Yahweh was seen rather as an enthronement than as a covenant between partners. This transplantation of Yahweh, from the god of Mount Sinai to the god of the people in Kades, turned him from a god of nature into a god of history.[85]

For G. Beer, Yahweh before Moses was a typical 'High God', known but barely worshipped. Beer distinguishes between Yahweh and the Holy mountain Sinai on the one hand and Jethro and the Midianite sanctuary Kades on the other. The Israelites took over the cult of Yahweh from the Midianites at Kades. Like Meyer, Beer thinks that Kades was the centre of an amphictyony after the style of the Greeks.[86] Many later Israelites will, like Moses (and Elijah), have journeyed to the sacred mountain. In the northern Negev, especially the southern Israelite

[81] *Mose und seine Zeit.* See note 64.
[82] *Mose. Ein Beitrag zur Untersuchung über die Ursprünge der israelitischen Religion.* Tübingen 1907[1]. Entirely revised edition: *Mose und sein Werk.* Tübingen 1932[2].
[83] 'So darf man den Aufenthalt in Kades als die Werdezeit Israels betrachten und Mose für den Schöpfer der politischen Einheit halten.' *Mose und seine Zeit,* S. 422.
[84] *Ibid.* S. 443 seq.
[85] 'Durch die Inthronisation in Kades wurde Jahweh der Gott Israels... Der Berggott des Sinaï löste sich von seiner altgewohnten Stätte, zog mit Israel und ward zum Landesgott Palästinas, dann aber löste er sich auch von Israel und Palästina ...' *Ibid.* S. 448. In this, Gressmann very much softens down the stress he had formerly laid upon the nature aspects of Yahweh. *Cf.* his *Das Erdgeruch Palästinas in der israelitischen Religion.* Berlin 1909.
[86] 'Kadesch ist von uns als Mittelpunkt einer Amphiktyonie zu denken, die unter der Vorhut der Midianiter stand,' *Mose,* S. 31. *Cf.* also *Welches war die älteste Religion,* S. 11 seq.

tribes will have visited the cultic centre Kades for the worship of Yahweh, for the jurisdiction there and for the annual markets that usually came to be held at such centres.[87] The difference between the relationship Yahweh-Midian and Yahweh-Israel was this, that the former relationship was 'natural' and the latter 'moral', that is tied to a choice and to conditions.[88] In a general way, however, Beer presupposes the Israelite tribes. The Joseph tribes departed from Kades for reasons unknown to us, and not until the song of Deborah do we have an indication that in the long run they linked up with the Leah tribes. Possibly the Joseph tribes only came into contact with Yahweh through Moses, while the Leah tribes had always known him (see above).[89]

The inconsistency of this foundation, whereby on one side Israel is supposed to result from the work of Moses, while on the other a pre-Mosaic Israel is ever again postulated in order to explain how Moses could act as he did, was set forth with great lucidity and emphasis by P. Volz. He rightly points this out as the flaw in the explanations given by Stade and Wellhausen of the origin of the true Israel.[90] Yet even someone like H. Gressmann did not escape this pitfall! Volz then concludes (already in the 1907 edition) that it is a mistake to ascribe the origin of Israel *as a people* to Moses. Moses did not found a people, he founded a religion.[91] In this matter the question whether Yahweh may have been known to the Israelites before Moses, is in itself irrelevant because:

[87] In his '*Mose*' Beer still regarded the Joseph tribes as the original partners in this amphictyony and as the first worshippers of Yahweh. In *Welches war die älteste Religion* he attributes this role mainly to Judah, as living in the south. Apart from the fact that it is very unusual to see so important a part given to a tribe that was generally considered to be young and to have a strong admixture of Canaanite blood, this is an unmistakable sign of his decided stand against the anti-Jewish tendency of many of his colleagues among the Old Testament scholars, who would not admit Judah to an important role. In the same speech Beer also attributes the familiar 'Judentyp' to admixture of Hittite blood (Aryans!), and then plainly states that there was no question of a 'Jewish race' in ancient Israel.
[88] *Mose*, S. 32.
[89] *Welches war die älteste Religion*, S. 17. While the J source supposes Yahweh always to have been known to the forefathers of the Israelites, Beer thinks that such was also the case for Judah. E, from the north, connects the introduction of Yahweh with Moses.
[90] Volz, *Mose*, S. 23 *seq*.
[91] 'Es ist daher ausgeschlossen, dass Mose die Hebräerstämme schon zu einem Volk vereinigt hätte. Er selbst war nicht Häuptling, sondern Prophet. Jedenfalls dürfen wir nie aus dem Auge verlieren, dass Moses Werk nicht die Gründung eines Volkes, sondern die Stiftung einer Religion war. Dies muss der leitende Gesichtspunkt bleiben, damit wir die Grundgedanken der mosaischen Schöpfung recht verstehen und nicht etwas zur Hauptsache machen, was in Wirklichkeit Nebensache war.' *Ibid*. S. 86.

'der Gott Moses seinen Inhalt und seiner Verehrung nach jedenfalls etwas Neues war!'[92] Volz himself leans to the former possibility. To Moses, however, this god reveals himself as the 'Gott des Willens', who appears primarily as god of the moral order. Only as such, we may indeed say that Yahweh, through the intermediacy of Moses, is the creator of the spirit of Israel, the law of Israel and the conscience of Israel.[93] In fact Volz here already ascribes to Moses what had formerly, in keeping with the old evolutionist schema, always been reserved for the great prophets: the founding of 'ethical monotheism'.[94] For the rest Volz also is convinced that 'Israel' was only really formed through the activity of Moses.[95] Therefore he justly asks himself what the relationship is of 'Religion und Volkstum innerhalb des Mosewerkes'.[96] The answer is: 'Wägt man bei diesem Nebeneinander des Religiösen und des Völkischen das Gewicht der beiden ab, so ist kein Zweifel, dass das Religiöse dem Völkischen wesentlich übergeordnet ist.'[97] In the outlook of Volz the political and national aspect always remains a *means* and never becomes an end in itself. From this point of view Volz can even speak of the

---

[92] *Mose und sein Werk*, S. 58. In the 'pan-Babylonian' school this problem of the 'old' and the 'new' Yahweh was usually solved by distinguishing between an old, originally Canaanite god Yahu or Yau and the new, universal Yahweh. On the basis of the J source this Yahu/Yau then naturally becomes the god of the bastard-tribe Judah. The Levites were the priests of this heathen god, who was a snake-god. For Winckler, see above p. 9-12. Very sweeping and decidedly anti-Jewish is also H. Schneider, *Die Entwicklung der Jahureligion und der Mosesagen in Israel und Juda*. Leipziger Semitistische Studien, Band V, 1, Leipzig 1909, S. 1-42. For Baentsch see under note 94. We find this contrast most grossly put by Friedrich Delitzsch, who rejects out of hand the identification God = Yahweh. Fr. Delitzsch, *Die Grosse Täuschung*, 2 Tle, Stuttgart/Berling 1921; espec. *I* S. 72 seq. and *II* S. 12 seq.

[93] *Mose und sein Werk*, S. 68.

[94] In *Mose und sein Werk* this is somewhat toned down again, as Volz, who in *Mose* had represented as the chief work of Moses the founding of a league of Yahweh as a kind of order of those who had learnt to know Yahweh in a new manner, now no longer restricts this league to the early times, but sees it as running on through the whole history of Israel as a Mosaic movement. *Mose*, S. 93 seq.; *Mose und sein Werk* S. 77 seq. espec. also 77[1].

We may remark that Volz, then, also sees Moses as the man who raised Yahwism to a 'higher', that is to say to an 'ethical' level. The same idea, resulting from quite a different chain of thought, is also found in B. Baentsch, *Altorientalischer und israelitischer Monotheismus*. Tübingen 1906, espec. S. 83.

[95] That 'Israel' was the name of the tribes united under Moses, is an idea that has found wide acceptance since W. Staerk, *Zur Geschichte der hebräischen Volksnamen*. Berlin 1899, S. 70. (= Studien zur Religions- und Sprachgeschichte des alten Testaments, Heft II).

[96] *Mose und sein Werk*, S. 74 seq.

[97] *Ibid.* S. 76.

'anti-national trait in Yahwism'.[98] For our subject it is highly important that because of this heavy stress upon the religious aspect, Volz also interprets the name 'Israel' taken by the united tribes as in the first place a *religious* appellation. On this point Volz certainly goes much further in 1932 than in 1907. 'Israel' is not just the name of a people, but a *profession of faith*: 'God rules' or 'May God rule'.[99] It is the name, the profession of faith and the programme of the Mosaic league of Yahweh in Israelite history. For this religious interpretation of the name 'Israel', Volz falls back upon the indeed very important studies of Sachsse[100] and Caspari[101] concerning the concept 'Israel', which we must now first consider.

Without doubt it is Eduard Sachsse who has made the most intensive and profound study of the phenomenon 'Israel'. His first little book (*Israel I*) contains an examination of the occurrence and the use of the name Israel. In *Israel II* Sachsse mainly goes into the content and the meaning of the name. In the Old Testament he distinguishes a threefold use of the name Israel. 1. Name of the patriarch; 2. Name of the people; 3. Name of the country. With regard to the first: an examination of the texts shows us that the use of Israel to indicate Jacob is comparatively young. Perhaps this use of the name may be explained as a secondary conclusion based on the expression $b^e n\bar{e}$ $yi\acute{s}r\bar{a}'\bar{e}l$. According to Sachsse this reasoning can at any rate be shown in P.[102] With regard to the second use of Israel, as the name of a people, we note first of all that it is sometimes $yi\acute{s}r\bar{a}'\bar{e}l$ and sometimes $b^e n\bar{e}$ $yi\acute{s}r\bar{a}'\bar{e}l$. In this connextion Sachsse speaks of a Y- and a B-source. Y is used mainly in historical and factual material, while theological reflection has a preference for B.[103] Since the intruding tribes may very well have brought the name of Israel with them, so that the country could only acquire that name after they had settled there, Sachsse takes the use of Israel as the name of a people to be older than its use as the name of the country.[104]

[98] *Ibid.* S. 76. *Cf.* also *Mose*, S. 92. 'Der Zweck Moses ist also nicht national. Es scheint seiner Schöpfung im Gegenteil von Haus aus etwas Uebernationales im Prinzip Antinationales anzuhaften. Jahwe ist nicht um Israels willen da, sondern Israel um Jahwes willen.'

[99] *Mose und sein Werk*, S. 78 *seq.*, espec. S. 88. For the translation of $yi\acute{s}r\bar{a}'\bar{e}l$ Volz refers to Noth, see below, chapter III, excursus on the etymology of this name.

[100] Ed. Sachsse, *Die Bedeutung des Namens Israel. I*, Bonn 1910. *II*, Gütersloh 1922. Cited hereafter as *Israel I* or *II*.

[101] W. Caspari, *Die Gottesgemeinde vom Sinaj und das nachmalige Volk Israel. Auseinandersetzungen mit Max Weber.* Gütersloh 1922.

[102] *Israel I*, S. 73 *seq.* See the quotation in note 104.

[103] *Israel I*, S. 56 *seq.* and 73 *seq.*

[104] 'Die nach Palästina einwandernden Stämme nannten sich (ganz oder teilweise) Israel. Der Name war Stammesname, ebenso wie etwa Moab oder Amalek.

Israel II makes a further examination of the conclusion reached in *I*: the use of the name Israel in the Old Testament can be best explained on the assumption that it dates from the time before the *Sesshaftigkeit*. Sachsse then shows that there are regions which in the time of the Judges and the early time of the Kings are regarded as less 'Israel' than other parts. This applies particularly to Transjordan. Transjordan was colonized from the west, and therefore all attempts to seek Israel's origins just there are doomed in advance. Starting from the phenomenon that the region considered to be Israel was not constant, Sachsse then very fully investigates the relation between Israel and Judah. We have already seen that it had become a general custom, certainly since Meyer and Luthet, to make an essential distinction between Judah and Israel. The main arguments for doing so are: firstly a totally different Conquest, but this, thinks Sachsse, may be quite well explained from military and tactical considerations. That J has no mention of a stay in Transjordan is an *argumentum e silentio*. Secondly: Judah's absence in the song of Deborah, which is also an *argumentum e silentio*. Nor is the third point at all convincing, that texts such as Gen. 38 and I Sam. 27:10 would make out Judah to be an ethnic conglomerate. For that Judah was of old resident around Bethelehem-Tekoa is contested by no one, that Caleb was then in Hebron and Jerahmeel in the Negeb is quite irrelevant to the relationship between Judah and Israel! Fourthly, Sachsse counters Luther's well-known 'brotherhood theory' founded on II Sam. 19:44, by adducing Judg. 20:13 where Benjamin and Israel are called brothers, while there also the two groups are opposed in enmity.[105] Against Meyer c.s. Sachsse postulates that Judah was always aware of a very close link with Israel, and that I Sam. 15 shows that it certainly also belonged to

Nach der Sesshaftwerdung wich die Stammesorganisation der territorialen Gliederung und die Stammesnamen wurden in gewissen Kreisen der Bevölkerung zu Landesnamen, während sich andere Kreise in dieser Hinsicht konservativer verhielten. Dies geschah jedoch vor der Zeit, in der die ältesten Stücke, die uns erhalten sind, schriftlich fixiert wurden. Es scheint, alsob gegen das Exil zu der Name *benē yiśrā'ēl* häufiger gebraucht worden ist. Dies kann daher kommen dass uns aus dieser Zeit die grosse B-Quelle P erhalten ist, zu der ungefähr die Hälfte von allen Stellen, an denen *yiśrā'ēl* vorkommt gehört (300× aus 620). ... Dazu kam eine zweite Entwicklung, deren Wurzel auf das Nordreich hinweist. Aus dem Namen *benē yiśrā'ēl* schloss man auf einen Vorfahren gleichen Namens. So wurde Israel der Beiname des Patriarchen Jakob. Doch diese Gleichung konnte keinen Einfluss auf den Sprachgebrauch im Südreich gewinnen. Denn erst nach den Exil fing man dort an, den Patriarchen häufiger Israel zu nennen; d.h. aber zur gleichen Zeit, wo der Name *benē yiśrā'ēl* in gewöhnlichen Verkehr durch den Namen *yehudīm* verdrängt wurde (Ezra-Nehemia-Esther).' *Israel I*, S. 74. See also A. Besters in *RB* LXXIV (1967) p. 1-23 and 321-355.
[105] *Israel II*, S. 59-67.

Saul's kingdom, probably as a result of voluntary association. We do best therefore to accept the witness of the Bible, which always counts Judah with Israel. Yet it is clear that the relationship between Judah and Israel is in many cases difficult to explain if one maintains 'Israel' as a politico-geographical concept. No, in all changing political and geographical circumstances Israel's unity was always a rallying-point, and there is no possible doubt that this unity was in the final instance determined by religion![106] Luther has attempted to explain the concept of 'Israel' as arising in the time of Ahab, but Edom, which at that time also belonged to 'Israel', was yet never regarded as 'Israel'![107] Israel simply must be the indication of the link that was felt because of 'der gemeinsame Gottesglaube'; this was already present in the early time of the Kings, and since its origin in the chaotic period of the Judges would hardly be explicable, it must be older. 'Der gleiche Gottesglaube, den wir in Nord und Süd in der ältesten uns unmittelbar erreichbare Geschichtsperiode antreffen, muss ein Erbe einer gemeinsam verlebten Vergangenheit sein.'[108] On these grounds Sachsse concludes that there must have existed before the Conquest a religious league of tribes. There is no reason at all to doubt the biblical reports attributing the foundation of such a league to Moses.[109] 'Für den Namen dieses Bundes kommt nur Israel in Betracht.'[110] Yet since no direct evidence can be found of the existence of this league 'Israel', Sachsse adduces quite a number of analogous developments from the history of the Germanic tribes.

Thus far E. Sachsse. The subtitle of Caspari's book makes it plain that this author's first concern is to contest some views expressed by M. Weber, the economist and sociologist whose influence has been so great.[111] Before treating Caspari, then, we must say a few words about Weber.

Weber also stresses that for earliest Israel Yahweh was a strange god,[112]

---

[106] *Israel II*, S. 72.

[107] See above p. 7; *Israel II*, S. 74 a. 90.

[108] *Israel II*, S. 78.

[109] 'Die gleiche Jahwe-Verehrung, die wir bei der Nord- und Südstämme fanden, setzt einen religiösen Bund voraus, den wir erschliessen müssten, selbst wenn uns keine Nachrichten von ihm mehr überkommen wären. Nun berichten die Quellen des Pentateuch einstimmig, dass die Stämme Israels einschliesslich der Südstämme durch Mose zu einen Bund zur Verehrung Jahwes zusammengeschlossen worden sind. Wie haben keinen Grund, die Richtigkeit dieser Tatsache zu bezweifeln!' *Israel II*, S. 90.

[110] *Ibid.* S. 90.

[111] M. Weber, *Gesammelte Aufsätze zur Religionssoziologie, Band III 'Das antike Judentum'*. Tübingen 1923².

[112] 'Nicht ein altvertrauter Orts- oder Stammesgott, sondern eine fremde und

24

but thereupon he makes a great effort to explain the further history of Israel and of Yahwism from the *Volkstum*, be it a very special *Volkstum* for Israel. Weber starts from a number of sociological given contrasts that are determinant for the developments in society. For Israel, these include the contrast between desert and cultivated land, and between town and country. In considering the religious, political and social forms of organization, Weber lays much emphasis upon the covenant that links the various groups and bridges over their contrasts. Thus it holds good that 'Israel selbst als politisches Gemeinwesen vor allem eine Eidgenossenschaft war.'[113] This confederacy had two main objects, a military and a cultic one. 'Was schliesslich die israelitische Eidgenossenschaft selbst anlangt, so war sie nach eindeutiger Überlieferung ein Kriegsbund unter und mit Jahwe als dem Kriegsgott des Bundes, Garant seiner sozialen Ordnungen und Schöpfer des materiellen gedeihens der Eidgenossen, insbesondere des dafür nötigen Regens. Der Name "Israel", sei es dass er (unwahrscheinlicherweise) ursprünglich "Jesorel" zu sprechen war und also der Gott bedeutete, "auf den man vertraut", bringt das zum Ausdruck. Ein Stammesname war "Israel" jedenfalls nicht, sondern der Name eines Verbandes und zwar: eines kultischen Bundes. Zur Bezeichnung eines Eponymos hat erst die theologische Bearbeitung der Legenden vom Heros Jacob den Namen Israel gemacht: daher der schattenhafte Charakter dieser Personifikation.'[114] This Israel federation really only functioned in time of war. Otherwise Yahwism, and thereby Israel, lived only in the family circle. At that level also we see all kinds of alliance. Thus families unite into clans, and clans into tribes. Judah is a plain example of such a tribe formed by union. Also Weber's general theories on the role of men's societies gained great repute. These men's societies everywhere play an important part in religious life. In Israel, too, Yahwism began as the secret doctrine of a men's society.

The attempts of Weber the sociologist to show in this way how and where Yahwism was rooted in Israelite social life, were opposed by Caspari the theologian with a mainly sociological argumentation. He began by maintaining than it was just in the Israelite's ordinary daily life that Yahwism was often quite unnoticeable. On the contrary, it was in the home that the old tribal cults and gods lived on tenaciously! The great fear of 'strange women' harboured by the Old Testament shows the awareness of this danger from within. Canaanite influences also were strongest on the level of ordinary family life. 'Im Gegensatz zum Hause

geheimnisvolle Gestalt war es, welche der israelitischen Eidgenossenschaft die Weihe gab.' *o.c.* S. 133.
[113] *o.c.* S. 82.
[114] *o.c.* S. 90.

war in Israel die Sippe der Hort der Jahwe Religion.'[115] Caspari then shows the fact that Weber seeks the seat of the Yahweh cult in 'men's societies' and the families, to be a result of his overestimating the influence of nomadic life on the later Israel. The same applies to Weber's idea that Yahweh was a war-god. Moreover, that is a quite mistaken conclusion from his own premiss, since the nomad in general wages war much less than the townsman, Caspari states. Why, Yahweh is nowhere called 'Fighter' or anything of that kind, only 'Fortress', 'Shield' or some other term from the art of defence: Yahweh was certainly never a war-god![116] If Weber saw Yahwism infiltrating into Israel as a kind of 'secret doctrine', Caspari sees the earliest Yahwism and Israel as a kind of movement around a leader, consolidating into a group through the experiences undergone as a group.[117] On the two points most important for our purpose, then, Weber and Caspari are heartily agreed: the first is that Moses never founded a people, nor did the foundation of the people result from the foundation of their religion. The people were always there, and at a given moment Yahwism came to them. The second point is that the formation of the later people of Israel must be seen as the association of formerly different groups for religious reasons. Israel therefore began as a *cultic league* of some groups, who in Caspari's view were to form the later tribes. For both, however, the name Israel is first of all a *profession of faith*!

This view of Israel as a religious community we also find in a slightly modified form in the work of E. Sellin.[118] He calls upon Volz and Weber, and in particular the idea of an original Yahweh league he borrowed from Volz. The origins of this league, or as Sellin calls it 'Jahweh-Koalition', he seeks in Transjordan, for Sellin too takes the E source as foundation of his historical reconstruction. 'Woher der Name Israel stammte, wissen wir nicht, er wird bei Peniel oder auch erst bei Sichem vgl. Gen. 33, 20 von einer Genossenschaft, die sich um ein Heiligtum sammelte, übernommen sein. Auch die ursprüngliche Bedeutung entzieht sich unserer sicheren Kenntnis.'[119] However, Sellin halts between two opinions: Peniel and/or Shechem. With Steuernagel he believes that the Genesis traditions contain historically reliable memories of the time of the Conquest, but he rejects his explanation of tribal history. A large part of the tribes only originated in Palestine. To operate with different

[115] Caspari, *o.c.* S. 107, *cf.* also S. 102.
[116] *o.c.* S. 112 *seq.*
[117] *o.c.* S. 157 *seq.*
[118] E. Sellin, *Gilgal*. Leipzig 1917. *Geschichte des israelitisch-jüdischen Volkes, I.* Leipzig 1924.
[119] *Geschichte*, S. 26. *Cf.* also M. Weber, *o.c.* S. 352.

tribal systems, as Steuernagel did for instance, only makes the matter more complicated.[120] That the attempts to make a generally acceptable reconstruction of the Conquest do not suceed, Sellin thinks due to the continual trying to treat Israel as a fixed entity, instead of as a term having a very variable meaning.[121] If the Yahweh league 'Israel' was formed in Peniel, a people 'Israel' only came into being after the entry. And that was after this variable 'Israel' had been united in a covenant with Yahweh by Joshua, at Gilgal near Shechem.[122] For Sellin the Yahweh league only has a function at the Conquest and Entry. Indeed, he sees Yahweh mainly as a war-god. At Shechem, Joshua converts the military league of Peniel into a cultic league: 'Eine gewisse Einheitlichkeit aller Stämme trotz aller zentrifugalen Kräfte und trotz des Mangels an einigenden politischen Organen ergab sich aus der alljährlich stattfindenden gemeinsamen religiösen Festen.'[123]

5. Between the two world wars

Continuing our general survey, we notice that in the earliest history of Israel as depicted by the Old Testament there are obviously three periods, each of which various scholars proclaim to be the great formative period of Israel. At the same time it is generally recognized that history itself, the three periods together, was of the greatest importance for the form Israel finally assumed. Yet for each of these periods evaluation continues to differ.

These three periods are:

Firstly: the time of the patriarchs. If Israel is considered to have originated in this period, or then to have existed in essence, the following questions, int.al., immediately arise: what is the relation between Israelites and Hebrews/Ḫabiru, and between the religion of the patriarchs and later Yahwism, and how is one to explain the phenomenon of the 'double Conquest'. For if one considers the cycles of Abraham and Jacob to represent old traditions of entry, then what is their relation to the Conquest attributed in the Old Testament to the whole of Israel under the leadership of Joshua? It nowhere appears in the book of Joshua that the entry was experienced as a return to the land of the forefathers.

---

[120] Sellin points out that one cannot make a division between an older Leah group and a younger Rachel group: already c. 1500 there was a tribe or place in Palestine called Joseph(el)! *Geschichte*, S. 45. *Cf.* also Ed. Meyer, 'Der Stamm Jakob und die Entstehung der israelitischen Stämme' and W. M. Müller, *Asien und Europe*. Leipzig 1893.

[121] *Geschichte*, S. 27.

[122] *Geschichte*, S. 98. *Gilgal*, S. 52 u. 90. Josh. 24 is the E version of Exod. 24 J!

[123] *Geschichte*, S. 138.

Secondly: the period of the Exodus and the wandering in the desert, culminating in the covenant with Yahweh at the Sinai. We saw above that here all the questions concerning the person of Moses at once come to the fore, and also the relationship to the Kenites and Midianites. Then there is the question which was first in 'Israel', the people or the religion. It is clear that however attractive it may seem, for instance, to seek Israel's origin at Kades – and indeed, since Stade and Wellhausen many have done so – yet all these traditions of exodus, covenant and desert, even the activity of Moses himself, seem to take the people for granted.

Thirdly: the time of and immediately after the entry of 'Israel' under Joshua. Israel as we meet with it in the Old Testament, only acquired its form in and through contact with the country where it went to live, and with the inhabitants and culture of that country. Here again the question rises of the spiritual unity such a Conquest surely supposes. And then the question: what was this Israel like? What are we to do with the tribal schemes and systems? An urgent question is, in how far the religiously so important traditions of the desert are still essential then. Further problems lie in the field of sedentarization and acculturation (to the Canaanite culture).

These questions mount up before those historians who would not confine themselves to a purely religious explanation of the phenomenon 'Israel'. Let us now turn to the chief 'histories of Israel' which largely dominated the time between the two world wars, and also to a few of the principal monographs on Israel's earliest history. Of the 'histories' published in that period, I call attention to those of Guthe,[124] Kittel,[125] Lods,[126] Olmstead,[127] Oesterley-Robinson[128] and Auerbach.[129] Of the monographs I will only mention those by Burney,[130] Schmidtke,[131] and

[124] H. Guthe, *Geschichte des Volkes Israel*. Tübingen 1914³.

[125] R. Kittel, *Geschichte des Volkes Israel. Erster Band*. Gotha 1923⁶.

[126] A. Lods, *Israël, des origines au milieu du VIIIe siècle*. L'Évolution de l'humanité, XXVII. Paris 1930.

[127] A. T. Olmstead, *History of Palestine and Syria to the Macedonian Conquest*. New York/London 1931.

[129] W. O. E. Oesterley and Th. H. Robinson, *A History of Israel. Vol. I, From the Exodus to the Fall of Jerusalem*, by Th. H. Robinson, Oxford 1932.

[129] E. Auerbach, *Wüste und Gelobtes Land. Geschichte Israels von den Anfängen bis zum Tode Salomons*. Berlin 1932. Although Auerbach was acquainted with the publications of M. Noth, it is desirable to discuss his work before that of Noth for two reasons. Firstly, Auerbach's work very clearly belongs to the series of pre-war 'histories', and secondly, Noth's theories and hypotheses are hotly contested and rejected, so exercised no influence.

[130] C. F. Burney, *Israel's Settlement in Canaan. The Biblical Tradition and its Historical Background*. The Schweich Lectures for 1917, London 1921³.

[131] Fr. Schmidtke, *Die Einwanderung Israels in Kanaan*. Breslau 1933.

Meek.[132] E. Sellin's work has already been discussed. The many researches of Alt and Noth, the greater part of which were carried out and published between the wars, will be considered separately.

Yet before we can discuss the works listed above, one point must be remarked on. Since the first world war, archaeological research in Palestine has been increasingly active. Especially owing to the very imperfect methodical and technical equipment of the excavations of that first period – they were often only carried out by Old Testament scholars, and hardly ever with the assistance of professional archaeologists! – the results were extremely meagre, with regard to Israel's earliest history in particular. And if there were any results, then these same methodical and technical reasons always caused them to be hotly contested. At this time also, with a few exceptions, there was hardly any understanding of the essential differences between facts of archaeological provenance and those supplied by literary historical research. Scholars were (and alas! still are) only too often inclined to make indiscriminate use of all this 'factual material' in an argumentation. Not until after the second world do we see a more widespread appreciation of the problems of methodic principle involved here. Especially in those books by the above-named which pay considerable attention to the archaeological material, such as those by Lods, Meek and Olmstead, this shows very plainly. They have not resisted the temptation of making no essential difference between the Bible and the spade!

Yet it is no small quantity of material that archaeology has supplied in the first four decades of this century, and it is indispensable for all research into the origins of Israel. Particularly the *Umwelt* in which ancient Israel must have arisen, became ever more known.[133] With regard to our special problem, however, the results of this intensive archaeological research really remainly rather negative. Perhaps the

---

[132] Th. J. Meek, *Hebrew Origins*. New York/London 1936.
[133] A survey of the pre-war material is to be found in: R. A. S. Macalister, *A Century of Excavation in Palestine*. London s.d. (1926). J. Garrow Duncan, *Digging up Biblical History*. 2 vols., London 1930. W. F. Albright, *The Archaeology of Palestine and the Bible*. New York/Chicago s.d. (1932). An excellent Dutch work is J. Simons, *Opgravingen in Palestina* Reeks 'Bijbelse Monografieën', Roermond 1936. In this last book, the pages 187-200 display a level-headed and critical attitude rarely seen before the second world war, and which is also directed to archaeological research. Especially with Anglo-Saxon scholars one often observes a too critical attitude towards historical and literary methods and results, beside a notable inability to judge critically of archaeological research also. Only consider the title of Garrow Duncan's work mentioned above! German scholars, on the other hand, were often extremely critical towards archaeology, resulting either in a negativistic attitude or in their being carried away by all kinds of wild (*e.g.* racist) theories!

29

most important point is that it was established, that in the period when Israel's Conquest must have taken place,[134] various cities in Canaan suffered heavily from warfare and often underwent serious destruction.[135] Yet it proved impossible to attribute this wave of destruction to new elements in the population.[136] In short, archaeology did not succeed in finding the Israelites through their identification with particular material remains. For some time an advantage was gained by the definite dating of the 'fall of Jericho' in 1407 B.C.E. by J. Garstang.[137] The negative results were not entirely balanced by the many excavations with positive results concerning the time of the Kings (Tell ed-Duwēr, Tell Bēt Mirsim, Tell el-Mutesellim, Tell Taᶜannek, Sebaṣṭje and many others).

Fortunately better results concerning Israel's earliest history came from the *Umwelt*. The latter proved far more complicated than had been imagined. A most important discovery was that of an entirely new ethnic and cultural factor in the Near East of the second millennium: the Ḫurrites.[138] The excavations at Nuzi and the texts found there, especially the juridical documents, were and are of great importance for our knowledge of the time when Israel came into being. In the course of the excavations at Tell Ta'annek, a lucky chance brought to light a few clay tablets containing many names. These showed that the Ḫurrites also formed one of the elements in the population of Palestine around 1400. Probably the Old Testament still speaks of them by the name of Horites.[139] In the third place there are the discoveries being made since

---

[134] This is now usually placed between a *terminus ad quem* in the Israel stela (*c.* 1220 B.C.E.) and a *terminus a quo* in the first half of the reign of Ramses II. For he was the pharaoh who built the towns Pithom and Raamses (Exod. 1:11), so that he was in all probability also the pharaoh of the oppression. The Entry is then dated between 1250 and 1220.

[135] Thus *e.g.* Bētin, Tell Bēt Mirsim, Tell ed-Duwēr.

[136] Perhaps Tell ed-Duwēr is an exception, because there are indications (though not decisive ones) that it was destroyed by the Philistines.

[137] J. Garstang, The Walls of Jericho. *PEQ* (1931), p. 186-196. J. Garstang, *The Foundations of Bible History, Joshua and Judges*. New York 1931, pp. 66, 146 *seq*. *Cf*. also J. and J. B. E. Garstang, *The Story of Jericho*. London/Edinburgh 1948², p. 135. *Cf*. also the discussion about the dating of the fall of Jericho, 'The Chronology of Jericho', *PEQ* (1931), p. 124-127, with L. H. Vincent. On the basis of the earlier German excavations, a date had formerly been accepted which was more than a century earlier! C. Watzinger, Zur Chronologie der Schichten von Jericho, *ZDMG* N.F. V. (1926) S. 131-136.

[138] Edw. Chiera and E. A. Speiser, A New Factor in the History of the Ancient Near East. *AASOR* VI (1926) pp. 75-92, Espec. also: E. A. Speiser, Ethnic Movements in the Near East in the Second Millennium B.C. *AASOR* XIII (1933) pp. 13-54.

1929 in Rās eš-Šamra, the ancient Ugarit. These excavations have given us a very great amount of new material concerning the language, culture and history of the Levant at the end of the Late Bronze Age.[140] Fourthly, the finding of many new texts enabled a common opinion to grow up with regard to the problem of the Ḥabiru, the word being now looked upon as bearing a social rather than an ethnic meaning. This insight was largely due to the texts found in Nuzi; in most of the works now to be reviewed Ḥabiru still functions as an ethnical term.[141] Only for the sake of completeness, we must finally mention the French excavations begun at Tell Ḥarīri, the ancient Mari, in 1933. Already before the second world war the texts found there began to throw an entirely new light upon the Middle Bronze Age, which very probably was the time of the biblical patriarchs. The process still continues, and we shall often have to refer to the Mari texts. In the works now to be reviewed they hardly play a part yet.

Of the studies we were going to discuss, it is really only that of Burney which fully belongs to our *group I*. Burney seeks the origins of Israel entirely in the time of the patriarchs. The people has two roots: on one side the Ḥabiru (Abraham and Isaac) and on the other Aramaean tribes (Rebecca, Rachel, Leah). From the combination of these two ethnic groups sprang Jacob/Israel.[142] The journey to Egypt, the Exodus, Sinai, were events that only a part of the Israelites experienced. The rest were living quietly in Canaan since the fifteenth century. Schmidtke offers us almost the same solution.[143] It is striking that in this monograph about the Entry of the Israelites there is nowhere any serious inquiry, what we are to understand by 'Israel'! Also the Exodus from Egypt, their residence there, the wandering in the desert, Moses and Sinai are passed over completely. The way Schmidtke and Burney treat the stories of the patriarchs plainly shows the influence of Steuernagel.

To the question: when and how did Israel originate and what are we to understand by 'Israel *in statu nascendi*', the historians Kittel and Robinson also give us an answer referring to the time of the patriarchs.

---

[139] Speiser, Ethnic Movements, pp. 26-31. A. Gustavs, Die Personennamen in den Tontafeln von Tell Taʿannek. *ZDPV* L (1927) S. 1-18. Gustavs still identifies these names as Hittite, however.

[140] This still holds good even if one hesitates to regard northern Ugarit as a prototype of Canaan.

[141] For the social sense first of all: Speiser, Ethnic Movements, p. 31-54 and M. Noth, Erwägungen zur Hebräerfrage. *Festschrift für O. Procksch*. Leipzig 1934, S. 99-113.

[142] Burney, *Settlement*, p. 85.

[143] Schmidtke, *Einwanderung*, S. 2 seq., 21, 65-67.

However, both also realize very well that the time at the Sinai, with everything which took place there, was of eminent importance for the 'form' of Israel. In essence, Kittel paints us a fairly traditional picture of Israel's earliest history. Again the origins lie with the Ḥabiru, whom Kittel equates with infiltrating Aramaean tribes![144] The Ḥabiru are again identical with the Hebrews. For these Hebrew tribes, Kittel introduces the term *'proto-Israelites'*.[145] These tribes already lived in Palestine in the Middle Bronze Age.[146] The centre lay by Shechem; there was also the sanctuary Gilgal.[147] Later these various Hebrew tribes and groups were fitted into a twelve-tribe system. Like Meyer, Kittel thinks the number twelve can best be explained from a tribal league having certain monthly duties towards a sanctuary such as Shechem/ Gilgal. Each tribe would then have the care of the deity for one month. Although the tribal system in its present form clearly dates from a time when the tribes no longer really functioned – that is to say, the later time of the Judges – it yet clearly contains older, historically reliable reminiscences, including the number twelve and the earlier classification according to Rachel and Leah.[148]

All this, however, refers to the proto-Israelites. True Israel originated when a small part of these proto-Israelites landed in Egypt and afterwards, during a time spent in Kades, came into contact with other groups of Hebrews and with a new religion. These events require a *Führer*, according to Kittel.[149] Through the experiences that had been shared (Oppression, Exodus, Sinai, Desert wandering, Entry) a new feeling of solidarity grew up which took the place of the former blood-relationship. This new, real Israel mainly consisted of the Rachel group. The Leah group had always remained in Palestine, and was the Israel that Merenptah found there.[150]

Robinson also sees Israel in the first place as an ethnic group. This is a point all have in common who seek Israel's origins in the time of the Patriarchs. For Robinson, the basis of solidarity as their common Aramaean descent.[151] The purest Aramaean tribes are found in the Leah

---

[144] Kittel, *GVI* I, S. 267-269.
[145] *o.c.* S. 293.
[146] Kittel points for this to the names Jacob-el and Joseph-el found on the pylons of Karnak, *o.c.* S. 261. *Cf.* also Ed. Meyer, *ZAW* V (1886) and Müller, *Asien and Europa*, S. 159-162.
[147] In this Kittel follows Sellin, *o.c.* S. 299.
[148] *o.c.* S. 296[5].
[149] 'Beim Auszug und in Qades ist Israel ein Volk geworden. Mose hat es dazu gemacht. Ohne ihn blieb Israel, was es war.' *o.c.* S. 379.
[150] *GVI* II, S. 9-11.

group. The Joseph tribe(s) had got into Egypt by other ways. When they came out of Egypt, they recognized the Kenites in Kades as distant relations. From these Kenites they also took over the god Yahweh, whom the Kenites in turn had probably borrowed from the southern Leah tribes. The work of Moses gave as it were a new identity to the Joseph tribe, and the instrument was religion.[152] As this Joseph/Israel was the Israel of the Old Testament, one may say that through the action of Moses a new people came into being, even if the elements are much older.[153]

Group II. Here Lods must be named first, who really stands quite close to Robinson. He only goes a little further in that he removes the whole time of the patriarchs to Kades. In the Negeb and the northern Sinai desert, Ḥabiru/Hebrews formed a 'confédération des Bené Israël'.[154] The expression Israel Lods still understands in an ethnic sense: it expresses a vague feeling of solidarity on the ground of common race. With Lods also the transition from race to people takes place through the means of Moses, whose activity he describes as the 'création d'un peuple par la fondation d'une religion nationale'.[155] This religion Moses took over from the Kenites.

It is plain that the most pronounced protagonists of the view that Israel originated at Sinai/Kades, really belong with the group of Sellin and Volz, discussed above. These, however, always allowed the religious to predominate over the national element. We have seen that they regarded 'Israel' as primarily a term of religion. If then we now discuss Auerbach here, that is because he does lay more stress upon Israel as a people than Volz or Sellin did. For Auerbach too, Israel's ancestors are descended from Aramaean emigrants. Possibly the time of the stories of the patriarchs reflects a period in Israelite proto-history when Israelite and/or related tribes were already in Canaan, but we know nothing certain of this time, nor is it essential.[156] The beginning of the actual people lies in the time of their bondage in Egypt, where quite different

---

[151] 'The controlling factor in her recognizing of herself as a nation was that supplied by Aramaean blood and, still more, by Aramaean tradition.' Robinson, *History*, p. 47.

[152] 'The instrument used by Moses was religion, in fact the only means by which he could have accomplished his purpose. It was in association with a new God, and in nothing else, that these tribes could find their unity, for the basic principle one people one God, seems still to have governed the policy of the tribes'. *o.c.* p. 90.

[153] *o.c.* p. 97.

[154] Lods, *Israël*, p. 214.

[155] *o.c.* p. 360.

[156] Auerbach, *Wüste und Gelobtes Land*, S. 52.

groups came into contact with one another. That they then coalesced and became a *real people*, is entirely the work of Moses.[157] That he did this work, Auerbach explains from the revelation that Moses had received.[158] The nucleus of his work lies in the laws he gave. From the beginning, the decalogue became the soul of the people that Moses created. 'Denn auch der Leib, der diese Seele trug, das Volk Israel, ist im wesentlichen das Werk des Mose. Aus dem Haufen entlaufenen Sklaven, aus den Sippen armseliger Beduinen hat er durch die Gewalt einer Idee ein Volk geschaffen. Diese Idee ist von Anfang an eine religiöse: "Israel" heisst: "Gott streitet". Es ist die Eidgenossenschaft derer, die sich zum ausschliesslichen Dienst des Einen und unsichtbaren Gottes verpflichtet haben.'[159] 'Die Form, in der uns in der literarischen Tradition diese Eidgenossenschaft Israel entgegentritt, ist das System der Zwölf Stämme. Hierbei aber begegnet uns die eigentümliche Erscheinung, das zwar die Idee der "Zwölf Stämme Israels" immer in der Theorie festgehalten wird, dass es aber in Wirklichkeit gar nicht immer zwölf und gar nicht die gleichen Stämme sind, die zur Volksgemeinschaft Israels gerechnet werden.'[160] Here Auerbach certainly comes very close to Volz and Sellin. The only difference is, that Auerbach's Israel is already a real people while wandering in the desert, being the twelve tribes: Simeon, Levi, Judah, Zebulun, Dan, Naphtali, Ephraim, Manasseh, Cain, Caleb, Rechab, Jerahmeel.[161]

Guthe's position, again, is on the border of Group II and III. He has an initial beginning of 'Hebräische Hirtenstämme in der Wüste", more especially in the southern desert.[162] Israel as we know it later, came from the tribe of Joseph, which spent a time in Egypt. Through the inter-

---

[157] 'Das der Ausbruch der Israeliten aus Aegypten nicht nur zu einer Vermehrung und Neuverteilung der nomadischen Wüstenstämme geführt hat, sondern zur Bildung eines Volkes Israel, das nach einem festen Plane das grosse Unternehmen der Eroberung Kanaans in Angriff nahm – das is das unsterbliche Werk einer grossen Führer-Persönlichkeit, des Mose ben ᶜAmram aus dem Stamme Levi.' *o.c.* S. 61. 'Jedenfalls aber hat sich in Kadeš das Schicksal Israels entschieden. Hier hielten sich die aus Aegypten kommenden Stämme etwa während der Dauer einer Generation auf, bis sie sur Eroberung Kanaans schritten, hier wurden sie, die bisher Nomadensippen und Sklavenhaufen gewesen waren, zu einem Volke!' *o.c.* S. 66.

[158] Hypotheses such as 'Yahweh was the god of the Kenites' or even 'a volcano-god' do not in fact explain the pith of the matter: with the Kenites Yahweh never became what, via Moses, He became in Israel!' *Cf. o.c.* S. 63 a. n. 1.

[159] *o.c.* S. 72.

[160] *o.c.* S. 73. On S. 72¹ there is a heated polemic with Noth's *Das System der zwölf Stämme Israels*! We shall return to this.

[161] *o.c.* S. 74.

[162] Guthe, *GVI*, S. 12.

mediacy of Moses the Kenite god Yahweh became the god of the tribe of Joseph. The Rachel group, with this Joseph tribe as its core, remained after the exodus from Egypt for some time in the oasis Kades. There this group melted into the Leah group, and thus Israel came into being. The central point in this was: 'die Unterwerfung der Stämme und Geschlechter unter die Gerichtsbarkeit, die Moses im Namen Jahwes ausübte und der Übergang zum sesshaften Wohnen.'[163] Yahweh himself at first principally functioned as god of war.[164] In the course of the Conquest this original unity is lost again.[165] Israel then forms for the second time under Saul. Also, new tribes originated in Palestine! The traditions of the patriarchs Guthe explains as 'die Aneignung und Umgestaltung kanaanitischen Gutes durch die Israeliten'.[166]

Group III. The Americans Olmstead and Meek are agreed that Israel in the true sense only came into being under David; only then were the different elements, Yahwism, Desert-traditions and Ḥabiru-traditions fused into a unity. Thus both only acknowledge a single Conquest, only Olmstead dates it in the time of Amarna[167] and Meek at the end of the thirteenth century. At the entry there was indeed no question of ethnic unity. 'Their common cause against a common foe tended to unite them more closely and in due course a confederacy or amphictyony of some of the tribes (probably only the Joseph tribes at first) was organized by Joshua at Shechem near Mount Gerizim ... In this northern Confederacy we have the beginning of what is later to be known as Israel.'[168] To this early Israel Judah originally did not belong.[169] Judah, though, had formed part of an amphictyony with Kades as centre, which had included the Kenites, the Simeonites, the Levites and the Jerahmeelites. There they worshipped Yahweh, who came from South

---

[163] S. 38.

[164] 'Im Kriege wird Israel seines Gottes gewiss.' *o.c.* S. 42.

[165] 'Alles, was bisher das Einheitsband der Stämme gebildet hatte, Gottesglaube, Kultus, Heerbann, Rechts- und Friedensordnung, war nicht dazu geeignet, um ein rasches und einheitliches Handeln der Gesamtheit herbei zu führen.' *o.c.* S. 87.

[166] *o.c.* S. 184.

[167] Attention was attracted by Olmstead's identification of the Ḥabiru chief Yashuya with Joshua. *History* p. 197. *Cf.* Meek, *Hebrew Origins*, p. 21.

[168] Meek, *o.c.* p. 25. 'The early *gērim* or immigrants had now become a people, a rebirth had taken place; the name of Jacob was changed into Israel' Meek, *o.c.* p. 26. Meek may have been acquainted with the work of M. Noth, but he nowhere mentions it. Moreover, the agreement with the older *History* of Olmstead remains so great that it is hardly probable.

[169] 'Israel and Judah were in their origin two separate and distinct peoples.' Meek, *o.c.* p. 76. Meek accepted the 'brotherhood theory' of Meyer and Luther. *Cf.* also *o.c.* p. 44.

Arabia. This Yahweh was introduced into Israel via Judah. The founder of the tribal league of Kades was Moses, the founder of that of Shechem was Joshua.[170]

6. A. Alt, M. Noth and G. von Rad

Beside the 'histories' discussed in the previous paragraph, the second half of the twenties witnessed the development of a new approach to the historical questions concerning earliest Israel. From the aspect of literary criticism this approach is very close to the methods developed by Gunkel *cum suis*, which made a name as *Formgeschichte* and *Traditionsgeschichte*.[171] Therefore this concerns on the one hand the continuation of the work of Sellin, Weber and others as already discussed, while on the other hand there is a great difference with that group of scholars, since history of religion and profane history are now more clearly distinguished, and because in general the methodical basis is far more solid. At the beginning of this development we find Albrecht Alt.

Although Alt's contributions towards solving the problem of Israel's origin are only of indirect effect, since he never went into details on this matter (he always assumed an already existent Israel), these contributions[172] are yet highly important, and that on five counts:
The first and most important concerns method. In the studies of Alt one really sees for the first time how the three different – and essentially different – sources of our factual material: the Old Testament, the world of the ancient Near East with its written traditions and archaeology, may all three be utilized to the full on a sound basis, *without doing injustice to any of the three*. But also: without any of the three *a priori* taking a higher place or being exempt from scientific criticism.[173] In the second place, by his discovery of the 'God of the Forefathers' as a phenomenon in religious history, Alt succeeded in giving a definite content to the concept 'religion of the patriarchs' as an earlier phase of Israelite religion. Before that, the religion of the patriarchs had always been the

---

[170] Meek, *o.c.* p. 110 *seq.*

[171] An excellent example of this method is the study of K. Galling, *Die Erwählungstraditionen Israels*. BZAW 48. Giessen 1928. It is also very important for our subject.

[172] The most important are: Die Landnahme der Israeliten in Palästina (1925). Now in: *KS I* S. 89-125. Der Gott der Väter (1929). Now in: *KS I* S. 1-78. Die Staatenbildung der Israeliten in Palästina (1930). Now in *KS II* S. 1-65. Die Ursprünge des israelitischen Rechts (1934). Now in *KS I* S. 278-332. Erwägungen über die Landnahme der Israeliten in Palästina (1939). Now in *KS I* S. 126-175.

[173] *Cf.* also Kraus, *Geschichte der historisch-kritischen Erforschung des Alten Testaments*, S. 370 *seq.* Only Alt is a little too uncritically applauded here!

subject of the most wild and unfounded theories, since nobody saw where and how the problem should be attacked.

Thirdly, there are Alt's masterly studies in territorial history. Especially in these extremely detailed studies it is clearly apparent how fruitful was the aforesaid work undertaken alike in the three fields of our knowledge. Thus his two studies concerning the *Landnahme* are so ordered, that he first carefully examines and arranges all we know of Palestine *before* the Israelites entered it, and then describes conditions there in the earliest time *after* the entry of which we have information, the later time of the Judges and the early Monarchy. On the basis of the essential differences observed, Alt draws highly important conclusions as to the nature of Israel's *Landnahme* and the way the Israelites inhabited the country in the first period after it.[174] The *Landnahme* proves to have taken place as a process of sedentarization, and the establishment of this fact forms the basis for comparisons with numerous analogous developments. In the fourth place, we have Alt's epoch-making study on Israelite law.[175] In this study, Alt comes closest to the problem of 'Israel'. We have seen how Alt's hypothesis that the religion of the patriachs belongs to a religio-historical type of 'gods of the forefathers', gave this religion of the patriarchs a legitimate place as an early stage before the later Yahwism. This transition from a primordial Israel to true Israel must have taken place before the *Landnahme*, for the latter presupposes it. Alt has hardly said anything about this transition itself. Thus earliest Israel existed just before and during the *Landnahme*, but precisely these two periods almost entirely escape our observation. Empiric Israel as we meet with it in the later period of the Judges has already taken many forms bor-rowed from the country they lived in, which was Canaan. Is it still pos-sible to recognize the genuinely Israelitish? Alt sees a possibility of this, *int.al.*, in law. To this end he introduces the famous distinction between law in a casuistic and an apodictic formulation. Law in the casuistic formulation contains juridical texts which posit a case and then deter-mine the punishment. There is usually a beginning such as: 'supposing that ...', or: 'if ...', followed by '... then (he) must ...'. This is therefore a very objectively formulated law, easy to administer and aimed at

---

[174] The studies of territorial history were mainly devoted to towns, *e.g.* Beth-Sean (1926), *KS I* S. 246-255. Jerusalem (1925), *KS III* S. 243-257. Megiddo (1944), *KS I* S. 256-273. Samaria (1954), *KS III* S. 258-303. Just by taking a non-literary subject as starting-point, Alt was able to integrate the results of archaeological research in such a far-reaching fashion. For in that way the essential gulf between archaeology and literary science is bridged over! *Cf.* also M. Weippert, *Die Land-nahme der israelitischen Stämme in der neueren wissenschaftlichen Diskussion.* FRLANT 92. Göttingen 1967, S. 14-51.
[175] See above, note 172.

providing for all eventualities. This law was intended for local jurisdiction 'in the gates'.[176] For this, casuistic law was intended, and from this practice it grew up.[177] It is notable that we find this law to be fairly neutral towards Yahwism; moreover, it is here that we find many parallels with the *Umwelt*, namely in the codex Ḫammurapi. Alt sees this as indications that the origins of this obviously generally valid law must be sought outside Israel. An additional point is that this law clearly presupposes the cultural, sociological and economic situation of the land of Canaan. Certain rules even seem entirely un-Israelitish, e.g. slavery because of debt. We have to suppose therefore that the casuistically formulated law was taken over from Canaan, after the *Landnahme*.[178] Then Alt made a fifth very important step forward by assigning to this historically observed phenomenon of the borrowing of Canaanite law, a *Sitz im Leben* in the *cult*. Alt elucidates this by making use of the parallel with the ancient administrators of law in Iceland.[179] This step, taken by Alt after H. Gunkel, is tremendously important. From then on, we shall again and again find the cult as the *Sitz im Leben* of all kind of (religio-) historical phenomena, and as the great transmitter of the Old Testament traditions.

Besides this casuistically formulated law of the ancient Orient, the Old Testament has law of apodictic formulation, the content of which is also much stricter. This includes the *ius talionis* and the 'thou shalt ...'. If a *casus* is given, then it is always followed by the stereotype *mot yumat*. For instance: *makkē 'iš wāmēt mot yumāt*.[180] Alt considers

---

[176] 'Der Umfang der im kasuistischen Recht behandelten Gebiete entspricht aufs beste dem Charakter der normalen israelitischen Gerichtsbarkeit. Diese lag, wie eine Fülle von Zeugnisse im Alten Testament lehrt, von Hause aus und bis in späte Zeiten in den Händen der freien Männer der einzelnen selbständigen Ortschaften mit den Ältesten, d.h. den Vertretern der führenden Geschlechter, an der Spitze und war somit Laiengerechtsbarkeit in dem doppelten Sinne, dass erstens ein beamtetes Richtertum fehlte und zweitens auch die Priesterschaft der Heiligtümer nur dann und nur insoweit zur Mitwirkung bei der Rechtspflege zugezogen wurde, wenn und soweit ein Rechtsfall der Gottheit zur Entscheidung überwiesen werden musste.' Die Ursprünge S. 16/17, *KS I* S. 289. The practice of this jurisdiction has been very finely described by L. Koehler in '*Die Hebräische Rechtsgemeinde*' an inaugural lecture of 1931, now included in the little volume *Der Hebräische Mensch*, Tübingen 1953.

[177] Laws concerning homicide, marriage and inheritance, slaves, injury to life and limb, injury to a third party (liability) *etc. etc.*

[178] Die Ursprünge S. 25/26, *KS I* S. 296.

[179] Alt borrowed this parallel from Aug. Klostermann, *Der Pentateuch*. Kap. III Par. 3 'Deuteronomium und Grágás'.

[180] Exod. 21:12. Cf. for the formula, Gen. 2:17; 3:4; 20:7; 26:11. Exod. 19:12, Exod. 21. Lev. 20, Num. 35:21, 31.

this law to be typically Israelitish and to stem from the desert, since everything is so much harder there. Its *Sitz im Leben* is the Levite preaching.

Actually Alt made a sixth important step, though it is the logical consequence of the above. It is, however, generally ascribed to Martin Noth, because he has worked it out so greatly.[181] His method of territorial history caused Alt to point out again and again that the *Landnahme* is the oldest phase of Israel's history that we can say anything at all certain about. This *Landnahme* proved to be a *process of sedentarization*, as we have seen. It was a matter of tribes who often acted very independently of each other, but who yet in some way or other knew they were 'Israel'. We also saw that Alt explicitly sets the origin of this 'Israel' before the *Landnahme*: in the desert. Even at a late date one of the principal elements distinguishing 'Israel' from 'Canaan' was just this consciousness of 'not being autochthonous'. Thus Alt considers this very essential. Yet how are we to imagine it in ancient times? Alt then takes up ideas of Meyer, Beer and Weber[182] and points to the analogy with the amphictyonies in ancient Greek and Italian history.[183]

---

[181] Certainly Noth never claimed to be the intellectual father of the amphictyony! He avowedly linked up with Alt. *Cf. Das System*, S. 47 (see below, note 184).

[182] For Meyer, see above p. 6 and note 27. Although Alt does not name these forerunners, the parallel with Meyer especially is striking, since Meyer also lays such heavy stress upon the processes of sedentarization. This is the foundation of the whole analogy with the Greek and Italic world! For Beer, see above p. 19; for Weber, p. 25. Besides Alt, Noth only names Gunkel and Weber as predecessors (*Das System*, S. 47). For Gunkel, see above note 42. Noth also comes rather close to Sellin and his Yahweh league, see above p. 26.

[183] 'Die älteste Verbindung der Stämme Israels zu einer höheren Einheit, aus der das historische Volk Israel erwachsen konnte, wird man sich am ersten nach der Art solcher Zusammenschlüsse in der Frühgeschichte Griechenlands und Italiens denken dürfen, d.h. in der Form sakraler Verbände um gemeinsame Heiligtümer (sogenannte '"Amphiktyonien"), die unter Umständen auch politischen Einfluss gewinnen konnten, ohne jedoch ihren Gliedern die Selbständigkeit ganz zu nehmen. Allem Anschein nach geht das mit geringen Veränderungen dauernd bewahrte System der zwölf Stämme Israels auf einen solchen Verband zurück, und zwar auf einen Verband aus sehr frühen Zeit da in ihm mehrere Stämme noch gleichberechtigt neben den anderen stehen, die nach der Einwanderung in Palästina schnell gesunken sind. Die mit Bewusstsein gewählte und festgehaltene Zwölfzahl, die auf der monatlichen Abwechselung der beteiligten Gruppen in der Versorgung des gemeinsamen Heiligtums beruht, ist für Zusammenschlüsse typisch. Wenn dieser Zwölfverbund, wie zu vermuten ist, wenigstens mit seinen Anfängen noch in Israels vorpalästinischen Zeit und zu einem Heiligtum ausserhalb des Kulturlandes gehört, so haben wir in ihm eine der ältesten nationalen Organisationsformen zu sehen.' *Die Religion in Geschichte und Gegenwart, 2. Aufl.* Tübingen 1929, III. Band, Sp. 438-439 *s.v.* Israel – politische Geschichte (A. Alt).

This idea of an ancient Israelite amphictyony was worked out further by Martin Noth, and Alt continues to handle it in the form given it by Noth. Noth did this in his *'Das System der zwölf Stämme Israels'*.[184] This work may be regarded as one of the most important and certainly one of the most influential contributions to the science of the Old Testament from the first half of the present century. At the same time it is a masterly synthesis and application of the studies by Alt mentioned above. For more than three decades 'Das System' almost completely dominated all conceptions of earliest Israel. Hence we must examine this work in detail. Our criticism, however, will be reserved for the following chapters.

'Das System der zwölf Stämme Israels' consists of two parts, one analysing, one postulating. In the first part Noth observes that when the Old Testament speaks of the tribes of Israel, personified as the twelve sons of the patriarch Israel, we always see a single *Traditionselement*, viz. the constant number twelve. There are not twelve traditions about tribes, but one tradition about twelve tribes![185] Though the tribes may interchange, the number twelve remains constant. This brings Noth to speak of a *system*. Now this system appears in the Old Testament in two forms, depending on whether Levi is counted in as one of the tribes. There is a system 'A', which includes Levi and speaks of Joseph, and a system 'B', which does not have Levi and has split up Joseph into Manasseh and Ephraim in order to make up the number.[186] The place left open by Levi is given to Gad in system 'B'. It almost goes without saying that Noth regards system A as older than system B. In the pure form we only find A in Gen. 49, B only in Num. 26 and 1. These passages clearly show a development in the system. B is used by preference for geographical enumeration of the tribes. Noth also remarks that in both systems the sons of Rachel and of Leah are neatly ordered, with the exception of the 'displaced' Gad in B. Noth considers all this so schematic that he can only imagine it to have originated in a time when the tribes were still real entities, so that a system of twelve tribes was also a real entity then.[187] So that must have been in the time before the state was formed under David. Yet as system A supposes the secular tribe of Levi, we must go back much farther still. *Terminus ad quem* then was David; the *terminus a quo* cannot be indicated otherwise than as 'the time when the song of Deborah was made, in which no system is to be seen'.[188] Thus the system existed during the whole period of the Judges. But to what reality does

[184] BWANT IV. F, 1. Stuttgart 1930. Fotomech. reprint Darmstadt 1966.
[185] *Das System*, S. 4.
[186] *o.c.* S. 13.
[187] *o.c.* S. 28 *seq.*
[188] *o.c.* S. 36.

this system correspond? And then we have the famous theory of Noth (and Alt) about the ancient Israelite amphictyony, meaning a league of twelve tribes, grouped around a central sanctuary.[189] Really then, a covenant between twelve tribes and one god. For this amphictyony, Noth gives detailed parallels from the Greek and Italic world (Delphi!). Thus far the first part.

In the second part Noth tries to demonstrate the existence of such an amphictyony in ancient Israel. He justly points out that under Saul there suddenly proves to be something called 'Israel'. So there was 'something' that mutually linked the tribes. Was that the common detestation of 'Canaan'? Or was it 'Yahwism'? Or even 'die Ideale Einheit Israels'?[190] Whatever that may have been! These all remain empty notions if they are not institutionalized in some way, Noth concludes. Well, this institution was the amphictyony.[191] What made Israel into 'Israel' was her religion – note the agreement with Volz and Sellin! – and religion, certainly in those ancient times, means cult. And if this cult were spread over many (tribal) sanctuaries, then instead of having a uniting 'Israel-forming' effect, it would have had a dividing and centrifugal effect. Thus a perfectly logical chain of reasoning leads Noth to the conclusion that there must have been a central sanctuary. He finds it, he finds it at Shechem. There, at Shechem, the Israelite tribal covenant was formed; there lay the centre, the central sanctuary.[192] The historical cause that led to the forming of the league of twelve tribes was the intruding of the house of Joseph. At Shechem Joseph made a covenant with an earlier six-tribe amphictyony, the Leah group. This amphictyony also had its centre at Shechem. Besides in Sellin, Noth also finds support here in Steuernagel, (see above p. 7-9). Moreover, the covenant made at Shechem – Joshua 24! – meant the introduction of the god of the house of Joseph as god of the whole amphictyony. This amphictyony was Israel, and the god of the house of Joseph thus became the god of Israel![193]

The amphictyony consists of six or twelve members, because one of the first tasks of an amphictyony is regular care of the central sanctuary, for periods of one or of two months. Later this central sanctuary was removed from Shechem to Shiloh. This was possible, because the actual sacred object of the amphictyony was the ark. But there is more to be said of this amphictyony: the covenant also implied a certain common

---

[189] o.c. S. 59.
[190] Thus B. Luther, *ZAW* XXI (1901) S. 20 *seq.*
[191] *Das System*, S. 62 *seq.*
[192] o.c. S. 66 *seq.*
[193] o.c. S. 79.

law.[194] We think of the expression 'a foolishness in Israel' or 'we do not do such things in Israel'. Furthermore the covenant has a military aspect, as each member has a right to assistance and the duty to assist in case of attack.

The theory sketched above of an ancient Israelite amphictyony found very many adherents, so many even that for about thirty years it practically ruled all possible conceptions of earliest Israel. The initial criticism soon died down, and was only to raise its voice again after 1960. That the hypothesis of an amphictyony was so generally accepted, also by scholars who were otherwise hotly opposed to each other, is mainly because it kills two birds with one stone: it explains the 'unity of Israel' before the monarchy and at the same time provides a splendid '*Sitz im Leben*' for all manner of institutions of earliest Israel, both social and profane. The method of *Formgeschichte*, which was gaining more and more ground since 1930, brought about an increasing need of a *Sitz im Leben* going as far back as that in the history of Israel.

Naturally Martin Noth also utilized this amphictyony hypothesis in his later publications on the origins of Israel and its most ancient history.[195] The hypothesis was significantly extended in 1950, when Noth thought he had tracked down in the O.T. an office termed 'Judge of Israel', and explained this office as having originally been the chief office of the ancient Israelite amphictyony.[196] After the foundation of the monarchy he supposed the office to have continued for some time, although the importance of its content was naturally much diminished.[197]

It was of great consequence for the speed with which this amphictyony hypothesis was accepted, that it was almost at once subscribed to in a number of important publications, such as those of Rost,[198] Balscheit[199]

---

[194] *o.c.* S. 97.

[195] *Cf.* espec. Die Gesetze im Pentateuch (1940), now in: *GSAT* München 1960², S. 9-141; espec. S. 32-53. *Das Buch Josua, HAT I*, 7, Tübingen 1953². *Geschichte Israels*, Göttingen 1966⁶, S. 11 *seq.* David und Israel in 2. Samuel 7 (1957), now in *GSAT²*, S. 334-345.

[196] Das Amt des 'Richters Israels'. *Bertholet Festschrift*, Tübingen 1950, S. 404-418. *Cf.* for further literature C. H. J. de Geus, De richteren van Israël. *NThT* XX (1965) p. 81-100.

[197] Noth thus explains passages such as Mic. 4:14 and Deut. 17:9. Das Amt des 'Richters Israels', S. 415-417.

[198] L. Rost, *Israel bei den Propheten*. BWANT 4. F 19. Stuttgart 1937.

[199] B. Balscheit, *Alter und Aufkommen des Monotheismus in der israelitischen Religion*. BZAW 69, Berlin 1938. Balscheit explains Israel's monotheism from the central consequence of the chiefly monolatric cult of the early Israelite amphictyony. In a way, he is the first here of a long series of authors, always managing to reduce other aspects of ancient Israel to the amphictyony.

and Möhlenbrink.[200] Highly influential was also the fact that G. von Rad subscribed to it, so that the amphictyony hypothesis gained an established and very important place not only in the field of history and of introductory studies to the Old Testament (as transmitter), but also in the religious history of Israel and in Old Testament theology.[201] Von Rad continues the line of Noth. Although the opinions of these two great scholars are certainly not always in parallel (they differ a good deal, for instance, with regard to the evaluation of the importance and the function of the Exodus traditions), yet Von Rad entirely accepts the amphictyony hypothesis. It is also the foundation of the outlook upon the historical development of Yahwism sketched in part I of his famous 'Theologie des Alten Testaments'. And it is Von Rad and his pupils who have made large-scale application of the amphictyony hypothesis for the explanation of religious phenomena in Ancient Israel.[202] Yes, a pre-monarchial central cult, not yet indeed exclusive but yet the focus of ancient Israel, is the basis of the great emphasis Von Rad lays upon the significance of the cult as the place where the old historic traditions of Israel were transmitted and relived.[203] Besides a much heavier stress upon the cult, Von Rad added something else to the amphictyony hypothesis, and that was a further elaboration of the concept of Holy War. Noth had already recognized war as an institution of the amphictyony,[204] but then either as a sanction against one of the membering tribes (Judg. 19-21) or as a war of defence or liberation, as waged by the Judges. Von Rad here adds the 'wars of the Lord', the wars waged to conquer Canaan and the wars against the 'nations', as e.g. Saul's war with the Amalekites. Von Rad identified old conceptions of and even directions for these amphictyonic holy wars (for they were waged in the name of the amphictyonic god!) in the

---

[200] K. Möhlenbrink, Die Landesnahmesagen des Buches Josua. ZAW LVI (1938) S. 238-268. And: Sauls Ammoniterfeldzug und Samuels Beitrag zum Königtum des Saul. ZAW LVIII (1940/41) S. 57-69. Epoch-making was also the study of K. Galling, Bethel und Gilgal. ZDPV LXVI (1943) S. 140-155 and LXVII (1944/45) S. 21-43.

[201] Von Rad gave a weighty impulse to the dissemination of the amphictyony theory with his article s.v. "ISRAEL", A: Israel, Juda, Hebräer im A.T. in ThWNT III, Stuttgart 1938, S. 356-360.

[202] G. von Rad, Theologie des Alten Testaments. Band I, Die Theologie der geschichtlichen Ueberlieferungen Israels. München 1957¹, espec. S. 1-110 Abriss einer Geschichte des Jahweglaubens.

[203] Cf. besides Von Rad also A. Weiser, Einleitung in das Alte Testament. Göttingen 1957⁴, espec. S. 21-24. A good and relevant example of this method of approach is seen in H. J. Kraus, Gilgal. Ein Beitrag zur Kultusgeschichte Israels. VT I (1951) S. 181-199.

[204] Noth, Das System, S. 100-108 and Exkurs IV S. 162-170.

instructions given for war in Deuteronomy and in the descriptions of the wars in the books Joshua to II Samuel.[205] Working with the *formgeschichtlich* method, Von Rad collected the literary elements which appear in these books with hardly any variation. On the basis of these literary elements, Von Rad reconstructed the 'theory of the holy war'. The sacred character of this theory is so strong that it looks rather more like a *liturgy!*[206] Although there is a great resemblance between the methods of Alt, Noth and Von Rad, and Von Rad leans heavily upon the work of Alt and Noth for the historical side, it is not right to take Von Rad and Noth together and speak of *e.g.* the 'method Von Rad-Noth', or the 'Noth-Von Rad school', as is sometimes done by a certain American school (see below).

7. G. A. Danell and H. H. Rowley

We now turn to two important works that both accept the amphictyony hypothesis, but explicitly dissociate themselves from Von Rad, *int.al.* on the point of the evaluation of the cult and of the Sinai traditions. The first is the afore-mentioned work of G. A. Danell.[207] Danell also supports the amphictyony hypothesis but, as we shall see, solely for the explanation of a single problem in the history of Israel: the unity of Israel before the monarchy. In chapter III we shall see how Danell explains the etymology of 'Israel' by reducing it to the old divine and tribal name Asher. According to Danell (following the trail of Naor) the names Asher, Jeshurun and Israel are essentially identical, although he at once admits that it is difficult to prove this.[208] The choice of this etymology, however, implies the taking up of a cardinal stand with regard to history, viz. that the name Israel is really 'pre-Israelitish', that is to say that it goes back to a time before there was any Israel in the usual meaning of the word. Danell follows Steuernagel in his view that the tribes streamed out as it were from the central mountain country of Ephraim, so he also assumes that Asher originally lived in the southern part of Ephraim. In this way he explains the fact that the name Israel is connected first of all with the region of Bethel and Shechem.[209] This original pre-Israelite-Canaanite Israel then, developed from the name of the god worshipped in Bethel and afterwards (sic! dG) in Shechem into

[205] Von Rad, Das Deuteronomium und der Heilige Krieg. *Deuteronomium-studien,* Göttingen 1948², S. 30-41. And: *Der Heilige Krieg im alten Israel.* Zürich 1951.
[206] *Der Heilige Krieg im alten Israel,* S. 6-14.
[207] *Studies in the Name Israel in the Old Testament.* Upsala 1946.
[208] *Cf.* below, chapter III, the excursus of the name Israel.
[209] *Studies in the Name Israel,* p. 27-38.

44

the name of the tribe especially worshipping him, and subsequently – also in pre-Israelite times! – into the name of a larger community centred on Bethel and later on Shechem, a pre-Israelite amphictyony 'Israel' consisting of the Leah tribes and the Israel of the Israel stela. Now what is the relation of that Israel to the tribes that afterwards came from the desert under Moses and Joshua? Here again Danell follows Steuernagel and Noth: the desert tribes are the Rachel tribes, they brought Yahwism with them. That they already bore the name 'Israel', however, Danell greatly doubts.[210] Probably the appellation 'Hebrew' at first only applied to them. Even at a much later time this group is still called so by the Philistines, according to Danell. In the traditions about the wanderings of the Hebrews, Danell finds reminiscences of the Hurrites, particularly in the stories about Abraham.[211]

It is worth noting how after extensive research Danell rejects the division between Israel and Judah, which before the war was generally accepted, and which as we saw goes back to Meyer and Luther. He considers it impossible to doubt that Judah already formed part of the kingdom of Saul.[212] The custom in the O.T. of using Judah and Israel as parallel concepts only dates from after 722 B.C.E. Yet there was a certain separate development before Saul. For on the one hand it seems impossible to detach Judah or Ephraim from a connection with Moses, while on the other it is quite clear that Joshua has no original ties with Judah, whose leader was Caleb. It is therefore most likely that both sections of Israel had their own traditions of the Entry, but being already united in the same cult, maintained friendly relations which were not forgotten after the Entries, but facilitated Judah's admission into the union of Israelite tribes under Yahweh.[213]

One cannot escape the impression of meeting with a great inconsistency here: two quite different reconstructions of the 'Conquest' are rather maladroitly linked up! Yet this view of Danell's is by no means unimportant. Danell has clearly shown that the term 'Israel' in the O.T. may very often be used to contrast the great majority of the people with a minority usually mentioned by name. Thus 'Israel' may have a variable meaning in the historical books![214] It is very clearly seen in

---

[210] o.c. p. 40.
[211] o.c. p. 36.
[212] o.c. pp. 47-50.
[213] o.c. p. 49.
[214] o.c. p. 66 and 75: 'There was then no opposition between Israel and Judah at this date. Both Israelites and Philistines – and Judaeans – considered Judah part of Israel and of the kingdom of Saul. His title characteristically enough is *melek yiśrā'ēl* and his kingdom is called *mamleket yiśrā'ēl*.' Cf. also p. 85 seq.

Judg. 19-21, where 'Israel' and 'Benjamin' are so contrasted, and in the same way Danell explains many passages in the Samuel books, wheie Israel in distinction from Judah need mean no more than the great majority of the rest of the people. Danell will not hear of the amphictyony living on after Saul and David; he does however take account of an earlier amphictyony at Kades, before the Rachel tribes migrated to Egypt. Danell's point of departure, a Canaanite, at least a non-Israelite (in the customary sense of 'Israel'!) origin of the term Israel, afterwards combined with Yahwism to become the real Israel of the Old Testament, he shares with those Old Testament scholars who regard the factor of religion as the decisive constituting element of 'Israel' and who detach this factor from ethnic considerations. The great difference is, though, that for Danell the name Israel pertains to the ethnic and not to the religious factor. We shall see this view appearing again also after Danell.[215]

The second book discussed here, and that like Danell's accepts the amphictyony hypothesis in a mitigated and limited form, is the work of H. H. Rowley 'From Joseph to Joshua', containing the Schweich lectures for 1948.[216] In a manner that excites our deepest respect almost the entire material until 1948 is summarized here. In these lectures, Rowley gives an excellent, clear and impressive status quaestionis of the whole complex of problems from the Exodus until and including the Entry. No wonder the work remained the last word on this problem for some twenty years. This was due in the first place to the overwhelming amount of material and literature that Rowley ordered and worked over, but also to his having made clear that the whole period from Joseph until and including Joshua forms a single problem, all aspects of which hang together.[217]

Rowley identifies the time of Jacob with the Amarna period. Jacob and his people form part of the Hebrews/Ḥabiru; the term Ḥabiru being interpreted as having a social meaning.[218] In Canaan, the Ḥabiru were concentrated in three areas: Galilee (Zebulun, Asher), the centre (Shechem) and the Negev. The main concentration was in the Negev, with

---

[215] For instance the surmise of M. A. Beek, Das Problem des aramäischen Stammvaters. *OTS VIII*, Leiden 1950, S. 193-213. See also in the discussion of Mendenhall and Seebass.

[216] H. H. Rowley, *From Joseph to Joshua. Biblical Traditions in the Light of Archaeology*. London 1950, 1964⁵.

[217] 'But, as I hope I have made plain, it is not merely a question of the date of the Exodus and of the movements into Palestine, but of relating the entries to one another and of explaining how all the tribes came to be Yahweh worshipping and why they thought of themselves as related to one another.' *o.c.* p. 109.

[218] *Cf.* above, p. 31. Fundamental for this view is always Noth's Erwägungen zur Hebräerfrage! *Procksch Festschrift*, Leipzig 1934, S. 99-113.

Kades Barnea as the probable epicentre. Here were Judah, Reuben, Simeon and Levi, together with Caleb and Kenaz. At a later stage these six formed an amphictyony with Hebron as its centre. Of the six, only the Levites shared in the Egyptian period and the Exodus. As a result of Gen. 34, the affair of Dinah and the Shechemites, Levi was driven away; part ended up in Egypt, and part fell back upon Judah with Simeon. In Egypt these Levites came into contact with the Rachel tribes Joseph and Benjamin.[219]

In Josh. 24 Rowley sees an old league between Canaanites and Ḥabiru. In its present form it is the renewal of the covenant of Sinai.[220] Yahwism is the real constitutive element of the biblical 'Israel', and that was introduced by the Rachel tribes. They, in turn, had taken over the worship of Yahweh from the Kenites/Calebites. The phenomenon 'Israel' as we meet with it in the Old Testament cannot be explained without a heavy emphasis upon the person of Moses and upon the role of religion as the unifying factor![221] After the Entry the tribes entered into a new amphictyony with those already present, which endured until the time of the Kings. Generally speaking, then, one may say that in Rowley's conception Israel originated by a very gradual process to which many factors contributed, but whose decisive moment did after all lie at Mount Sinai.

Both in their method of work and in their results Danell and Rowley really form the transition between the older historians such as R. Kittel and the modern German scholars such as M. Noth and G. von Rad. Although they both make use of the results of Alt and Noth, their methods mark them as belonging to the earlier period. Not meaning, of course, that one might speak of their having taken a step backward. Next comes a group of scholars whom many consider as the great opponents of the method of Alt and Noth, but who on closer examination do not offer a real alternative; we mean the mainly American school of W. F. Albright.[222]

---

[219] *From Joseph to Joshua*, p. 123 and 160.

[220] *o.c.* p. 128.

[221] *o.c.* p. 153-163.

[222] After the last world war Albright's manner of approach was mainly followed outside the U.S.A. in Israel, particularly by Y. Aharoni, A. Malamat, B. Mazar and Y. Yadin. Yet in Europe also he does not lack followers, especially among those who because of theological motives have never felt quite happy about the examination of the Old Testament by means of literary criticism. By many, this methodical criticism is mistakenly felt as scepticism (or perhaps personally so experienced?) and as a result the examining of separate parts of the O.T. by means of literary criticism is acceptable, while all the vials of wrath are immediately poured out upon those who consistently approach the whole Old Testament

8. The school of W. F. Albright

Albright is renowned first of all as one of the greatest inspirers of Palestinian archaeology. Although many of his own, sometimes rather hasty conclusions and reconstructions founded on excavations he visited, advised, or carried out himself could not be maintained when the sites were afterwards re-examined[223] and although many of the data he calls to aid were published much later or not even yet,[224] there can be no doubt of the very great services Albright rendered to archaeology, oriental studies and biblical science. We need only regard Albright's role in stimulating the American share in these sciences for half a century! His excavations

according to one particular critical, which in this context means scientific, method. Compare for instance the always highly negative judgement pronounced upon authors such as Wellhausen, Eissfeldt and Noth, while far more is accepted from Meyer and Alt! The expression 'minimalists' favoured by such people, meaning that Wellhausen and his followers understand by Old Testament science the 'minimalizing' of the O.T. through a consistent refusal (*sic*) to use archaeological material, is only too eloquent in this respect. Moreover, the term suggests that the ultimate historical reconstruction is the norm by which it judges. All this is not only impermissible and irrelevant, but also completely arbitrary! Ed. Meyer certainly did not arrive at a so much more orthodox reconstruction of Israel's earliest history than Wellhausen did. A lucid synopsis of the current opinions regarding the problem of the Conquest, with a good survey of the stand taken until then by Albright, is now to be found in: M. Weippert, *Die Landnahme der israelitischen Stämme in der neueren wissenschaftlichen Diskussion*. FRLANT 92, Göttingen 1967.

[223] Compare *e.g.* the results and conclusions of Albright's pupil L. A. Sinclair of a re-examination at one of Albright's first sites in Palestine: An Archaeological Study of Gibeah, *BA* XXVII (1964) p. 52-64, with those of the (also American) archaeologist P. W. Lapp, Tell El-Fûl, *BA* XXVIII (1965) p. 1-10. The use of these different topographical names really tells us enough!

[224] The definitive report of the excavations at Bethel only appeared in 1968. It was put together as best he could by J. R. Kelso: *The Excavation of Bethel*. AASOR XXXIX, Cambridge Mass. 1968. We find that it is decidedly not possible to draw those historical conclusions which Albright thought he was justified in drawing in the thirties, in his polemic with M. Noth. *Cf.* especially *BASOR 56* (1934), *58* (1935) and *74* (1939). Albright's call upon the results of the excavations at Shiloh, where he was adviser to the third campaign, also proves to be unfounded. Marie-Louise Buhl and S. Holm-Nielsen, *Shiloh. The Danish Excavations at Tall Sailūn, Palestine, in 1926, 1929, 1932 and 1963. The Pre-Hellenistic Remains*. Copenhagen 1969. *Cf.* also below, note 228. The most striking is, that the famous radical 'cultural gap' between the Late Bronze Age and the Iron Age proves quite to disappear in practice. These very reports now published about Bethel and Shiloh clearly show that we have to do here with processes of considerable extension in time. *Cf.* also the – for an American! – very sharp criticism and reappreciation of Martin Noth by W. G. Dever, Archaeological Methods and Results: a Review of Two Recent Publications. *Or XL* (1971) p. 459-471.

at Tell Bēt Mirsim, and their publication, are still held in honour.[225] His vast knowledge of ancient Semitic cultures and languages enabled Albright to survey and combine the data from the whole ancient Middle East in a way that few can equal. Indeed, with even more justice than Sir Flinders Petrie, Albright may be called the 'king of Palestinian Archaeology' in the period between the two world wars. Since the greater part of his archaeological activity lay before 1940, it would be unfair to complain that modern science must disallow many of his results and conclusions, now that archaeology has acquired so much more fine-grained methods and improved techniques. On this point the criticism of especially English scholars like Dame Kathleen M. Kenyon and Sir Mortimer Wheeler is not quite fair.[226] Besides as an actual excavator, Albright has also become known as an orientalist, and as a theologian who has tried to build up a scientific approach to the Old Testament in which, as he viewed it, more justice would be done to the archaeological data. In a number of articles in the bulletin of ASOR, Albright attempted to give a reconstruction from this angle of Israel's earliest history in particular, which might serve as an alternative to that of Alt and Noth.[227] Yet in this respect also it must be said that Albright was chiefly a *stimulator*. His arguments are too incidental and lacking in consistent method really to affect the standpoints of Alt and Noth. Also, Albright fairly often revised his own views, and in the course of a few decades defended many contrasting beliefs. Generally speaking, one may say that the picture of Israel's earliest history that Albright always had before him, has a far more evolutionist trait than is customary in Europe.[228]

[225] Published as *Tell Beit Mirsim I, Ia, II* and *III*, in respectively AASOR XII, XIII, XVII and XXI-XXII. New Haven 1932-1943. *Cf.* also Albright's *The Archaeology of Palestine*. Pelican A 199, London 1949[1] and often reprinted since.
[226] This applies especially to Sir Mortimer Wheeler, *Archaeology of the Earth*. Pelican A 356, London 1961[3]; but also to P. W. Lapp, who in his *Biblical Archaeology and History*, Cleveland 1969, calls all pre-war excavations unscientific!
[227] Archaeology and the Date of the Hebrew Conquest of Palestine. *BASOR 58* (1935). Further Light on the History of Israel from Lachish and Megiddo. *BASOR 68* (1937). And especially in: The Israelite Conquest of Canaan in the Light of Archaeology. *BASOR 74* (1939). In these three articles the main point is how literary and archaeological data may be combined and in what way they can supplement one another. Further they are particularly directed against the aetiological method as utilized by Noth in his Joshua commentary (see above, note 195). Statements of principle are also found especially in the first chapters of Albright's famous *From the Stone Age to Christianity*. New York 1957[2]; and now also in his *Archaeology, Historical Analogy and Early Biblical Tradition*. Baton Rouge 1966. And in *Yahweh and the Gods of Canaan*. London 1968.
[228] This is seen most plainly in '*The Biblical Period. From Abraham to Ezra. A Historical Survey*'. Originally a chapter from L. Finkelstein ed., *The Jews: Their History, Culture, and Religion*. New York 1949. Frequently reprinted separately.

To understand what Albright was really aiming at, we can best turn to his pupil J. Bright, who has treated these problems systematically in his 'Early Israel in Recent History Writing.'[229] The method defended there is also the foundation of his 'History of Israel'.[230]

Both with Albright and with Bright we notice how much is in fact taken over from Alt and Noth and from the earlier introductory science since Wellhausen. Bright stresses his appreciation of the work of Noth and particularly of the fact that it is so firmly rooted in the method of literary criticism. Also the traditio-historical approach and the quest for an original Sitz im Leben is positively appraised. So is the Formgeschichte and the distribution over the Pentateuch sources G, J and E. Bright accepts the amphictyony hypothesis and even Noth's point of departure, that all traditions referring to Israel's oldest past have been transmitted to us via the league of the twelve tribes.

Hence M. Weippert can observe 'dass die "Schulen" von Alt und Albright mit demselben Quellenmaterial und prinzipiell auf dem Boden derselben Methodik... arbeiten'.[231] That they yet arrive at such a totally different picture of Israel's history, is mainly a matter of evaluation. After Bright has set forth where his views agree with Noth's and expressed his appreciation of Noth's work, he introduces his criticism as follows: 'has Noth succeeded in presenting a satisfying picture of the origins and early history of Israel? The answer must be: no. On the contrary, his presentation leaves one distinctly dissatisfied. Is this really all that an objective historian can say?'[232] His criticism falls under three heads.

I The historical evaluation of the hexateuch traditions produces too little 'history'. Little can be said historically of the patriarchs and of the Exodus and Sinai traditions of Moses. The Entry took place in quite a different way than is described in the book of Joshua. Yet if Noth were right in this, then the phenomenon of Israel and its religion would remain entirely without an adequate explanation![233] The answers of Noth are unsatisfactory. If the tribes only came into being after the Entry and joined together in an amphictyony, then what was that solidarity based upon? Why did they so quickly accept the new religion? According to Noth we lack the data to reply to these questions, but we do have the data! The solidarity of all the tribes, the

[229] Studies in Biblical Theology, No. 19, London 1956. Here Bright also discusses the conservative approach of Y. Kaufmann (see below, par. 9). Noth's reply is found in Der Beitrag der Archäologie zur Geschichte Israels. SVT VII, Leiden 1960, S. 262-282. Cf. also Die Welt des Alten Testaments. Berlin 1962⁴, S. 127-132.
[230] London 1960.
[231] M. Weippert, Die Landnahme der israelitischen Stämme, S. 59.
[232] Early Israel, p. 83.
[233] O.c. p. 84.

pan-Israelite tendency is already present in 'G', that is to say at the end of the period of the Judges! Is not in that case the period of the amphictyony far too short to be both subject and creator of these traditions concerning the whole of Israel? According to biblical tradition 'Israel' did exist before the Entry.[234] Not only the pan-Israelite tendency, but also the combination of the themes Exodus and Sinai and the role of Moses in both are already found in 'G' so that they are very old. These old amphictyonic traditions therefore give an explanation of Israel's origin and the source of her faith, which is quite simply more probable and in any case more satisfactory that the negative replies of Noth.

II   The evaluation of the archaeological data and those from the *Umwelt*. Of course archaeology cannot prove anything, but it can give a picture of the milieu *e.g.* in the time of the patriarchs, and thus provide much indirect information. Here it is always a matter of the 'balance of probability', a combination of archaeological and literary data is sometimes required because of intrinsic probability.[235] Noth's puritanical attitude on this point sometimes leads to an underestimation of the possibilities of archaeology. In fact, Bright suspects Noth of a negative combination: 'We have no archaeological evidence bearing upon the conquest narratives of Joshua because, *ex hypothesi* (i.e. on the basis of literary criticism, dG) there can be none.'[236]

[234] Noth does reckon with a previous history of the Yahweh amphictyony, but does not let it function in any way. We shall have to express the same criticism in chapter III.

[235] *O.c.* p. 87-89. If on the one hand we have a series of towns that were destroyed, and on the other a literary tradition about a Conquest in the same period, then a combination of these two is the most probable possibility, though of course it can never afford a strict proof. For that matter, one can hardly escape the impression that Bright (like Albright before him) simplifies the problems here. For instance, when he cries out: 'Can it (*scil.* archaeology) not tell a Philistine occupation from an early Israelite one? Or a Late Bronze Age Canaanite one from an Early Iron Age one? Can it not tell if there has been an appreciable gap between destruction and re-occupation?' (*o.c.* p. 88) Every knowledgeable person knows this is not so simple, and that to these questions many specialists are inclined to answer if not simply 'no', at any rate 'yes, but ...' Moreover many archaeologists, especially those Anglo-Americans schooled in scientific methods of excavation, are opposed on principle to connecting specific finds with specific ethnic units. In one of the most important handbooks of recent years, the producing of 'imitation history books' by archaeologists is even seen as a kind of 'fall' of archaeology, and the historical interpretation of finds as one of the chief causes of the present crisis in this discipline: D. L. Clarke, *Analytical Archaeology*. London 1968, p. 11. Yet see also M. I. Finley, Archaeology and History. *Daedalus*, winter 1971, p. 168-186. Also Noth's view, note 229.

[236] *O.c.* p. 89.

III The literary methods. Bright criticizes Noth upon the following points: Noth too often makes impermissible use of an opposition between *saga* and history. For instance with regard to the stories of the patriarchs, whereas these tales combine both aspects. Well-known is also Bright's criticism of the use of the aetiological factor in the old tales as the *formative* factor.[237] Furthermore, Alt and Noth's insistence upon the *Ortsgebundenheit* of the traditions is untenable. The same applies to the way they divide the Pentateuch into five themes.

Examining the picture drawn by Bright himself of ancient Israel, we find there is no question of a real alternative to the amphictyony. Nor, indeed, could such be expected to result from the same methodic approach. Both Bright and Noth distinguish between an 'Israel' in the theological sense as the true essence, and an 'Israel' as a historical and political entity, constituting the outward form of this essence. Noth keeps all this very vague: the time of the patriarchs and the pre-Yahwistic Israel-amphictyony of the Leah tribes hardly function in his description. Bright places the origins at the migration of the 'Amorites', at the beginning of the second millennium.[238] True Israel, however, began with the covenant at the Sinai, which was also joined by non-Israelite groups. For Bright, the league of twelve tribes was far more than a sacred covenant, it was the nucleus of a commencing political organization.[239] Israel was not a specific race and only for a short time was it a nation (political unity), but it was always a people (cultural unity). The decisive criterion was religion. The roots thereof lie before the Entry, so that Bright has *a priori* a more positive attitude towards the traditions of the Pentateuch. This he describes as a 'balanced examination of internal and external evidence'.[240] Is it really so certain that the tribes only originated in Palestine? According to Bright, that cannot be proved of a single tribe. Is it not more likely that for instance the first places

[237] See first of all once more the remarks and the literature in M. Weippert, *o.c.* S. 132-139. Then the review by S. Herrmann in *ThLZ* LXXXIX (1964) Sp. 813-815. Especially for the Old Testament: B. S. Childs, A Study of the Formula 'Until this Day'. *JBL* LXXXIII (1963) p. 279-292. S. Mowinckel, *Tetrateuch, Pentateuch, Hexateuch.* BZAW 90, Berlin 1964, espec. S. 78-86. B. O. Long, *The Problem of Etiological Narrative in the Old Testament.* BZAW. 108, Berlin 1968. R. Smend, *Elemente alttestamentlichen Geschichtsdenkens.* Theol. Stud. Heft 95, Zürich 1968. F. Golka, Zur Erforschung der Aetiologien im Alten Testament. *VT* XX (1970) S. 90-98.
[238] C. H. J. de Geus, The Amorites in the Archaeology of Palestine. *Ugarit-Forschungen* III, (1971) S. 41-60.
[239] *Early Israel*, p. 113. See also the ending of this chapter.
[240] *O.c.* p. 123.

in the system for Reuben and Simeon go back to a time when these tribes held a leading position? [241]

Apart from a different evaluation of the Exodus, Sinai and Moses traditions, Albright and Bright therefore in no way offer a real alternative. For our subject, the most essential is that the amphictyony, be it with more stress upon the political aspect, is accepted.

The approach of Albright and Bright we find again practically unchanged in the work of one who was perhaps Albright's most important pupil, and his successor in the archaeological field in Palestine: G. E. Wright.[242] One may say that Wright, in spite of his archaeological background, pays even more attention to 'biblical theology'. For Wright the true Israel, Israel as a religious community, was the bearer of Yahwism. In respect of history, Wright hardly differs from Bright. The same may be said of the Israelian archaeologist Y. Yadin.

In a certain sense one might say that the last and most consistent step in the direction of Israel as a religious community, was taken by G. E. Mendenhall.[243] For him, 'Israel' is only a religious term, hence he sees the beginning of Israel as the joining of converts from all kind of different groups. In the long run, this religious community became a people. To seek for a pre-history of Israel before the Entry, that is before the combining of the inhabitants of Canaan and the Hebrews with Yahwism, is therefore senseless. Thus this Albright-pupil finally again arrives at the standpoint we already know from Volz and Sellin! Mendenhall really wants to explain the phenomenon of Israel by sociological means.[244] We shall have to return to Mendenhall in chapter III.

The contrary path, in 'Du groupe ethnique à la communauté religieuse', with the also sociological approach of Causse and Nyström, falls outside the scope of this book, since the subject studied is religion, and not the history of the people.[245]

[241] O.c. p. 115-118. See for my own view the ending of chapter II. When Bright posits that it cannot be proved which was there first, Ephraim as a geographical name or as the name of a people, he is right. In this instance, the probability lies with the former case. Nothing can be proved here, so that this point can hardly be adduced as an argument on either side. It is indeed so that Palestine is derived from the Philistines and not the other way round. On the other hand it is practically certain that the ethnic appellation is secondary in the case of 'Amorites' and 'Canaanites'. Cf. the essay named in note 238.
[242] G. E. Wright, The Literary and Historical Problem of Joshua 10 and Judges 1. JNES V (1946) p. 105-114. Biblical Archaeology. Philadelphia and London 1957. Archaeology and Old Testament Studies. JBL LXXVII (1958) p. 39-51.
[243] G. E. Mendenhall, The Hebrew Conquest of Palestine. BA XXV (1962) p. 66-87.
[244] See also the discussion of Mendenhall's attempt to find a tertium datur beside Albright and Noth in Weippert, Landnahme, S. 59-66.
[245] A. Causse, Du groupe ethnique à la communauté religieuse. Strassbourg 1937.

9. Criticism begins

This last paragraph will chiefly summarize the criticism that began in the sixties. We have seen in the previous paragraph how even the influential school of Albright and Bright, claiming to present an alternative on so many points to the picture of Israel's earliest times as designed by German scholarship, yet accepted the amphictyony hypothesis. Although we must name two scholars who strongly criticized the very principles of the amphictyony hypothesis before the second world war, it is yet justified to speak of beginning criticism with regard to the sixties. In spite, indeed, of two developments which should really have effected the contrary. The first of these is the increasing tendency to discover more and more 'amphictyonic' offices, institutions and traditions, so that we may well say Noth's hypothesis ran wild. The second thing is the fact that a whole series of research projects directed at particular amphictyonic institutions as these were posited by Noth, practically always rendered a negative result, which is really a negative result for the amphictyony hypothesis. I am thinking here of studies concerning the central sanctuary, the ark, the tribal league and the Holy War, the amphictyonic ethos, the judges, etc. etc.

With regard to the first development: strictly speaking mis-use is no counter-argument. The standpoint of M. Weippert is illustrative here, who subscribes to the amphictyony hypothesis while admitting that it has grown rank.[246] It is a pity he did not verify how this rank growth was possible! There is no suggestion yet of fundamental criticism.

Criticism as to details, concerning the various amphictyonic institutions, named above in the second place, will not be discussed in this paragraph. The matter will be fully examined in chapter IV, which is devoted to these institutions.

Yet it remains strange that a hypothesis so radically affecting the reconstruction of Israel's earliest history was so little criticized.[247] Perhaps one explanation might be, that this hypothesis did not spring up as something totally new. It was indeed already present *in nuce* in the

---

S. Nyström, *Beduinentum und Jahwismus.* Lund 1946. This applies also to the essay by G. Fohrer, Zur Einwirkung der gesellschaftlichen Struktur Israels auf seine Religion. In: *Near Eastern Studies in Honor of W. F. Albright.* Baltimore 1971, S. 169-186.

[246] For Weippert *cf.* note 222. He speaks of the amphictyony on p. 46[2], calling it an otherwise 'überzeugend entwickelte These'.

[247] The only important contemporary reviews of *Das System* that I could find were those of H. W. Hertzberg in *OLZ* XXXI (1931) Sp. 852-855, of J. Meinhold in *ThLZ* LVI (1931) Sp. 411-414, of F. Horst in *ThBl* XII (1933) Sp. 104-107 and of K. Galling, in *DLZ* LII (1931) Sp. 433-440.

previous century. Thus Noth's formulation of the hypothesis was really the outcome of a certain tendency, not the beginning of a new one. To retrace clearly what went before is one of the aims of this chapter.

There was, indeed, some criticism. In par. 5 we already mentioned E. Auerbach. His criticism of Noth can be summed up on two counts. In the first place he reproaches Noth with attaching too little weight to the work and the personality of Moses. Fusing a group of Aramaeans with a number of other elements into the people of Israel, is entirely the work of Moses. The Yahweh league at Kades under Moses' leadership was Israel's first political *form*, not its *origin*!

The second count is more important. Auerbach points out that the amphictyonies of classical antiquity never caused the forming of a nation. He calls Noth's theories mere 'flights of fancy'. A comparison with the Arabian tribal league under Mohammed could at a pinch have passed muster. If there had been an Israelite amphictyony, it would also have had to rest first upon the *ethnos*![248]

After Auerbach the next important critic was Otto Eissfeldt. He never dropped his objections to the amphictyony hypothesis, so his work forms a bridge to the sixties.[249] Eissfeldt's objections can also be summed under two heads: a) the amphictyony has not been proved, and b) the amphictyony cannot prove what according to Noth it should prove!

Eissfeldt points out that there are really only two passages on which Noth supports his theory: Judg. 19-21 and Josh. 24. He then challenges Noth to prove that the pan-Israelite tendency, that everywhere else in the book of Judges is so obviously secondary, must be original just

---

[248] *Wüste und Gelobtes Land I*, S. 72. That the amphictyony presupposes the *ethnos* has already been remarked about other amphictyonies. From two quite different points of view, the idea has also been mooted that an amphictyony was the form suited to ethnic minorities, who in this way tried to keep their own identity. In: W. E. Mühlman, *Staatsbildung und Amphiktyonien in Polynesien*, Stuttgart 1938, S. 111-112. Also: R. W. Williamson, *The Social and Political Systems of Central Polynesia*. 3 vols, Cambridge 1924. For the classical world: J. P. Harland, The Calaurian Amphictyony. *AJA* XXIX (1925) p. 160-171, espec. p. 166. We already find similar ideas in the old standard work by H. Bürgel, *Die Pylaeisch-Delphische Amphiktyonie*, München 1877. Original 'founders' of the amphictyony were Doric tribes. See also ch. IV. In the Netherlands M. A. Beek comes closest to the standpoint of Auerbach. Perhaps he lays a little more stress upon the ethnic element: the common Aramaean descent. *Wegen en Voetsporen van het Oude Testament*. Delft 1954[2]; *Van Abraham tot Bar Kochba*, Zeist 1964[3].
[249] His polemic with Noth is chiefly to be found in: Die geschichtliche Hintergrund der Erzählung von Gibeas Schandtat (Judges 19-21). In: *Festschrift G. Beer*. Stuttgart 1935, S. 19-40. Israel und seine Geschichte. *ThLZ* LXXVI (1951) Sp. 335-340. The Hebrew Kingdom. *CAH*[2] vol. II, chapter 34, Cambridge 1965, espec. p. 12-17.

here in Judg. 19-21. Also that terms such as *qāhāl* and *'ēdā*, elsewhere always considered to be late, should just here indicate that the text is very ancient. Why is there precisely here no mention of the tribal league, and why does no 'ruler of Israel' come into action here? Notwithstanding these questions, Eissfeldt agrees with Noth that the story must have some historical nucleus. This he seeks elsewhere, though: in the memory of Benjamin coming to be an independent tribe.[250] This would have occurred as a result of rebellion on the part of some (in reality probably more than one) South-Ephraimite town. Armed conflict then arose, which resulted in the termination of *connubium* by the rest of Ephraim. At that moment, the 'birth' of a new tribe was a fact.[251] Eissfeldt also points out that there is no evidence at all that Israel consisted of exactly twelve tribes in the time of the Judges. With regard to the lists of eponyms he also seeks the historic substratum somewhere else than Noth does. It is a highly arbitrary proceeding on the part of Noth to call the sets of twelve of *e.g.* Shalmaneser III 'a stereotype phrase', while finding a whole institution represented in those of the Old Testament![252]

Therefore the amphictyony cannot be proved. But then would it explain the unity of Israel as a people and her action as a political unity under Saul and David? In his review of Noth's *'Geschichte Israels'* Eissfeldt particularly discusses this question. For he is well aware that to all the questions put above, Noth would have answered: the amphictyony just did not function primarily in the political and military field, but above all in the ethical and religious field. Yet, says Eissfeldt, Noth then comes into conflict with what he himself so clearly set forth in his introduction to the *'Geschichte Israels'*, viz. that the concept 'people' *does* precisely belong to the political and military sphere, *not* to the ethical and religious, nor to the sphere of blood-relationship. Eissfeldt then seriously criticizes this separation of spheres of life. He reproaches Noth with not having taken sufficient account of the fact that the texts of the Old Testament express a theocratic idea.[253]

Eissfeldt fully agrees with Noth that a people originates as a result of historical and political factors. Therefore the amphictyony, even if it had existed as Noth postulated, could never explain the historical phenom-

[250] In saying thus, Eissfeldt undermines another part of Noth's argument. For Noth imagines Benjamin as already coming into the country as a tribe in the fifteenth century, *Das System*, S. 7[2]. This idea of Noth's is no longer supported by Schunck, *Benjamin*, BZAW 86, S. 18-47. Schunck does reckon, though, with a joint Conquest by Ephraimite and Benjaminite groups.

[251] For the tribe as endogamous group, see chapter III.

[252] *Cf. Geschichte Israels*, Göttingen 1956[3], S. 225[1].

[253] *Israel und seine Geschichte*, Sp. 340. One might also wonder whether Noth was perhaps led astray here by Luther's doctrine of the Two Rules.

enon of a 'people of Israel'. The amphictyony too, therefore, pre-supposes other binding factors. In this connexion Eissfeldt points to the absence of the Kenites in the tribal system, while it is often apparent how closely the Israelites felt themselves related to the Kenites.[254] This can only mean that the Kenites were not part of the political unity 'Israel' at the moment when the tribal systems were formed. And this moment was, according to Eissfeldt, the early monarchy under David.

That these arguments of Eissfeldt's were so little regarded, is due, I think, to two causes. In the first place the amphictyony hypothesis with its primacy of religion, is of course particularly tempting to theologians. In the second place, the questions that really underlie Noth's hypothesis[255] are only answered by Eissfeldt in a very vague manner: 'But there did exist a theoretical community of some sort consisting of about twelve tribes, before Israel became a state ....[256]

The political disjunction during the period of the Judges is very much stressed by H. M. Orlinsky.[257] He energetically attacks the amphic-tyony, remarking that it is not once mentioned in the whole Book of Judges. A feeling of unity was only present on the grounds of a common religion and a common language. The autonomous tribes and little city-states only worked together in so far as was necessary to make head against common problems.

These views of Orlinsky nowhere seriously face up to the problems set by Noth, so that they hardly impair his thesis. I only name Orlinsky here because we saw in par. 6, with surprise, that most Americans accept the amphictyony hypothesis.

Quite a different approach is that of Y. Kaufmann.[258] This Israelian scholar developed a highly original conception of Israel's earliest history. The method of literary criticism Kaufmann only accepts to a limited extent. What he actually does, is to demonstrate in a most ingenious and original manner – his attitude towards the text being quite un-critical – that the information in the Old Testament about the Entry is in the main quite apposite. Where it does not cover the facts, this is due not to the tradition as such, but to the design of the *Conquest* not having

[254] In this connexion Eissfeldt mentions I Sam. 15:6; 27:10 and 30:29. The Hebrew Kingdom, p. 16.

[255] See for this the introduction to chapter III.

[256] The Hebrew Kingdom, p. 17.

[257] H. M. Orlinsky. The Tribal System of Israel and Related Groups in the Period of the Judges. In: *Studies and Essays in Honor of Abraham A. Neuman*. Ed. by Meir Ben-Horin, Bernard D. Weinryb and Sol. Zeitlin. Leiden 1962, p. 375-388.

[258] Y. Kaufmann, *The Biblical Account of the Conquest of Palestine*. Jerusalem 1953. *Cf.* also the treatment of this little book in J. Bright, *Early Israel in Recent History Writing*. London 1956, p. 56-78.

been fully carried out: part of it remained Utopian! Highly original is his distinction of five different, successive conceptions of the land of Israel. He even speaks of five different 'maps'.

Although his method sets Kaufmann aside from the discussion as carried on upon the matter, while he certainly does not offer an acceptable alternative, his work is full of valuable remarks. For instance, about the aetiological method, and his emphasis upon the opposition Israel-Canaan already in the earliest times.

Kaufmann will have none of the amphictyony. He only speaks of their living and being organized in tribes. Yet in this little book, at least, he does not make plain how he imagines that to have functioned.

A dissident voice of quite another calibre is put forth by another German, S. Herrmann. He follows the trail of Eissfeldt. In a whole series of articles Herrmann has attacked the amphictyony hypothesis and tried to find an alternative.[259] For him too the chief objection is that it is impossible in principle to prove the hypothesis. His main counter-argument lies in establishing that the hypothesis supposes mutual contacts in the time of the Judges which are extremely dubious, even if only because of the geographical disjunction of the Israelite territory. This disjunction was not only caused by the political and geographical situation in Canaan, it was also rooted in the past. That is to say, it was due in part to a different *Conquest*. The various entries led to different traditions of the Entry. With regard to religion also, the developments in the north and the south were different. In the north, there was great emphasis upon the Exodus, Moses and the Mountain of God; in the south mainly upon the ark, the tent of the Presence, and Kades.[260] This discord in Ancient Israel, and particularly the difference between the south (Judah) and the north, plays a dominant part in Herrmann's opinion. He will not hear of a twelve-tribe system in the time of the Judges: it is an attempt of the Davidic-Solomonic state to give a genealogical basis to the political unity then in existence.[261] From the same period dates also the feeling of unity as we see it in the traditions of the Pentateuch.

---

[259] S. Herrmann, Das Werden Israels. *ThLZ* LXXXVII (1962) Sp. 561-574. Israel in Aegypten. *ZAeS* XCI (1964) S. 63-79. Neuere Arbeiten zur Geschichte Israels. *ThLZ* LXXXIX (1964). Sp. 813-825. Der Name JHW₃, in den Inschriften von Soleb. *Proceedings of the Fourth World Congress of Jewish Studies, Vol. I.* Jerusalem 1967, p. 213-217. Autonome Entwicklungen in den Königreichen Israel und Juda. *SVT* XVII (1969) S. 139-159. *Geschichte Israels in alttestamentlicher Zeit.* München 1973.
[260] Das Werden Israels, Sp. 570-573.
[261] Autonome Entwicklungen, S. 153.

This approach of Herrmann was protested against by R. Smend Jr.[262] Smend points out that under the personal union the feeling in the northern kingdom was definitely unfavourable for the formation of such a pan-Israelite tendency.[263] He is convinced that in the time of the Judges Judah really did form part of 'Israel', so that it is impossible to attack the amphictyony hypothesis from that angle.[264] Generally speaking, Smend considers Herrmann's approach really quite old-fashioned.

Then how does Herrmann explain the unmistakable tendencies towards unity and the common worship of Yahweh? For he sees quite well that this is where the amphictyony hypothesis exercises its great attraction. How about the unity of Israel, even if one joins with Herrmann in thinking that the song of Deborah does not suppose this unity, but is calling for it?[265] Herrmann explains the common worship of Yahweh more or less as a chance effect of history. Yahweh is the god of the inhabitants of Midian and the north-eastern Sinai. Judah came into contest with this god at Kades. The Joseph group made his acquaintance on their southward wandering which was finally to lead them to Egypt.[266] In support of this, Herrmann refers to the appearance of the divine name JHW_3^o, in the inscriptions of Soleb under Amenophis III.[267] What it comes down to is, that he sees the basis of Israelite unity in common historical recollections of the 'Proto-Israelites' from the time before their sojourn in Egypt.[268] The 'Proto-Israelites' were ultimately Aramaean nomads.[269]

[262] R. Smend, Gehörte Juda zum vorstaatlichen Israel? *Proceedings of the Fourth World Congress of Jewish Studies*, Vol. I. Jerusalem 1967, p. 57-62.
[263] *O.c.* p. 58-59.
[264] *O.c.* p. 62. This conclusion we already find, with far more elaborate argumentation, in G. A. Danell, *Studies in the Name Israel in the Old Testament.* Uppsala 1946: 'There is never a shadow of doubt in the Old Testament, that Judah of old belonged to Israel in the wider sense of the name, and this view is probably of very ancient date' p. 48.
[265] Das Werden Israels, Sp. 568.
[266] *O.c.* S. 573. Israel in Aegypten, S. 76.
[267] Der Name JHW_3^o, in den Inschriften von Soleb, S. 213-216. The god 'Shasu Jhw$_3^o$, is described as a Midianite mountain-god. *Cf.* also R. Giveon, Toponymes Ouest-Asiatiques à Soleb. *VT* XIV (1964) p. 239-255. The Shosu of Egyptian Sources and the Exodus. In: *Fourth World Congress of Jewish Studies*, Vol. I. Jerusalem 1967. p. 193-196. And now also: *Les Bédouins Shosou des Documents Egyptiens.* Leiden 1971, p. 235-239, 261-271.
[268] Israel in Aegypten, S. 74-78.
[269] With Herrmann, we return to the romantic view of the Beduin: a god like Yahweh has nothing to do with the life of farmers in Canaan, 'Jahwe hat viel mehr Züge jener vital-beduinischen Ursprünglichkeit an sich, die seine Verehrer auszeichnete, eine Ursprünglichkeit und schöpferische Kraft, wie sie nicht selten gerade

Very recently Herrmann has published his *Geschichte Israels*.[270] Therefore his conclusions can now be studied in the context of his reconstruction of Israel's history. Essential remains the dichotomy Judah-Israel. In reality Judah was never Israel. Israel originated in the central Palestinian mountains as a loose association of tribes. But the new element Herrmann brings in in this book, is his view that Israel came into existence at the moment(s) on which some of the tribes became aware of their own ethnic identity. And this used to happen in the – defensive – confrontations with the Canaanites. Of this awareness sings the Song of Deborah.[270a]

The twelve-tribe system has always been a theory, see above. That an "all-Israel" had existed, consisting of exactly twelve tribes, is a still younger theory.

The amphictyony hypothesis was greatly strengthened, when W. W. Hallo thought he had discovered a Sumerian parallel.[271] This seemed to obviate an important objection, viz. the fact that no other amphictyonies in the ancient Middle East had ever been demonstrated. Meanwhile, however, it has been pretty well established that Hallo's parallel really only holds for the Solomonic system of monthly supplies delivered to the court.[272] The word 'amphictyony' is totally misplaced here. Towns are named of which it is not certain whether they were all autonomous political units; there are a good many changes in the towns taking part, and their rights and duties were not the same: some supplied nothing, others a double quantity.[273]

in den Grenzgebieten zwischen Wüste, Steppe und Kulturland beheimatet ist und deren Bewohnern zu Leistungen von bleibender Bedeutung befähigte.' Israel in Aegypten, S. 72.

[270] S. Herrmann, *Geschichte Israels in alttestamentlicher Zeit*. München 1973. Espec. S. 160-164 and 188-190.

[270a] Quite near to Herrmann in their view of how Israel came into existence are: T. Ishida, The Leaders of the Tribal Leagues "Israel" in the Pre-Monarchic Period. *RB* LXXX (1973) p. 514-530 and A. D. H. Mayes, Israel in the Pre-Monarchy Period. *VT* XXIII (1973) p. 151-170.

[271] W. W. Hallo, A Sumerian Amphictyony. *JCS* XIV (1960) p. 88-114.

[272] I Kings 4:7-20. *Cf.* now for this T. N. D. Mettinger, *Solomonic State Officials*. Lund 1971, p. 111-127.

[273] Critical judgement must be brought to bear upon political parallels between Israel and ancient Sumer. Such parallels have been drawn, *int. al.*, by Th. Jacobsen, Early Political Development in Mesopotamia. *ZA* NF XVIII (LII) (1957) S. 91-141. And A. Malamat, Organs of Statecraft in the Israelite Monarchy. *BA* XXVIII (1965) p. 34-65. For criticism of this see D. G. Evans, Rehobeam's Advisers at Shechem, and Political Institutions in Israel and Sumer. *JNES* XXV (1966) p. 273-279.

Another publication, which was also regarded as supporting the amphictyony hypothesis, was from the hand of B. D. Rahtjen.[274] Rahtjen maintains that Ancient Israel could, strictly speaking,[275] hardly be called an amphictyony,[276] since all known amphictyonies are of cities and never of tribes. Never is a central sanctuary so mobile as the ark in Israel. In the final outcome, Rahtjen would not deny the Israelites their amphictyony, but he sees a far closer parallel to the classical amphictyonies in the Philistine pentapolis: cities, an Indo-Germanic background and a permanent central sanctuary in the Dagon temple at Ashdod. De Vaux was later to remark with justice,[277] that there is not the slightest evidence of such a Philistine amphictyony, or that Ashdod was a central sanctuary. The latter also seems unlikely since Dagon was not a Philistine god. I would add here, that if such an amphictyony did exist, it certainly failed completely in keeping the Philistines together as an ethnic unity.

The first really fundamental criticism of Noth's amphictyony hypothesis that found a hearing, was voiced in 1966 by G. Fohrer.[278] Fohrer again begins by first pointing out the weaknesses of the thesis itself: it is not a single hypothesis, but a whole conglomeration of unproven hypotheses.[279] Next, Fohrer remarks that the manner in which the hypothesis formulated by Noth functions at present in Old Testament scholarship, can only be termed a riotous growth. Especially the abuse of the

---

[274] B. D. Rahtjen, Philistine and Hebrew Amphictyonies. *JNES* XXIV (1965) p. 100-104.

[275] In this context Rahtjen speaks of 'the European norms'.

[276] Naturally this depends on what definition of an amphictyony is used. If one wishes also to apply the term amphictyony outside the Graeco-Italic world, the pronouncement is not correct. In the ancient Germanic world tribes could be members of an amphictyony, but also regions (Sweden). *Cf.* also note 293. If one goes far back into the past of the Delphic Amphictyony, then this also was founded by tribes and not by cities! Bürgel *o.c.* S. 22.

[277] R. de Vaux, Le thèse de l'Amphictyonie Israélite'. *HThR* LXIV (1971) p. 415-436, espec. p. 421.

[278] G. Fohrer, Altes Testament – 'Amphiktyonie' und 'Bund'? *ThLZ* XCL (1966) Sp. 801-806, 893-904. And: *Geschichte der israelitischen Religion.* Berlin 1969, S. 75-91.

[279] In the first place it rests upon earlier views regarding a central sanctuary with an amphictyony in the time of the patriarchs. It assumes the displacement to the time of the Conquest, and the transfer from the purely religious sphere to the politico-military field by Weber. Noth then pushes it on to the time of the Judges, and lays more stress again upon the cult. Finally it is completely institutionalized and smaller amphictyonies are assumed as earlier stages (Hebron, Shechem, Kades, Gilgal, Bethel).

postulated amphictyony as a 'Sitz im Leben' is severly censured by Fohrer.[280]

Fohrer, too, then points out that the most important conditions for an amphictyony in ancient Israel: the number of twelve tribes and the existence of a central sanctuary, cannot be proved for the period of the Judges. Moreover, the function of the ark is still extremely uncertain. In view of the above, the analogy with the Graeco-Italic amphictyonies becomes highly dubious. It must be added that it is surely very strange the Hebrew has no name for such an important institution. And that a Yahweh amphictyony, deliberately founded with a Yahweh sanctuary (the ark) as centre, should be called 'Israel', that is called after El, Fohrer considers most unlikely indeed![281]

The covenant made in Joshua 24 does indeed suppose a 'Gemeinschaftsbewusstsein', but that cannot be explained from the period of the Judges. It must be older. It was in the time of the Judges that this sense of unity was in danger of being lost, owing to the crisis of sedentarization. The process of sedentarization is very important in Fohrer's view.[282] Yet if the amphictyony hypothesis is so weak in its formal aspect, then why was it so generally accepted? Fohrer explains this from the theology of the covenant, which played such a great part between 1930 and 1960. This theology, however, lies open to some of the same objections as the amphictyony hypothesis. Before the deuteronomistic period, says Fohrer, we find no concrete idea of a covenant. Nor is it permissible to conjure it up in a *formgeschichtlich* way, *e.g.* via the ancient eastern pacts of vassalage. The covenant of Sinai was of course a fact, but it only served to constitute Israel as a people, afterwards it hardly plays a part at all.[283] Finally, Fohrer finds it strange that if 'Israel' was already a certain unity before Saul, Saul did not then become king over the whole of Israel at once. Hence Fohrer concludes the amphictyony hypothesis does not by any means explain what it pretends to explain: 'Insgesamt ergibt sich für die Richter – und den Übergang zur Königszeit ohne

---

[280] 'Nehmen wir alles in allem, so bleibt in einer fast tausendjährigen Geschichte Israels kaum etwas übrig, was nicht als eine ursprüngliche Einrichtung oder als eine Folgeerscheinung der Amphiktyonie erschiene.' *ThLZ* XCI (1966) Sp. 804.
[281] Sp. 807.
[282] *Cf.* for this ch. III. Fohrer's conception of the tribal systems, which he regards primarily as genealogical systems, is discussed in ch. II.
[283] Sp. 899. His Geschichte der israelitischen Religion S. 53-62, shows that the actual participants in the Covenant of Sinai only formed quite a small group: the Moses group. The great majority of the Israelites were then already living in Palestine or occupied in settling there.

Verwendung der Amphiktyonie-Hypothese und der *berīt*-Vorstellung als tragender Ideen ein ebenso klares Bild wie mit ihnen.'[284]

In the beginning of this paragraph we said that research concerning details would be treated in chapter IV. Let us make an exception here for a few studies that we merely wish to name, because they show that it is possible, also by means of literary criticism, to make more concrete pronouncements regarding the time of the patriarchs. The most important of this series are the studies of Zobel, Seebass, Weippert and De Pury.[285] All are concerned with the earliest history of the Israelites in the time of the 'Conquest' and before. A highly important conclusion is drawn by Seebass, who shows that Israel's connexion with Shechem is very ancient, and probably already dates from the middle of the second millennium,[286] as indeed that of Jacob with Bethel does also. The studies of Zobel, Seebass and De Pury demonstrate once more the antiquity of the tie with the central Palestinian mountain country.

From another angle also more light has come to fall upon the time of the patriarchs, as more and more has become known of what is usually called, incorrectly, 'the Amorite milieu'.[287] The importance of the texts from Mari, especially, can hardly be overestimated.[288] The combination of these two recent developments now renders it, I think, both possible and necessary to speak of the time of the patriarchs as a more concrete historical reality. Now that the location of their histories proves to have been mainly Palestine, these certainly ought to be treated as part of the history of Israel.

Of recent years two very direct attacks have appeared upon the amphictyony hypothesis. In the first place that of G. W. Anderson.[289] Anderson bases his criticism on the essay of Fohrer. He also is surprised

[284] *ThLZ* CXI (1966) Sp. 904.

[285] H. J. Zobel, *Stammesspruch und Geschichte*. BZAW 95, Berlin 1965. H. Seebass, *Der Erzvater Israel und die Einführung der Jahweverehrung in Kanaän*. BZAW 98, Berlin 1966. M. Weippert, *Die Landnahme der israelitischen Stämme in der neueren wissenschaftlichen Diskussion*. FRLANT 92, Göttingen 1967. A. de Pury, Genèse XXXIX et l'histoire. *RB* LXXVI (1969) p. 1-49.

[286] Seebass, *o.c.* S. 10-11. Of course the patriarch Israel here represents an Israel group! With justification, Seebass refers here to C. Steuernagel, who many years ago already demonstrated that the expression *'elohē yiśrā'ēl* belongs to Shechem. BZAW 27, Berlin 1914, S. 343 *seq.*

[287] See for this ch. III, and in Weippert S. 102-123.

[288] For that matter, Martin Noth was one of the first scholars who realized the importance of the Mari texts! See especially his *Die Ursprünge des alten Israel im Lichte neuer Quellen*. Arbeitsgemeinschaft für Forschung des Landes Nordrhein-Westfalen, Band 16, Heft 94, Köln 1961.

[289] G. W. Anderson, 'Am, Ḳāhāl, 'Ēdāh. In: *Translating and Understanding the Old Testament. Essays in Honor of H. G. May*. New York/Nashville 1970, p. 135-151.

how little has been or can be proved and how much is speculation. The lack of a Hebrew term for the amphictyony also surprises him. He agrees with Fohrer that it is impossible for it to have been called 'Israel'. His argumentation, however, is more formal: he inquires whether an amphictyony is really referred to. According to Noth, Joshua 24 describes how, as the result of a common experience (scil. the Conquest), the twelve tribes, with the 'house of Joseph' as a nucleus, made a covenant around a central sanctuary (the ark). Yet is this interpretation of Joshua 24 correct? Even if it were, a confederation is by no means an amphictyony. Noth cannot prove the existence of a central sanctuary. His sole argument to support the whole analogy with the classical amphictyony, is that the tribes were twelve in number. Yet the number twelve is not at all essential; we know of amphictyonies with 5, 6, 7, 10, 11, 12 or even 15 members. Anderson follows Rahtjen's reasoning in this. The essential point is and remains the common celebration of the cult at the central sanctuary, and this Noth cannot demonstrate.

In his view of the time of the Judges, Anderson follows Orlinsky: any form of centralization is unthinkable in this period. It can at best have been an ideal. Therefore it is not only a mistake to speak of an amphictyony, but even of a confederation of tribes.[290] Thus also Anderson comes to the conclusion that the feeling of solidarity of the Israelites cannot possibly be explained from the period of the Judges. Therefore it must be older, which presupposes contact between Judah and Joseph before the Entry into Palestine. In Anderson's eyes the unity of the Israelites goes back to the Sinai: 'if the arguments advanced are sound, and if Israel's consciousness of itself as a unity (a union of tribes) dates from the period before the settlement, then to look for the establishment of that unity elsewhere than in the institution of the Sinai covenant is to disregard the testimony of tradition in the interest of airborne guesswork. But to find the origins of Israelite unity in the Sinai covenant is not to exclude the admission to it, after the invasion, of diverse elements, tribal and other. Of this, Josh. 24 may well contain a record.'[291]

A more recent attack was made by R. de Vaux, and also his approach betrays the influence of Fohrer.[292] His argumentation is again almost the same:

[290] Yet even such a confederation would be based on a mistaken interpretation of Joshua 24. Moreover, it is nowhere evident that such a confederation existed in the time of the Judges. *O.c.* p. 149.
[291] *O.c.* p. 150. The tenor of these pronouncements hardly seems to agree with the appreciative words about Noth on p. 141! Here we again see the Anglo-American spirit of animosity towards German science.
[292] R. de Vaux, La Thèse de "l'Amphictyonie Israélite". In: Studies in Memory of Paul Lapp. *HThR* LXIV (1971) p. 415-436.

1) The number twelve in itself has no particular significance. There are amphictyonies enough with a different number of members.
2) All the amphictyonies we know of belong to the Indo-Germanic sphere and date from the first millennium B.C.E.[293]
3) It is an absolute condition that a central, common cult can be shown to have existed at one or more common sanctuaries.
   a) *Shechem* was still Canaanite in Judges 9, and it cannot be proved that the ark ever stood there. The town was certainly a point of contact for northern tribes.
   b) *Bethel* does not originally belong in Judg. 19-21.[294] The 'fear of the Lord' is not exclusively connected with the ark.[295] There is no indication whatever of a central cult at Bethel.
   c) *Gilgal* is not mentioned in the Book of Judges. It is important under Saul, but the ark is not there then.
   d) *Shiloh* makes a first appearance at the end of the period of the Judges. There was a temple here with the ark, but there is no indication that this sanctuary was of importance outside the territory of Ephraim.
   e) *Mizpah* on the other hand would be a far more likely site.[296] Yet here there is nothing to suggest the presence of the ark.
   Therefore: we cannot point out a central sanctuary. On the contrary, we are struck by the number of sanctuaries. Even the Book of the Covenant, which should then form the basis of the amphictyonic law, takes local sanctuaries for granted!
4) Noth's interpretation of Joshua 24 is forced. What Josh. 24 describes is the integration, by means of a covenant, of the Joseph group.[297] At that moment, the others were already long settled in Canaan. There is no question in Josh. 24 of establishing an amphictyony.
5) The *nasi'* was indeed a leading figure within the tribe, but he had no religious function.

---

[293] This remark again depends upon the definition chosen. With regard to the Philistine pentapolis and Nippur De Vaux is right. Yet see also the Polynesian amphictyonies (see above, note 248), the origins of the Delphic amphictyony and examples such as that of the Ghuzz (M. Th. Houtsma, Die Ghuzenstämme. *WZKM* II (1888) S. 219-233). There 24 tribes were linked in six groups of four in a religious organization, by means including totem animals and a common cult. After they embraced Islam, the Ghuzz disappeared as an ethnic unit.
[294] *Cf.* for this A. Besters, Le sanctuaire central dans Jud. XIX-XXI. *EThL* XLI (1965) p. 20-42.
[295] This contra A. Alt, Die Wallfahrt von Sichem nach Bethel. *KS I*, München 1953, S. 79-88.
[296] In this connexion De Vaux mentions Judg. 20:1-3; 21:1-5, 8; I Sam. 7:5-12.
[297] This Joseph group was also the bearer of Yahwism and of the Sinai tradition.

6) An action undertaken by all tribes together cannot be demonstrated anywhere.
7) Elsewhere[298] De Vaux has reasoned that the 'tribe' of Judah only originated during the early monarchy. This argument might be brought up here too, at least to counter the argumentation of Noth and Herrmann.

Now his *Histoire ancienne d'Israël* has appeared[299] – to my deep regret posthumously and unfinished – we find the above mentioned articles incorporated as chapters.[300] Therefore the *Histoire ancienne* does not bring us much new information on De Vaux's views. Very important for his very detailed reconstruction of Israel's origins are the postulated nomadic past of Israel and the following process of sedentarization. This is the framework in which the oldest history of Israel is told.

According to De Vaux originally there were only associations and federations of tribes, without much structure or organization. The feeling of identity arose only after the Conquest. De Vaux mentions three factors that were of special importance: 1. the ethnic factor: the memory of common descent; 2. the religious factor: Yahwism and 3. the pressure from outside which forced the tribes to cling together.[301] As one will notice, here are many points of agreement with the latest book of Herrmann.

It would seem useful to end this paragraph by briefly setting forth the arguments of a defender of the amphictyony hypothesis, the R. Smend already referred to.[302] He discusses the three main objections advanced against the hypothesis of Noth:
1) The system of twelve tribes did not yet exist in the time of the Judges.
2) In itself, the system of twelve tribes has nothing to do with an amphictyony.
3) The evidence is lacking for the institutions and actions of an amphictyony.

With regard to the first point, Smend is thinking particularly of Herrmann and Mowinckel. He points out that a tribal system beginning with Reuben, Simeon and Levi can hardly reflect a political situation

---

[298] R. de Vaux, The Settlement of the Israelites in Southern Palestine and the Origins of the Tribe of Judah. In: *Translating and Understanding the Old Testament*, p. 108-134.
[299] R. de Vaux, *Histoire ancienne d'Israël*. Vol. I, Paris 1971, vol. II, Paris 1973.
[300] Volume I, part III, chapter 2 and volume II, chapter 2.
[301] Vol. II, p. 63-64.
[302] R. Smend, Zur Frage der altisraelitischen Amphiktyonie. *EvTh* XXXI (1971) S. 623-630. *Cf.* also G. Schmitt, *Du sollst keinen Frieden schliessen mit den Bewohnern des Landes*. BWANT 91, Stuttgart 1971, S. 84[5].

of the time of the early monarchy. Even if it might be proved that in the time of the Judges Judah did not belong to 'Israel', it would still be impossible to show that 'Israel' did not then consist of twelve tribes. An amphictyony of ten tribes has to do without the analogies with the classical world! (contra Mowinckel).

In discussing the second point, Smend mainly tries to counter the argumentation of Fohrer. Positing a system with Dinah and without Benjamin, and describing Yahwism as chiefly connected with the tribes of Rachel, Fohrer concludes that there must have been a system of twelve tribes before the introduction of Yahwism. Yet why should not the amphictyony, asks Smend, already in its earliest phase have worshipped El?[303] This would at once do away with Fohrer's objection to the name of 'Israel' for the amphictyony. Smend also points out that the analogies with the classical amphictyonies made use of by Noth, are not to be taken so strictly as if they represented actual parallels. Besides resemblances, there are just as many differences. If Fohrer wants to interpret the tribal systems as genealogical systems, and gives them the function of expressing the 'Gesamtheit Israels', then Smend is fully justified in asking what this 'Gesamtheit Israels' means in actual fact.

And in the third place there is no evidence. Smend explicitly points out once more – quite rightly! – that the amphictyony hypothesis is a consequence following from Noth's entire work, and that it does not rest upon one or two passages of textual evidence. The amphictyony was a sacred covenant, and not a political institution. Therefore Orlinsky's argumentation is simply forcing an open door. The most important institution was the central sanctuary, and although Smend admits that this function cannot be ascribed to the ark, he still maintains that something of the kind probably existed. Also with regard to the office of a 'Judge of Israel' Smend, in spite of Richter, considers it more probable that this was an amphictyonic office.[304]

Finally, Smend reminds us that Noth himself already pointed out that the value of the amphictyony lay in the fact of its existence, and that it would really be unlikely for many concrete memories to become attached to an institution having so few concrete qualities.[305]

To conclude, I would remark upon the rank growth of the amphictyony hypothesis outside the study of the Old Testament. Now that the amphictyony of ancient Israel has penetrated into all kind of handbooks

[303] Smend here points to the alternation of the epithets 'El the god of Israel' and 'Yahweh the god of Israel'.
[304] See for this ch. IV. The reference is to W. Richter, Zu den 'Richtern Israels'. *ZAW* LXXVII (1965) S. 40-72.
[305] Smend quotes at length from Noth, *Das System*, S. 64-65.

as practically an accepted fact, we need not be surprised to see the amphictyony described as, for instance, an intermediate stage between tribal forms of organization and the formation of a real state.[306] In this way the model of Israel is given application outside Israel. The same fallacy now leads archaeologists to discover 'Tribal League Shrines' both within and outside Palestine.[307]

[306] Cf. for this G. Buccellati, *Cities and Nations of Ancient Syria*. Studi Semitici 26, Roma 1967.
[307] *E.g.* E. F. Campbell-G. E. Wright, Tribal League Shrines in Amman and Shechem. *BA* XXXII (1969) p. 104-116.

CHAPTER II

THE SYSTEM OF
THE TWELVE TRIBES

The previous chapter has shown that the amphictyony hypothesis of Martin Noth was not a matter of spontaneous generation. We saw that it was already to be found in the works of Ed. Meyer and G. Beer;[1] while E. Sellin, R. Kittel and E. Auerbach came very close to it.[2] In reconstructing Israel's earliest history, most other authors also gave a fairly important place to a league of tribes or Yahweh league. A critical evaluation of Noth's hypothesis, with which the present chapter is concerned, might well begin by remarking that in *Das System der zwölf Stämme Israels* far too little transpires of this anterior history. We must at once admit, though, that Noth never claimed to have been the discoverer of an analogy with the Italic and ancient Greek amphictyonies.[3] It might be objected that, in contrast to Noth's hypothesis, all these earlier covenants of the tribes, leagues and amphictyonies had always been imagined as prior to the entry into Canaan, usually as having their centre in Kades, or sometimes in Transjordan. Yet also H. Winckler and R. Kittel already placed their tribal leagues after the Entry, and in Palestine.[4] The peculiarity of Noth's hypothesis, however, is that he no longer regards the amphictyony or tribal league as a phase to be postulated in the vague past of Israel, but depicts it most concretely as a living institution, whose influences may be pointed out even far into the time of the kings. Indeed, he goes further still, and ascribes the very origin and formation of Israel to this amphictyony!

Now it is easy enough to dismiss this hypothesis out of hand because of the lack of convincing evidence for it. Nowhere in the Old Testament

[1] See above, p. 6 and 19 *Cf.* also H. Gunkel, Genesis 1922[5].

[2] PP. 26, 32, 34 *seq.* Noth's famous hypothesis is already present *in nuce* in Alt's *RGG* article of 1929, but it may also be that Alt is already dependent on his pupil there. Olmstead too may be dependent on Noth, though this need not be so; I find it impossible to check the matter.

[3] See above, p. 40-43

[4] See above, p. 10 and 32.

is the amphictyony explicitly named, it has to be postulated. This is the case both for the amphictyony itself and for its 'institutions', such as the central sanctuary, the turn of maintenance of the twelve tribes, the amphictyonic offices, amphictyonic law, an amphictyonic ethos etc. etc. Noth, by the way, never went beyond proposing a possible analogy with the classical amphictyonies and using this analogy as a hypothesis. Really relevant criticism must therefore begin with Noth's own argumentation.[5] One may then go on to ask whether the evidence supporting this hypothesis is as strong as Noth *c.s.* held it to be. In this chapter, we shall therefore first examine Noth's most important starting-point: the existence of a system of twelve tribes as an independent and extremely ancient component of the Old Testament tradition.

The existence of such an extremely ancient element of tradition is the main support on which Noth built up his hypothesis. A second equally essential point of departure is more an assumption *a priori*; it is the supposed necessity of seeing some concrete expression of the 'unity of Israel' in pre-monarchic times'. This second point will form the subject of chapter III. It will then also be discussed what exactly we are to understand by the term 'tribe'.

1. The tribe of Joseph

In the Old Testament there is not one system of twelve tribes, but two. Noth himself clearly pointed that out.[6] Only recently Helga Weippert

---

[5] M. Weippert, *Die Landnahme* S. 46[2] is perfectly right when he remarks that much of the criticism is mainly directed against the outward form of the amphictyony and hardly touches the core of Noth's thesis. This also applies to my own criticism in 'De richteren van Israël', *NThT* XX (1965/66) p. 81-100.

[6] Noth, *Das System*, S. 23-28. The system 'A'. with Levi and Joseph, is found in Gen. 29:31-30:24; (35:16-18); 35:23-26; 46:8-25; 49:3-27; Ex. 1:2-4; Deut. 27: 12-14; Ezra 48:31-35; 1 Chr. 2:2. System 'B', without Levi and Joseph but with Ephraim and Manasseh, is found in Num. 1:5-15; 20-43; 2:3-31; 7:12-83; 13:4-15; 26:5-51; Josh. 13-19; 21:4-7, 9-39. Combinations of A and B are found in Num. 10: 14-28; 1 Chr. 4-7; I. Chr. 12:24-38; 1 Chr. 27:16-21. These are all passages where the number twelve has been maintained. Deut. 33 is a separate problem, see below p. 91. We must agree with Noth in dismissing attempts to reconstruct a third system on the basis of Gen. 29 and 30. *Cf. Das System*, S. 9. This third system would contain Joseph, but omit Benjamin, the daughter Dinah being inserted between the group of the sons of Leah and the others. Noth is right, I think, to point out that the lack of an etymology of the name Dinah is very striking in the context of Gen. 29:31-30:24, and forms a clear indication that Dinah was added later: in order to complete the number twelve. The name Dinah comes from Gen. 34. The absence of Benjamin may be explained from the fact that an old and well-known story of the birth of this son of Jacob was already contained in Gen.

has shown that from the material that was not used by Noth a third system can be reconstructed. But since this third system is also very clearly a geographical system and therefore a variant of Noth's system "B", this does not alter the fact that Noth was certainly right in his distinction of *two kinds* of tribal systems![6a] The great difference between the two systems is that two tribes which appear in system 'A', have disappeared in system 'B'. These are Joseph and Levi. In order to keep to the number twelve the second, younger system sets Ephraim and Manasseh in the place of Joseph. According to Noth this is the result of adaptation to altered conditions, being the disappearance of Levi as a secular tribe and the splitting up of (the house of) Joseph into the two

35:16-20. Hence one can only confirm Noth's finding that Gen. 29 *seq.* presupposes system 'A'. This idea was already attacked by C. Steuernagel. *Die Einwanderung der israelitischen Stämme*, S. 3, and recently again by G. Fohrer, Altes Testament 'Amphiktyonie' und 'Bund'? *ThLZ* XCI (1966) Sp. 812-814. Fohrer repeated his view again in his *Geschichte der israelitischen Religion*. Berlin 1969, S. 78-83. To refute Fohrer's reasoning that this 'third system' (which Fohrer even puts first!) which has not yet got Benjamin while it does contain the otherwise unknown tribe of Dinah must therefore be very old, one need only point to the arguments of Noth, to which Fohrer makes no reference whatever. Moreover, Gen. 29 does not deal with *tribes* at all, but with the children of Jacob. There is no question here of a list of tribes, it is a genealogical system. That is a very important difference to which we shall return. Although Fohrer does clearly distinguish between lists of tribes and genealogical lists, he makes the mistake of disregarding the distinction here with reference to the three forms of the duodecimal schema. *Cf.* also J. Muilenberg, The Birth of Benjamin. *JBL* LXXV (1956) p. 194-201. A. de Pury, *Genèse* XXXIV et l'histoire *RB* LXXVI (1969) p. 5-49, esp. p. 38-39. Finally, it must be mentioned that Fohrer himself has changed his mind in so far as he now regards all three of his 'Tribal systems' as genealogical lists. *Geschichte der israelitischen Religion*, S. 82.

[6a] Helga Weippert, Das geographische System der Stämme Israels. *VT* XXIII (1973) S. 76-89. This system "B2" is to be found in Num. 34:19-29; Josh. 21:4-8; 21:9-42; 1 Chr. 6:40-48 and 49-66; Judg. 1; 1 Chr. 12:25-38; Deut. 33:1-29. The system "B2" has always Judah in first position, Benjamin in the third and at the end the order Asher-Naphtali.

On the other hand we cannot accept a third system as is put forward by R. de Vaux in his *Histoire ancienne d'Israël*, vol. II, p. 38 and 46-49. According to De Vaux a third "territorial" system is presented mainly by Josh. 13-19, and further by Num. 34 and Ezek. 48. His main arguments are however only the different order in which the tribes are enumerated and the division of Manasseh. So actually we do not have here a real third system, but again only the *possibility* of another variant of the geographical system "B". In my opinion Noth was certainly right in rejecting the enumeration of Josh. 13-19 as a separate system (*Das System*, S. 18-19). Josh. 13-19 was only pressed into the tribal system by a rather late redactor (*i.e.* in system "B") and he succeeded only partly in this, because Josh. 13-19 in its present form counts fourteen tribal territories. Therefore his source(s) did not know the frame of the geographical twelve-tribe system.

separate tribes of Ephraim and Manasseh. This would make the second system later than the first. This latter supposition, however, concerning the origin of Ephraim and Manasseh, which Noth shares with nearly all the pre-war Old Testament scholars, cannot stand up to criticism. We shall therefore begin our attack on this point.

E. Täubler has advanced a number of arguments which make it impossible any longer to regard the tribe of Machir as merely a part split off from the tribe of Joseph, as was always customary.[7] Machir was probably a tribe inhabiting the north-western part of the Ephraimite mountain country around the town of Dothan since the Amarna period. The tribal name Machir is closely related to that of Issachar. In both cases the tribal name is an indication of the social position of these two tribes, who had to labour in the service of others. Thus a tribe 'Machir' would really belong to the Leah group. In the long run the tribe was partly absorbed, partly driven away by the tribe of Manasseh which arose later.[8] Moreover, Täubler already showed that probably the name 'House of Joseph' did not come into use until the early monarchial period, and was always directed against (the House of) Judah.[9] Täubler's thesis that the term 'House of Joseph' marks the end of a development and not its beginning, while it can moreover be dated with fair certainty in the early monarchial period, perhaps even in the latter time of the judges, was confirmed and adopted by a number of later scholars. It is shared also by Kaiser,[10] Schunk,[11] Zobel,[12] Herrmann[12a] and Mayes,[12b]

---

[7] *Cf. e.g.* Ed. Meyer, *Die Israeliten und ihre Nachbarstämme*, S. 291.

[8] E. Täubler, *Biblische Studien, Die Epoche der Richter.* Hrgb. von H. J. Zobel, Tübingen 1958, S. 176-214, esp. S. 190-203. Zobel himself also uses this reasoning in his *Stammesspruch und Geschichte.* BZAW 95, S. 114. *Cf.* also A. de Pury, *o.c.* p.46.

[9] Täubler does distinguish, though, between the late 'House of Joseph' and the 'Josephites', which may be earlier: 'Auf Grund dieser Beispiele kann es als sicher gelten, dass der Ausdruck Haus Joseph für Manasse und Ephraim in der früh-königlichen Zeit üblich war und dass er die einheitliche genealogische Komplementär-Bezeichnung für die einheitliche territoriale der Vogtei gewesen ist. Damit ist nahe gerückt, dass er auch erst in dieser Zeit entstanden ist.' *o.c.* S. 199.

[10] O. Kaiser, Stammesgeschichtliche Hintergründe der Josephsgeschichte. *VT* X (1960) S. 1-15.

[11] K. D. Schunck, *Benjamin. Untersuchungen zur Entstehung und Geschichte eines israelitischen Stammes.* BZAW 86, Berlin 1963, esp. S. 13-18.

[12] H. J. Zobel, *Stammesspruch und Geschichte.* BZAW 95, Berlin 1965, S. 112-126, esp. S. 113, 120, 128.

[12a] S. Herrmann, *Geschichte Israels in alttestamentlicher Zeit.* München 1973, espec. S. 125 and 144. Herrmann also considers the tribe/house of Joseph as a younger combination of the older tribes Ephraim and Manasseh, but he does not give any arguments for this view.

[12b] A. D. H. Mayes, Israel in the Pre-Monarchy Period. *VT* XXIII (1973) p. 154[6].

while Ruppert,[13] without really pronouncing on the actual historical problems, also views matters in this light. Ruppert continually points out that in the E version of the Joseph cycle there is a clear anti-Davidic, anti-Judaic tendency. This tendency must have been strong outside Judah in the earliest time of the Kings.[14]

Needlessly, perhaps, we should yet like to re-examine this new view of Joseph, since it concerns one of the principal *a priori's* underlying the thesis of Noth, and the place of Joseph is of fundamental importance in judging the system of the twelve tribes.

That for Noth the splitting up of an original tribe of Joseph into the later tribes of Ephraim and Manasseh (and Machir) was a principle accepted without question and requiring no argumentation whatever, is abundantly evident from the way he treats Josh. 16 and 17. Chapters 13-20 relate how the country, here regarded as having come wholly into the possession of the Israelites, was divided among the tribes by lot at the sanctuary in Shiloh. Two additional chapters deal with the cities of refuge (20) and the cities of the Levites (21). The most important descriptions of the tribal boundaries are chiefly found in ch. 15, 16 and 17.

Although the genesis of the second half of the book of Joshua is highly complicated, it has been considerably elucidated by the work of A. Alt, and not least by that of Noth himself.[15] In approaching the problem

[13] L. Ruppert, *Die Josephserzählung der Genesis* StANT XI, München 1965, S. 215 soq., S. 226-231.

[14] For this also A. Weiser, *Samuel. Seine geschichtliche Aufgabe und religiöse Bedeutung.* FRLANT 81, Göttingen 1962, S. 23.

[15] There is an extensive literature dealing with these chapters, including much detailed research in the topographical field. Here I only list what seems the *most important* literature, and especially that dealing with the tribes of Joseph: A. Alt, Judas Gaue unter Josia. (1925) *Kl. Schriften II*, München 1953, S. 276-288. Das System der Stammesgrenzen im Buche Josua. (1927) *Kl. Schriften I*, München 1953, S. 193-202. K. Elliger, Die Grenze zwischen Ephraim und Manasse. *ZDPV* LIII (1930) S. 265-309. M. Noth, Studien zu den historisch-geografischen Dokumenten des Josuabuches. *ZDPV* LVIII (1935) S. 185-255. *Das Buch Josua.* HAT 17, Tübingen 1953². Überlieferungsgeschichtliches zur zweiten Hälfte des Josuabuches. *Alttestamentliche Studien Fr. Nötscher zum 60. Geburtstage.* BBB I, Bonn 1950, S. 152-167. S. Mowinckel, *Zur Frage nach dokumentarischen Quellen in Josua 13-19.* Oslo 1946. *Tetrateuch-Pentateuch-Hexateuch.* BZAW 90, Berlin 1964, esp. S. 51-76. J. Simons, The Structure and Interpretation of Josh. XVI-XXII. *Orientalia Neerlandica*, Leiden 1948, p. 190-215. F. M. Cross and G. E. Wright, The Boundary and Province Lists of the Kingdom of Judah. *JBL* LXXV (1956) p. 202-226. Eva Danelius, The Boundary of Ephraem and Manasseh in the Western Plain, *PEQ* LXXXIX (1957) p. 55-67; XC (1958) p. 32-44 and 122-144. E. Jenni, Historisch-topographische Untersuchungen zur Grenze zwischen Ephraim und Manasse. *ZDPV* LXXIV (1958) S. 35-40. Z. Kallai-Kleinman, The Town Lists of Judah, Simeon, Benjamin and Dan. *VT* VIII (1958) p. 134-160. *The Tribes of*

of the tribal boundaries in Joshua we still take our departure from Alt's essay *'Das System der Stammesgrenzen im Buche Josua'* of 1927. Alt here advances three new points of view which are essential to understand how the present form of these traditions came into being. First of all Alt breaks with the customary solution of literary criticism by means of the Pentateuchal documents.[16] He convincingly shows that Josh. 13-20 was directly based on two different kinds of documents: a description of the boundaries of the tribes and lists enumerating the principal towns situated in the various tribal territories. Secondly, Alt makes it quite plausible that these lists or documents each describe a situation which must have actually existed, so that they must be founded on particular historical conditions.

Alt's finding for the date of the list of tribal boundaries is the latter period of the Judges. The matter is more complicated for the lists of place-names, but according to Alt that of the tribe of Judah must surely go back to its division into administrative provinces under Josiah.[17]

A third point is that the text as we now see it displays a peculiar tension between on the one hand the faithful rendering of a particular historical situation as it must once have existed, and on the other the later theory of the twelve tribes and the occupation and division of the entire country.[18] This tension results from the redaction and was not present in the original documents used by the author or adapter. In

Israel. A Study in the Historical Geography of the Bible. Jerusalem 1967. E. Täubler, *Biblische Studien.* Tübingen 1958. Y. Aharoni, The Province List of Judah. *VT* IX (1959) p. 225-246. *The Land of the Bible: A Historical Geography.* London 1966, esp. p. 221-245. G. Wallis, Taanath-Silo. *ZDPV* LXXVII (1961) S. 38-45. A. Kuschke, Historisch-topographische Beiträge zum Buche Josua. *Gottes Wort und Gottes Land.* Hertzberg Festschrift. Göttingen 1965, S. 90-109. R. de Vaux, *Histoire ancienne d'Israël*, vol. II, p. 46-49. O. Bächli, Von der Liste zur Beschreibung. *ZDPV* LXXXIX (1973) S. 1-14.

[16] *Cf.* for this O. Eissfeldt, *Hexateuch-Synopse.* Leipzig 1922/Darmstadt 1962, S. 75-78; 230*-241*.

[17] The position of Mowinckel, who denies particularly the existence of documents the author might have used, is extremely weak. See also Noth's answer in the Nötscher Festschrift. The theses of Alt are in the main also accepted by the American and Israelian scholars, though these usually set a earlier date: Cross-Wright in the time of Jehoshaphat, Kallai-Kleinman under David, and Aharoni in the time of Uzziah. Everyone is agreed, however, on the principle that the list is based on the administrative regions of Judah.

[18] Alt even speaks of a 'getreues Spiegelbild unerfunden Wirklichkeiten', *Das System*, S. 196. He demonstrates this by means of the examples Kiriath-jearim and Tappuah *o.c.* S. 200. The concomitant acknowledgment that the system of tribal boundaries as it now lies before us also contains a large theoretical part, greatly irritated Israelian and American scholars in particular. This annoyance was aroused even more by M. Noth.

several places it must have given the author a lot of trouble to adapt his material to the later theories. The most important result of Alt's researches is, that these chapters may no longer be written off as 'clerical fiction' – for they are traditionally ascribed to P – but that they are shown to have a reliable historical core.

A further step was taken by K. Elliger, who showed that the boundary between Ephraim and Manasseh as described in Josh. 16 and 17 cannot possibly have been a frontier drawn at some time in order to split up Joseph into Ephraim and Manasseh.[19] The boundary described must undoubtedly refer to a situation that once existed, when the boundary was obviously by no means firmly fixed but fluctuated a good deal. Moreover that situation makes it clear that the splitting up of Joseph, as Elliger says, did not take place without tension between Ephraim and Manasseh![20]

On certain points Alt's views have been rectified by M. Noth.[21] Thus Noth was able to show that in the final instance the boundary descriptions also go back to lists of place-names, so-called *Grenzfixpunkte*, the connection verbs having been put in afterwards. Noth lays more stress upon the fact that the boundary descriptions we now have were completely theoretical: the country was never entirely Israelite territory so that it could have been divided up as a whole. Like Alt and Elliger, Noth emphasizes that in the boundary descriptions transmitted to us attention is concentrated upon the tribes in Central Palestine. With regard to Joseph Noth then posits – and that is what interests us here – that the boundary description begins with a theoretical unit 'Joseph', but in fact only describes two tribes. All the problems that arise in reconstructing the boundary between Ephraim and Manasseh Noth explains from this theoretical framework. At the same time Noth retracts a little in saying that there never was a real frontier between these territories, and therefore no factual boundary description either; here Noth disagrees with Alt and Elliger.[22] On the other hand Noth holds that *within* the original single territory of Joseph a *Sondergebiet* was reserved for Ephraim. In other words: Josh. 16 and 17 show us as it were the process at work of the division of Joseph. This hypothesis of a separate territory for Ephraim inside Joseph/Manasseh is essential to Noth's

---

[19] So commonly regarded. *Cf. e.g.* the very authoritative commentary of H. Holzinger on this; KHAT VI, Leipzig-Tübingen 1901.

[20] Elliger, *o.c.* S. 300, 301[1].

[21] Chiefly in *ZDPV* LVIII (1935) and in the introduction to his commentary on Joshua. See above note 15.

[22] *ZDPV* LVIII (1935) S. 204-210.

treatment of these chapters.[23] The argumentation is really very weak, though, it rests practically entirely upon 16:9 which Noth translates as follows: 'Die abgeteilten Städte gehören den Ephraimiten inmitten des Erbbesitzes der Manassiten, alle Städte mit ihren Gehöften.'[24] Together with 17:9a[B], verse 16:9 is supposed to make it clear that 'dem Ephraim nur "innerhalb des Besitzes von Manasse" eine Reihe von Städte zugewiesen wird'.[25] At the same time, Noth claims, the chapters 16 and 17 always maintain that the entire territory should legally fall to Manasseh as the first-born. Noth holds that 17:1-7, where the essential unity of this whole territory is stipulated once more from the point of view of the laws of inheritance, was inserted on purpose to stress that unity. According to Noth then, 16:9 and 17:9a[B] are duplicates or recapitulations of what went before: the territory of Ephraim may be summarized as 'the cities reserved for the Ephraimites within the patrimony of the Manassites'.

Yet it is very doubtful whether that is what the text intends.[26] Noth seems to regard the waw of $w^e h e^\cdot \bar{a} r \bar{\imath} m$ as an explicative waw, but it is far more likely to be an ordinary copulative waw: vs. 9 is an addition to what went before, and most translations have always taken it as such. Verse 9 is very closely connected with vs. 8: '*Furthermore* the cities reserved for the Ephraimites within the patrimony of the Manassites'.[27] The same intention is expressed in 17:9a[B]. Noth translates: '... südlich des Tales liegen (   ) Städte Ephraims inmitten der Städte Manasses und das Gebiet Manasses liegt nördlich des Tales.' Noth regards the $h\bar{a}$'$\bar{e}l\e$ as secondary, and therefore will not insert an article before '$\bar{a}r\bar{\imath}m$, as is generally done.[28] With regard to this verse also Simons has made it perfectly clear that this translation is forced, and moreover nonsensical: how can Ephraimite cities lie in the territory of Manasseh to the south of the wadi Kanah, if the Manassite territory only begins to the north of that wadi?[29] As the verse now stands the lack of an article in front of '$\bar{a}r\bar{\imath}m$ is a clear indication that something is wrong with the text. Simons

[23] This was rightly emphasized by J. Simons, *o.c.* p. 190 *seq.*
[24] *Das Buch Josea*, S. 100; *cf.* also *BHK*[3]. That this translation is a distortion of the Hebrew is not only the opinion of Simons, but also of Y. Kaufmann, *The Biblical Account of the Conquest of Palestine.* Jerusalem 1953, p. 31.
[25] *Das Buch Josua*, S. 102.
[26] *Cf.* especially the essay of Simons.
[27] H. W. Hertzberg in *ATD* 9, S. 100: 'Und (dazu) die Städte'. Simons translates 'besides', Alfrink in *BOT* III 'bovendien' (moreover); *SBJ*: 'autre'. The *NEB* has now: 'There were also cities reserved for the Ephraimites within the patrimony of the Manassites...'
[28] *Das Buch Josua*, S. 98. *Cf.* also *BHK*[3]. The *NBG* also cheated a little with its 'aldaar' (there). *NEB*: 'these cities: *prob. rdg.*'
[29] Simons, *o.c.* p. 210 *seq.* Also Kaufmann, *o.c.* p. 34-36.

restores the article and in front of the first *lannaḥal* inserts *miṣṣe̯fōn* which may have dropped out through haplography. He then translates as follows: 'The border went down to the river Kana, southward (*negbā*) – "north" of the river were those cities of Ephraim among the cities of Manasseh because (*we̯*) the territory of Manasseh was north of the river – and it (the border) went out to the sea.' This brings Simons somewhat into conflict with 16:8, which explicitly states that the wadi Kanah lies *west* of Tappuah.[30] It seems best to leave the text as it is, only perhaps inserting the article. I think Y. Kaufmann comes closest to the solution when he explains the condition of this verse as a 'scar'. For these words might well have served as the closing formula of the list(s) of place-names now lacking for Ephraim and Manasseh.[31] It would be a fitting close to that part of the list which enumerated Ephraimite towns either forming enclaves in Manassite territory, or penetrating into that territory as wedges to the north of the wadi Kanah.

Noth's appeal to 17:1-7 is also sharply criticized by Simons. We have seen that this pericope also plays an important part in Noth's argumentation. In Noth's view, the purpose of these verses is to explain 'warum das Gesamtgebiet der "Söhne Josephs" nicht einfach in zwei Teile ging, sondern dem Machir zufiel; das wird mit dem Erbrecht des Erstgeborenen begründet'. These verses must also serve to explain why this territory is yet not called Machir, but Manasseh.[32] In other words, Noth ascribes pericope 17:1-7 largely to the author or adapter of Josh. 16 and 17, although he himself repeatedly admits that the genealogical argumentation in these verses is clearly secondary and derived from Num. 26 and 27. Kaufmann, by the way, has clearly shown that no such law of inheritance ever existed in Israel! The eldest son was merely entitled to a double share (Deut. 21:17). The gravest objection, however, is again to Noth's translation. Simons points out that Noth made far too much of the word *kī*, which is used twice, by translating it both times in 17:1 as 'for' (denn). In reality we have to do here, certainly the second time, with an affirmation. Josh. 17:1 and 2 is meant to explain why Machir gets *nothing*: Machir already had the two territories in Transjordan. This explanation was necessary, though, for an audience still associating Machir with the country west of the Jordan.[33] The author's point of

---

[30] Tappuah is generally identified with Sheikh Abū Zarad.
[31] Kaufmann, *o.c.* p. 35 *seq.* The absence of such lists for these two tribes Kaufmann ascribes to a later Judaean redaction of the book of Joshua.
[32] *ZDPV* LVIII (1935) S. 205 *seq.*
[33] Simons, *o.c.* p. 191-196. Compare also the translations. S. Mittmann, *Beiträge zur Siedlungs- und Territorialgeschichte des nördlichen Ostjordanlandes*, S. 213-215, places the migration of the Machirites fairly late: otherwise they would surely

departure, as Noth also sees it, was a single territory which really ought to be called Machir, but of which part had fallen to Ephraim. Noth has to admit that the old list of *Grenzfixpunkte* already shows Ephraim and Manasseh/Machir existing side by side. He is certainly rather inconsistent here.[34] Noth's argumentation on the basis of Josh. 16:9, 17:9a[B] and 17: 1-7 therefore is not in the least convincing; it rests entirely on certain presuppositions regarding the history of the tribes, and particularly regarding the 'splitting up' of Joseph.

Another point in the discussion is always the singular suffix in 17:10a *gᵉbūlō*. This can really only refer to the preceding word Manasseh. Yet that does not properly agree with the plural *yifgeʿūn* in verse 10b. Also, the effect of keeping to the singular suffix would be that only a southern boundary was named for the territory of the Josephites. If we read a plural, then v. 10 would give the northern boundary of the Josephite territory, being the northern boundary of Ephraim and Manasseh together. Elliger already regarded this as proving that the boundary description originally concerned two *independent* entities: Manasseh and Ephraim.[35] The plural form of the verb is a later redactional adaptation. Since the verses 7-10a deal entirely with the territory of Manasseh, while 11-13 enumerate the Manassite cities (claims) outside the tribal region proper in Issachar and Asher, one might well take 10b to be a later gloss explaining that Manasseh borders on Asher in the north and on Issachar in the east. If one dismisses Noth's interpretation, then one must hold with Alt, Elliger and now also Aharoni, that the original boundary description referred to two independent regions Ephraim and Manasseh.

Elliger, moreover, has brought forward a number of arguments to show that originally the two tribes were named in the reverse order in Josh.

have found better places, and closer to their original habitation. M. Ottosson, *Gilead*, p. 140-142, also thinks of developments which cannot lie too far back in the past.

[34] See also *Das Buch Josua*, S. 102 *seq.*

[35] *ZDPV* LII (1930) S. 271. Noth puts down the difference in number as due to carelessness, *Das Buch Josua* S. 104. Simons, *o.c.* alters the suffix into the plural *gᵉbūlām*, simply because he wishes at any cost to take the orginal unity of the region of Joseph as given. He also has some philological arguments: *a.* LXX + S read the plural MT as singular. *b.* The singular suffix is contradicted by the plural form of the verb. *c.* One can more easily imagine a copier writing a singular after Manasseh, than his writing *gᵉbūlō* after he had heard *yifgeʿūn*. *Ad a.* One can no longer argue in this way on the basis of the translations since the rehabilitation of MT after World War II. *Ad b.* If verse 10b is a later addition, this argument falls out. *Ad c.* Verse 10a speaks of Ephraim and Manasseh; Ephraim's border also is regarded as continuing to the sea! The sing. *gᵉbūlō* is most certainly the *lectio difficilior* here.

16 and 17. The most convincing of these is the case of Tappuah, a town treated as known in the territory of Ephraim in 16:8, while it is not fully discussed until the description of Manasseh in 17:7.[36] There is general agreement with Elliger on this point. Yet what could have been the meaning of this reversal? Elliger and his followers always explained it as stemming from a compulsion to follow the system set forth in Gen. 48. Yet it must be doubted if such a compulsion was indeed so strongly felt.[37] It is clear that at a certain moment Manasseh was outstripped by Ephraim and that since then the sequence was reversed. In this text, though, it was rather a drastic measure.

It seems possible to me to find a quite satisfactory solution of this and similar problems regarding Josh. 16 and 17 by starting from the hypothesis of Täubler, that the mention of the Josephites in 16:1-3 is a later addition and that the original boundary description only counted independent tribes. Indeed, that giving the territory of Ephraim and Manasseh the collective name of 'Joseph' is not ancient, but on the contrary late.[38] Joseph is not at the beginning of a chain of development, but at the end! Simons seems to suggest that the region of origin did indeed form a whole under the name of Machir, but this is improbable. The territory of Ephraim seems to have 'lain fallow' until a fairly late period. We know that Ephraim is one of the youngest tribes, if not the very youngest. At any rate it is a tribe which was only constituted in the settled country and took its name from the *har 'efrayim*.[39] Ephraim was an extremely militant, aggressive and expansionist tribe. This is touched upon in various places in the Book of Judges.[40] The settlement and rise of Ephraim seem to have been partly at the expense of other Israelite tribes, particularly Manasseh – considering the enclaves – and Benjamin.[41] The process of Ephraim's rise can be followed since the song of Deborah, where Ephraim is named beside the far older Machir and compared with Amalek.[42] After the troubled times of Gideon and Jephthah, we see in

---

[36] Elliger, *o.c.* S. 267.

[37] *Cf.* also 17:10 and 11 with Asher–Issachar and Issachar–Asher respectively. Also Num. 32:1 and 2.

[38] Täubler, *o.c.* S. 188 *seq.*

[39] See for this esp. K. D. Schunck, Ophra, Ephron und Ephraim. *VT* XI (1961) S. 188-200. Also: *Benjamin. Untersuchungen zur Entstehung und Geschichte eines israelitischen Stammes.* BZAW 86, Berlin 1963, esp. the Exkurs, S. 15-18.

[40] Judg. 8:1-3; 12:1-6. The chapters 19-21 must also certainly go back to a tribal war between Ephraim and Benjamin, the former being the aggressor. Schunck, *Benjamin*, S. 57-70. Zobel, *Stammesspruch und Geschichte*, S. 115-126.

[41] Cf. also J. H. Grønbaek, Benjamin und Juda. *VT* XV (1965) S. 435 *seq.*

[42] Judg. 5:14a[B] where I translate with *bēt-essentiae*: 'their shoots/scions are like Amalek'.

I Kgs. 4:7-19 that in the central hill-country only one district is instituted: Ephraim.[43] Finally, we have the later usage of calling the whole northern kingdom simply Ephraim. Obviously Ephraim was the one that counted in the northern realm. Putting Ephraim's name before that of Manasseh marks a phase in this development, so that in my opinion the change-over should be given a purely political explanation and not a cultic one, *e.g.* Ephraim's possession of the sanctuaries Bethel and Shiloh, as is still constantly done.[44] It is clear that militant Ephraim already had political aspirations in the time of the Judges.

With regard to Josh. 16 and 17 it may be said that at a certain moment someone reversed the order of Manasseh-Ephraim and stuck the verses about the Josephites in front. In this way the unity of the whole region was claimed, not as an original unity, but either as a programme or as adaptation to an existing situation. In order to choose between these two possibilities, it is necessary to review the whole system of the boundary descriptions. These begin with Judah, whose description gives rise to the following remarks:[45] the description of the boundary on the east, south and west is very brief, of that on the north fairly detailed. The southern boundary we also find in Num. 34. Actually, these are not the boundaries of the *tribe* of Judah, but of a Greater Judah. It is improbable that these boundaries could be regarded as the political claim of an older southern amphictyony, as Noth would have it.[46] Aharoni is more likely to be right in assuming that these boundaries, with the exception of the northern boundary, were not described at all in the original document; they are simply the southern boundaries of the land of Canaan, used here *in order to add a boundary description of Judah.*[47] Judah's northern boundary is the same as the southern boundary of Benjamin. It is to be questioned, therefore, whether Judah originally appeared at all in the *Vorlage* with the original boundary descriptions! In any case this originally only contained boundaries between tribes and no outward frontiers. At any rate, the *Ortsliste* used for Judah in Josh. 15 does not go back to the time of the Judges, but clearly presupposes the kingdom of Judah.[48] However, it is not only Judah's presence in the

---

[43] Moreover, Ephraim is the first department named! *Cf.* A. Alt, Israel's Gaue unter Salomo. (1913), *Kl. Schriften II*, München 1953, S. 76-89, esp. p. 85.

[44] Not so long ago by E. C. Kingsbury, He set Ephraim before Manasseh. *HUCA* XXXVIII (1967) p. 129-136.

[45] For the following particularly Noth, *Das Buch Josua*, S. 85-100. Aharoni, *The Land of the Bible*, p. 227-235.

[46] M. Noth, *Das Buch Josua*, S. 89.

[47] Aharoni, *The Land of the Bible*, p. 233.

[48] Alt already deliberately left open the possibility of these classifications going back to a far older register. This possibility must always be kept in mind.

system which is doubtful, but also that of Dan. Dan's former territory seems to have been divided among Judah, Benjamin and Ephraim, while the system attempts, in a very artificial manner, yet to leave a region open for Dan. This view of Alt and Noth has often been hotly contested, especially in Israel, but it is now also adopted by Aharoni.[49] One observes a knowledge in the system of Dan's former southern residence. Nor is a description given of Dan's later northern dwelling-place. Whether the system of tribal boundaries also contained a description of the regions in Transjordan is very problematic, and is still vehemently debated.[50] No description of Issachar is given either.[51] One may therefore conclude that the ancient document gave a description of the internal boundaries of the following six tribes in Central Palestine: Benjamin, Manasseh, Ephraim, Zebulun, Asher, Naphtali. Together with the towns or regions in Transjordan, this region is not very different from the 'Israel' which remains true to Ishbosheth in 2 Sam. 2:9. Aharoni justly points out that these tribes, with the exception of Benjamin, are also the tribes that aid Gideon. Benjamin's absence there may be explained, but not that of Issachar, whose territory was the main scene of the conflict! The enumeration of just these tribes therefore forms a very strong indication that the original system of boundary descriptions does indeed date from the later period of the Judges, as Alt already remarked. With this dating in the background, one can be fairly certain that the addition of the 'boundary description' of Judah together with the note about the Josephites presupposes the situation after the splitting up into two states. As a result of this addition, Ephraim and Manasseh were reversed and Benjamin was moved to ch. 18. There is no question of Joseph's other boundaries being 'suppressed' as Elliger called it; the only boundary requiring description was the southern boundary with Judah, because of the usual antithesis between Joseph and Judah. Elliger quite rightly remarked, though, that the boundary description in 16:1-3 is that of an eminently political frontier continuing to the sea, whereas the original boundary descriptions remain purely geographical and are confined to the central hill-country.[52]

We must now check whether these conclusions concerning the 'tribe'

[49] Noth, *ZDPV* LVIII (1935), S. 194 f.
[50] Many deny it. Alt did so already in *Das System der Stammesgrenzen*. Aharoni now also does, *The Land of the Bible*, p. 231 *seq*. On the other hand Noth always maintained that there were also boundary descriptions for the Transjordan tribes; see esp. *ZDPV* LVIII (1935) S. 230-255.
[51] Opposed to Noth in this matter are Alt, *Das System*, S. 193; Elliger, *ZPDV* LIII (1930) S. 302; Aharoni, *The Land of the Bible*, p. 233.
[52] Elliger, *o.c.* S. 301-308.

of Joseph can be maintained after examining the other passages where (the house of) Joseph or the Josephites are named. We shall begin with the prose and leave the poetic texts to the last.

There is an addition to Josh. 17:14-18 which relates how the territorial aspirations of the house of Joseph were sanctioned by Joshua.[53] Clearly, this episode is now transmitted in a double form, *i.e.* 14+15 and 16-18. The first two verses are rather a secondary extension than a parallel, we have the original tradition in the verses 16-18.[54] We are struck by the rather laboured enumeration 'to the house of Joseph, to Ephraim and Manasseh'. The most commonly proposed solution is always to strike out 'to Ephraim and Manasseh' as a later explanatory gloss,[55] and that is indeed not inaccurate. To strike out Joseph in v. 16 and v. 18 would require too drastic an alteration of the text. Moreover, the matter concerns Ephraim in the first place and not also Manasseh. The gloss should I think, be understood as a reminder that 'Joseph' is not a real tribal name, but a comprehensive indication of the real tribes Ephraim and Manasseh. The whole formulation of the verses 16-18, for that matter, with the expression 'sons of Joseph/Josephites' seems fairly late[56] and is probably from the same hand as the beginning of chapter 16. This need not conflict with the comparison between Joseph. 17:16-18 and Judg. 1, already formerly drawn and once more explicitly set forth by S.

[53] For the authenticity of Joshua's part here, see A. Alt, Josua (1936), *Kl. Schriften I*, München 1953, esp. S. 189-192. This authenticity is not impaired by the consideration that in its present form the tradition really supposes the time of the kings, since the Josephites are named and territorial extension is desired in the valleys of the Canaanites. The original tradition will have dealt with internal boundaries, *i.e.* boundaries with other Israelite groups.

[54] Noth, *Josua²*, S. 106. Eissfeldt, *Hexateuchsynopse*, S. 77, 236*. *Cf.* also S. Mittmann, *Beiträge zur Siedlungs- und Territorialgeschichte des nördlichen Ostjordanlandes*, S. 209-214. According to Mittmann this tradition concerns Transjordan, which is referred to by *har.* It is worthwhile pointing out that in Transjordan there is never any mention of Joseph or Josephites, though there is of runaway Ephraimites. (Judg. 12:4). See now also the somewhat different solution by Götz Schmitt, *Du sollst keinen Frieden schliessen mit den Bewohnern des Landes.* BWANT 91, Stuttgart 1971, S. 89-97.

[55] Noth, *Josua²*, S. 102 a. 106.

[56] Täubler, *Biblische Studien I*, S. 197-203, imagines a much more complicated procedure: first the words were only 'house of Joseph'; later this was replaced by 'sons of Joseph', and that was then explained as Ephraim and Manasseh. All the same, Täubler's dating of Judges I places the expression 'house of Joseph', as the first redaction of these verses, in the early time of the kings. *Cf.* also above, p. 22, where we saw that Ed. Sachsse already observed that the expression *beně yiśrā'ēl* is younger than the collective *yiśrā'ēl*. This conclusion of Sachsse we find corroborated by A. Besters, "Israel" et "Fils d'Israël" dans les livres historiques (Genèse – II Rois). *RB* LXXIV (1967) p. 5-23, 321-355.

Mittmann.[57] Judg. 1 is not directly dependent on these notes in the book of Joshua, for both go back to the same source, a document or an oral tradition in anecdotal form. In most cases the passages in the book of Joshua are older and better preserved than those in Judg. 1.[58]

Concerning the other three passages in the book of Joshua we may remark: in 14:4 we are told that the Josephites formed two tribes, Manasseh and Ephraim. This rests upon the number of twelve according to Noth's system A, that which has Joseph and Levi. In fact, however, Joseph consists of Manasseh and Ephraim.

In 18:5 we again meet with the 'house of Joseph', here in obvious parallel with Judah. The same applies to verse 11, where Judaeans and Josephites are contrasted. This chapter also clearly shows that the opinion, often expressed, that Benjamin as son of Rachel belonged to the house of Joseph, is mistaken. This also Täubler has sufficiently demonstrated, followed by Schunck.[59]

Finally, the mention of Joseph's grave in Josh. 24:32 is clearly a literary matter of a secondary nature. It stems from Gen. 33:19, 50:25 and Exod. 13:19. Historically, though, the existence of a tradition concerning the grave of Joseph, and that particularly in or near Shechem, is an extremely interesting point to which we shall have to return.

After those texts referring to the tribes in the book of Joshua, the next in importance are those in the book of Numbers. A mere glance at the passages where Joseph or the Josephites[60] are mentioned, shows that the naming of Joseph is only original in the younger additions to this book, *i.e.* 27:1; 34:23; 36:1, 5, 12. All other passages were inserted later.[61] The old traditions always have Ephraim and Manasseh existing side by side. The principal source of nuncupatory material in the book of Numbers is the 'list of $n^e \dot{s}i'\bar{\imath}m$' in 1:5-15. This list is perhaps a little older than the list to which Num. 26 goes back. Yet this early dating of the

[57] S. Mittmann, *Beiträge*, S. 211.
[58] C. H. J. de Geus, Richteren 1:1-2:5. *Vox Theologica* XXXVI (1966) p. 32-54.
[59] Schunck, *Benjamin*, S. 15. Schunck does reckon with a temporary annexation of Benjamin by the house of Joseph, as a consequence of the events in Judg. 19-21. S. 70-80.
[60] Num. 1:10, 32; 13:11; 26:28, 37; 27:1; 32:33; 36:1, 5, 12. See for all Noth, *UP*, S. 233[574] and *Das Vierte Buch Mose*, Göttingen 1966.
[61] In Num. 13:8-11 the text is disordered. This is due to the later addition of the tribe of Joseph, together with the reversal of the order of Manasseh and Ephraim. The patronymic of Igal the Issacharite has also dropped out. *Cf.* Noth, *Das Vierte Buch Mose*, S. 87-92. Noth's translation in verse 11 'und zwar vom Stamme Manasse' is misleading. See also *UP*, S. 143-150. The nomenclature here is mainly young and secondary.

list 1:5-15 rests entirely upon the names. In general, these may, well be ancient names, but as this is not at all a necessary conclusion it is an assumption and therefore no proof! For instance, there is not yet one among them composed with the divine name of Yahweh. If one accepts the methodic consideration that such names must have been transmitted in a particular context, in this case in an authentic document such as this 'list of $n^e\check{s}\bar{i}'\bar{i}m$', then one must settle upon the early time of the Kings as *terminus ad quem* for dating this list.[62] A *terminus a quo* on the other hand is hard to find. Noth himself already pointed out that the list contains quite a number of names of what he proposes to call proto-Aramaic origin. These are names of types that we already find in Mari and also in many other texts of the second millennium. They are West-Semitic names that most probably are not Canaanite. It is impossible to say how long these names remained in use, or how long they may have been traditionally remembered. This same list could also furnish the proof that names of this kind stayed in use for a long time! That Noth yet dates the list with such conviction to the time of the Judges, rests solely upon the fact that in verse 16 these men are called $n^e\check{s}\bar{i}'\bar{i}m$. And according to Noth the $n\bar{a}\check{s}\bar{i}'$ is one of the principal functionaries of the ancient Israelite amphictyony. The names in this list are possibly old, but it is not permissible to date it so decisively or assign it so definite a function only on the basis of verse 16. The list may very well appear in a secondary context here, while it may also be questioned whether the office of $n\bar{a}\check{s}\bar{i}'$, *Sprecher*, *i.e.* representative of a tribe, ever existed in the manner Noth imagined it.[63] No one doubts that the words 'of the sons of Joseph' in verse 10 are a later addition. Meanwhile, D. Kellermann has now greatly queried these views of Noth.[64] According to him verse 16 is certainly secondary and fairly young, but he cannot regard the list of names 5b-15 as old and authentic either.[65] However, if the list was originally transmitted in a different context, I think it quite possible it is much older. Though Kellermann may show that the individual names are also found in a much later period, yet the whole group of just these twelve names still points to an earlier time of origin.

[62] Noth, *Personennamen*, S. 107, 113-114. *Das System*, S. 15-16.
[63] For this, the excursus in *Das System*, p. 151-162. This interpretation of the $n\bar{a}\check{s}\bar{i}'$ has been justly contested by J. van der Ploeg, Les chefs du peuple d'Israël et leurs titres. *RB* LVII (1950) p. 40-62, esp. p. 47-51 and E. A. Speiser, Background and Function of the Biblical Naśi'. *CBQ* XXV (1963) p. 111-118.
[64] D. Kellermann, *Die Priesterschrift von Num. 1:1 bis 10:10.* ZAW 120, Berlin 1970, S. 5-7.
[65] Kellermann, *o.c.* the excursus on p. 155-159. And now also the very important study by Th. L. Thompson, *The Historicity of the Patriarchal Narratives.* BZAW 133, Berlin 1974, p. 22-51 and 317-318.

The same must be said with regard to Num. 26. Noth has brought forward more than enough evidence to show that this list cannot have simply sprung from the imagination of some priestly scribe. The document probably reflects a situation such as may have existed at the end of the period of the Judges. And again in the original version of Num. 26 Joseph did not in any wise appear.[66]

In Deut. 27:11-13 we find the twelve tribes enumerated in two groups, containing Joseph and Levi, and in a passage which has always seemed not to be in the original context.[67] The verses speak of both blessing and cursing, while the continuation gives only the ritual curse. In the list Levi is one of the twelve, whereas v. 14 *seq.* only speak of the Levites as pronouncing the ominous words. Deut. 27:11-13 might perhaps be meant as an introduction to chapter 28, and many so regard it, but that does not solve the problems, since the content is also very remarkable. These verses are undoubtedly the *Vorlage* of Josh. 8:30-35. Yet like Deut. 11:29, Josh. 8 supposes a text of Deut. 27:11-13 not yet containing the list of tribal names. The list itself is also remarkable, and supposes a Judaean outlook upon political geography. From the literary aspect the list depends upon Gen. 49. One may well suspect that in these verses also the original text only spoke of Levites.[68] In agreement with Gunneweg one is forced to conclude that there is no question here of a tradition that may be put to direct historical use.[69]

Next, the house of Joseph is twice mentioned in the first chapter of the Book of Judges, in 1:22 and 35. Old Testament scholars have always looked upon Judg. 1 as a first-class historical source. An authentic enumeration of negative results of the *Landnahme*, imagined either as a remainder of the Entry reported by J, or with Noth as a conglomerate of quite disparate elements of traditions, each in itself authentic and reliable. I am firmly convinced that this classic view of Judg. 1 is quite

[66] *Das System*, Exkurs I S. 122-132. The phenomenon that former Canaanite city-states appear as clans in the genealogies of Num. 26, and especially with Manasseh, suggests the later time of the Judges for the origin of this document. Shechem already plays the part here of an Israelite family! The essay of G. E. Mendenhall, The Census Lists of Numbers 1 and 26, *JBL* LXXVI (1958) p. 52-67, also assigns it to the time of the Judges.

[67] For literary analysis of Deut. 27, see in the first place Noth, *Das System*, Exkurs II; Literarische Analyse von Jos. 24 und Dtn. 11, 29. 30; 27, 1-13; Jos. 8, 30-35. Also Ed. Nielsen, *Shechem*, p. 67-85.

[68] In agreement with Nielsen, *o.c.* p. 72 *seq.*

[69] A. H. J. Gunneweg, *Leviten und Priester*, Göttingen 1965, S. 69 *seq.*

untenable.[70] Judges 1 is a document cleverly composed and antefixed to the already existing Book of Judges in the deuteronomic period.[71] Its purpose is to make clear that the dangers to Yahwism are by no means less internally, *i.e.* from the remaining Canaanite enclaves, than from without. The whole composition of this document supposes the existence of the two states. The content was largely derived from the deuteronomic historical work, supplemented by anecdotal material probably stemming from oral tradition. Judges 1 is definitely not the authentic historical source from the latter time of the Judges which it was always believed to be. This means then, that we may not conclude from Judg. 1 that the expression 'house of Joseph' was current in the period just after the Entry, as conjoining Ephraim and Manasseh.

Really ancient, however, is II Sam. 19:21; that is to say, this text very probably dates from the early time of the Kings. It is doubly interesting because it is the crucial text to prove that Benjamin was formerly also reckoned as belonging to the house of Joseph.[72] Yet this nowhere appears in the Old Testament genealogies; the conclusion that *therefore* we evidently have an extremely ancient tradition here is highly premature.[73] Nor may it be concluded from the order of the army in Num. 2:18-24 and 10:22 *seq.* or from Psalm 80:2. Neither does Täubler provide a solution with his apodictic: 'Es ist zu übersetzen: früher als das ganze Haus Joseph'.[74] This translation I do not consider possible, since *rīšōn* followed by *le* always means 'first of ...'.[75] If the verse is taken in a genealogical sense it remains a puzzle, as it is an established fact that Shimei was a Benjamite and related to the house of Saul. Verse 21b must however be read in its context, and that context is a political confession of guilt, culminating in a *Rebellenbekenntnis*[76], introduced by *ḥāṭāti*. This formula also expresses submission, *cf.* the words of Hezekiah in II Kgs. 18:14. Shimei comes to offer his submission as the first of the political constellation opposing David. This constellation is called here

[70] For this C. H. J. de Geus, Richteren 1:1-2:5, *Vox Th.* XXXVI (1966) p. 32-53.
[71] We do not mean to say that separate books already existed at this time. The chapter Judg. 1 was inserted between the elements 'Joshua' and 'Judges' in the deuteronomist history, disturbing their sequence. One often observes in the O.T. that later additions have been placed in front of a particular text instead of after it, as would seem more logical to us.
[72] Ed. Meyer, *Die Israeliten und ihre Nachbarstämme*, S. 290.
[73] Thus *e.g.* H. P. Smith, *The Books of Samuel*, p. 363. *Cf.* also W. Caspari. *Die Samuelisbücher*, KAT VII, S. 595.
[74] Täubler, *o.c.* S. 198.
[75] *Cf.* Exod. 12:2; II Sam. 19:44; Isa. 41:27.
[76] This expression is taken from R. Knierim, *Die Hauptbegriffe für Sünde im Alten Testament*. Gütersloh 1965, S. 25 *seq.*, 257.

'house of Joseph'. The word 'house/*bayit*' has not a genealogical but a political content here and stands in contrast to 'house of David'. In that sense Benjamin still belonged to the house of Joseph then, but the usual genealogical systems have nothing to do with it.

The same conclusion must be drawn with regard to 1 Kgs. 11:28, apart from the fact that much is not yet clear in these verses.[77] Here again we find the expression 'house of Joseph' in a context of anti-Judaean, anti-Davidic activities. It is certain that in I Kgs. 11:14-40 two traditions appear which lie a little outside the Deuteronomist; they were either admitted by the Deuteronomist or added afterwards. It is striking that Jeroboam ben Nebat appears in such a favourable light here. On the one hand there is a tradition about three political opponents – *śeṭānīm* – Hadad, Rezon and Jeroboam,[78] on the other that of Jeroboam's meeting with the prophet Ahijah from Shiloh. Now it is customary to construct from verses 26 + 40 a little report about Jeroboam rising against Solomon and failing. Verse 27 and 28 are then regarded as the connective introduction to the Ahijah episode.[79] Yet these two verses should rather be regarded as a secondary explanation of v. 26, so that 26 (27 + 28) and 40 belong together.[80] In any case it is clear that Solomon places Jeroboam in a position where he could exercise much political power and influence, whether he did or did not attempts to seize power.[81] Jeroboam clearly abused the confidence of Solomon. The function of inspector of the 'labour force' of the 'house of Joseph' gave him plentiful opportunity of travelling over the whole country and making himself popular.

[77] Besides the commentaries: A. Jepsen, *Die Quellen des Königsbuches*. Halle 1956². M. Noth, *Überlieferungsgeschichtliche Studien*. Tübingen 1957, S. 72, 80. Ed. Nielsen, *Shechem*. Copenhagen 1959, p. 171-174, 205-208. Ina Plein, Erwägungen zur Überlieferung von Reg. 11²⁶-14²⁰; *ZAW* LXXVII (1966) S. 8-24. H. Seebass, Zur Königserhebung Jerobeams I. *VT* XVII (1967) S. 325-333. J. Debus, *Die Sünde Jerobeams*. FRLANT 93, Göttingen 1967, esp. S. 3-8. S. Herrmann, Geschichte Israels, Möglichkeiten und Grenzen ihrer Darstellung. *ThLZ* XCIV (1969) Sp. 641-650.

[78] As Debus rightly remarks, *o.c.* S. 3¹. Jeroboam is commonly separated from the traditions about Hadad and Rezon.

[79] Noth still took this view, *Könige*, BK XI, 4 Neukirchen 1968, S. 244-258.

[80] As Debus puts it, *o.c.* S. 4.

[81] H. Seebass makes the interesting proposal to read, in agreement with the LXX: *weḥū' mitnaśśē' 'el hammelūkā*. There would then have been no question of an earlier rebellion by Jeroboam against Solomon, but of presumption on the part of Jeroboam, who regarded himself as a pretender to the crown and behaved as such, *VT* XVII (1967) p. 326. Yet this also rests upon the supposition that the source of 11:14 *seq.*, an ancient list of adversaries (Jepsen), did not mention Jeroboam. Moreover, the addition 27 + 28 clearly supposes the present Masoretic Text.

Unfortunately we cannot exactly date the addition of v. 27 + 28, so that v. 28 does not definitely show whether the expression 'house of Joseph' was current at the time of the united monarchy or not. Neither can the precise content of the concept 'house of Joseph' be determined. But Ephraim must surely have belonged to it. It was in Ephraim that Solomon undertook great building operations: Gezer, Beth-Horon. Yet it may also have signified the whole non-Judaean area, and then one thinks of the extensive works in Galilee (Hazor). In any case it is quite evident the whole house of Joseph is prepared to follow Jeroboam in his striving against Solomon (and Jerusalem).

The tribe of Joseph is named four times in Ezekiel, viz. in 37:16, 19; 47:13 and 48:32. Ezekiel 37 deals with the reunion of the two parts of the state, which had become topical again after Josiah. Here again Joseph is parallel with Judah, representing the northern and the southern states respectively. The unity of Israel was highly important to Ezekiel, and he only applied the name Israel to the two states together. The mention of Ephraim in both verses is due to a later gloss. The *šibṭē yiśrā'ēl* should probably not be translated as 'tribes' here, but as 'staves'. The expression explains the wooden objects as staves of office.[82]

The mention of Joseph in 47:13 rests upon a gloss intended to harmonize 48:1, which lists the tribes with the inclusion of Ephraim and Manasseh, with the late 48:32.[83] The 'gate of Joseph' in 48:32 listed among 11 other gates named after the tribes, is in a very late appendix to Ezekiel. The order of the tribes seems to be totally arbitrary here.[84]

In Chronicles, the name Joseph appears four times in the long genealogical introduction I Chr. 1-9. In I Chr. 2:2 we find an enumeration of the twelve sons of Israel, taken from Gen. 35 with two changes.[85] Apart from the very numerous additions, this genealogical introduction is basically altogether dependent upon the Pentateuch tradition. 5:1 *seq.* seems to present an independent tradition relating how the right of primogeniture passed from Reuben to Joseph. This is the more strange, since the Chronicles very clearly regard Judah as the leading tribe. Possible Chronicles did indeed conclude that the blessings of Reuben must have

---

[82] W. Zimmerli, Israel im Buche Ezechiel. *VT* VIII (1958) S. 75-90 espec. S. 83. *Ezechiel.* BK XIII, 12 Neukirchen 1965, S. 903-920.

[83] *Cf. BHK³.* Zimmerli, *Ezechiel.* BK XIII, 15 Neukirchen 1968. S. 1202-1235. H. Gese, *Der Verfassungsentwurf des Ezechiel.* BHTh 25, Tübingen 1957, S. 95-100, 107.

[84] For a possible solution: Noth, *Das System*, S. 13².

[85] Israel instead of Jacob (LXX harmonizes) and the position of Dan (due to careless copying?). *Cf.* Noth, *Üb. Stud.* S. 117-122, 132 *seq.* W. Rudolph, *Chronikbücher*, HAT I 21, Tübingen 1955.

passed to Manasseh and Ephraim because of Gen. 48 and of Gen. 49:3 *seq.*, where Reuben is at once blessed and cursed. Or perhaps the reasoning was just purely juridical: Joseph really consists of two tribes, and receives two shares. Well, Deut. 21:17 shows that the double share was the right of the first-born. The expression $n^e\!z\bar{\imath}r$ '*ẹḥāw* in Gen. 49:26 and Deut. 33:16 might also have led to the view that Joseph was the first-born. This is even explicitly stated in Jer. 31:9 and 20, though not of Joseph, but of Ephraim. However, the content of the title *nāzīr* was mainly religious, whereas the $b^e\underline{k}\bar{o}r$ in Jer. 31 is used in a figurative sense. Only here in Chronicles the word $b^e\underline{k}\bar{o}r$ clearly stands in a genealogical context, unless one were to adopt the conjecture in II Sam. 19:44, where it is proposed to read $b^e\underline{k}\bar{o}r$ instead of $b^e\bar{d}\bar{a}wid$; this seems to me unnecessary and far-fetched. Considering, however, the preponderant place taken in Chronicles by Judah, Rudolph's conjecture that *lō lō* has dropped out in 5:2 is more likely to be right. This brings the factual content of 5:2 in agreement with that of Ps. 78:67 *seq.* (see below). Nor need this conflict with the above: after 5:1 it is all the more striking that the right of primogeniture among the sons of Israel did *not* pass to Joseph. We must also bear in mind that in Chronicles the polemic with the Samaritans already comes into play.[86] That I Chr. 7:29 is a later addition is evident at once. This genealogy is founded upon Num. 26, and there also Joseph was only added afterwards.

If we now turn to the poetic parts of the Old Testament where we may find mention of the tribe of Joseph, we must first consider those references that are of prime importance. These are the pericopes concerning Joseph in the blessing of Jacob and the blessing of Moses, Gen. 49:22-26 and Deut. 33:13-16. We may be quite certain that these blessings are built up of separate, independent emblematic typifications belonging to different *Gattungen* and not all of the same age, while moreover they still confront us with great philological problems. An almost incalculable amount has been written about these blessings. Fortunately we can in the main subscribe to the very thorough examination made by H. J. Zobel. There and in the commentaries the further literature is listed, especially the very numerous studies of detail.[87]

---

[86] *Cf.* Rudolph, *o.c. ad loc.* On the other hand H. J. Zobel assumes because of these texts that Joseph did indeed count as the first-born during the divided monarchy. Chronicles expresses in genealogical language what Gen. 49 and Deut. 33 put in mythological language. *Stammesspruch und Geschichte*, S. 123 *seq.*
[87] H. J. Zobel, *Stammesspruch und Geschichte*. BZAW 95. Berlin 1965. The same author: Die Stammessprüche des Mose-Segens (Dtn 33, 6-35). Ihr 'Sitz im Leben'. *Klio*, XLVI (1965) S. 83-92. *Cf.* also: J. Coppens, La bénédiction de Jacob. Son

The Joseph pericope in Jacob's blessing is not a unity either; it consists of three parts: verse 22, 23 + 24 and 25 + 26. Of these, only v. 22 properly be called an emblematic typification. The pun upon the root *prh* – see also Gen. 41:52 – and the rhyme upon ... *ʿayin* have led to an almost general consensus that the qualification was originally formulated to apply to Ephraim. Unfortunately, the translation still remains problematic. Zobel translates the first words *bn prt* as: 'eine junge Fruchtrebe ist "Ephraim". This is supported by the way *gęfęn* and *poriyyā* appear side by side in Ezek. 19:10 and Ps. 128:3. Besides, Hos. 10:1 might then be a paraphrase of Gen. 49:22. A very serious objection to the translation 'fruit-tree' is, however, that the old qualifications of the tribes are characterized by animal similes. And indeed, such is the simile employed for Joseph in the blessing of Moses. It is desirable therefore to follow Salo's recent suggestion and return to the old translation 'Sohn der Färse'.[88] This image of the young bull is used also in the blessing of Moses, and is eminently suited to Joseph. The actual emblematic typification, v. 22, is then extended in a narrative style in v. 23 + 24. Such extensions are also seen in the verses 9-12, 14-15, 20, 21; they are certainly of later date.[89] Coppens has pointed out that especially these later extensions of the original qualifications contain very much Canaanite mythological material.[90] It is particularly interesting, therefore, to meet with the name of Jacob in this context.[91] In contrast to v. 22, the name of Joseph does indeed originally belong to the blessing in v. 25 + 26. These verses constitute an independent unit.[92]

cadre historique à la lumière des parallèles ougaritiques. *SVT IV*, Leiden 1957, p. 97-115. O. Eissfeldt, Silo und Jerusalem. *SVT* IV, Leiden 1957, S. 138-147. A. H. J. Gunneweg, Über den Sitz im Leben der Sog. Stammessprüche. *ZAW* LXXVI (1964) S. 245-254.

[88] V. Salo, Joseph, Sohn der Färse. *BZ* XII (1968) S. 94-95. The form *prt* can be explained as an old fem. ending. *Bnt* is now known in Ugaritic in the meaning 'Erzeignis'. Salo then translates: 'Sohn der Färse ist Joseph, Sohn der Färse an der Quelle, Geschöpf derer, die schreitet an der Seite des Stieres'. In giving up Zobel's translation, we also obliged to relinquish his historical reconstruction, S. 115 seq.

[89] Zobel, *Stammesspruch und Geschichte*, S. 116-120. Gunneweg, Sitz im Leben, S. 252.

[90] Coppens, *o.c.* p. 102-105.

[91] Zobel's historical reconstruction based on verse 24b is extremely speculative. The *rōʿę ʾębęn yiśrāʾēl* remains a crux at present, unless one would see a case of the prosthetic aleph here, a yod being lost through haplography, thus: *zōʿę benē(y) yiśrāʾēl*. Cf. H. A. Brongers and A. S. van der Woude, Wat is de betekenis van ʾĀbnāyîm in Exodus 1:16? *NThT* XX (1965/1966) p. 241-254, esp. p. 252. A remark one cannot help making, though, is that *benē yiśrāʾēl* instead of *yiśrāʾēl* seems strange in a text of this kind.

[92] Zobel, *Stammesspruch und Geschichte*, S. 24 *seq.*

They suppose a situation in which Joseph is seen as a leading tribe, probably especially in the cult (*nāzīr*). Careful comparison with the Joseph pericope in the blessing of Moses shows moreover that Gen. 49:25 + 26 may be regarded as a later elaboration of Deut. 33:13-16; it is evident from the content, style and vocabulary.[93] This is rather striking, since on the one hand the blessing of Moses is certainly older as a literary unit than that of Jacob, as is apparent at once from the haphazard listing of the nine tribes for Moses' blessing, while the blessing of Jacob is already based on a fixed system of twelve tribes, yet on the other hand the blessing of Jacob has in most cases preserved an older form of the emblematic typification.[94] Thus the Joseph pericope in Deut. 33 also comes to stand in a noticeable cultic context, while its language is rich in mythological imagery. These aspects alone put Deut. 33:17 into considerable contrast with what goes before. As in the real original qualifications, the matter is formed by the depiction of profane, political conditions in metaphorical language of the animal world. Formally also the connexion is disjointed, for the suffix of *šōr* cannot but refer to Yahweh. That this animal comparison does not refer to Joseph but to Ephraim (and Manasseh), is explained by the unmistakable gloss 17b. This is indeed most plausible. Zobel rightly pointed out that the mere proportion of the numbers in 17b shows that 17a refers in the first place to Ephraim. Moreover we again find the metaphor of the young bull, that is used for Ephraim in Gen. 49:22, to add to Zobel's argumentation. Finally the picture presented here of a militant and aggressive tribe is in excellent agreement with what we know of the rise of Ephraim (see above, p. 79). Deut. 33:17b is therefore another example of a factually correct gloss. Reviewing the pericopes concerning Joseph in chronological order, one sees that Gen. 49:22 and Deut. 33:17a are undoubtedly the oldest. They may very probably go back to the time of the Judges. Gen. 49:23 + 24 are a later amplification, then comes Deut. 33:13-16, and Gen. 49:25 + 26 as a later development. For our purpose it is highly important to observe that the ancient emblematic typifications in Gen. 49:22, Deut. 33:17a and probably also Gen. 19:23 *seq.* originally referred to Ephraim and not to Joseph. Here again we see that Joseph is only part of the original text in the younger additions. Yet the difference is not only chronological; one sees that the content of

---

[93] Zobel, *Stammesspruch und Geschichte*, S. 36 *seq.*
[94] Zobel, Die Josephsspruch des Mose-Segens, S. 87. On the basis of a reconstructed orthography, Cross and Freedman place the blessing of Moses in the tenth century. Fr. M. Cross and D. N. Freedman, The Blessing of Moses. *JBL* LXVIII (1958) p. 191-210.

the true Joseph pericopes is far more theological, whereas that of the tribal qualifications is otherwise secular.[95]

The prophets only mention Joseph a few times: Amos 5:5, 15; 6:6; Obad. 1:18 and Zech. 10:6. There is no doubt that in Amos (the house of) Joseph means the northern kingdom.[96] Like (the house of) Jacob, it is a poetical expression for (the house of) Israel. This always means the northern kingdom. It is remarkable that Amos never names Ephraim. And also, that in Amos we thrice find the name Joseph in a very polemic context. For to Amos the great sin of Joseph/Israel was the falling away from Jerusalem, both in politics and in religion.[97] Zech. 10:6 belongs to a later period, but to a similar background. The hope of Israel's return to Jerusalem and the house of David, already expressed by Amos, was not given up after 722. It even became highly topical in the time of Josiah, to whose period Otzen dates cap. 10:6-10 of Deutero-Zechariah, together with 9:11-12.[98] As with Amos, Joseph here represents the northern kingdom, as *apostatic*. In the last days of Judah there was in Jerusalem a great hope that the 'true Israel' might be restored, as is very evident, for instance, with the prophet Jeremiah (cap. 31!). This hope is also strong in the prophets Ezekiel and Deutero-Isaiah, as we have already seen in discussing Ezek. 37:16 and 19,[99] but the religious content of the concept

[95] Many premature conclusions concerning Israel's earliest history have been drawn from Deut. 33:16, just as they were from Gen. 49:24b[B]. The starting-point is always the religious or cultic meaning of *nāzīr*. 16a[B] is connected with this, and the 'dweller in the thorn-bush' interpreted as Yahweh, because of Exod. 3. As in the introductory hymn to the blessing of Moses, Deut. 33:1-6, there would be a reference here to the traditions of the Sinai. Hence some would conclude that these traditions were especially the spiritual heritage of Joseph. Yet this linkage is most precarious. Far more probable is the opposite course: Beek suggests that Exod. 3 was influenced by far older ideas. That such earlier ideas were indeed entertained in the northern kingdom has been demonstrated by Eissfeldt. It is therefore unnecessary to follow Beek and think of old traditions of the desert. *Cf.* L. Baeck, Der im Dornbusch Wohnende. *Aus drei Jahrtausenden.* Tübingen 1958, S. 240-242. O. Eissfeldt, Ein Psalm aus Nord-Israel, Micha 7:7-20. *ZDMG* CXII (1962) S. 259-268. G. Fohrer, *Ueberlieferung und Geschichte des Exodus. Eine Analyse von Ex. 1-15.* BZAW 91, Berlin 1964, espec. S. 34. M. A. Beek, Der Dornbusch als Wohnsitz Gottes (Deut. XXXIII 16). *OTS* XIV (1965) S. 155-161. Also H. Schmid, *Mose.* BZAW 110, Berlin 1968, espec. S. 28-31.
[96] The authenticity of these passages in Amos has often been combated, but is at present fairly generally accepted. *Cf.* Eissfeldt, *EAT*[3]. F. Hesse, Amos 5:4-6, 14 *seq. ZAW* LXVIII (1956) S. 1-17 and K. W. Neubauer, Erwägungen zu Amos 5: 4-15. *ZAW* LXXVIII (1966) S. 292-316.
[97] See for this especially G. A. Danell, *Studies in the Name Israel*, p. 136.
[98] B. Otzen, *Studien über Deuterosacharja.* Copenhagen 1964. Espec. p. 127-134.
[99] See above, p. 88.

'Israel' as a cultic community became more and more dominant over its political meaning.[100]

The book of Obadiah is really too short to permit of our finding a satisfactory solution to all its problems.[101] As to its date, however, there is fairly general agreement: we have to do with prophecies (or: a prophecy) against Edom because of the betrayal by this people, with whom Israel once felt most closely linked, after the fall of Jerusalem in 587. It is fairly certain therefore that Obad. 18 was composed in exile. Here again the house of Joseph is put into parallel with the house of Jacob, and most commentators equate it with the northern kingdom. Only it is not easy to decide here whether the parallel of Zion and Jacob in v. 17 is meant to be antithetic or synonymous. In the latter case this would be the only passage where the appellation Joseph would, like Jacob, have been extended to Judah.[102]

Finally, the name of Joseph appears a few times in the Psalms: Ps. 77:16; 78:67-69; 80:2-3; 81:6 and 105:17. In his commentary on the Psalms, H. J. Kraus defends the view that in the Psalms 'Joseph' is always the poetic name for 'Israel in Egypt'.[103] Actually such is only the case in Ps. 105. In Ps. 77, which very probably dates from the time of exile, we see the sons of Joseph in parallel with the sons of Jacob. Here again Jacob and Joseph are poetic synonyms of Israel. Perhaps Joseph is named here because of the mythological reference to the passing of the sea in v. 17-20, though it is not necessarily so. We may compare the language of Obadiah. Nor can this text form a reason for linking Joseph in particular with the Exodus or the sojourn in Egypt.[104]

In Psalm 78 Joseph again appears in a familiar context. The date of this psalm is still much debated, and proposals vary from the time of the splitting of the kingdom (Eissfeldt) to post-exilic times (Kraus).[105]

---

[100] That this pan-Israelite expectation was cherished by most of the pre-exilic prophets, has been clearly shown by G. A. Danell, *Studies in the Name Israel.* Cf. esp. p. 289.

[101] W. Rudolph, Obadja, *ZAW* XLIX (1931) S. 222-231. J. Gray, The Diaspora of Israel and Judah in Obadiah v. 20, *ZAW* LXX (1953) p. 53-59. G. Fohrer, Die Sprüche Obadjas. *Studia Biblica et Semitica Th. C. Vriezen Dedicata*. Wageningen 1966, p. 81-93.

[102] Cf. the use of 'Israel' and 'Jacob' in Ezekiel and Deutero-Isaiah.

[103] H. J. Kraus, *Psalmen*. BK XV, Neukirchen 1960, S. 557-565.

[104] Cf. above, note 95 and Noth, *Ueb. Pent.* S. 231[571].

[105] Besides the commentaries: H. Junker, Die Entstehungszeit des Ps. 78 und des Deuteronomiums, *Biblica* XXXIV (1953) S. 487-500. O. Eissfeldt, *Das Lied Moses Deuteronomium 32, 1-43 und das Lehrgedicht Asaphs Ps. 78 samt einer Analyse der Umgebung des Mose-Liedes.* BSA 104, 5 Berlin 1958/1959. J. Schildenberger,

Though the latter dating is rather extreme, it is impossible to date the psalm very early because of its resemblance to Deuteronomy and its literary form of didactic poetry. It would seem to fit best in the latter time of the kings.[106] The way 'Joseph' is used here is clear: on one side Joseph is in parallel with Ephraim, on the other in violent contrast to Judah and Zion. One notices that v. 67 certainly seems to suppose claims to political power on the part of Joseph/Ephraim, as also appears from the Joseph cycle in Genesis (Gen. 37:5-12). An important point is the connecting of Jacob or Israel, here the entire people, with David in v. 70-71.

A particular difficulty is constituted by Psalm 80:2, first of all because the psalm is very difficult to date. It is generally held to date from the time before the Exile.[107] In spite of some typical Judaean peculiarities in this psalm, it yet seems best to keep to the idea that 'Joseph' in v. 2 is a poetical expression for the northern state, i.e. especially for Ephraim, Benjamin and Manasseh, the Rachel group (v. 3). This trio is a little surprising, since after the splitting of the state Benjamin joined Judah. That the Rachel group formed the nucleus of Israel, however, is undisputed. The same three tribes also represent the northern kingdom in 2 Chr. 31:1. It is improbable that Joseph could be used here to personify 'Israel in Egypt'. The theme of Egypt is not taken up until v. 9-12.[108] Psalm 81 is a pre-exilic festive liturgy. Here also Joseph (spelt as Jehoseph!) is primarily a poetic designation of Israel. Jacob/Joseph/Israel are parallel concepts. 'Joseph' may not simply be understood here as

---

Psalm 78 (77) und die Pentateuchquellen. 'Lex tua veritas', Festschrift Junker, Trier 1961, S. 231-256. H. J. Cook, Pekah. VT XIV (1964) p. 121-135. F. N. Jasper, Early Israelite Tradition and the Psalter. VT XVII (1967) p. 50-60.

[106] Junker and Schildenberger date Psalm 78 to Hezekiah.

[107] O. Eissfeldt, Psalm 80. Geschichte und Altes Testament, Albrecht Alt zum 70. Geburtstag dargebracht. Tübingen 1953, S. 65-78. And: Psalm 80 und Psalm 89. WO III (1964/1966 (1964)) S. 27-31. Cf. also Schildenberger's above-mentioned essay.

[108] This simple and almost automatic identification of Joseph with 'Israel in Egypt' is also much impeded by the consideration that although the calling out of Egypt is a repeated theme in Hosea, the prophet never once uses the name Joseph. Hosea always calls the northern kingdom Ephraim, alternating with 'Israel' or 'Jacob'. This terminology follows from the fact that the main centre of the northern kingdom lay in Ephraim, and the Ephraimites formed its chief support. I think it is stretching the point quite too far to conclude from this use of the name Ephraim that Hosea knew a tradition in which the tribe of Ephraim was especially linked with Egypt, at least in the sense that those who came from Egypt afterwards only constituted the tribe of Ephraim. Hosea does not use the name Ephraim in such a specific sense. Thus G. A. Danell, Studies in the Name Israel, p. 45. H. H. Rowley, From Joseph to Joshua, p. 142-144. O. Kaiser, Stammesgeschichtliche Hintergründe der Josephsgeschichte. VT X (1960) S. 13.

the northern kingdom, the name is now clearly used for the whole nation.

Only in Psalm 105:17 do we at last find explicit mention of the Joseph from the Joseph story in Genesis. The form of this psalm relates it closely to 78, 106 and 107; it is again a historical didactic poem, very probably of post-exilic date. Remarkably enough, this is the only passage in the Old Testament that refers back directly to the story of Joseph; deutero-canonical and later literature does so much more often.[109]

The above examination has more than confirmed Täubler's theory that we cited on p. 72. The expression 'house of Joseph' first crops up in the early time of the Kings, and it has an anti-Davidic sound. It has proved possible, though, to go further: we find that the O.T. gives us no occasion to think there was an ancient independent tribe of Joseph. Everywhere it could be shown that mention of a tribe of Joseph was either late, or secondary. The earliest traditions have only Ephraim and Manasseh.[110] Joseph is, however, mainly associated with Ephraim. Zobel saw this clearly, though he still reckons with a tribe Joseph supposed to have existed in some distant past. He always speaks of Ephraim-Joseph to indicate the identity of the two names. The starting-point of any re-construction of the history of the appellation 'Joseph' must be that it was almost certainly a real personal name.[111] It seems perfectly evident to me that originally Joseph was just as much a person as Jacob, for instance. A pointer to this is also the tradition of his grave.[112] The expression 'house of Joseph' also suggests people were still aware of his being a person. It is this man Joseph that the Joseph cycle of Genesis

---

[109] L. Ruppert, *Die Josepherzählung*, S. 239-243. A quotation, or rather a purely literary allusion, is perhaps to be seen in Zech. 9:11 in the words 'the pit with no water in it), cf. Gen. 37:24. Thus Otzen, *Deuterosacharja*, S. 240 seq. Ruppert does not mention this text.

[110] Doubt of a tribe of Joseph ever having existed is also voiced by J. Hoftijzer, Enige opmerkingen rond het Israëlitisch 12-stammen-systeem. *NThT* XIV (1959/1960) p. 255 (but compare p. 258!) and by A. H. J. Gunneweg, *Leviten und Priester*, S. 60. He does not work it out any further, though. See also the despair of M. Weippert, *Die Landnahme der israelitischen Stämme*, S. 50-51.

[111] M. Noth, Gemeinsemitische Erscheinungen in der israelitischen Namengebung. *ZDMG* N.F. VI (1927) S. 1-45, espec. S. 23[1].

[112] See above, p. 83. As Mowinckel says, *Von Ugarit nach Qumran*, S. 142-145, we must reckon with the possibility that this grave may date from pre-Israelite times. Then there are two possibilities: the grave may have been afterwards connected with the person of Joseph in the Israelitic period, or it was originally so connected. In the former case we have to do with the linking of an old native tomb tradition with the proto-Israelitic figure of Joseph. In the latter case both are of non-Israelite origin. Since in the Old Testament Joseph seems to belong to the trio Israel-Jacob-Joseph, however, the first possibility seems the most probable.

goes back to.[113] As the O.T. has not transmitted to us any memories of this 'historical Joseph', it does not seem likely that he lived after Joshua, who in historical times was the great hero of the tribe of Ephraim. The form of the name Josephel (?) also suggests that we have to do with a legendary figure of the second millennium, who could still be evoked centuries later. One might compare him to a figure like Daniel.[114] There were undoubtedly more patriarchs than the three the Old Testament has now transmitted to us.[115] If this is right, then the connexion with Ephraim, so evident in the O.T., is secondary. Not only the date points to this, but also the fact that Shechem, the site of Joseph's grave, was not reckoned to be in the territory of Ephraim until a fairly late period. An explanation of the connexion might be that the name Ephraim was too evidently a geographical term to serve as the name of an eponym. That the name of Joseph crops up at the splitting of the state is undoubtedly connected with the ideological foundation of the Northern Kingdom. An appeal to the past is typical of political innovations!

In the early time of the Kings, probably until 722, the term '(house of) Joseph' has a rather negative sound, directed against Jerusalem. Is that why the name is so strikingly left out by the north-Israelite prophet Hosea? Yet after the fall of Samaria the hope of restoration revives and the use of the name Joseph has a far more positive aspect. The end of the development is that in and just before the Exile the names Jacob, Joseph and Israel can be used almost indiscriminately of the existing people.

The question at once arises, how the two systems of twelve tribes are to be fitted into this development. Before making any statements about this, we shall first have to consider the tribes of Levi and Gad. It is already clear, though, that a system containing Joseph – Noth's system 'A' – cannot possibly be very old and can certainly not date from the time of the Judges.

---

[113] In the whole of the Pentateuch the Joseph cycle is one of the youngest parts, really already supposing the existing Pentateuch (Tetrateuch). Thus Noth, *Ueb. Pent.* S. 226-232. Von Rad has very happily connected the Joseph tales with the wisdom literature: Josephsgeschichte und ältere Chokma. *SVT* I Leiden 1953, S. 120-127. R. N. Whybray, The Joseph Story and Pentateuchal Criticism. *VT* XVIII (1968) p. 522-528, now rightly points out that after this insight it is inconsistent still to divide the Joseph cycle over these two documents. Whybray suggests a younger date.
[114] Named together with other legendary figures of the past, Job and Noah, in Ezek. 14:14, 20 and 28:3. *Cf.* also the legendary king Dn'l of Ugarit. It is doubted nowadays whether the name already appears in Egyptian sources in the time of the Hyksos. M. Weippert, *Die Landnahme der israelitischen Stämme*, S. 13.
[115] M. Noth, *GI*[3] S. 118.

2. The secular tribe of Levi

The generally accepted earlier dating of system 'A' than of system 'B' (without Joseph and Levi), follows from the current solutions to the problem of 'Levi'. There are two of these, which appear to be mutually exclusive.[116] The one preferred is that based on a lost secular tribe of Levi. A number of traditions in the Old Testament seem hard to explain if the 'Levi' mentioned is the sacerdotal tribe; these are the typification of Levi in the blessing of Jacob, Levi's role in Genesis 34, and the mention of Levi as one of the twelve sons of Jacob in the twelve-tribe system. At the same time, of course, in the great majority of instances Levi is the eponym of the Levitical priests. The second solution denies the existence of a secular tribe of Levi. The fact that Levi appears in the system of tribes is seen as a later fiction intended to give the Levites the same rights as the other tribes.[117] Of the first solution, which Gunneweg simply calls the *Untergangstheorie*, we have an older and a younger form. The old traditional theory was that the former secular tribe of Levi ceased to exist through some catastrophe or other – a connexion with Gen. 34 is often suggested – and the survivors, having lost their possessions, found a new way to earn their living as priests. This idea is really sufficiently gainsaid by Wellhausen's ironical remark that there can hardly have been so many sacerdotal offices vacant at that moment. Wellhausen assumes on the contrary that the former secular tribe of Levi (he wonders if it is the masculine form of Leah) and the eponym Levi of the Levites originally had nothing to do with one another.[118] Wellhausen sees no historical continuity, but simply two names that happen to be the same. This is really Noth's view also, though he does not definitely pronounce himself upon the matter. He would, however, go so far as to assume a historical and traditional link between the two Levis, the sacerdotal caste of the Levites taking over a number of the

---

[116] See for the following especially A. H. J. Gunneweg, *Leviten und Priester. Hauptlinien der Traditionsbildung und Geschichte des israelitisch-jüdischen Kultpersonals*. FRLANT 89, Göttingen 1965, esp. S. 52-64. The other relevant literature is also listed there.

[117] This latter view was defended, *int.al.*, by S. Mowinckel in *RGG²*, Band III, Tübingen 1929, *s.v.* Levi und Leviten. Also by many who would regard 'Levite' as only an appellative in the earliest times. One of these is W. F. Albright, in whose eyes for instance Samuel is a typical Levite, although he is not called one before very late texts. 'Reconstructing Samuel's Role in History', in: *Archaeology, Historical Analogy and Early Biblical Tradition*. Baton Rouge 1966, p. 42-66.

[118] *Prolegomena*, S. 137. The connection between the two Levis is not entirely fortuitous, but is formed by the person of Moses.

traditions (and aspirations) of the ancient tribe of Levi.[119] Noth insists, however, that the Levi in the twelve-tribe system is the old secular tribe of Levi, that in a far-distant past even formed part of the six-tribe Leah amphictyony. After the loss of Levi,[120] the tribal system was adapted to the altered situation, resulting in system 'B' without Joseph and Levi, but with Ephraim and Manasseh, while Gad came to take the place left open by Levi. This was not only an adaptation to the loss of Levi, it was also a sign that the character of the tribes was changing: they were becoming more geographical entities. Noth's view of the problem 'Levi' really makes out the central point of his reasoning, for if Levi had not been a secular tribe, then the system 'A' would not have been a true tribal system. The only alternative would be to suppose Levi to be everywhere the eponym of the Levites, and as the rise of the Levites can still be followed in the O.T., it would become impossible to date a system containing Levi to the time of the Judges. Therefore, if no secular tribe of Levi existed, Noth's entire construction falls to the ground, as he himself was fully aware![121]

One must realize that the whole question, often so hotly debated, as to whether a secular tribe Levi did or did not exist, is determined by the amphictyony hypothesis. We shall see that it is hardly of interest for the exegesis of the Old Testament, unless one were to postulate a special tie between Yahwism and the Levites. Nor is it important for the reconstruction of Israel's history – apart from the amphictyony; when reconstructing the historical development of priesthood and the Levites in Israel, it remains a theoretical and fairly speculative inquiry. After all, nobody defends the view that there were once two distinct Levis at the same time! Yet according to the view of Noth this should be possible. The whole discussion only makes sense if one begins by assuming there were twelve equal tribes according to Noth's system 'A'. The discussion is hampered by the lack of a clear understanding as to the meaning of 'tribe' in this context. Chapter III deals extensively with this matter.

Starting from Noth's problem, we again ask: is there a secular tribe of Levi in the Old Testament? This question falls into two parts: do the

[119] Das System, S. 33 seq. GI³, S. 86¹. Ueb. Pent. S. 197⁵⁰³. This view of Noth has been worked out further in the traditio-historical manner by his pupil H. Strauss, Untersuchungen zu den Ueberlieferungen der Vorexilischen Leviten, diss. Bonn 1960. Zobel, Stammesspruch und Geschichte, S. 17, is really still an adherent of the Untergangstheorie in its older form, only like Ed. Meyer he removes the locale of the transition from a secular to a sacerdotal tribe to Kades. M. Weippert, Die Landnahme der israelitischen Stämme, entirely follows Noth, p. 48⁸, and indeed on p. 27² he even goes a little further.
[120] Noth, too, leaves an open question as to the cause of this fatality. GI³, S. 86¹.
[121] Cf. Das System, S. 34, especially note 1.

famous passages (Deut. 33:8-11), Gen. 34 and Gen. 49:5-7 really necessitate the existence of a secular tribe of Levi? And secondly: is a secular tribe of Levi a necessary conclusion from the naming of Levi in the twelve-tribe system?

It is practically certain that the blessings may be regarded as our earliest source of information about the various tribes. Judg. 5 does not mention Levi. However, Levi does appear in Deut. 33 and Gen. 49. In the blessing of Moses we notice at once that there is no essential difference between the verses about Levi and those about the other tribes, yet Levi here is clearly the eponym of the Levites, he is addressed in the singular, there are puns upon the names of places, altogether the blessing makes a most authentic impression.[122] Yet for linguistic reasons we may not give it a very early date.[123] It is at any rate clear that the blessing concerns the Levites, and not a secular tribe of Levi. As to whether such a tribe might have existed, Deut. 33 tells us nothing. On the other hand the blessing of Moses reduces the function of this Levi to the office of voicing the divine will by means of the Thummim and Urim. At the time of this author – no Levite himself! – the Levites were obviously already attached to sanctuaries as priests. They served the divine law and gave the oracle of Yahweh. Yet these Levitical priests had by no means gained the monopoly of sacrifice. On the contrary, the Levites have enemies who do not acknowledge their claims.[124] All this sets a date a quo in the latter time of the Judges. Nevertheless, the 'rule of the Levites' (Gunneweg) in v. 9, also found in an earlier form in Exod. 32, certainly makes the impression of being older.[125]

Matters are more complicated with regard to Gen. 49:5-7. In the blessing of Jacob an oracular curse is addressed to Levi as a prophet might do.[126] One thing is certain about the Levi spoken to here, that is that he is 'dispersed'. The Levites meant are living dispersed among the other Israelites without a territory of their own, and probably without owning any land. This 'being dispersed' the Levites have in common with the Simeonites. Zobel thinks it out of the question that these

---

[122] Besides the analysis of Gunneweg, we can fall back upon the very thorough discussion of the blessing of Levi by Zobel, *Stammesspruch und Geschichte. Cf.* also H. Schmid, *Mose.* BZAW 110, Berlin 1968, S. 91-94.
[123] F. M. Cross and D. N. Freedman, The Blessing of Moses. *JBL* LXVII (1948) p. 191-210. We have already seen that it is not permissible to regard Deut. 33, as Noth did, as a very young text, in which the twelve-tribe system had already run wild. *Das System,* S. 21-23 and above note 94.
[124] Thus Zobel, *o.c.* S. 68.
[125] Gunneweg, *o.c.* S. 40.
[126] Zobel, *o.c.* S. 9.

Levites here could be any others than the later Levites.[127] The great objection formerly made to this interpretation, the improbability of the sacerdotal tribe of Levi being cursed in the O.T., no longer holds now that it is generally realized that the rise of the Levites did not go un-opposed, as witness Deut. 33. Gunneweg comes to the same conclusion: what is judged of here is the same thing as in Deut. 33, the special social status of the Levites. The only difference is that here the judgement is negative! Gen. 49:5-7 therefore drops out as a text which might prove the existence of a secular tribe of Levi: a statement is made regarding the result of a certain historical development. As to earlier stages we can say nothing whatever upon the evidence of these verses. Now the deed of violence referred to in Gen. 49:5-7 is always related to the action of Simeon and Levi in Gen. 34. In other words: is the *tertium comparationis* of the combination Simeon and Levi only the social situation in which these tribes were living, or (also) certain events in their common past? On the basis of earlier research, Zobel thinks the latter answer must be right.[128] He does, indeed, place the events described in Gen. 34 in a time far removed: some centuries before the author of Gen. 49:5-7. Yet since this is the only passage in the O.T. that might be held to per-petuate a direct memory of secular Levites, those explanations of Gen. 34 (and thereby also of Gen. 49:5-7 that harks back to the same event) which start from the possibility of the Levites in this case also being 'ordinary' Levites, have an *a priori* advantage. A very serious and in my opinion succesful attempt at such an explanation has been made by Ed. Nielsen,[129] who explains Gen. 34 as being originally only a Simeonite tradition. Later Levi was connected with Simeon because of the intensely anti-Canaanite attitude of the Levites. This would make it a later harmonization on the grounds that the Simeonites once did what was afterwards considered typical of the Levites. Nielsen also suggests that the Simeonite expedition may have been inspired, perhaps even ac-companied, by Levitical priests.[130] Gunneweg takes practically the same course, though he does assume that Simeon and Levi were connected of old in the tradition of Gen. 34. Obviously he is unconvinced by Niel-sen's reasoning, thinking it an inconsistency that Nielsen is willing to

[127] *o.c.* S. 70. Yet Zobel clings to a secular tribe of Levi, because of Gen. 34. Following Wellhausen, Meyer and others, he regards the Levites as the priesthood of Kades.
[128] 'Jene Erzählung aber lässt keinen Zweifel daran aufkommen, dass Simeon und Levi weltliche Stämme waren'. Zobel, *o.c.* S. 70.
[129] Ed. Nielsen, *Shechem, A Traditio-Historical Investigation*. Copenhagen 1959, p. 241-286. *Cf.* also The Levites in Ancient Israel. *ASThI* III (1964) p. 16-27.
[130] Nielsen, *o.c.* p. 282-284.

reckon with Levite priests as instigators.[131] Nor does Gunneweg accept the very detailed analysis of Gen. 34 by S. Lehming, who argues *in extenso* against both Simeon and Levi being original in Gen. 34. Lehming holds that the verse only spoke of anonymous 'sons of Jacob'.[132] Gunneweg thinks it more important, however, to settle clearly what may *not* be deduced from Gen. 34! And that is first of all the 'perishing' of the tribes Levi and Simeon. The only loss here is that of Shechem. 'Auch dass Levi in Gen. 49 und 34 eine andere Grösse als die Leviten meinen *müsse*, ist, noch von allen Unsicherheiten von Gen. 34 abgesehen, nicht zwingend aus diesen Texten abzuleiten. Gen. 49, wo man immerhin festeren Boden unter den Füssen hat, lässt sich auf jeden Fall ohne Schwierigkeit, ja leichter als Spruch über die Leviten verstehen.'[133] Thus Gunneweg ultimately pronounces a *non liquet* as to the historical question.[134] A similar *non liquet* in this matter is spoken by A. de Pury.[135] After a very thorough literary analysis of Gen. 34 and 49:5-7, De Pury reaches the same kind of conclusion as Lehming: literary historical study will not admit Simeon and Levi to Gen. 34 in its primal form. The pronouncement in Gen. 49:5-7 refers to a different event, an act directed against fellow-countrymen and still fairly fresh in the memory of its victims (Judah?). Everything indicates that we have to do here with a raid carried out by 'semi-nomads' against a sedentary people.[136] We know that the original home of the tribe of Simeon was in the extreme south of Judah. Our earliest information about Levi seems to point to the same region, perhaps even further to the south. Such a raid, then, would be very much in character for Simeon. But for Levi? Then is Levi appearing here as a secular tribe just like Simeon? Some scholars attach much importance to the fact that in Num. 26:58 three families are regarded as Levites whose habitat is clearly South-Judah: Hebron,

---

[131] Gunneweg, *o.c.* S. 48[3].

[132] S. Lehming, Zur Ueberlieferungsgeschichte von Gen. 34. *ZAW* LXX (1958) S. 228-250. This conclusion regarding Levi and Simeon is now also shared by A. de Pury, Genèse XXXIV et l'histoire. *RB* LXXVI (1969) p. 5-49.

[133] Gunneweg, *o.c.* S. 51.

[134] This of course is also a consequence of the method he chose!

[135] A. de Pury, Genèse XXXIV et l'histoire. *RB* LXXVI (1969) p. 5-49. De Pury's point of view has now also been adopted by R. de Vaux, The Settlement of the Israelites and the Origins of the Tribe of Judah. In: H. Th. Frank and W. L. Reed eds., *'Translating and Understanding the Old Testament'. Essays in Honor of H. G. May*, Nashville/New York 1970, p. 108-134, esp. p. 114 and 117. (= *Histoire ancienne d'Israël*, vol. I, part III, ch. 2).

[136] De Pury, *o.c.* p. 31 draws attention to the remark of W. Krebs on Gen. 49:6 '... and they hamstrung oxen' that to hamstring (root *'ḳr*) large animals, horses or cattle, which they do not carry off as being no use in their economy, is a characteristic of raiders.

Libna and Korath.[137] Yet it is a somewhat radical proceeding to subjoin v. 58 to the 'census list' and then declare it to be ancient.[138] This brings one into conflict with the tradition that precisely this region was Calebite in ancient times.[139] On the other hand Exod. 32:38 also shows that the Levites were not averse to exercising violence against people of their own nation, and it is not impossible that precisely this was the *tertium comparationis*, even though the motives may have differed.

In summary: I agree with Nielsen that against the background of nearly all the other O.T. texts where Levi never appears as a secular tribe or group, it is impossible to conclude the existence of a secular tribe of Levi on the basis of *this* passage. The material does not permit of such a conclusion; it is not a necessary hypothesis for the understanding of Gen. 49:5-7. We must be content with a *non liquet*.

At a moment when the aforesaid scholars have concluded that owing to lack of data there is no sense in endless discussions about secular or sacerdotal tribes of Levi, A. Cody comes to declare anew the secular origin of the Levites.[140] To declare it, for Cody's style of reasoning is somewhat apodictic. He concludes: 'The positive testimony of the Old Testament documents (1), the connected evaluation of the Dedan inscriptions which once were understood as indicating that *lēwī* might have been an appellative (2), and the definite evidence that Levi existed in the Ancient Near East not as an appellative but as the initial element of certain personal names, of which, therefore, it could in all normality serve as a hypocoristicon, should be enough to persuade us of the solid probability that there was a secular tribe of Levi which bore that hypocoristic personal name as its gentilitial name (3).'[141]

Ad. 1. The profound and subtle analyses of Nielsen, Gunneweg, Lehming and De Pury are simply swept aside. Cody makes automatic use of Noth's classification of the texts as belonging to system 'A' or system 'B', and follows the old propaedeutic formula according to which all that is 'P' is young, and all that is not 'P' is old. Although Cody rejects

---

[137] Thus *e.g.* De Vaux in the essay cited in note 135. *Cf.* also his Sur l'origine kénite ou madianite du Yahwisme. *EI* IX (1969) p. 28-32. Further Ae. Cody – see note 140 – on p. 34-38.

[138] K. Möhlenbrink, Die levitischen Überlieferungen des Alten Testaments, *ZAW* LII (1934) S. 184-231, espec. S. 196.

[139] See for this the two aforesaid articles by R. de Vaux. The other way round, that former Calebite possessions were afterwards regarded as Levite, is far more probable.

[140] Ae. Cody, *A History of Old Testament Priesthood*. Analecta Biblica 35, Roma 1969.

[141] Cody, *o.c.* p. 36 (*numbered by me, dG*).

Hoftijzer, there is no sign anywhere that he knows what Hoftijzer's arguments are![142]

Ad. 2. Quite right, and so this no longer plays a part in the discussion at present.

Ad 3. Here again Cody is perfectly right: the word *lēwī* is best explained as a proper name. Yet in the genealogizing tribal form of organization of ancient Israel, where tribes and groups are called after more or less fictitious ancestors, nothing else is to be expected. As a possible alternative, one might think of a name derived from some geographical designation. A true appellative designation is *a priori* not to be expected in the period, at least certainly not in the genealogical system. *Cf.* also the designation 'Rechabites'.

Cody is really arguing from two suppositions: the first is again the amphictyony hypothesis – the Levites were not a sacerdotal tribe at the moment of origin of the twelve-tribe system (p. 36), as this originated together with the amphictyony (Noth), the amphictyony requires twelve equivalent tribes, etc., etc. The second assumption is his own conclusion[143] that the cultic task of the Levites had a historically marked beginning, *viz.* their appointment by Moses himself. So before that they did not have such a task!

I agree with Cody, though, that the qualification of the earliest known Levites as *gērīm* is an essential point.[144] Yet whether this status was caused by the loss of a former tribe of Levi, or through their not really belonging to the nation,[145] or whether as guardians of the cult of Yahweh they were *gērīm qualitate qua* are as yet unanswerable questions. With regard to the *historical* aspect of the matter we conclude again to a *non liquet*.

The first of our two questions: do (Deut. 33:8-11), Gen. 34 and 49:5-7 *necessarily* demand the existence of a secular tribe of Levi, has now received an answer, and a negative one. These passages are easier to explain if one assumes that they also deal with the same Levites who appear in the rest of the O.T. The first member of the question having thus been answered in the negative, it seems an obvious step to do the same with the second member: must we necessarily postulate a secular tribe of Levi because Levi appears in the twelve-tribe system? Yet this step is usually not taken, because the only imaginable alternative then seems to

[142] Cody, *o.c.* p. 25[116]. Hoftijzer's essay is also lacking in the list of literature, as is also Nielsen's article in *ASThI* III (1967).

[143] Cody, *o.c.* p. 50-52.

[144] Cody, *o.c.* p. 55-61. *Cf.* also Gunneweg, *Leviten und Priester*, S. 14[80].

[145] De Vaux thinks in this direction, *EI* IX (1969) p. 28-32.

be that Levi was put into the system as a fictitious tribe of priests.[146]

That is precisely what Noth was always so vividly opposed to; in his eyes the twelve-tribe system is not just a later construction, a young theory, but transmits an *authentic* tradition regarding an ancient Israelite amphictyony. The twelve-tribe system reflects a situation that must once have existed in reality. Yet even if not looking upon the inclusion of the sacerdotal tribe as a young theory but as an authentic tradition, one still comes into fatal conflict with Noth's amphictyony hypothesis, because the principle of twelve essentially equal tribes is then broken down. Quite apart from the problems raised by trying to place a whole tribe of priests in that early period. And if one gives up the essential equality of the twelve tribes one gets into difficulties, for instance, with the idea that the central sanctuary was cared for by each in turn for a month, so filling up the year.[147] It is most interesting to observe Noth's immense influence demonstrated in the way Gunneweg simply accepts the amphictyony hypothesis as quite incontestable. Yet for Gunneweg also matters would certainly become simpler if he did not feel so tied to this hypothesis. 'Dass aber dieser Levi unter den Jakobssöhnen und als einer von ihnen erscheint, *das* ist es, was die Eponymtheorie nicht zu erklären vermochte, und das wird desto rätselhafter, wenn die Namen der Jakobssöhne Eponymen von Stämmen sind, die zusammen die Israel genannte Amphiktyonie darstellen und wenn deshalb die Systeme von Eponymen nicht einfach als späte Theorie, sondern als Niederschlag echter, alter, amphyktyonischer Ueberlieferung zu betrachten sind. Hieran wird man auf jeden Fall mit Noth festhalten müssen. Die von ihm herangezogenen ausserisraelitischen Parallelen, aber auch die trotz aller Verschiebungen auffällige Konstanz, mit der bis in die jüngsten Schichten der alttestamentlichen Ueberlieferung hinein die offensichtlich vorgegebene Zwölfzahl, aber auch die Eponymen selbst tradiert werden, machen es allein schon mehr denn unwahrscheinlich, dass es sich hier nur um eine blasse Reflexion oder Fiktion oder Theorie der späteren Zeit handeln könnte. Hält man die Systeme wohl für spätere Theorie, so taucht ja sofort die Frage auf, aus welchem Interesse eine solche Theorie entstanden sein soll.'[148] For the same reasons he rejects any suggestion to date Noth's system 'B' before 'A'.[149] For it is surely unthinkable that living and

[146] *Cf.* also the remarks of Gunneweg, *o.c.* S. 45[6] u. S. 58.

[147] Noth, *Das System*, S. 78 *seq.* and Gunneweg, *o.c.* S. 59. Here Gunneweg notes a serious inconsistency when Noth yet leaves open the possibility that some tribes really hardly existed any longer!

[148] *o.c.* S. 55; *cf.* also p. 59.

[149] Thus *e.g.* A. Menes, *Die vorexilischen Gesetze Israels*. BZAW 50, Berlin 1928, S. 1-19. And J. Hoftijzer, Enige opmerkingen rond het Israëlitische 12-stammensysteem. *NThT* XIX (1959/60) p. 241-260.

flourishing tribes like Ephraim and Manasseh should afterwards be replaced by the so much vaguer and older 'Joseph'? And must not a system only containing sons of Jacob be much more original and sound than one that also includes grandsons? That in texts with the system 'B' we often find the Levites in secondary additions is seen as a result of 'systemitis': it was not so easy to dismiss the tribe of Levi.[150] It is interesting to see how, reasoning from Levi's inclusion in system 'A', Gunneweg at last concludes that there never was a secular tribe of Levi, and yet manages to escape the dreaded alternative of a sacerdotal tribe. Through accepting the amphictyony hypothesis, Gunneweg comes to a dead end in the contrast between a sacerdotal and a secular tribe.[151] Moreover, Gunneweg several times links the Levites in particular very closely with the ancient Israelite amphictyony (e.g. in connexion with Deut. 27 and 33). The great constituent element of the amphictyony is the number twelve. The tribes themselves may be interchanged, some of them can hardly be called tribes any more, having become purely traditional entities, but the number twelve remains. The same may be said of the parallels outside Israel. From this Gunneweg draws what I regard as the only correct conclusion, that system 'A' is not concerned with twelve actual tribes, but with the twelve sons of Jacob. System 'A' is a system of *eponyms*![152] True, Gunneweg thinks it a list of members of the amphictyony, but the members are eponyms, and not tribes in actual existence at the time the list was drawn up.

Was there ever a tribe of Joseph, was Judah ever a tribe like the others?[153] 'Wie dem aber im einzelnen auch sei, man wird das System

[150] Gunneweg, o.c. S. 56. Another argument, that 'A' is found in an older literary layer, is not very convincing either. Firstly that gives us at most a *terminus a quo* in the early monarchy, and secondly it is now generally realized that precisely P gives very much old and authentic material in its lists and other documents.

[151] Gunneweg, o.c. S. 57: 'Die Problemstellung lautete bisher: gab es einen weltlichen Stamm Levi, so muss dieser untergegangen sein, denn die Leviten bilden keinen weltlichen, sondern einen – fiktiven – "Priesterstamm"; dieser konstituierte sich aus den Resten oder aus Priestern des ehemaligen weltlichen Levistammes; oder auch: diese Leviten haben mit dem untergegangen Levi nichts zu tun – so die "Untergangstheorie". Gab es niemals einen weltlichen Stamm Levi, so ist der in der alttestamentlichen Ueberlieferung so genannte "Stamm Levi" im Gegensatz zu den realen, weltlichen Stämmen *als* Stamm eine fiktive Grösse – so die "Eponymtheorie".'

[152] Gunneweg, o.c. S. 59. In my 'De richteren van Israël' (NThT XXII(1965/1966) p. 84) I already pointed out, if in a rather summary manner, this essential difference between Noth's systems 'A' and 'B'.

[153] Gunneweg, o.c. S. 60. In his 'The Settlement of the Israelites and the Origins of the Tribe of Judah', De Vaux sees the tribe of Judah originating as a result of David's kingship in Hebron! See also below, p. 112.

mit Levi als Mitgliederliste der Amphiktyonie und nicht von vornherein als Verzeichnis von zwölf Volksstämmen verstehen müssen. Die zwölf Eponymen meinen primär die Glieder dieser Amphiktyonie, und zwar als solche, in ihrer Bezogenheit auf "Israël", das sie als "Brüder" und "Söhne Israels" miteinander repräsentieren, und nicht primär "weltliche Stämme".'[154]

It follows that the Levites were also seen from the first as one of the twelve constitutive elements of 'Israel'. In this way it also becomes perfectly plain why Levi is absent in system 'B': that is a system of territorial entities, and of course Levi could not be placed in that. System 'A' still reflects the amphictyonic situation, system 'B' does not really do so any more.

Thus far the highly astute solution of Gunneweg, which indeed contains many true and very valuable remarks. Yet this solution is not acceptable. Firstly, it must be rejected on methodological grounds, because the amphictyony is taken *a priori* to be an unassailable established fact. One cannot help wondering in how far the amphictyony hypothesis can stand up, if the twelve-tribe system is after all turned into a more or less theoretical construction. Is this not circular reasoning on the part of Gunneweg himself? The second reason for rejection is, that in this argumentation also it is essential for the date of 'A to be anterior to 'B', which we cannot accept. 'B' is more easy to place in a historical context, because it contains entities of a more definite historical situation. That system 'B' reflects conditions that must have existed at the end of the time of the Judges and the beginning of the time of the Kings, seems indisputable to me. According to Gunneweg's reasoning 'A' reflects a considerably earlier situation, which we consider impossible because it is in 'A' that we find Joseph. That is why we cannot help inquiring whether it is really impossible to give 'B' an earlier date than 'A'.

That such a sequence has been suggested, we have seen above.[155] Besides the aforesaid arguments, another reason which always leads Gunneweg to reject the possibility of the system with Levi being younger, is that the later inclusion of the eponym of the Levites among the other eponyms would be a purely theoretical construction. With some justice he remarks that Hoftijzer does not give a proper answer to the question as to what the object of such a theory could have been. It is indeed true that Hoftijzer only states his observation, but his observations are

[154] Gunneweg, *o.c.* S. 61.
[155] *Cf.* above note 149. Unfortunately the many sensible remarks made by Menes were often not taken seriously because of his historical materialism. He was the first to form a correct estimate of the social implications of 'being a Levite'. Gunneweg's book constitutes a rehabilitation of Menes in more than one respect.

correct![156] If a secular tribe of Levi ever did exist, it was certainly not in a period we have any definite knowedge of; that is, it must have been long before the song of Deborah. On the other hand the traditions in which system 'A' functions often also show a clear preference for Joseph. The enumeration of tribes – as Hoftijzer still puts it, eponyms or sons of Jacob would be better – reflects a situation such as must have existed at a certain moment before the fall of the Northern Kingdom.

Well, if Levi ever existed as a secular tribe, it was certainly not at that time! If we assume that the tradition of regarding Israel as an entity consisting of twelve tribes was then already in force, it is perfectly reasonable to suppose that at some moment the need was felt to include the eponym of the Levites also. This must have been at a juncture when the Levites were looked upon as one of the constitutive elements of Israel, or when such a claim could be made a point of action.[157] We owe to Gunneweg a splendid summary of the rise of the Levites. Beginning as 'foreigners' and often despised, with a lower juridical status, they yet become more and more the particular priests of Yahweh. So they become the characteristic Israelite caste of priests, which according to the earliest texts of the O.T. had to carry on a stiff fight against the old-established sacerdotal families of the principal sanctuaries, such as the Aaronites in Bethel and the Zadokites in Jerusalem. The definitive victory of the Levites is seen in Deuteronomy. 'Hier wird am Ende aus dem Programm eine programmatische Theorie, nach welcher 'ganz Levi' ein Volksstamm von Priestern sein soll'.[158] Our investigation of Levi thus brings us to the same period we reached for Joseph: after 722, though not much later. This not only answers the question when Levi was included, in other words when system 'A' originated, but also why. System 'A' is the expression, the programme of a desire for restoration after 722, inspired

---

[156] Hoftijzer, o.c. p. 256-260.

[157] This was all the more easy, since the designation was very probably felt as a real name and not as an appellative. The inscriptions of El-Öla that are always being adduced afford no proof to the contrary nor any indication of a Levitism outside Israel, for these texts are fairly young. The unmistakably Jewish names in them point to close Jewish contacts (R. de Vaux, 'Lévites' minéens et 'Lévites' israelites. In. Festschrift Junker 'Lex tua veritas', Trier 1961, S. 265-273. A possible connexion with Lawi', of the Mari texts is not yet clear (H. B. Huffmon, Amorite Personal Names in the Mari Texts. Baltimore 1965, p. 225 seq.), especially as the etymology of this Lawi' is still much debated. However, we know now from Ugarit as well as Mesopotamia that such social groups could have eponyms just as ethnic groups could. The formation of such 'guilds' is clearly of great antiquity in the ancient Near East. These guilds were generally organized like ordinary tribes, with the same terminology. Cf. for Israel also the Kenites and the Rechabites (R. de Vaux, Les Institutions de l'Ancien Testament, I, p. 32-33. Cf. also Zobel, o.c. S. 69).

[158] Gunneweg, o.c. S. 222.

by the Deuteronomist movement. We can plainly see that the theory represents a programme, for the theory is that of a new reunited Israel. One sixth of the passages in the O.T. that mention a tribe or tribes (about 180) are in Deut. or in typically Deuteronomist formules. It is obvious from this that 'A' is younger than 'B'. Indeed, the reasoning requires that there should already be a tradition of twelve tribes, *i.e.* 'B'. The original function and *Sitz im Leben* of system 'B' will be considered more fully below.

3. Gilead or Gad

It was Noth's thesis that the place of Levi in system 'B' had been taken by Gad.[159] If we assume with Hoftijzer, however, that the changed order in Num. 26 has to do with the placing of the standards in Num. 2, then the change of place is easily explained. It was simple in this way to prevent the tribe of Judah coming under the standard of 'Reuben'. The fact that an *eastern* division of 'Judah' stands at the beginning, points very clearly in this direction.[160] If the place of Gad is explained in this very plausible manner, there is no longer the slightest necessity to postulate, because of Num. 26, an earlier form of the tribal system consisting of the six Leah tribes.[161] Now Gad is also one of the tribes lacking in the song of Deborah. The absence of Judah and Simeon is usually explained from the North-Israelite origin of the song. From system 'A', that according to Noth's dating might certainly be expected here, the tribes Joseph, Levi and Gad are lacking. Instead of Joseph we find Ephraim and Machir, a certain sign that this song is ancient. It follows from the above that the same may be said of the absence of Levi.[162] Yet if the absence of Joseph, (Manasseh) and Levi does not then constitute an insurmountable obstacle, the absence of Gad does! It is usually solved by postulating that in this song the regional name of Gilead has been used instead of the tribal name Gad. Noth himself already pointed out, though, that this is a little too simplistic.[163] There are three questions to be answered: a) what is the relation between Gilead and Gad? b) what

[159] Noth, *Das System*, S. 14. Cf. Num. 1:20-43; 2:3-31; 26:5-52.
[160] Hoftijzer, *o.c.* p. 259-260.
[161] Thus Noth, *Das System*, S. 75-78. This signifies the failure of R. Smend's attempt to ascribe the element *Jahwekrieg* to the Rachel tribes, and the *amphictyonic* element to the six Leah tribes. *Jahwekrieg und Stämmebund*. FRLANT 84. Göttingen 1963, S. 77.
[162] In view of Gen. 34, the supposed 'special character' of the Levites can hardly explain their absence. Does not Deborah sing above all of the battle of Yahweh?
[163] Noth, *Das System*, S. 36¹. According to Noth, Gilead is a purely geographical term in the O.T.

do we know historically about these two entities? And c) what does this mean for the twelve-tribe system?[164]

Ad. a. Here again we can make grateful use of the lucid expositions of Hoftijzer. He has indeed convincingly shown that the original version of Num. 32 did not yet link Reuben + Gad with Gilead. The remarks about Gilead were added afterwards. This original version probably dates from the time before 722. On the other hand Josh. 13 supposes a text of Num. 32 in which the link with Gilead is already present. In origin Gilead and Gad are therefore two different entities that existed side by side in the time of the early monarchy, 'the district of Gad and Gilead' (I Sam. 13:7). The only possible explanation of Gad's absence in Judg. 5 is, that for the author 'Gad' did then not yet belong to 'Israel', or only vaguely so![165] The principal part of the region of Gad probably lay in the southward extensions. These parts were only added to Israel under David![166] Ottosson also keeps to the principle that in the early time of the Kings and before, Gad and Gilead were different entities. In Judges 5 'Gilead' is simply used as a tribal name. With regard to I Sam. 13:7 Ottoson points out that Gad and Reuben were particularly noted as tribes that kept flocks (Num. 32), and that Reuben was practically absorbed by Gad, so that the words 'the district of Gad and Gilead' may well be intended in a wider sense to mean the plains and the highlands of Transjordan.[167] It is true that in the Deuteronomistic division of land the tribe of Gad does indeed receive a large piece of Gilead.[168] A single glance at the map included by Z. Kallai shows us that this was largely a theoretical contruction and not a condition that could have obtained during the early monarchy.[169]

[164] Besides the literature listed by Hoftijzer on p. 244[1], cf also E. Täubler, *Biblische Studien, I.* Tübingen 1958, S. 248-254. M. Noth, *Gilead und Gad. ZDPV* LXXV (1959) S. 14-73. A. H. van Zyl, *The Moabites.* Leiden 1960. K. D. Schunck, Erwägungen zur Geschichte und Bedeutung von Mahanaim. *ZDMG* CXIII (1963) S. 34-40. A. Kuschke, Historisch-topographische Beiträge zum Buche Josua. *'Gottes Wort und Gottes Land'. Hertzberg-Festschrift.* Göttingen 1965, S. 90-109. Y. Aharoni, *The Land of the Bible.* London 1966. Z. Kallai, *The Tribes of Israel.* Jerusalem 1967. M. Ottosson, *Gilead. Tradition and History.* Lund 1969.
[165] Hoftijzer, *o.c.* p. 248-254. S. Mowinckel also shares this view in his *Israels opphav og eldeste historie,* Oslo 1967, p. 136 seq. Also now S. Mittmann, *Beiträge zur Siedlungs- und Territorialgeschichte des nördlichen Ostjordanlandes.* ADPV, Wiesbaden 1970, S. 208-246.
[166] Mittmann, *o.c.* S. 240.
[167] Ottosson, *o.c.* p. 137 seq. and 199. Mittmann comes to practically the same conclusions, *o.c.* S. 239-241.
[168] Ottosson, *o.c.* p. 137.
[169] The large areas enclosed in the west, the north and the east, can hardly be

Ad b. 1) Gad. We see from I Sam. 13:7 that Gad, although a tribal name, could be used to indicate a tribal territory in Transjordan, distinct from Gilead. The same appears in II Sam. 24:5 *seq*. Num. 32:1 shows that Gad was closely associated with Jazer, a town whose location is not yet certain. According to Noth it must have been situated in the wadi Kefrēn.[170] Another reliable source is line 10 of the Mesha stone,[171] where king Mesha of Moab (c. 840) states that the Gadites lived 'of old' in the region of Ataroth.[172] Now this 'of old' must be understood in the sense of 'as far as memory reaches', *i.e.* about three generations. This brings us to the beginning of the tenth century, a date that agrees excellently with I Sam. 13.

Thirdly, there is the mention of Gad in the blessings of Moses and Jacob. We note that Deut. 33 has only praise for Gad. Obviously the tribe is here depicted in its prime. In Gen. 49, however, it is threatened by other groups, though still able to cope with them. The typification of Gad in the blessing of Moses is probably younger than that in the blessing of Jacob. According to Zobel the rise of Gad is connceted with conquests to the cost of Reuben, being the execution upon Reuben of a divine punishment. It is striking that in neither collection is Gad given a blessing in the form of the 'old tribal qualifications' (Zobel) with an animal comparison. Both Gen. 49:19 and Deut. 33:20 must be regarded as comparatively young.[173] We learn something of Gad's end from the inscription of Mesha, where line 1 tells us that Mesha himself came from Dibon. According to Num. 32:34 Dibon belonged to Gad, so the tribe suffered increasing pressure from Moab![174]

Ad b. 2) Gilead. Although clearly a geographical designation, Gilead is used in Judg. 5 as a tribal name. Gilead's central territory was the northern Belqa and the southern 'Adschlūn. Later, in the time of the Kings, the region to the north of the 'Adschlūn was also colonized (Half Manasseh). This was then also called 'Gilead'. This is the position we find back,

understood otherwise than as political claims. The meeting-point of the territories of Judah, Benjamin and Reuben at the northern point of the Dead Sea, for instance, also seems quite theoretical.

[170] Noth, *ZDPV* LXXV (1959) S. 62-70. The most recent suggestions are those of R. Rendtorff to locate Jazer at Tell 'Arème, (Zur Lage von Jaser. *ZDPV* LXXVI 1960, S. 124-135) and of M. Ottosson, who seeks the town somewhere 'on the es-Salt route' (*o.c.* p. 85).

[171] *TGI*², S. 51-52.

[172] Ataroth = Chirbet 'Aṭṭārūs, 15 kilometres north-west of Dībān. *Cf.* also Num. 32:3, 34.

[173] Zobel, *Stammesspruch und Geschichte*, S. 97-100.

[174] Noth, *ZDPV* LXXV (1959) S. 29.

int. al., in Solomon's provinces (I Kgs. 4:13 and 19). The Israelites must have inhabited ancient Gilead at a very early date.

Ad c. This means that from the Old Testament we can reconstruct not only the rise of Ephraim and Levi, but also that of Gad, if less clearly. As with Ephraim, this rise was probably largely to the cost of another Israelite tribe, of Reuben.[175] Ottosson shows that Num. 32 describes a condition when Gadite cities were situated both north and south of Reuben.[176] For the tribal systems this signifies that both systems, as they both contain Gad, must be younger than the song of Deborah. Yet if Gilead and Gad are clearly distinguished entities, and Gileadites are seen to play an important part in the early time of the Kings, then why is Gilead lacking in system 'B'? Surely 'B' is then dropping a part of 'Israel' from the system? The reason is that Gilead had always been a colonized region, and the Israelites were always aware that it was inhabited by Benjamite, Ephramite and probably also Reubenite clans. A name such as Machir ben Ammiel (II Sam. 9:4; 17:27) suggests that remnants of the ancient tribe of Machir also found a refuge here.[177] A highly important difference emerges here between the haphazard listing of tribes as in Judg. 5, and the two tribal systems 'A' and 'B': that is the increasing tendency to use genealogical concepts instead of geographical ones. The course of this development, then, was in a direction exactly contrary to that posited by Noth and Gunneweg.

4. The two twelve-tribe systems

We may summarize the results of our investigation of the two different systems as follows: 'A' is younger than 'B', indeed, 'A' presupposes 'B'. We were also able to determine that 'B' is in any case younger than the song of Deborah, for the situation it supposes can only have existed towards the end of the time of the Judges. System 'A' was interpreted as a theoretical construction with programmatic intent: the return of Joseph, Levi as equal of the other eponyms. Now, therefore, we must inquire into the meaning and function of system 'B'. Let us again begin with the questions posed by Martin Noth: does system 'B' correspond to a

[175] According to J. B. Curtis, Some suggestions concerning the history of the tribe of Reuben, *JBR* XXXIII (1965) p. 247-250, however, Reuben was absorbed into Judah.
[176] Ottosson, *o.c.* p. 80.
[177] See for the population of Gilead especially Schunck, Mahanaim, *ZDMG* CXII (1963) S. 34-40. Mittmann, *o.c.* S. 224, also stresses that Gilead was populated by immigrants.

concrete organization of twelve tribes as it must once have existed in the time of the Judges, or is it theory again?

Now as B. Stade already remarked, it is very unlikely that there were ever exactly twelve tribes at the same time. Tribes like Reuben and Simeon had almost disappeared when others such as Ephraim, for instance, were only just rising.[178] Recently R. de Vaux once more defended the old view that the tribe of Judah was fairly young and was created by David.[179] This dynamic aspect of the tribes has repeatedly come to the fore in the researches of Zobel, that we have already often referred to. It must be kept firmly in mind and strictly adhered to, in consideration also of what was said in the previous paragraph.[180] For this reason, Stade regarded the twelve-tribe system as a later fiction on the part of the priesthood. While acknowledging the fact, Noth sees the compulsive maintenance of the number twelve as a schematic device that must have had some definite concrete function. 'Schematisch und fiktif dürfen für den Historiker nicht identische Begriffe sein'.[181] We already pointed out that by admitting that the set of twelve always contained a few 'traditional entities', Noth was actually seriously undermining his comparison with the amphictyonies of classical antiquity![182]

If we consider the data, we are struck by the fact that in the time of the Judges the set of twelve nowhere appears, not even where it might reasonably be expected. It has long been known that the stories about the so-called great Judges originally had a very restricted horizon and were only afterwards extended in a pan-Israelite sense. Even in these

---

[178] Thus B. Stade already in *Geschichte des Volkes Israel I*. Berlin 1887, S. 145. Also interesting is the conclusion of K. D. Schunck, *Benjamin*, S. 75, that during the greater part of the time of the Judges this tribe hardly existed, only becoming independent again after Saul.

[179] R. de Vaux, *The Settlement of the Israelites and the Origins of the Tribe of Judah*. (= *Histoire ancienne d'Israël*, vol. I, part III, chapter 2). Even though his arguments are mostly quite old, this does not make them erroneous. I cite: 1) the later 'Judah' consisted of a conglomeration of groups, a) ancient Israelite, such as remnants of Simeon, perhaps Levite groups round Hebron, local clans around places like Tekoah and Bethlehem and possibly Ephraimite groups; b) Calebites, Jerahmeelites, Kenites; c) Canaanite elements. 2) There is no ancient boundary description of Judah, the boundaries now given are simply the southern and south-western frontiers of Canaan. On the east there are natural boundaries. The northern boundary of Judah reflects conditions under David (*cf.* Y. Aharoni, *The Land of the Bible*, p. 227-235. Z. Kallai, *The Tribes of Israel*, p. 295-303). 3) There is no tradition at all about an Entry or Conquest.

[180] Zobel, *Stammesspruch und Geschichte*, S. 127-128.

[181] Noth, *Das System*, S. 41 and 77 *seq.*

[182] See above, note 147. Also: R. Smend, *Jahwekrieg und Stämmebund*. FRLANT 84, Göttingen 1963, S. 12.

extensions there is no mention anywhere of twelve tribes; the horizon of the reviser(s) remains confined to the Central Palestinian and Galilean tribes.[183] Even Judg. 19-21, which Noth regards as a pre-eminently amphictyonic tradition,[184] is not about twelve tribes, but about a conflict between Benjamin and 'Israel'. This Israel is only described geographically as 'from Dan to Beersheba and out of Gilead also'.[185] Precisely the detail of the Levite cutting his concubine into *twelve* pieces is a fairly late addition, as was demonstrated by Schunck.[186] No more than in I Sam. 11:7, did the original text give the number of pieces. One notes the preference in both traditions for the expression $g^e\underline{b}\bar{u}l$ $yi\acute{s}r\bar{a}'\bar{e}l$!

Of quite a different kind, though again we cannot put it to immediate use, is the tradition of the twelve stones at Gilgal. One can hardly avoid accepting Noth's conclusion here, that the present text of Josh. 4 is a combination of two variants of an etiological tradition: one speaking of twelve stones *in* the Jordan, and one of the twelve stones at Gilgal.[187] The first variant clearly supposes the later Deuteronomist view of the Conquest, the etiological explanation of these twelve stones being afterwards extended also to the twelve stones at Gilgal.[188] For such an etiology to come into being, the actual presence of the twelve stones seems to me a truly necessary condition![189] The connexion with the tribes is clearly secondary. It is not really required to imagine a kind of *cromlech*. More probably the twelve stones were stelae (massebas) attendant on an altar, or perhaps they even formed an altar. One might at least conclude this from I Kgs. 18:31, where in a younger extension of the Carmel

---

[183] R. Smend, *Jahwekrieg und Stämmebund*, S. 10-19 *Cf.* also W. Richter, *Traditionsgeschichtliche Untersuchungen zum Richterbuch*. BBB 18, Bonn 1963, S. 330-333.

[184] *Das System*, S. 162-170 Exkurs IV, Literarische Analyse von Ri. 19-21.

[185] Noth's interpretation of Judg. 19-21 was already criticized before the war by O. Eissfeldt, Der geschichtliche Hintergrund der Erzählung von Gibeas Schandtat. *Festschrift G. Beer*, Stuttgart 1953, S. 19-40, esp. S. 25 *seq.* Besides Noth's analysis, see also that of A. Besters, *Het centraal Heiligdom. Historisch-literair-kritisch Onderzoek van Jud. XIX-XXI.* Leuven 1964; *cf.* by the same author *EThL* XLI (1965) p. 20-41. Further of course K. D. Schunck, *Benjamin*, S. 57-59

[188] Schunck, *Benjamin*. S. 64.

[186] Gilgal has still not been satisfactorily located! For criticism of the customary identification with Chirbet el-mefdschir, see H. J. Franken, Tell es-Sultan and Old Testament Jericho. *OTS* XIV (1965) p. 189-200.

[188] Thus Noth in *Das Buch Josua*², S. 25-27.

[189] A. R. Hulst's opinion that in the etiology of Josh. 4:4 *seq.* the number of twelve is not original, seems unacceptable to me. Der Jordan. *OTS* XIV (1965) S. 162-188. The actual presence of 12 stones/massebas seems essential to me for the etiology to originate. Schunck thinks somewhat on the same lines, *Benjamin*, S. 46[165]. The originality of the twelve stones is defended, *int. al.*, by J. A. Soggin, Kultätiologische Sagen und Katechese im Hexateuch, *VT* X (1960) S. 343. Also B. O. Long, *The Problem of Etiological Narrative in the O.T.* BZAW 108, Berlin 1968, p. 78 and 82.

tradition the restored altar on Mount Carmel is described as consisting of twelve stones 'one for each tribe of the sons of Jacob, the man named Israel by the word of the Lord'.[190] This definitely pre-Deuteronomist verse is an extension of the original version, which Steck dates in the eighth century or even later.[191] Another indication that at this time the twelve-tribe system functioned to designate the whole of Israel. Here again one may well suppose that the twelve stones first had a cultic significance, and were only afterwards associated with the twelve tribes of Israel, even though this interpretation is already a matter of course for the author of I Kgs. 18:31. Perhaps the twelve stones in the breast-plate of the high priest constitute a similar case.[192] A possible answer may be found in Exod. 24:4. Exod. 24:3-8 is an appendix to the Book of the Covenant that is definitely pre-deuteronomic and makes an impression of great antiquity. Noth even regards this pericope as an integral part of the Book of the Covenant, as its conclusion.[193] The question whether the number of massebas here was originally one or twelve was raised a very long time ago. It is indeed striking that maṣṣēḇā has the singular form, though this is not grammatically impossible. Yet one cannot help suspecting this strange singular form has come from Josh. 24:26 *seq.* The whole ritual indeed strongly recalls what we know of the ritual at Shechem. One may also wonder whether there have not been two changes in the function of these stones. At first the stones were set up to mark the sacred spot of the Covenant and the revelation.[194] An example of this is seen in Deut. 27:1-10, where indeed the number of stones is not mentioned, but may be accounted twelve on the grounds of v. 11-26, the twelve curses. The remarkable thing is that the sacred words were written on these stones.[195] In all these cases one might say that the massebas re-present what is sacred, as is *a fortiori* the case when a single stela repre-sents the deity. Now it is striking that both in Josh. 24:26 *seq.* and in Exod. 24:3 *seq.* the holy words are written in a book (or roll)[196] and the stones have changed their function to represent the participants in the

[190] Translation *NEB*. The combination tribes and Jacob is rarely found, *cf.* Isa. 49:6. The term suggests system 'A'.
[191] O. H. Steck, *Ueberlieferung und Zeitgeschichte in den Elia-Erzählungen.* WMANT 26, Neukirchen 1968, S. 17² und 134¹. *Cf.* also Noth, *Ueb. Stud.* S. 106².
[192] Exod. 28:21; 39:14.
[193] In his *Ueb. Pent.* S. 33¹¹⁵ Exod. 24:3-8 still forms a 'sekundärer Anhang', in the Exodus commentary ATD 5 S. 161 it is joined to the Book of the Covenant.
[194] *Cf.* Gen. 28:18; 31:46; 35:14.
[195] Excavations in Shechem have brought to light a number of very large massebas, upon which a fairly long text could easily be written. See G. E. Wright, *Shechem*, figs. 36-39.
[196] H. Seebass, *Mose und Aaron, Sinai und Gottesberg.* S. 115.

cult! They have become stelae of the Covenant, and in that case one is sufficient. If this supposition is correct, then the number twelve is also original in Exod. 24:4, and their interpretation as representing the tribes is secondary. A second change of function may have come about when the character of the stones as memorial stones had been forgotten and they came to be regarded as building-stones of an altar, as in I Kgs. 18:31.[197] That Exod. 24:3-8 transmits a ritual closely related to, perhaps even identical with that of Shechem may be taken as an established fact.[198] Thus we not only find ancient traditions of Shechem, but also a possible explanation how the number twelve came to be associated with the tribes.

One of the earliest passages held to demonstrate the functioning of the set of twelve, is the tradition of the meeting of Jeroboam ben Nebat with Ahijah from Shiloh, I Kgs. 11:29-39. Many recognize in Ahijah a defender of the old 'amphictyonic ideal' as Samuel had formerly been.[199] Not long ago now, Noth has argued that the pericope I Kgs. 11:29-39 does not represent an independent old prophetical tradition but comes from the Deuteronomist and is intimately related to the verses 1-13. That it has long been regarded as an independent whole is due to its rather inadequate linkage with what follows and what goes before.[200] Seebass on the other hand considers that the present pericope was formed by the fusion of two traditions of different origin, one strongly pro-Jeroboam, promising him the entire realm of Solomon, and a second only

---

[197] Though an altar of massebas certainly existed also! See K. Galling, Erwägungen zum Stelenheiligtum von Hazor. *ZDPV* LXXV (1959) S. 1-13.

[198] Of the very abundant literature on this subject I will only mention: Ed. Nielsen, *Shechem*. Copenhagen 1959, p. 351. W. Beyerlin, *Herkunft und Geschichte der ältesten Sinaitraditionen*. Tübingen 1961, S. 44-59. H. Seebass, *Mose und Aaron, Sinai und Gottesberg*. Bonn 1962, S. 114 *seq.* J. L'Hour, L'Alliance de Sichem. *RB* LXIX (1962) p. 355-361. G. Schmitt, *Der Landtag von Sichem*. Arb. z. Theol. I, 15, Stuttgart 1964, S. 71.

[199] *Cf. e.g.* J. Bright, *A History of Israel*, p. 211.

[200] Noth in *Könige*, BK XI 4, Neukirchen 1968, S. 245 *seq.*, 258 *seq.* He has therefore entirely reversed the opinion expressed in *Ueb. Stud.* S. 72 u. 79, where this pericope dealing with Ahijah is still treated as an independent prophetical tradition. That 29-39 is by the Deuteronomist, is also the conclusion of Ina Plein, Erwägungen zur Ueberlieferung von I Reg. 11:26-14:20, *ZAW* LXXVIII (1966) S. 8-24. She takes into serious account, however, that there may have been an old report, whereas Noth looks upon I Kgs. 11:29-39 as a free composition by the Deuteronomist based on data from 14:1-18, which does go back to an old prophetical tradition. An old nucleus afterwards worked up as a sermon by the Deuteronomist is also the assumption of Brongers and Debus. H. A. Brongers, *I Koningen*. Nijkerk 1967, p. 123-125. J. Debus, *Die Sünde Jerobeams*. FRLANT 93, Göttingen 1967, S. 3-5. These two, then, take Noth's former standpoint.

promising him ten tribes.[201] The second variant is then looked upon as a later correction, having regard to the actual course of events. It seems to me, then, that Ina Plein is most likely to be right in regarding the pericope as embodying an originally northern pro-Jeroboam tradition in a southern rendering, the whole remaining a composition of the Deuteronomist. She very rightly posits that the arithmetic of $10 + 1 = 12$ constitutes such a crux that it really must go back to an ancient tradition, since no text-critical solution can be provided. For surely any later reviser would have been inclined to correct the 'sum'.[202] Yet this does not remove the crux! Temerarious as it is, I would hazard adding a new solution to those already proposed.[203] I start with Noth's attempt to find a solution outside the traditional tribal schema, in the style of II Sam. 19:44 'The men of Israel answered, "We have ten times your interest in the kind and, what is more, we are senior to you;"'[204] For it is certain that ten tribes were assigned to Jeroboam. Now may we not suppose, on the basis of the tens in two ancient northern traditions, Judg. 5 and Deut. 33,[205] that besides the schema of 'twelve' there also existed a schema of 'ten' which for some time could also be used to indicate the totality of Israel?[206] There is then no point in inquiring exactly which tribes these were, for the set of ten was just as schematic and theoretical as the set of twelve. Ten tribes, or twelve tribes, meant: all the tribes, in the sense of 'the whole of Israel'. Observe that the tribe of Judah

[201] H. Seebass, Zur Königserhebung Jerobeams I. *VT* XVII (1967) S. 325-333. Also: Die Verwerfung Jerobeams I. und Salomos durch die Prophetie des Ahia von Silo. *WO* IV₂ (1968) S. 162-183.

[202] Ina Plein, Erwägungen, S. 19 und 24.

[203] The solutions usually proposed are 1) the missing tribe is Levi, left out here to simplify things, as it is clearly a matter of territory. 2) Judah is lacking, not being under discussion, and the one tribe is Benjamin which 'passed to the other side'. 3) The missing tribe is Simeon, because it no longer existed. None of these solutions is satisfactory. Ad 1) the author will certainly have been thinking here of a system in the style of 'B', which does not contain Levi. Ad 2) Surely it is highly probable that in the original tradition Jeroboam was designated as Solomon's successor, so that Judah was also assigned to him. Ad 3) this would really also apply to Reuben and probably already to Issachar too. Like Simeon, these 'tribes' only survived as genealogical concepts. *Cf.* also K. Galling, Bethel und Gilgal I. *ZDPV* LXVI (1943) S. 148-150.

[204] Translation *NEB* (there II Sam. 19:43). *G.* also Noth, *Könige*, S. 260.

[205] In Deut. 33 the headings over the individual blessings are secondary. Verse 12 is therefore anonymous. That verse 17b is a gloss we have already seen (*cf.* above p. 91) Even if one would not join Schunck in defending anew the old thesis that verse 12 is the beginning of the blessing for Joseph/Ephraim, the fact remains that originally only ten tribes were *named!* (Schunck, *Benjamin*, S. 72). Zobel, *Stammesspruch und Geschichte*, S. 34 *seq.* does assign the anonymous blessing to Benjamin.

[206] Zobel, *o.c.* S. 128 connects both songs with the cult on Mount Tabor.

is not named in Judg. 5, though it is in Deut. 33.[207] A division into north and south would be too simplistic a solution here with regard to the prophecy of Ahijah, and would moreover misconceive the nature of the *schema*.[208] The relevant arithmetic is not $10 + 1 = 12$ but $10 - 1 = 9$. Expressed in terms of the tribal schema it forms an exact parallel to the position taken in II Sam. 19:44: Israel is ten times more important than Judah.[209] In this way Ahijah's symbolic treatment of his cloak also becomes more comprehensible; it is entirely in keeping with such actions by Samuel and David.[210] That the text now speaks of twelve pieces must be set down to the Deuteronomist. With this, our question is really answered. Both the set of ten and the set of twelve were theoretical schemas meant to express the totality of Israel, the *whole* of Israel. This does not by any means signify that all the ten or twelve named were real tribes, or that there could not be other tribes than the ones named. The number is more important than what is counted.[211] The origin of the number

[207] Since the headings of the blessings are most probably secondary (see above note 205), Judah cannot be denied its place in the original list on account of the different heading. The content of the verse fits very well into the context of this collection. *Cf.* also Zobel, *Stammesspruch und Geschichte*, S. 26-30.

[208] One may not conclude from this set of ten that there must have been an amphictyony with ten members. Noth's whole analogy with the amphictyonies of classical antiquity depends upon the number twelve! R. Smend has rightly pointed this out. *Jahwehrieg und Stämmebund*, S. 12 and Gehörte Juda zum vorstaatlichen Israel? *IVth World Congress of Jewish Studies I.* Jerusalem 1967, p. 57-58. Such a ten-tribe amphictyony was assumed *int. al.* by S. Mowinckel, 'Rachelstämme' und 'Leastämme'. *Von Ugarit nach Qumran.* BZAW 77, Berlin 1961², S. 167. A. Weiser, Das Deboralied. *ZAW* LXXI (1959) S. 96 and K. D. Schunck, *Benjamin*, esp. S. 53.

[209] *Cf.* also I Sam. 11:8.

[210] I Sam. 15:27 *seq.*; I Sam. 24:5, 21.

[211] Compare for instance the set of twelve sayings appearing in Deut. 27:15 *seq.* beside the familiar forms of the decalogue. See also the articles 'ten' and 'twelve' in the encyclopaedias. This also applies to the sets of twelve transmitted to us by the O T. from Israel's surroundings: the twelve primal tribes of the Aramaeans (Gen. 22:20-24); the twelve Ishmaelite tribes (Gen. 25:13-16); the Edomite tribal eponyms deriving from the wives of Esau (Gen. 36:10-14). Then in Gen. 25:2 we have six names of Arabian tribes. Very probably six is also the basis of the Horite list in Gen. 36:20-28. (M. Noth, *Das System*, S. 44.) J. R. Bartlett (The Edomite Kinglist of Genesis XXXVI 31-39 and I Chron. 43-50. *JThSt* XVI (1965) p. 301-314) also includes Gen. 36:31-39 in this series: he considers that two originally separate lists have been joined together. Yet see also G. Fohrer, Altes Testament – 'Amphiktyonie' und 'Bund'? (*ThLZ* XCI (1966)Sp. 808³³). The custom of listing kings, peoples or tribes according to a duodenary schema is seen very plainly in the royal inscriptions of Shalmaneser III (*ANET* p. 276-282). On the prism B of Esarhaddon the sets of ten and twelve alternate (*ANET* p. 291). The function of twelve as a representative number is also demonstrated in the Old Testament when twelve men fight for each side in II Sam. 2:8-17.

twelve in this function could be surmised to lie in the ancient cults of sanctuaries such as Gilgal and Shechem, where in the course of time the twelve stones or massebas were interpreted as representing the partici-pants in the cultic ceremony. It is interesting therefore to note that Schunck remarks on the ten stelae in a Late Bronze Age sanctuary found at Hazor![212]

Are we then compelled to look upon the twelve-tribe system as a later fiction? We have seen that also Gunneweg, following Noth, very def-initely rejects the possibility of its being theoretical, arguing that no one has yet been able to show what the sense of such a theory could have been.[213] This remark is not quite justified: Gunneweg does review the opinion of S. Mowinckel, who attributed a function to the system of tribes in the ideology of the Davidic-Solomonic empire, pointing out many weak spots in Mowinckel's reasoning, but he does not deal with Hoftijzer who arrives at the same conclusion on better grounds. S. Herrmann may also be added to this row. Then it is worth while to mention the opinion of Zobel, who gives the system of tribes a function in the ideo-logical conflict after the splitting of the kingdom.[214] Helga Weippert is of the opinion that her second geographical system – called by me "B2" – was originally a ten-tribe system of Northern origin. In the early monarchic period it was extended to a twelve-tribe system by the ad-dition of the Southern tribes Judah and Simeon. These two tribes were placed before the existing system, of Northern tribes. In its present form it therefore also represents the situation of the United Monarchy.[214a] What it comes down to in both cases is, that the system of tribes was created to form an artificial framework connecting groups that formerly were politically fairly independent of each other. This view is still most clearly set forth in the deservedly classic little work by Galling, 'Die Erwählungstraditionen Israels'.[215]

If we then see the *system* of the tribes originating during the early mon-archy, it might be objected that this says nothing as to the history of the various tribes. Might their history not have been such, that the origins of Israel must be sought elsewhere? In this connexion, of

[212] Schunck, *Benjamin*, S. 53[32]. For this set of ten K. Galling, Erwägungen zum Stelenheiligtum von Hazor. *ZDPV* LXXV (1959) S. 1-13.
[213] See above, p. 104.
[214] S. Mowinckel, 'Rachelstämme' und 'Leastämme', S. 150. J. Hoftijzer, Enige opmerkingen rond het Israëlitische 12-stammen-systeem, p. 262. H. J. Zobel, *Stammesspruch und Geschichte*, S. 129. S. Herrmann, Autonome Entwicklungen in den Königreichen Israel und Juda. *SVT* XVII, Leiden 1969, S. 152.
[214a] Helga Weippert, Das geographische System der Stämme Israels. *VT* XXIII (1973) S. 87-89.
[215] K. Galling, *Die Erwählungstraditionen Israels*. Giessen 1928, S. 63-92.

course, the traditions of the desert are always brought up.[216] Now the tribes and the nature of their tie with the land and with one another will be discussed in the next chapter. The 'dogma' of sedentarization that has obtained ever since Ed. Meyer will then in particular be indicted. Here we will stress once more that the enumerations are always based on a geographical principle. First came, nearly always, Reuben and Simeon, even when these tribes had long vanished from history. Yet this need not be an indication of an earlier phase of the system; the explanation of the phenomenon is purely geographical.[217] Descriptions of regions and boundaries simply began by preference in the south-east. A similar 'compulsion' is seen in the case of the last two tribes. These are in the great majority of instances Asher and Naphtali. Sometimes Naphtali and Gad, in which case the movement is retrograde. It means no more than that these tribes were known once to have lived there. When that was, we cannot tell.

Of course we do not mean to say that the traditions concerning the Exodus, the Sinai and the Wandering in the desert are just later 'fictions'. Yet even if it is possible to find a common traditio-historical or even historical basis for the traditions of the Exodus and the Sinai,[218] it is still not possible definitely to identify a particular group as the bearer of these traditions. In view of the central place taken by these 'themes' in Yahwism, I am personally inclined to think first of all of the Levites here. With regard to the actual desert-traditions, I subscribe to the conclusions of V. Fritz.[219] They are to be explained from the geographical conditions in the northern Negev, the scene of the earliest history of the southern tribes. The theme of the whole of 'Israel' in the desert is indeed a 'literary fiction', according to Fritz.[220] These traditions do *not* contain any memories of a time before the *Landnahme*.

---

[216] See our discussion of J. Bright's *Early Israel in Recent History Writing*, in chapter I, par. 8.
[217] Thus for instance Bright, *o.c.* p. 118.
[218] Cf. for this view A. S. van der Woude, *Uittocht en Sinaï*. Groningen 1960. C. H. W. Brekelmans, Het 'historisch Credo' van Israël. *TTh* III (1963) p. 1-11. H. Schmid, *Mose*. Berlin 1968.
[219] V. Fritz, *Israel in der Wüste*. Marburg 1970, S. 97-134.
[220] Fritz, *o.c.* S. 113.

CHAPTER III

THE UNITY OF ISRAEL

1. Introduction

We have seen in the first chapter how round about the turn of the century there was a change of focus in viewing the origin and the earliest history of Israel. Instead of starting from the genealogies of Gen. 10 and 11 and explaining the development of Israel as a more or less gradual evolution, younger historians began to lay more and more stress upon the discontinuity in its historical development, and upon the religion of Israel as the principal cohesive element, even as the constituent principle *kat' exochēn*.[1] Thus between 1900 and 1930 we found many variations of the view that the subsequent people of Israel originated when various groups or tribes were united in a religious covenant. Whether this covenant is thought to have come about in Canaan or at Kades or the Sinai is a minor matter. It was a covenant with one another and with the new god. The fact that the worship of Yahweh was introduced into Israel, was not 'natural', is greatly stressed and much interest is aroused in the work and the person of Moses; we saw that some even regarded him as *founder* of the nation.[2] It is pre-eminently the period in which attention is focused upon problems of religious history and theology[3] rather than upon purely historical matters. Only with this background in mind can we understand that a work such as Noth's '*Das System der Zwölf Stämme Israels*' could become so influential and yet could meet with so little criticism.[4]

---

[1] This development is already seen very plainly in Wellhausen, *cf.* the quotation on p. 4-5.
[2] See for this ch. I par. 4 and the literature cited. Also *int. al.* K. Koch, Der Tod des Religionsstifters. *KuD* VIII (1962) S. 100-123.
[3] One need only recall the part played by the idea of Berith before the Second World War, and still played by it now in a new shape! It may suffice here to cite the critical remarks of G. Fohrer, Altes Testament – 'Amphiktyonie' – und 'Bund'? *ThLZ* XCI (1966) Sp. 801-816, 893-904.
[4] The only really contemporary critics of Noth's amphictyony hypothesis we have

Since for the historian Israel does not appear in the world as an empiric entity, as an organized people with a religion of their own, until the time of the early monarchy, the time of Saul and David, the historiography of ancient Israel offered an unsatisfactory and incomplete picture of the preceding period. On the one hand the independent existence of the various tribes in the time of the Judges was greatly stressed. Moreover it was almost generally accepted, since Ed. Meyer, that the southern tribes, i.e. principally Judah, hardly had any common history with the northern tribes in the period before David. On the other hand it was realized that the way several tribes would stand together in the time of the Judges, *e.g.* in the battles against Sisera and against the Midianites, and the fact that all tribes united against the Philistines – including those tribes who were not themselves directly threatened – and especially of course the acceptance of Saul's kingship, showed that all the same all Israelite tribes felt themselves to be linked in some manner.

An obvious explanation of this feeling was to ascribe it to 'Yahwism' or still more vaguely to a kind of consciousness of a 'common fund of thought'.[5] Noth rightly dismisses this as far too abstract for ancient Israel.[6] Yet indeed Noth also sought the unifying element in the religious sphere, so his objections were directed rather against the form than against the principle itself: 'Nur muss man sich darüber klar sein, dass religiöse Verbundenheit der Stämme noch nicht konstatiert ist, wenn man ihnen allen den abstrakten Begriff des "Jahwismus" zuschriebt. Man kann überhaupt im Blick auf den hier behandelten Fall nicht von "Religion" reden, ohne in erster Linie an ihre Äusserung im Rahmen bestimmter konkreter Formen, an einen an besondere Stätten gebundenen, geregelten Kult zu denken'.[7] In this way Noth assigns a definite form to the 'religious unity of Israel' and a concrete *Sitz im Leben* in a cult. In the same way, however, he can also fully maintain the old viewpoint of the dichotomy Israel-Judah and of the great political disintegration and independence of the various tribes in the period of the Judges. Both aspects – union in the cult and political disintegration – are apparently connected in a perfect manner by the amphictyony hypothesis. Thus

---

been able to find are E. Auerbach, *Wuste und gelobtes Land*. Band I, Berlin 1936, S. 72-73 and O. Eissfeldt, Der geschichtliche Hintergrund der Erzählung von Gibeas Schandtat (Richter 19-21). *Festschrift G. Beer*, Stuttgart 1935, S. 19-40.
[5] *Cf.* for this S. 61-64 and 109-121 of *Das System* and the examples given there. Also *e.g.* R. Kittel, *Geschichte des Volkes Israel*, Band II, S. 16.
[6] 'Freilich, hätte man die Zeitgenossen der Debora oder des Gideon gefragt, was der "Jahwismus" oder "die ideale Einheit Israel" eigentlich sei, ich fürchte, sie hätten es nicht gewusst'. *Das System*, S. 62. It is remarkable that Noth offers no arguments in support of this statement.
[7] *Das System*, S. 63.

the problem posed by Noth in part II of *'Das System'*, whether such an institution as an ancient Israelite amphictyony is really conceivable in the time of the Judges, is reversed to become the thesis that such an amphictyony should be supposed a priori! In masterly manner, Noth's amphictyony hypothesis again advances the primacy of religion in Israel's earliest history.[8]

We notice that in this argumentation Noth constructs a considerable difference between the content of the religion of the Israelites at that moment of their history, and its outward form in the cult! If the religious factor is rejected as the main principle to explain the 'unity of Israel', then the same objection applies to using 'the cult' for that purpose. This is simply advancing the unknown in explanation of the unknown. Naturally religion may be expressive of a national concept, but it does not call either the national concept or the nation itself into being. The line followed by Noth leads him to somewhat disregard the question of the relation of Yahwism to the totality of forms and traditions already present at the moment Yahwism was introduced.[9]

The considerations sketched above are those which in our time still induce many scholars to work with the amphictyony hypothesis. A clear example is afforded by W. F. Albright and his school, otherwise so greatly opposed to Noth, who freely adopt the amphictyony hypothesis.[10] More consistent in this matter is a work such as *'Das Königtum in Israel'* by J. A. Soggin. Here the author lays great emphasis on its being merely a working hypothesis. A working hypothesis which Soggin requires to solve the embarrassing problem of 'unity – diversity'.[11] A direct and well-founded continuation of the hypothesis as set up by M. Noth, in the function already given to it by Alt, is now seen again in the excellent survey by M. Weippert, *'Die Landnahme der israelitischen Stämme in der neueren wissenschaftlichen Diskussion'*. Weippert begins, however, by explicitly admitting that the amphictyony hypothesis has

[8] This primacy of religion is heard very plainly already in 1929 in the first sentences of Alt's famous study Der Gott der Väter: 'Die Entstehung des Volkes Israel beruht historisch auf dem Zusammenschluss seiner Stämme in der Verehrung des Gottes Jahwe. Mögen die Stämme oder wenigstens einzelne Gruppen von ihnen sich auch schon früher als Verwandte betrachtet haben, so ist doch offenbar erst durch diese Einigung das alle umfassende Gemeinbewusstsein in ihnen erweckt worden, das ihrer Geschichte als Volk die unentbehrliche seelische Grundlage gab.' *KS* I, München 1953, S. 1.

[9] See for this the discussion between Caspari and Weber in the beginning of the twenties. *Cf.* Ch. I, p. 24-27.

[10] This inconsistency on the part of Albright, Bright, Wright a.o. was already pointed out in Ch. I, par. 8.

[11] BZAW 104, Berlin 1967, espec. S. 9-14.

run wild. Following Noth, he bases it mainly upon literary arguments: reference to a twelve-tribe system. He acknowledges that much modern criticism is justified – int.al. that of R. Smend – but he does not think the hypothesis is essentially affected by it.[12]

For Götz Schmitt too the necessity to explain the unity of Israel before the monarchy forms the main argument to adhere to the amphictyony hypothesis. Significant is however, that Schmitt feels himself compelled to *defend* this hypothesis![13]

We have also seen in chapter I that the way one reconstructs Israel's earliest social, economic and political organization is of fundamental importance for the picture that is drawn of Israel's earliest history. For years, there has existed a more or less unspoken common opinion regarding this social and economic organization, and in this matter Noth merely reflects the view of the great majority of Old Testament and Oriental scholars. Since we regard these presuppositions as *fundamental*, the greater part of this chapter will be devoted to a critical inquiry after the earliest known social, economic and political structures and forms of organization of Israel. This will show that the reasons usually assigned for denying the earliest Israelites a national identity of their own are far from compelling. There are no convincing arguments against the unity of the Israelites having of old been primarily *ethnic*. The strongest argument in favour remains the fact that the Israelites themselves have always felt it to be so! Since the amphictyony hypothesis is intimately connected with the problems of the Conquest, being needed to explain how formerly alien groups became a unity in Palestine, we must also examine a second equally fundamental presupposition: *viz.* that the Israelites are not autochthonous in Palestine. This is again closely linked with the view taken of Israel's earliest social structure. The conclusion will be that Israel may well owe its ethnic and national identity to living in Palestine, but that this came about several centuries earlier than Noth imagined!

According to the opinion of Noth and many others, then, in the period between the Conquest and the Monarchy the people of Israel consisted of twelve tribes, in principle independent and having equal rights, who were united in a sacred covenant. What bound them together was the common cult of a common, central sanctuary and the ensuing obligations. For the rest, the tribes went very much their own way. The first question

---

[12] FRLANT 92, Göttingen 1967, S. 46-49, espec. S. 46[2]. After 1970, however, Weippert does not consider the term "amphictyony" any longer adequate (sachgemäss). *Biblica* LII (1971) S. 425[2]. See also *infra*, chapter IV, paragraph 1.
[13] Götz Schmitt, *Du sollst keinen Frieden schliessen mit den Bewohnern des Landes*. BWANT 91, Stuttgart 1971, S. 84[5].

that now seems necessary, and which curiously enough has only very rarely been put, is this: what are we to understand by the concept 'an Israelite tribe'? We shall find this question extremely difficult, while no really satisfactory answer can be found. Its discussion will occupy the greater part of this chapter. Only then does the question arise whether we have any indications that these tribes functioned as politically independent units in the period of the Judges, and whether they had the necessary political organization to do so.

2. The problem of the original social and economic structure

All reconstructions that have been made of the earliest social and economic structure of the Israelites – 'earliest' meaning the time before the entry into Canaan – were and are dependent upon the opinion held as to the problem of the 'original' social and economic structure of the Semites in general. This problem is again intimately connected with that of the 'Ur-Semiten' and their 'original milieu'. Obviously these opinions again depend upon all kinds of presuppositions and/or antiquated standpoints in the field of cultural and social anthropology.[14] To keep the present study within bounds, we shall merely summarize the most important results of research in this field since the Second World War, in so far as they apply here.

I. The idea that an agrarian, sedentary way of life was always or usually preceded by a non-sedentary herding phase has been generally abandoned. The sequence[15] is now held to have been that food-gathering came before food-producing, the earliest phase being that of non-sedentary hunters and food-gatherers. From collecting wild grain,[16] agriculture developed. In the Middle East agriculture developed two forms, one

---

[14] A very clear and topical summary of these problems is to be found in J. Henninger, *Über Lebensraum und Lebensformen der Frühsemiten*. Arbeitsgemeinschaft für Forschung des Landes Nordrhein-Westfalen, Heft 151, Köln/Opladen 1968.
[15] First of all for this: C. Daryll Forde, *Habitat, Economy and Society. A Geographical Introduction to Ethnology*. London/New York 1934[1], 1961[13], esp. p. 460-72. Also H. von Wissmann, Ursprungsherde und Ausbreitungswege von Pflanzen- und Tierzucht und ihre Abhängigkeit von der Klimageschichte. *Erdkunde* XI (1957) S. 81-94 u. 175-193. E. A. Hoebel, *Anthropology: The Study of Man*, 1972[4] esp. p. 195-223. Modern views are tersely summed up, with an extensive bibliography in: R. Herzog, *Sesshaftwerden von Nomaden*. Forschungsbericht des Landes Nordrhein-Westfalen, Nr. 1238, Köln/Opladen 1963, esp. S. 23-29. Also in B. G. Trigger, *Beyond History: The Methods of Prehistory*. New York/Chicago 1968.
[16] Such gathering of wild grain can yield considerable quantities, as demonstrated in: W. van Zeist, *Oecologische aspecten van de neolithische revolutie*. Groningen 1969.

dependent on rain, the other located in oases. There are indications that the former is older than the latter, although the former will have been longer able to maintain the character of a gathering economy.[17] In the Middle East, this primitive agriculture was very soon accompanied by the keeping and breeding of sheep, goats and donkeys.[18] From the beginning of neolithic times, the keeping of these animals was an important element of economy. In addition, cattle and swine were kept, though the indications for these animals do not go quite so far back. The existence of neolithic tribes of nomad herdsmen, on the contrary, has never yet been demonstrated.[19]

II. For the Semites, these general data may be specified as follows: at our first sight of the Semites, their chief means of subsistence are agriculture and flock-keeping. There are increasingly strong indications that this was also their way of life at the time that, probably from the north-west, they began to spread over the Middle East.[20] The view so often heard, and continually repeated *e.g.* by R. de Vaux, that we first meet with the Semites as flock-herding nomads in the Syro-Arabian desert, must be dismissed as no longer tenable!

III. Generally in ethnology, as well as in the special case of the Semites, keeping large flocks and herding cattle[21] is to be regarded as a later

[17] For this, first of all Von Wissmann, Ursprungsherde, and Bauer, Nomade und Stadt im islamischen Orient. In: *Die Welt des Islam und die Gegenwart*, Hrgb. v. R. Paret, Stuttgart 1961, S. 22-63. Also: A. J. Jawad, *The Advent of the Era of Townships in Northern Mesopotamia*. Leiden 1965. R. McAdams, *The Evolution of Urban Society*. London 1966. Agriculture itself was not the decisive impetus towards urbanization! It was still unknown in earliest Jericho. Interesting finds were made in the pre-neolithic village Tell Mureybit in Syria. The inhabitants gathered grain at a very considerable distance from their dwelling-place. *Cf.* Van Zeist, *o.c.* p. 11 and M. N. van Loon, The Oriental Institute Excavations at Mureybit, Syria. Preliminary Report on the 1965 Campaign. *JNES* XXVII (1968), p. 265-82.

[18] Discounting the dog, the first 'livestock' to be kept were animals formerly hunted: gazelles and antelopes. In the Levant these were replaced by the goat, in Mesopotamia by the sheep. The earliest indications of the keeping of goats and/or sheep are little later than the first signs of agriculture. See for this particularly Von Wissmann, *Ursprungsherde*. Also F. Hančar, Zur Frage der Herdentier-Erstdomestikation. *Saeculum* X (1959) S. 21-27 and B. Brentjes, *Die Haustierwerdung im Orient*. Wittenberg 1965, esp. S. 22-31. *Cf.* also the literature specified in note 15.

[19] Honesty compels one to admit that the reverse also holds true!

[20] For this especially Henninger, *Über Lebensraum und Lebensformen der Frühsemiten*. *Cf.* also J. Aro, Gemeinsemitische Ackerbauterminologie. *ZDMG* CXIII (1963) S. 471-80.

[21] There is some indication that the keeping of cattle originally had a religious

development and specialization stemming from agriculture, concomitant with taking into use tracts of ground which were formerly of hardly any economic value.[22] 'Historically, pastoral nomadism is best described as a specialized offshoot of agriculture that developed along the dry margins of rainfall cultivation'.[23]

IV. The emergence of mounted nomads, according to modern definitions the mark of true nomad herding societies,[24] is a comparatively recent development dating from the transitional period between the Bronze Age and the Iron Age (in the Middle East). Their appearance in Central Asia also dates from the 14th and 13th centuries B.C.E.[25]

V. The typical camel nomadism of the present-day Beduin is fairly recent. It did not arise until the first centuries of our era. The connection was not with the domestication of the camel in general,[26] but with the development of a saddle fastened upon the hump of the dromedary, and not in front of, behind or beside it. Only when this saddle – the šadād saddle – came into use did the camel or dromedary become altogether the riding mount of the desert and an equivalent to the horse. It was a decisive step towards the Beduin way of life when this saddle was developed. Dostal demonstrated that under the influence of the Parthian horsemen this manner of riding spread from the Syrian desert – Palmyra probably being the epicentre – towards the south, where the extreme

rather than an economic function. Cattle, and the bull in particular, play a great part in a complex of concepts and rites concerning fertility of an otherwise typically agrarian nature.

[22] For this especially the books of Daryll Forde and Herzog named in note 15.
[23] Johnson, *The Nature of Nomadism*, p. 2.
[24] The term nomads derives from νομάς/νομαζειν = roaming about for pasture.
[25] Besides the literature specified in note 15: E. D. Philips, New Light on the Ancient History of the Euroasian Steppe. *AJA* LXI (1957) p. 269-80. R. Ghirshman, Invasions des nomades sur le Plateau Iranien aux premiers siècles du Ier millénaire avant J.-C. In: *Dark Ages and Nomads c. 1000 B.C.* Ned. Hist.-Arch. Instituut, Istanbul 1964, p. 3-8. And: K. Jettmar, Die Entstehung der Reiternomaden. *Saeculum* XVII (1966) S. 1-11. According to Phillips the Scythians were the first mounted nomads who threatened the Near East! E. D. Phillips, The Scythian domination in Western Asia: its record in history, scripture and archaeology. *World Archaeology* IV (1972) p. 129-138.
[26] There is still no certainty as to the date of this domestication. More and more authors incline to the idea that camel and dromedary were imported from Iran already domesticated. *Cf.* the review of the most recent literature in J. Henninger, *Lebensraum und Lebensformen*, S. 15-23. The point at issue, however, is not *when* the animal came into use, but *what* it was used for! The dromedary seems to have been known as a beast of burden from very early times.

126

southeast and southwest have not even yet been reached.[27] The other important step which enabled the Beduin to develop their mode of existence was the construction of the famous 'black tent'. This is first depicted and mentioned in the first century of our era. It is notable that all those tribes of the South-Arabian hinterland where the šadād saddle is not yet in use, do not have tents either.[28]

VI. It is indisputable that *all* tribes in the Arab world now known as semi-nomads, were once entirely nomadic. Therefore it is quite inadmissible to use their way of life as a prototype of that of the primal Semites or the patriarchs.[29] Under heading II above, and repeatedly in our first chapter, we have observed that to do so is a general custom. The concept of transhumance or *'Weidewechsel'* belongs to a sedentary context and should be clearly distinguished from the phenomenon of nomadism![30]

VII. Those social functions – especially in Israel – which until recently were held to be typical of nomadic life, are not so at all! The most characteristic example is that of the 'patriarchal extended family', the *bēt 'āḇ*,

---

[27] We owe this new insight mainly to the lengthy researches of Caskel and Dostal. Important publications are: W. Caskel, Zur Beduinisierung Arabiens. *ZDMG* CIII (1953) S. 28*-38*. W. Dostal, The Evolution of Bedouin Life. *L'Antica Società Beduina*; racc. da F. Gabrieli. Studi Semitici 2, Roma 1959, p. 11-34. Also particularly this author's: *Die Beduinen in Südarabien. Eine ethnologische Studie zur Entwicklung der Kamelhirtenkultur in Arabien.* Wiener Beiträge zur Kulturgeschichte und Linguistik, Bd XVI, Wien 1967. *Cf.* also the publications of Henninger and Herzog already referred to. Also in: *L'Antica Società Beduina*: Maria Höfner, Die Beduinen in den vorislamischen Inschriften; and J. Henninger, La société bédouine ancienne; resp. pp. 53-68 and 69-94. Fr. Altheim-Ruth Stiehl, Beduinisierung. In: *Antike und Universalgeschichte.* Festschrift H. E. Stier, Münster 1972, S. 294-301.

[28] W. Dostal, *Die Beduinen in Südarabien,* see previous note.

[29] Very important for the semi-nomads is still the study of T. Ashkenazi, *Tribus semi-nomades de la Palestine du Nord.* Paris 1938. Ashkenazi plainly shows that these semi-nomads were formerly real nomads (*cf.* p. 3-47, 162-5). For the conclusion see again Henninger, *Lebensformen und Lebensraum.* Thus also already M. Frhr. von Oppenheim, *Die Beduinen* Bd. I, S. 22-23. For this reason a warning must be given to use the Shammar as an example of a semi-nomadic tribe, as often done. The Shammar do indeed have sections which are semi nomads now or which have even completely settled down. But we know that this is a development of the last hundred years! For the Shammar: L. Stein, *Die Schammar-Gerba.* Berlin 1967. See further on those so-called semi-nomads: H. Klengel, *Zwischen Zelt und Palast.* Leipzig 1972.

[30] 'The literature indicates that a village of permanent buildings occupied by all or part of the population all of the year, rather than a mobile tentcamp, forms the nucleus of a transhumant society.' Johnson, *o.c.* p. 18. See further *infra,* paragraph 6.

as it is indeed found in Israel. This *bēt'āb* with its typical authoritarian structure has no equivalent among the Beduin.[31] Since this is an important point, we will treat it a little more fully. The mobility of the Beduin prevents the group living in one tent from becoming larger than some five persons.[32] It is true that such a tent-group or family rarely lives alone, but forms a communal living and working group with other tents. Usually such a communal group consists of closely related families. Its size depends upon various factors. The true camel nomads, who need a fairly large herd of camels to live on, often live several hundred together, sometimes even more than a thousand persons. Among flock-keeping nomads the groups are far smaller. Since the number in one tent is not enough to form a sufficient economic basis in the desert, while it is the normal procedure for a married son to set up his tent beside his father's (though this is certainly not a binding rule), the 'camping unit' forms the primary Beduin organization. Especially with smaller groups there will be consanguinity in such a unit, but it is not essential.[33] Many factors determine who is finally included in the camping unit, economical and political, but also psychological factors. A man who cannot get on with his brothers joins a different unit. This is possible because of a second essential difference with the sedentary 'extended family': the ownership of the herds is not strictly collective. While the *'camping unit'* or *'tribal section'* as rule has a brand of its own and the animals are cared for collectively, it is still fairly simple for any man to demand his personal share and go and join another group. Obviously matters are very different in the case of landed property.

The distinctive mark of the 'extended family', however, is not that a fairly large number of relations live together, nor that the principal means of production may be collectively owned, but the authority of the father. Yet since the young Arab can at any moment pack up his tent

[31] We owe this insight especially to the pioneering work of J. Henninger, *Die Familie bei den heutigen Beduinen Arabiens und seiner Randgebiete*. IAE XLII, Leiden 1943, esp. S. 121-3, 129. Then by the same author, *Über Lebensraum und Lebensformen der Frühsemiten*, S. 34-38. The patriarchy of the Beduin has been very greatly stressed in the discussion with those who supposed that the ancient Arabs had a matriarchy. The fact alone that the discussion regarding an ancient Arab matriarchy was carried on for more than half a century, shows that matters are less eloquently 'patriarchal' than is often suggested to us! *Cf.* for the Israelitish *bēt'āb* par. 3.

[32] Johnson, *o.c.* p. 162 and Henninger, *Die Familie* S. 122, make the basic assumption that each tent will have a mean content of five souls. Modern administrations assume the same number. Oppenheim (*Die Beduinen*, I, S. 12-13) hesitatingly goes up to seven.

[33] Louise E. Sweet, Camel Pastoralism in North Arabia and the Minimal Camping Unit. In: *Man, Culture and Animals*, p. 146-147.

and depart with his own animals,[34] such authority does not stretch very far here. Robertson Smith already remarked in general terms: 'There is no part of the world where parental authority is weaker than in the desert.'[35] Henninger also points out that just because parental authority is so weak, the clans became so important.[36] The latter phenomenon, I imagine, should rather be ascribed to the economic reason indicated by Louise Sweet.

In the *tribal section* or clan as *camping unit*, the tents of the members of a family usually stand together, and such a group of tents is called *'ahl*. It is obvious, however, that such an *'ahl* is not equivalent to the *bēt 'āb*! There is one factor, though, which has a strong cohesive effect within such an *'ahl*, and that is the institution of the *bint al 'amm* marriages. Yet there is nothing corresponding to this institution in the *bēt 'āb*! Moreover, the right of primogeniture – often a clear indication of a strictly patriarchal structure – is not strongly developed in any Semitic culture. It has, indeed, more force among sedentary peoples than with the Beduin, where it is practically lacking.[37] That the organization in clans is in itself no indication of a sedentary or non-sedentary, an agrarian or non-agrarian way of life, will be shown by examples from South Arabia.[38]

Another point we may touch upon here, since the same line of reasoning is followed, is religion. Religion also has often been considered to afford evidence that all the Semites originally had a nomadic way of life, while conversely various phenomena in the different religions have constantly been explained as rudiments of an originally nomadic existence. Particularly with regard to Yahwism this has always been done on a large scale, as was clearly seen in chapter I. In this matter, however, we cannot yet make such positive statements as we can regarding social structure. Thus it is impossible to say, on the basis of our knowledge of the god El,

[34] 'When a man has acquired camels, a tent, and a wife, he is not obliged to remain with his father's or brother's or uncle's cluster ... but may independently move with others. A poor man who has no camels seeks a wealthier man and works for him as a herdsman. Each year he receives an animal or two as part of his compensation, and he expects, after seven or eight years of good fortune, to be independent.' Louise Sweet, o.c. p. 145.
[35] W. Robertson Smith, *Kinship and Marriage in Early Arabia*, London 1907², p.68.
[36] *Die Familie*, S. 130.
[37] J. Henninger, Zum Erstgeborenenrecht bei den Semiten. *Festschrift für W. Caskel*, hrgb. v. E. Gräf, Leiden 1968, S. 162-83.
[38] It is typical, however, of cultures with a unilateral system of descent. Cf. note 66 and M. Fortes, The Structure of Unilineal Descent Groups, *The American Anthropologist* LV (1953) p. 17-41. Fr. Altheim and Ruth Stiehl also argue with the example of South-Arabia: Beduinisierung, in: *Antike und Universalgeschichte* (Festschrift für H. E. Stier), Münster 1972, S. 294-301.

whether his background was originally an agrarian or a pastoral god. The most we can say is that El was worshipped in the whole Semitic region.[39] It may be stated, though, that 'traces of a non-agrarian way of life' were formerly assumed far too easily and far too much *a priori*.[40] Even the earliest data we have regarding Semitic religions clearly display agrarian traits. Beside El, the grain-god Dagān appears to be one of the very oldest Semitic deities.[41] In the mythologies, evaluation of the desert is extremely negative. Desert and land of the dead are often direct synonyms.[42] The old Semitic custom of referring to the gods in terms of kinship such as *'āḇ, 'āḥ, 'amm, dōd etc.* need not perforce indicate a non-agrarian way of life, as is clear from the above. On balance, our knowledge of the Semitic religions still has too many lacunae to allow of positive statements. It must be concluded that it is certainly not permissible either to make pronouncements regarding certain phenomena in the verious religions, declaring them to be rudiments from a different way of life!

VIII. The ethnographical and historical presuppositions noted above, are closely associated with the idea that a tribal form of organization is a more or less necessary preliminary stage of the formation of a state. This way of reasoning is also often reversed, a tribal phase being postulated as having preceded the formation of some particular state. As was done at the symposium *Dalla Tribù Allo Stato* in Rome, 1961.

This idea that the tribe functioned as a state *in statu nascendi* was long regarded as so self-evident, that it has only quite recently been realized such is by no means the case.[43] It is now seen more and more clearly that

[39] See again the summary in Henninger, *Über Lebensraum und Lebensformen der Frühsemiten*, S. 38-44.
[40] *Cf.* for this C. Widengren's fully documented criticism of the view of S. Moscati (as chiefly given in his contribution La questione delle antiche divinità semitiche to the collection *L'antiche divinità semitiche*, ed. S. Moscati, Roma 1958) in *JSS* V (1960) pp. 397-410. The views of Moscati largely parallel those of De Vaux; both regard the Semites as primarily flock-keeping nomads.
[41] *Cf.* the remarks of W. von Soden in Henninger, *Über Lebensraum und Lebensformen der Frühsemiten*, S. 52-55.
[42] A. Haldar, *The Notion of the Desert in Sumero-Accadian and West-Semitic Religion.* Uppsala Universitets Årsskrift 1950:3. Haldar's detailed criticism of Nyström's *Beduienentum und Jahwismus* (Lund 1946) has unfortunately been little regarded. I do hope that Haldar's arguments in esp. the chapters III-V of his *Who were the Amorites?* (Leiden 1971), will receive better attention!
[43] Academia Nazionale dei Lincei, Anno CCCIX-1962: 54. See especially the contribution by S. Moscati, Dalla tribù allo stato nel vicino oriente antico, p. 55-65. Further G. E. Mendenhall, Tribe and State in the Ancient World: the Nature of the Biblical Community. *The Tenth Generation.* Baltimore 1973, p. 174-197.

a) far from being a first step towards the formation of a state, the tribe constitutes a considerable obstacle on the way, and b) that in a tribal society the real political power does not rest with the tribes. A few short remarks upon this point are in order. With regard to a) it may be pointed out that of those peoples originally organized in tribes, only those proceeded to form real states, who had succeeded in breaking up their tribal organization. Since the concept of tribe is not primarily a political, but in the first place a juridical (see ad IX) and secondly an economic and social concept, and since these are structures which usually prove exceptionally tough, we see in practice that a tribal ordering, once established, is incredibly difficult to break down. As it has been trenchantly put: "tribalism is an evolutionary cul-de-sac".[44] We hardly ever see tribes at the origin of states, but persons or 'gangs' and leagues, *i.e.* groups formed for a particular political purpose, regardless of tribalism. In Israel, such figures as Jephthah and David are striking examples.

With regard to b), it must be realized that within unilateral kinship systems – and these are altogether dominant in the Semitic world – each tribe is composed of several distinct unilateral groups. These fractions are inclined to compete with each other, if they are not already organized in a vertical order, and as a result classes originate. In the first case actual political power will after some time pass from one clan to another, in the second case it is structurally linked to a particular clan. Even if power is supposed to be exercised for the whole tribe, yet in both cases it actually resides in a single clan.[45] The clans are the true bearers of political power.[46]

It is worth remarking in this connexion that the formation of tribes is by no means always an 'automatic' development, but that it is often imposed from without. Also, it was often the result of a common reaction against a common enemy. Thus the colonial powers brought many tribes into being, and firmly embedded any existing tribalism in the colonial policy of divide and rule. In the Arab world many tribes similarly owe their origin to the fact that for instance a rebellious ambitious *šēḫ*

---

[44] M. H. Fried, On the concepts of 'tribe' and 'tribal society' *Essays on the problem of tribe*, AES, Seattle/London 1968, p. 17. The problem as a whole is treated in the essay from the same collection: II. S. Lewis, Typology and progress in political evolution, p.101-10.

[45] An attempt to lessen the mutual competition of the clans is undoubtedly part of the motive prompting the frequent and very striking phenomenon of the exogenous *šēḫ* families among present-day Beduin. On this matter see E. Bräunlich, Beiträge zur Gesellschaftsordnung der arabischen Beduinenstämme. *Islamica* VI (1934) S. 68-111 und 182-229.

[46] M. Fortes, The Structure of Unilineal Descent Groups. *The American Anthropologist* LV (1953) p. 17-41, esp. p. 28.

promised a higher tax yield, or that it was considered (by representatives of the Caliphs, the Sultans or the Queen of England) that some tribe was too large and should be split up.[47] Researchers such as Caskel, Bräunlich and Dostal have paid much attention to the role played by such politico-historical factors in the foundation of tribes. Caskel and Dostal also point out the part played by the Parthians and the Romans in the origin of Beduin tribes in the Syro-Arabian desert.[48]

IX. Extensive genealogies and complicated genealogical systems are typical of societies with a unilateral and/or unilineal kinship system. A unilineal clan may be characterized in two ways: as a 'corporate group' and by means of the concept 'continuity'.[49] From a juridical point of view, a unilineal kinship group counts as a single person at law. To out-siders, all members of such a group are, juridically speaking, identical. The members share in all rights and duties of the group. This is the found-ation of the vendetta and the *ius talionis*. The concept of continuity represents the fact that the group retains its identity regardless of the continual replacement of individuals through death and birth. This living continuity is expressed by the genealogies. We have already seen that genealogical systems orientate as it were a unilateral group with respect to other groups. Fortes stresses that this system is seen to func-tion particularly when the corporate group as such holds the ownership of the principal means of production! This may be land, or a large com-mon herd, but also a monopoly of certain technical crafts that are in-herited in a particular clan (*e.g.* in the case of smiths);[50] it may also be the holding of particular posts or offices which is hereditary in a clan. The condition is always the presence of some permanent and collective property, of whatever kind it may be. The ancient Israelite expressed

[47] Examples in M. H. Fried, *o.c.* and in Em. Marx, *Bedouin of the Negev*. Manchester 1967.
[48] For the studies of Caskel and Dostal, see note 27. A survey of the question in R. Herzog, *o.c.* S. 16-19.
[49] For the following see M. Fortes, *o.c.*
[50] We already pointed out in ch. II that also in Israel the old tribal terminology and social class structure still survives in certain craft-guilds, see above, ch. II note 157. A very plain example of the phenomenon that the principal means of production was the property of the whole corporative group, is seen in the following rule of the codex Hammurapi: 'If a member of the artisan class took a son as a foster child and has taught him his handicraft, he may never be reclaimed. If he has not taught him his handicraft, that foster child may return to his father's house.' Laws 188 and 189. *ANET*[2] p. 174-5. Quoted in D. B. Weisberg, *Guild Structure and Political Allegiance in Early Achaemenid Mesopotamia*. YNER I, New Haven/London 1967, p. 77.

132

this notion in the concept *naḥ^alā*, which in Israel was intimately connected with the ownership of land.

X. The historical value of the genealogies is slight. Formerly, deeply impressed by the long genealogies that even little boys could recite by rote, scholars greatly overestimated their historical value. In cases where such genealogies could be checked, *e.g.* among the Beduin of Cyrenaica, they proved to have little historical significance, and moreover to be constructed according to set rules.[51] The same applies to the famous genealogies of the Pacific, which are often cited in this connexion.[52] This historical unreliability is now generally accepted, on the understanding that they are not primarily destined to function in the historical sphere. Their function is first of all juridical: genealogies establish the rights of the individual in the common property. They also assign the individual his place in the totality of the people. *Mutatis mutandis* this also applies to the rights of the clan in the larger totality of the tribe or people. This is a natural consequence of point IX.

3. Family, Clan, Tribe

It is a widespread misunderstanding that Josh. 7:16-19 provides a realistic and reliable picture of the social organization of the ancient Israelites: tribe – clan – family. Innumerable examples in the Old Testament show us that the 'descent' of men names the father and grandfather, while the family or clan may be added, but is frequently omitted.[53] Outside the priestly tradition, mention of the tribe a man belongs to is extremely rare, and when it occurs nearly always serves to indicate his geographical place of origin. Here in Josh. 7 and even more plainly in I Sam. 10:17-21, mention of the tribe in a genealogical sense serves to maintain the fiction – probably attributable in both cases to Dtr – that all the twelve tribes are present.[54] Checking through the tribes in the

---

[51] M. Fortes, *o.c.* p. 27.

[52] From archaeological data it is now possible to reconstruct the history of the archipelago in outline. In doing so, it became more and more evident that the genealogies were historically impossible. *Cf.* B. G. Trigger, *Beyond History*, p. 10-11.

[53] The word 'tribe' is used to translate both *šēbeṭ* and *maṭṭē*. From now on the Hebrew *mišpāḥā* is rendered as 'clan'. See also note 65.

[54] The tradition of Achan was adapted by Dtr to fit into this context. Originally it no doubt circulated independently. Reminiscent of that is probably the use of the term *mišpāḥā* in verse 2, the choice of the term *šēbeṭ* being due to Dtr, at any rate in verse 1. *Cf.* also Noth, *Ueberl. Gesch. Stud.* S. 58, and *Das Buch Josua*, S. 43-47. For I Sam. 10:17-21 (27a) *cf. Ueberl. Gesch. Stud.* S. 54-55. The term *ule'alfēkęm* was apparently necessary to make it clear that the word *šēbeṭ* is used

Concordance, one is struck by the fact that – again apart from the typical priestly tradition and the tribal systems – they are used almost exclusively in a geographical sense.[55] There is an essential difference between the tribe, functioning primarily as a geographical unit, the territory of a particular group of people connected by political and historical factors, and the clan as the largest social unit. At the same time, we find again and again that in certain cases the frontiers may overlap, so that the two concepts may coalesce.

To elucidate this matter, it is desirable to discuss the three concepts 'family', 'clan' and 'tribe' somewhat more thoroughly here. It will perhaps be possible to shed a little light upon the problem of the social and political organization of the Israelites in early times.[56] The smallest social unit in ancient Israel was the *bēt 'āḇ*.[57] This concept comprises more than a family of three generations. The best rendering of the Hebrew expression 'father's house' is: 'extended family', consisting of grandparents, parents, children,[58] with the horizontal addition of various,

in the genealogical sense. It has been well said that 'it is difficult to discover in the sources which give us the most historically reliable accounts of Israelite culture any defined pattern by which several "households" make a "family" and several "families" a "tribe", and it appears probable that such a pattern, at least in its fully developed form, is an artificial creation which hardly reflected the actual facts.' J. R. Porter, *The Extended Family in the Old Testament*, p. 7. After completing this chapter, I found a number of the views expressed in it already advanced in H. Schaeffer, *Hebrew Tribal Economy and the Jubilee, as illustrated in Semitic and Indo-European Village Communities*. Leipzig 1922.

[55] In these cases the tribal name is often defined with *gᵉḇūl* or *'ereṣ*, sometimes in combination with the prepositions *'al* or *min*. See also *infra* p. 145.

[56] More general literature apart from the articles in the lexicons: Johs. Pedersen, *Israel, Its Life and Culture*. London/Copenhagen 1926, I p. 29-96. D. Jacobson, *The Social Background of the OT*. Cincinnati 1942. J. Henninger, *Die Familie bei den heutigen Beduinen Arabiens und seiner Randgebiete. Ein Beitrag zur Frage der ursprünglichen Familienform der Semiten*. IAE XLII, Leiden 1943. C. Umhau Wolf, Terminology of Israel's tribal Organization. *JBL* LXV (1946) p. 45-50. T. Ashkenazi, La tribu arabe: ses éléments. *Anthropos* XLI-XLIV (1946-1949) p. 657-67. L. Köhler, *Der Hebräische Mensch*. Tübingen 1953. W. Dostal, Die Ṣulubba und ihre Bedeutung für die Kulturgeschichte Arabiens. *AVK* XI (1956) S. 15-42. R. de Vaux, *Les Institutions de l'Ancien Testament*, vol. I, Chap. I. J. H. Chamberlayne, Kinship Relationships among the early Hebrews. *Numen* X (1963) p. 153-67. F. J. Andersen, Israelite Kinship Terminology and Social Structure. *The Bible Translator* X (1969) p. 29-39.

[57] Besides the literature cited in the previous note, attention must be drawn here to two special studies on the *bēt 'āḇ*: K. Elliger, Das Gesetz Leviticus 18. *ZAW* LXVII (1955) S. 1-25 and J. R. Porter, *The Extended Family in the Old Testament* London 1967 (quoted in note 54).

[58] According to Elliger, *Leviticus*. HAT I 4 S. 239, the *bēt 'āḇ* normally even consisted of four generations.

mostly unmarried, uncles, aunts and cousins. This 'extended family' was kept together by the principle of actual consanguinity. At the same time, the limits of the extended family were determined by the fact that it naturally also formed a unit of production and habitation. Even in the case of the smallest unit the social, economic and geographical aspects cannot be separated, although the idea of real consanguinity dominates all. In olden times, when this extended family still functioned completely, its principle was exogamy. Since this has often been contested, most recently by Porter, it is necessary to present the arguments for this more fully. In the first place it must be pointed out that living together was as important for the *bēt 'āḇ* as blood-relationship. Thus also slaves and strangers, even cattle may be counted among the *bēt 'āḇ*. The ground-plans of Iron Age dwellings that have been excavated, however, do not allow of at all a large number of persons belonging to a *bayit*.[59] Even if we only allow a single room to each family of parents and children, the number of persons inhabiting one house can rarely have been more than twenty. A style of building with compounds or with several floors for the various families has not been found in Palestine. Porter assumes that the *bēt 'āḇ* can therefore hardly have originated in Palestine and among sedentarized Israelites. It must have had its origin under semi-nomadic living conditions.[60] Yet though Porter also bases himself on 'extended families' of a comparatively restricted size, this is no solution of the problem. There is not the slightest indication that the semi-nomads – if there were any – of those early times lived in larger houses. Moreover, it is extremely unpractical for nomads to live in fairly large groups.[61] But if one accepts this restricted size of the Israelite *bēt 'āḇ*, then endogamy certainly becomes highly improbable! And indeed, Porter himself rightly suggests that Lev. 18 does not refer to marriage, but to illicit sexual relations within the *bēt 'āḇ*.[62] All the various degrees of affinity are enumerated in Lev. 18 for completeness' sake and not

[59] *Cf.* the ground-plans of dwelling-houses in *BRL* and *BHH*. Especially too the ground-plans of the early Iron Age from Tell Deil Miroim published by W. F. Albright (vol. III, *AASOR* XXI-XXII, New Haven 1941-1943). The ground-plans, however, are always of upper-class dwellings. *Cf.* also the houses which have now been found in Taanach, *BASOR* 195 (1969) p. 2-49.

[60] Porter, *o.c.* p. 8. Porter's argument follows the familiar course: the rules concerning the *bēt 'āḇ* use no arguments or norms derived from Yahwism, therefore they are older, and therefore (*sic* dG) they still date from the semi-nomadic period! This reasoning supposes that Yahwism must have creatively intervened in the social structure of Israel. Just that is so questionable!

[61] Henninger points out that the extended family is hardly found among Beduin, though it is among sedentarized Arabs. *o.c.* S. 129. *Cf.* also *supra* par. 2 ad VI and VII!

[62] Porter, *o.c.* p. 9. The same applies to Lev. 20:17 and Deut. 27:22.

because they were present in every normal *bēt 'āḇ*. Lev. 18 is chiefly concerned with the cultic purity of the members of the extended family, or with 'rules of the house'. Not with marriages. All the same, the existence of such prohibitions against incest, founded on the cult, will hardly have helped towards marriages between members of the same *bēt 'āḇ*! Nor is there any counter-evidence in the history of the patriarchs, the levirate or the story of Tamar (II Sam. 13:13). After all, the stories of the patriarchs do rest upon the social and juridical prescripts of a different period, while even then a good deal of trouble was taken to obtain a bride from elsewhere. The levirate was not a normal marriage and need not remain within the *bēt 'āḇ*. II Sam. 13:13 is not representative either, and does not even confirm that a marriage between brother and half-sister was considered permissible. A royal *bēt 'āḇ* cannot simply be compared to that of commoners.[63] Not only have we thus to do with an exogamic group, but the *bet 'āḇ* can also be said to be an institution typical of a sedentary population whose economy is mainly agrarian. As urbanization proceeded, the importance of the *bēt 'āḇ* seems to have declined.[64] Obviously such an extended family cannot exist independently; anthropologically speaking, it is based on the existence of a larger group.[65] Since it is a general rule that people are compelled to marry within the culturally defined group to which they belong, the exogamic extended family must form part of a larger endogamic unit, the clan.[66] Such a clan was formed in Israel by the *mišpāḥā*. That the

[63] For that reason we do not consider the argumentation convincing that a text such as II Sam. 13:13 and the marriage of Abraham and Sarah date from a period when such a marriage was acceptable, as *e.g.* De Vaux would have it *o.c.* p. 47-49. All the more, since also De Vaux regards Lev. 18 as a regulation for *marriages*. All the examples that are brought forward again and again in defence of such marriages between members of the same *bēt 'āḇ* come from royal dynasties or are clearly theoretical 'desperate measures', as in the case of Lot (Gen 19:30-38) or in that of Bu-Zaid cited by Patai (*Sex and Family in the Bible and the Middle East*, New York 1959, p. 25-26). *Cf.* now also J. Hoftijzer, Absalom and Tamar: A Case of Fratriarchy? In: *'Schrift en Uitleg'. Studiën aangeboden aan W. H. Gispen.* Kampen 1970, p. 55-61. H. J. Boecker, Anmerkungen zur Adoption im Alten Testament. *ZAW* LXXXVI (1974) S. 86-89.
[64] Elliger thinks this already demonstrable from Lev. 18: insertion in P caused an evident change of emphasis. 'Nicht mehr soll die Grossfamilie in ihrem Zusammenleben geschützt, sondern jetzt soll die Gemeinde in ihrer Kultfähigkeit erhalten werden.' Das Gesetz Leviticus 18, S. 18.
[65] For the anthropological definitions: see the 'glossary' in: E. A. Hoebel, *Anthropology: The Study of Man.* New York 1972[4].
[66] Hoebel's definition of a clan is: 'A unilineal kinship group that maintains the fiction of common genetic descent from a remote ancestor, usually legendary or mythological.' *O.c.* p. 691.

mišpāḥā was the most important form of organization and the most important way of living in the social context in ancient Israel was and is agreed on all sides, with hardly any differences of opinion. With the extended families, the elements which constitute it and of which it is an extension, the clan has two essential characteristics in common: in the first place the clan, too, consists of individuals. This rule may also be reversed: each individual belongs to a clan. Through the intermediary stage of *gēr* ('stranger') an individual may pass from one clan to another. An Israelite from Ephraim is *gēr* in Gibeah in Benjamin, Judg. 19:16. In the same way the Levites can be called *gērīm*.[67] Secondly, the clan, too, constitutes a real community of living and dwelling. Although the distinction between *bēt 'āb* and *mišpāḥā* is sometimes wavering, this should not be exaggerated. It is true there are several places in the Old Testament where a family is named when one would expect a clan and vice versa. Yet all these passages can be sufficiently explained from the context, or are at most due to rather inexact terminology.[68] As stated above, the extended family is always part of the clan, a part which cannot really exist by itself.[69] The clan is the unit, and in the time of the Judges the clan was still fully functional. If we try to work out exactly how these clans functioned in ancient Israel, then as we have seen they prove to have formed groups which were voluntarily endogamic. That endogamy was compulsory we cannot say for lack of prescripts and because of a fairly high number of exceptions.[70] But we can say that it was the rule.[71]

[67] In the very great majority of cases, of course, the *gēr* was someone who did not belong to the people at all! *Cf.* for this R. de Vaux, *Les Institutions de l'Ancien Testament*, vol. I, p. 25-26.

[68] Pedersen, *Israel I*, pp. 47-48 gives too much weight to the differences he sees and suggests that *bēt 'āb* and *mišpāḥā* can also be used interchangeably. Yet in the passage cited, Gen. 24:38-41, *bēt 'āb* and *mišpāḥā* lie so close together that where there is one, the other is also, since it was Abraham who departed! This says nothing as to synonymity. In Deut. 29:17 mention is made of 'man, woman, clan, tribe' clearly representing the three degrees; man and woman stand for the family. In I Sam. 9:21 and I Sam. 18:18 the use of 'clan' instead of 'extended family' is obviously a polite form of speech, which moreover is neutralized if the difference between the two is disclaimed. In the pericope of the Passover (Exod. 12:21-28) 'your clans' in v. 21 is a very common expression to indicate the whole people, and may certainly not be played off against the 'houses' of the following verses.

[69] That is, I think, the purport of texts such as Gen. 24:38 and Judg. 9:1.

[70] The only prescript in this matter concerns the high priest. In Lev. 21:14 *'ammīm* cannot but be a parallel to *mišpāḥā*. In the context, we may have to do with a rudiment of a former general rule. *Cf.* also Elliger, *Leviticus*, S. 278.

[71] Gen. 24:3; 28:1-2 and Judg. 14:3 are often quoted in evidence of this undoubtedly correct thesis. Yet all these cases concern extraneous marriages. The contrast is between one's own kindred and foreigners. Yet these and similar cases clearly show that in earlier times the injunction to take a wife of one's own people

It can also be said that in early times clan and dwelling-place, which in the conditions of ancient Israel means clan and town, often coincided. We must imagine the numerous townlets of the countryside each preponderantly inhabited by members of the same clan. Often, too, one clan inhabited several townlets. In that case the clan coincides with a district. This also explains the fact that comparatively few clans are noted for each tribe. One should remember that in Palestine the politico-geographical condition is far more a given entity than in a flat country like Holland. Political units are far more coincident with geographical ones: a valley, a fertile mountain-ridge, if these are given little can be changed. They may pass into other hands, but always in their entirety. The frontiers lie where inhabitable and economically useful land passes into desert country. Thus it is not at all surprising that in the history of Palestine historical geography often displays a remarkable continuity. The find of the Samarian ostraca is very important in this context. They enable us to demonstrate from the administrative practice of the Northern State how at the end of the ninth and the beginning of the eighth century, old clan names still serve to indicate certain districts.[72] These ostraca

was less stringent than it afterwards became. The custom among present-day Beduin where a girl is expected to marry an uncle on her father's side, the so-called 'bint-'al 'amm', cannot be accepted as an analogy with ancient Israel. For one thing, Num. 27, with which it is always compared, is an explicit exception in the Old Testament. Also, the custom is not only an anthropologically fairly unique phenomenon, but also an institution which can and should be completely explained from the specific Arab Beduin culture. Hoebel, o.c. p. 406-408. F. Barth, Father's brother's daughter marriage in Kurdistan. *Southwestern Journal of Anthropology* X (1954) p. 164-171. F. R. Murphy and L. Kasdan, The Structure of Parallel Cousin Marriage. *The American Anthropologist* LXI (1959) p. 17-29. In his very interesting article: *Mārat ilim*: Exogamie bei den semitischen Nomaden des 2. Jahrtausends, *AFO* XXIV (1973) S. 103-108, J. Renger demonstrates that in the so-called Amoritic milieu of the Old Babylonian period and also in the biblical patriarchal traditions, marriages with relatives within the lineage of the father were avoided. Marriages, however, with relatives of the mother's lineage were preferred. Renger calls marriages of the *bint-'al-'amm*-type endogamous, and those of the *ḫāl*-type exogamous.

[72] M. Noth, Das Krongut der israelitischen Könige und seine Verwaltung. *ZDPV* L (1927) S. 211-44. Y. Aharoni, *The Land of the Bible*. London 1967, pp. 325-7. These ostraca have been variously dated between Ahab and Jeroboam II on the basis of their orthography. In 1927 Noth placed them in the time of Ahab (o.c. S. 219), afterwards somewhat later (cf. *Die Welt des ATs*, 1962⁴, S. 197). The date of ca. 800 now seems acceptable, for some peculiarities of the Samarian ostraca, int. al. the way the *yōd* is written, have also been found on ostraca of Arad which have a firmer archaeological dating. Y. Aharoni, Arad: its Inscriptions and Temple. *BA* XXXI (1968) p. 10. Aharoni does not, by the bye, assume a few years between the two groups of Samarian ostraca, but a whole generation.

contain short notes concerning supplies of wine and oil to the court of Samaria, all from the region of Manasseh. Of the six clans of which Manasseh consisted according to the Old Testament,[73] Asriel, Abiezer, Helek, Shechem, Shemida, Hepher, only the last is lacking. Of the Zelophehadites related to Hepher, however, the sub-tribes Noah and Hoglah are named. Aharoni's remark: 'The most interesting fact is that all of the clan names appear in the Bible as children of Manasseh, which is illuminating evidence for the existence of the ancient clan divisions that had maintained their integrity even late in the Monarchial period. This, in turn, shows that the agrarian social structure had continued to prevail,'[74] with the conclusion he draws seem to me completely justified, and they are in the main in agreement with Noth. A. Alt's researches in territorial history enable us to state that those clans which typically represent districts, are older Israelite clans than those which in fact represent the territory of town-states that were incorporated later, as in this case Shechem.[75]

Like the townlets, the clan was ruled by a council of elders, the $z^e q\bar{e}n\bar{i}m$,

---

[73] Num. 26:30-33; Josh. 17:2-3; I Chron. 7:14-19. The reading (A) zrl, determined by Albright and Cross, is now generally accepted instead of the earlier srq. Cf. for this F. M. Cross in BASOR 163 (1961) p. 12-14. Also G. E. Wright, The Provinces of Solomon. EI VIII (1967) esp. p. 60*-64*, who is in full agreement with Cross and Albright on these points.

[74] Aharoni, The Land of the Bible, p. 324. Cf. also Noth, ZDPV L, S. 237. One hardly sees how this continuity is maintained when Aharoni identifies the place-name Elmattan from the ostraca with the modern Immatin to the south of Samaria. Here he also places the territory of the Abiezerites. Owing to his identification of Ophrah with 'Affuleh in the plain of Jezreel, he is then compelled to assume the migration of part of this clan, o.c. p. 241. Now the identification of Elmattan and Immatin only rests upon a possible identity of name, and is decidedly doubtful. Gideon's Ophrah must certainly have been situated in north-east Manasseh. Identification with 'Affuleh brings us into conflict with the tribal frontiers of Manasseh: it would be a Manassehite enclave in the territory of Issachar, but the known Manassehite enclaves in the north are all areas of ancient town-states. A possible solution here might be to take it as a sign of Manassehite imperialism: we already remarked that the tribe is really inexplicably absent in the tales of Gideon (above, ch. II p. 81). See for this Josh. 17:11-18. According to Kallai-Kleinman, p. 355-7, the two tribes fought over the region around 'Affuleh. Following this track, one would conclude that Abiezer was originally an Issacharite clan, and there would be no suggestion of a later habitat in the south. Migration must not, of course, be excluded but in this case it would seem highly unlikely. The familiar instance of Dan certainly shows that even after such a migration the ancient name of Dan is preserved for a very long time in the old territory.

[75] For an excellent summary of Alt's findings and of the problems connected with this matter: Weippert, Landnahme, S. 14-28; cf. also above, ch. I par. 6, and note how the name Shechem remained the same through all vicissitudes!

comparable to the Latin *senator*, not *senex*![76] The elders formed a council of free, landowning burghers, the *ba'alē hā'īr*. We must certainly not think of their rule as democratic, but rather oligarchic or even aristocratic. Those members of the council actively concerned in government are called *śārīm* or *šōfeṭīm*.[77] Besides the elders of a town, we also meet with elders of a region, a people or a tribe. Besides the frequent mention of the 'elders of Israel', I Sam. 30 speaks of those of Judah, Num. 22 of those of Midian and Moab. It is a very old misunderstanding to make a contrast between this institution of the elders, and the town. The terminology does indeed derive from the ruling of the clan, but clan and town were parallel in the time of ancient Israel. The rule of a council of elders is indeed in contrast with the feudal and monarchial system in the town-states of Canaan, but not with the town in itself! Nor must we forget that the Canaanite town-states had their heyday in Palestine in the Late Bronze Age, while some continued into the Iron Age. Nor is the size of these towns to be compared with that of the Israelite townlets of the Iron Age. It is an unfortunately deep-rooted habit always to try to reduce the social and political structure of ancient Israel to a (semi-) nomad structure.[78] Yet the elders are in the first place the *ziqnē hā'īr*![79] When we come across the elders of a certain region, they are the delegates of the towns of that region, who in some particular situation must take action together, as is quite evident, for instance, in Judg. 11.[80] From the functioning of the institution of elders in the Old Testament and from the fact that they also formed a ruling class, whose members could be referred to as *gibbōrē ḥajil*, we may conclude that clan and town or district did not automatically and completely coincide. The clans whose names we know are those of the landowning families. Clans as enumerated in Num. 26 or Josh. 17 are somewhat larger units. In the whole region, however, they were the ruling group. The Old Testament also speaks of the *mišpaḥat gēr*.[81] In general it is very difficult to situate an individual in the clan systems as they are transmitted in the Old Testament. That in the country clan and town long continued to form an exclusive entity, may perhaps be shown from I Sam. 25:3. Nabal the Calebite carries on his activities in Carmel, clearly as owner of extensive pastures. Yet he lives in Maon. This might be due to the fact that Nabal was a Calebite,

---

[76] A. Malamat, Organs of Statecraft in the Israelite Monarchy. *Biblical Archaeologist Reader III*, New York 1970, p. 163-198.

[77] C. H. J. de Geus, De richteren van Israël. *NThT* XX (1965-66) p. 81-110.

[78] This more fully above, par. 2.

[79] *E.g.* Deut. 19:12; 21:3; Josh. 20:4; I Sam. 16:4; Ruth 4:2.

[80] De Geus, *o.c.* p. 87-90.

[81] Lev. 25:47.

and hence not acceptable to the inhabitants of Judaic Carmel as co-dweller, *i.e.* as one of themselves.

Not only did the clan function for the ancient Israelites as the largest, voluntarily endogamic kinship group and as a community which, at least for the landowning and therefore ruling group, practically coincided with the town they lived in, it also had two other important functions. One was the part played by the clan in jurisdiction. Justice was administered 'in the gates' and also formed part of the task of the elders. Nowadays it may well be regarded as *communis opinio* that in ancient Israel, as indeed in the whole of the ancient Orient, administration and jurisdiction were two aspects of the same thing.[82] With regard to this system of jurisdiction exercised by the council of elders as representing the (blood-related) community, we must always remember that this system originated in and for a time with no central state authority. That was why the members of the clan were also called upon for redemption and vendetta. The solidarity of the clan was the most important force sanctioning ancient Israelite justice. This is very vividly described in II Sam. 14:1-17, esp. verse. 7. Though the case described is fictitious, it was undoubtedly constructed in accordance with everyday practice. Closely linked with the vendetta is the system of redemption, intended to check the alienation of in the main real property, though it may also apply to persons. The connection shows how closely linked were blood and land.[83]

In discussing A. Alt in chapter I we already drew attention to his famous antithesis between casuistically and apodictically formulated rules of law. The former he supposed to derive from jurisdiction 'in the gates'. This law has many parallels with ancient Eastern law, hence Alt supposes it to be largely of Canaanite origin. The apodictic law of Yahwistic inspiration, on the other hand, Alt regards as law that functioned principally in the cult, these strict rules being ultimately drawn from

---

[82] De Geus, *o.c.* p. 81-86, for the root *špṭ* which expresses both notions.
[83] That administration and jurisdiction were the task of the elders appears from very old texts such as Exod. 17, 18, 24; Num. 11; Deut. 19, 21, 22. The book of Ruth vividly illustrates how this worked. *Cf.* also L. Köhler, *Die hebräische Rechtsgemeinde*, 1931 (now in: *Der hebräische Mensch*. Tübingen 1953). Also: D. A. McKenzie, Judicial Procedure at the Town Gate. *VT* XIV (1964) p. 100-105. Besides this jurisdiction by the elders, justice was done of old by means of divine ordeals and oracles, Judg. 4:4-5. For the vendetta, the *ius talionis etc.* see the lexicons and esp. De Vaux, I p. 221-251. Also A. Alt, Zur Talionsformel. *KS* I, München 1953, S. 33-40, and B. van Oeveren, *De vrijsteden in het Oude Testament*. Kampen 1968. For I Sam. 14: 1-17 *cf.* J. Hoftijzer, David and the Tekoite Woman. *VT* XX (1970) p. 419-44.

desert life.[84] In the last two decades this distinction has met with increasing opposition. A whole series of scholars has shown that the apodictical form of law was by no means exclusively Israelitish, but in general use in texts of alliance and in state treaties. There is the *Sitz im Leben* of this literary form. Moreover, the distinction into apodictically and casuistically formulated commands and prohibitions is not so simple as Alt would have had us believe.[85] E. Gerstenberger has shown that just the apodictically formulated commands, and particularly the negatively put prohibitions – 'thou shalt not ...' – originally show no national or religious tie at all! Then what is their background? Gerstenberger speaks of an international *'Sippenethos'*.[86] He is followed in this by Schottroff who concludes that formulas such as *bārūk* and *'ārūr 'attā* also belong to the social context of the clan.[87] Gerstenberger demonstrates this in the first place from Jer. 35:6-7 where we find the well-known command of the leader of the Rechabites, Jonadab ben Rechab, and then from the commands of Lev. 18, which we have already seen most probably to be very ancient, and to stem from rules intended to regulate life within an extended family. The authority behind the prohibitions of the Old Testament is the patriarch, the head of the extended family. Since the majority of the elders of the clan will have been such *'ābōt*, this conclusion of Gerstenberger's seems very acceptable to us, and even evident.[88] Unfortunately, simply because of the fact that jurisdiction 'in the gates' is not mentioned in connexion with the prohibitions, and also of course because of a prejudice regarding Israel's social structure, Gerstenberger thinks it necessary again to place this *'Sippenethos'* in the 'Nomaden- und Halbnomadenzeit Israels'. For it was only in that time that the clan relationship formed the true constitutive element of the people.[89] We shall return to this misunderstanding. There is a considerable dis-

---

[84] A. Alt, Die Ursprünge des israelitischen Rechts. Now in *KS* I, S. 278-332. See also above, ch. I par. 6.

[85] A survey and summary of the criticisms levelled at Alt in E. Gerstenberger, *Wesen und Herkunft des 'Apodiktischen Rechts'*. WMANT 20, Neukirchen 1965, S. 1-22. Cf. also K. Baltzer, *Das Bundesformular*. WMANT 4, Neukirchen 1960. Also important is the critical survey in R. Hentschke, Erwägungen zur israelitischen Rechtsgemeinde. *Theol. Viat.* X (1965/66) S. 108-133. Hentschke very rightly warns against hasty conclusions as to socio-economic and religious conditions founded on the form of the rules of law.

[86] Gerstenberger, *o.c.*, S. 110-115.

[87] W. Schottroff, *Der altisraelitische Fluchspruch*. WMANT 30, Neukirchen 1969.

[88] All the same, Gerstenberger, appealing to Pedersen, is too indefinite about the distinction between the extended family and the clan, *o.c.* S. 115. This treatment is due to the need he feels to project this social structure in the desert.

[89] Gerstenberger, *o.c.* S. 114. The same objection holds good for Schottroff, *cf.* note 87.

crepancy here in Gerstenberger's reasoning, for he quite follows Alt's view that the prohibitions do not belong to public jurisdiction. In disagreement with Alt he then postulates that it was family law, or rather, family ethics. Obviously, in that case any mention of the gates might be excluded *a priori*. For the rest we need only conclude that Gerstenberger's study has convincingly shown the important function of the clan in ancient Israelite law.

The fourth and final point to be mentioned is how the clan functioned in the field of cult and religion. The clan also had a communal cult. This is evident *e.g.* from the absolute necessity for a person to be present at the religious ceremonies of his clan, as David pretends in I Sam. 20: 6, 29. For a very long time the feast of the Passover was only celebrated within the clans.[90] It was, however, celebrated by all in the country at the same time on its appointed date. Besides the Passover, there were religious festivals which each clan and town community celebrated independently. Such is the case in I Sam. 20, but also in I Sam. 9:12. These are clan ceremonies which clearly fell outside the 'national calendar of festivals'.[91] Unfortunately the Old Testament is completely silent as to the content of such a festival.[92] Was it celebrated in memory of the mythological ancestor? There is some indication that the so-called 'gods of the fathers' belong to such clan-cults.[93] An interesting detail supplied

---

[90] J. B. Segal has greatly stressed this in his *The Hebrew Passover*, London 1963. He regards the feast as an ancient New Year festival. In it, the head of the clan functions as mediator between god and man. The festival kept its place in the spring, in contrast to the later official state New Year festival in the autumn, in which the king had such an important role. According to Segal there is a conscious polemic here.

[91] Such a sacrificial feast is called z^ebah $hayy\bar{a}m\bar{\imath}m$, specified in I Sam. 20:6 as $misp\bar{a}h\bar{a}$. It is also mentioned in I Sam. 1:21 and 2:19. R. Rendtorff's work, *Studien zur Geschichte des Opfers im Alten Israel* ((WMANT 24, Neukirchen 1967) once more clearly shows the difference between the public cult attached to official sanctuaries with *e.g.* the '$\bar{o}l\bar{a}$ sacrifice, and the cult within the clan, the setting of the z^ebah. That this correct observation leads to the conclusion that the z^ebah sacrifice is a legacy from Israel's nomadic past, is a mistake and typical of the general trend: we saw exactly the same reasoning in Gerstenberger with regard to the *Sippenethos*, *o.c.* S. 241-50.

[92] For all these data, unfortunately without interpretation, see M. Haran, $Zebah$ $hayyam\bar{\imath}m$. *VT* XIX (1969) p. 11-22.

[93] A. Alt, *Der Gott der Väter* (1929), *KS* I München 1953, S. 1-78. Weippert maintains (*Landnahme*, S. 104-105) that a god could only be imagined under this aspect in a milieu of nomads and semi-nomads. This seems exaggerated, as is also his theological distinction of a 'Religion des Ortes' and a 'Religion des Weges', a fine instance of the romanticizing of Beduin life which was justly criticized by G. E. Mendenhall (*BA* XXV (1962) S. 66-87). This distinction approaches to the

by I Sam. 9:22 is that about thirty people have been invited to partake of the sacrificial meal. We know the custom of inviting guests to religious meals. In agreement with Haran we may suppose these thirty to have been the heads of the families of Rama with the addition of some important guests from elsewhere. This certainly tells us something of the size of such a community.[94]

A third aspect of the cultic function of the clan comes to the fore in the study of Gerstenberger already referred to. Although his conclusion that that Yahwism was an amphictyonic affair is most disputable, his observation that the *Sippenethos* was fairly indifferent towards Yahwism is important in this context. At the same time the existence of prohibitions concerning religious and cultic purity shows that the authority of the elders of the clan also extended over these spheres of life.[95]

All this would seem to make it very clear that the *mišpāḥā* was the principal form of organization and social grouping in ancient Israel, and that for landowning Israelites it practically coincided with the town. It was around the extended family and the *mišpāḥā* that life revolved for an Israelite of the time before the monarchy. When we inquire what a tribe was at that time, the contours at once become much vaguer than for the extended family or the clan. It is not permissible, though, to explain this *a priori* in historical terms by saying that the tribes were then already melting away as real entities, or contrariwise that they were just coming into existence. We must first see wether the tribes functioned in the time of the Judges, and if so, how. On checking over the use of tribal names in the older texts, it is quite obvious that they function primarily

ideas of Buber, and in Holland was also defended by B. Gemser, *Vragen rondom de Patriarchenreligie*, Groningen 1958, p. 18. Weippert refers back to E. Lehmann and J. Hempel (S. 104[4]), and at any rate Lehmann may have been Buber's source, though he does not name him. (*Cf.* M. Buber, *Königtum Gottes*. Heidelberg 1956[3], S. 61-71.)

[94] Haran, *o.c.* p. 17-18.

[95] 'Das Jahwegebot hat nie völligen Eingang in die Sippenordnung selbst gefunden' (Exod. 22:27), Gerstenberger, *o.c.* S. 114. It is rather interesting here to recall the old discussion between Weber and Caspari (see above, ch. I, par. 4). What Gerstenberger posits here is quite in Weber's line. He, too, regarded the clans as indifferent in the matter of Yahwism, which was rooted in a religious union of tribes (Das antike Judentum, *Ges. Stud.* III, Tübingen 1923[2], S. 82-100). On the other hand it was just in the clans that Caspari imagined Yahwism beginning to flourish, while the danger lay in the families with their cults that could not be known or checked. After all that has gone before, we cannot help saying that Caspari makes too much of the contrast between the clan and the extended family, and has too little appreciation of the specific clan cults. (W. Caspari, *Die Gottesgemeinde von Sinaj und das nachmalige Volk Israel.* Gütersloh 1922, S. 86-107).

as territorial indications. This shows most plainly where the expression used is 'the land of Benjamin/Zebulun/Naphtali' *etc.*[96] It was of the greatest importance that the various groups living together in any particular region should do so with as little competition and strife as might be, in view of their many common interests. The first of these was safety upon the roads. The safety of travel and trade is to the interest of all. The desolate condition caused by its lack is vividly painted in Judg. 5:6. Next comes the common use of pastures and wells. There must have been all kinds of agreements in this matter both among the Israelites themselves and with other groups such as the remaining Canaanite enclaves. Thirdly, solidarity of whole region must have been highly desirable when danger threatened from without. The testimony of the Book of Judges shows that this solidarity in particular was sometimes far from complete. It can be said that in most cases the striving to be independent dominated over the rational consideration of assisting one another. As to this, though, it must always be remembered that the territory of the Israelite clans did not form a coherent whole. Larger unions were usually temporary, coming into being through concerted action when a man of strong character or a powerful clan or town took the lead and obtained a following. The true power behind such authority did not reside in the tribe, but always in the town or clan of the leader, the 'Judge'. Thus is the rise of the Judges to be explained. In the beginning the *šofᵉṭīm* and *śārīm* were the leading figures of the early Israelite townlets, and some of them attained to a prestige and power far transcending their original function. Yet this power and this prestige were always temporary and bound up with the person of the *šōfēṭ*. The office of *šōfēṭ* in itself is not connected with the tribe, but is rather related to the *mišpāḥā*.[97]

Two things are evident from the above: the tribe as territorial unit may serve to explain incidental solidarity with regard to a few concrete communal problems, but this solidarity applies only to these problems and is not lasting. Moreover it is not exclusively Israelitish. The second thing is that in regard to these functions of the tribe *actual consanguinity* has been quite abandoned, while it is *history* and politics that count. Which clans at a certain moment form a tribe together is the consequence of certain historical developments. In this, the essential difference

---

[96] *E.g.* Judg. 12:13; 1 Sam. 9:16; Isa. 8:23.
[97] For this more in full: C. H. J. de Geus, De richteren van Israel. *NThT* XX (1965-66) p. 96-100. R. de Vaux, in his *Histoire ancienne d'Israël*, vol. II, p. 67-86, considers the Judges as having been the leaders of confederations of tribes. His arguments are derived from the Mari letters.

between a tribe and a clan should be borne in mind: the clan consists of individuals, the tribe of collectives.[98]

Now it is very striking in the Semitic world that the tribes, which literally and formally speaking have nothing to do with 'descent' and consanguinity, have yet been brought into genealogical systems and function as blood-related groups, though in many cases this is quite fictitious. Thus one may even posit: tribe and tribal system are indivisible. The tribe undoubtedly owes its *origin* to historical factors, and one of these historical factors *may* have been the factor of actual consanguinity. The *function* of the tribe, however, apart from being territorial, is primarily that of a fictitious consanguineous group, for in the Semitic world solidarity was always connected with the blood.[99] This fiction of blood-relationship within the tribe has three functions: in the first place the tribal system forms a compulsory endogamous group. Probably each tribe was originally endogamous, while this role was afterwards taken over by the whole system.[100] In reality ancient Israel only had the tripartition: extended family – clan – people. The fact that both clan and people might be called *'amm* clearly shows that the two ideas were conterminous and largely coincided in daily life.[101] For the Israelite it was

---

[98] This distinction and awareness of the fact that 'tribe' and 'people' are historical concepts, is also found in Noth, *Welt des Alten Testaments*, Berlin 1962⁴, S. 58-59. Anthropologists lay more stress upon the criterion of culture than upon history. A tribe is: 'A social group speaking a distinctive language or dialect and possessing a distinctive culture that marks it off from other tribes. It is not necessarily organized politically.' Hoebel, *o.c.* p. 704. This definition of Hoebel's is a good deal attacked at present, especially for the linguistic norm used in it. See below, p. 150 and the symposium *'Essays on the Problem of Tribe'*. AES, Seattle/London 1968. Esp. D. Hymes, Linguistic problems in defining the concept of 'tribe', p. 23-48. Nevertheless, this definition was long an accepted formula, and we can use it as a starting-point here.

[99] Interesting in this connexion is the use of the term 'brother' in Gen. 26:31.

[100] Quite another matter is what that system was like. It came into being at the moment when persons 'from somewhere else', were accepted as belonging to the people. This function of genealogies was referred to above, on p. 133. *Cf.* also the examples in Patai, *o.c.* p. 31-39. With regard to this aspect one can indeed say the principle of *'aṣīl* among present-day Beduin is a most ancient Semitic heritage.

[101] 'Wenn die Familie des Einzelnen als Anfangszelle eines Volkes angesehen wird, dann ist es möglich, die gleiche Grösse, die als Volk bezeichnet wird, auch *mišpāḥā* "Grossfamilie, Sippe" zu nennen; denn das Volk ist dann einer ausgeweiteten Grossfamilie gleich und die einzelnen Volksglieder sind Brüder, wie es das Deuteronomium will. Fällt freilich der Blick auf die tatsächliche Gliederung eines Volkes, dann treten die einzelnen Sippen hervor, die es in sich schliesst'. L. Rost, Die Bezeichnungen für Land und Volk im Alten Testament. *Festschrift O. Procksch*, Leipzig 1934, S. 138. This is also the explanation of the Old Testament predilection for referring to the nations as *mišpāḥōt*, clans. *Cf. e.g.* Gen. 12:3; Exod. 20:32.

146

a way of orientating himself in the world, all groups with which he came in contact being placed in systems of fictitious blood-relationship. In this the tribes only function in so far as they express regional distinctions, which of course always existed. The Israelite lives primarily in his *mišpāḥā*. The tribal system does not come into play until he goes beyond his clan. Then one of its functions is to constitute an exclusive endogamous group. Palestine society in the Iron Age was extremely 'racist'! And indeed other Semitic cultures share this characteristic. The whole genealogical system served to maintain the idea of the people as one large, closed family. A marriage with a woman not belonging to the people was disapproved of, the whole system was geared to prevent this as far as possible. Gen. 34:22 is interesting in this context, where the condition attached to a *connubium* is that the two groups shall become *le'amm 'eḥād*. The background is clear: a marriage is only possible withing the *'amm*. If the *connubium* of Gen. 34 had become effective, an alteration in the genealogical system would clearly have been required. While still unnecessary in Gen. 34, Num. 26 shows that this afterwards took place all the same.[102] It would seem that in olden times the content of the expression *'iššā zōnā* was: 'a woman from outside Israel'. Surely this is very plain in Judg. 11:1; if Jephthah had really been the son of a prostitute, his father would undoubtedly have remained unknown. The concepts 'whore' and 'other woman' coincide. 'Other' is used here just as in the well-known expression 'other (*scil.* strange) gods'.[103] Also of interest in this connexion is the ancient tradition in Num. 25, esp. verse 1.[104] In Lev. 21:7 and Deut. 22:19 we find the requirement of purity greatly stressed for the *Israelite* girls; any sexual

In this connexion a correction must be suggested in H. J. van Dijk, *Ezekiel's Prophecy on Tyre*, p. 4-10. Van Dijk attempts to show by means of many examples from Hebrew and Ugaritic that the words *'īr* and *'amm* may be synonyms, *i.e.* that in certain cases *'amm* means 'city'. Now anyone will immediately be convinced by the examples collected by Van Dijk that in these instances it might be better to translate *'amm* as 'city'. But that is a mere matter of translation! For the Israelites and the inhabitants of Ugarit the concepts of 'city' and 'people' were so close that they were to some extent interchangeable in a particular clearly defined context. But this does not imply that in itself, outside that context, *'amm* could mean 'city'!

[102] *Cf.* A. de Pury, Genèse XXXIV et l'histoire. *RB* LXXVI (1969) p. 5-49. Also: E. A. Speiser, 'People' and 'nation' of Israel. *JBL* LXXIX (1960) p. 157-63.

[103] It is unimportant in this connexion whether one regards v. 1a as a gloss, as *e.g.* W. Richter does, Die Ueberlieferung um Jephtah, Ri. 10, 17-12, 6. *Biblica* XLVII (1966) S. 485-556, or as original as *e.g.* M. Ottosson does in *Gilead, Tradition and History*. Lund 1969, p. 157-160.

[104] *Cf.* esp. F. Langlamet, Israël et l'habitant du pays. *RB* LXXVI (1969), esp. p. 500-03.

contact with a man who is not of her own people is whoredom just as much as forbidden sexual contact within the *bēt 'āḇ*. We are convinced – though it is difficult to demonstrate this from the texts – that in the historical background of the ancient[105] text Ex. 34:15-26 the sexual, or if preferred, the ethnic aspect is primary, while the religious foundation is secondary.[106] From the text Judg. 11:1-3 one can also see that Israelite law did not actually recognize such a marriage; the children of 'another woman' had the same status as those of a concubine. Several passages in the Old Testament show that the status of women of non-Israelite origin was that of concubine. Thus Rizpah, of Hivite origin, the concubine of Saul.[107] In I Chron. 1:32, 33 Keturah, the certainly non-Israelite ancestress of the Midianites, is also called the concubine of Abraham. Judg. 8:31[108] and I Chr. 7:14[109] also afford clear evidence in this matter.

Not only was the tribal system highly important for the concluding of purely Israelite marriages, the tribal solidarity based on fictitious blood-relationship was necessary at a time when central authority was lacking or ineffective, and the law was sanctioned by vengeance and vendetta. A large, powerful group was required for the security of not only individuals, but also of the separate clans. Certainly the system of the vendetta must already in ancient Israelite times have been one of the chief factors leading to the formation of larger units.[110]

[105] Langlamet has now made this seem highly probable. According to Schmitt this pericope is to be ascribed to the Jahwist. The prohibition of making a pact with the Canaanites must have originated quite soon after the Conquest. G. Schmitt, *Du sollst keinen Frieden schliessen mit den Bewohnern des Landes.* BWANT 91, Stuttgart 1970, S. 24-25 and 112.

[106] So also Langlamet, *o.c.* esp. p. 500-07.

[107] In Gen. 36:2 and 24 Aiah is connected with the Hivites. We know that these also lived in Central Palestine.

[108] It might well be that the problem of the early Israelite *beena* marriage can be explained by the wives of Samson and Gideon refusing to take second place in the *mišpāḥā* of their husbands, and consequently remaining in their own family.

[109] We may here refer to Hos. 1:2-3, which speaks of the famous *'ēšet zᵉnūnīm Gomᵉr bat Diḇlāyim*. The great majority of exegetes has always interpreted the strange name of Diblaïm as a reference to her sexual morality. Yet, apart from the possibility of reading *Dbl-jm* (Rudolph), the idea that the ending *-āyim* indicates a place of origin should also be considered. One may then compare a name such as Shamgar ben Anath (Judg. 3:31), which is also usually explained as Shamgar from Beth-anath. Diblaïm would then stand for (beth) Diblathaïm, the place in Moab named in Num. 33:46 and Jer. 48:23. Hos. 1:3 would then also concern a non-Israelite woman!

[110] Besides the literature mentioned in note 83, see esp. S. Nyström, *Beduinentum und Jahwismus.* Among the later Arab Beduin the existence of the vendetta was also one of the principal factors in forming the various tribes as groups of fictitious

In the third place it is an established fact that also in ancient Israel the principle of blood-relationship functioned in the cult. We already saw this on a smaller scale with the clan, when solemnities of the cult were celebrated *in* the clan. An indication in this direction may also be that tribes are apt to bear the name of a god; in Israel Asher and Gad, perhaps also Zebulun. The well-known phenomenon in the West-Semitic world of a great many terms expressive of family relationship being used for gods and goddesses – 'father', 'mother', 'brother and fellow-tribesman' –clearly illustrates that the system of (fictitious) consanguinity extended into the field of the cult. Celebrating the cult together (not so much the local *zebah* as the *hag*, a festival to which one goes up) must have greatly worked towards the solidarity of the clans within a particular region. Here again the fiction of consanguinity prevailed: the great solemnities in the temples or on mountain sanctuaries such as the Gerizim, the Tabor or the Carmel, were finally 'family ceremonies' and the participants are 'brethren' ('*āḥīm*).

The tribes, then, are first of all an expression of blood-relationship. They can only be said to have had a true political function in so far as it was considered desirable to belong to a powerful tribe. If a tribe could no longer provide the safety a clan thought they had a right to, such a clan would join another tribe. This started a process in which the large tribes tended to grow still larger.[111] It is interesting to observe that two of the 'lost' tribes were typical herding tribes, Reuben and Simeon. They will have disappeared because on the one hand they had to part with more and more of their territory, while on the other their economic basis was affected.[112]

One may conclude therefore that an Israelite tribe was always a

blood-relationship, and it was also the reason for the disappearance of tribes: one cannot afford to belong to a weak tribe! W. Caskel, *Gamharat an-Nasab. Das genealogische Werk des Hišam ibn Muhammad al-Kalbī*. Band I, Leiden 1966, S. 63. *Cf.* also J. Henninger, Altarabische Genealogie (review of Caskel's aforesaid work). *Anthropos* LXI (1966) S. 852-70, esp. S. 856.

[111] The instance always given of the instability of the tribes is that of the clan Hezron, which in Num. 26:6 is counted with Reuben and in Num. 26:20 with Judah. In Num. 26:20 the clan Zerah is counted with Judah, and in 26:13 with Simeon (in Gen. 36:13, 33 even with Edom!). One must take account of the fact, though, that the disappearance of precisely Reuben and Simeon also comes into play here. It is interesting too that Gen. 46:21 and I Chron. 7:6 reckon the clan of Becher with Benjamin, which is undoubtedly correct, thereby correcting Num. 26:35 where Becher (which *nota bene* was the kin of Saul!) is attributed to Ephraim. No doubt Numbers 26 here represents the period of the commencing monarchy, when the tribe of Benjamin had almost entirely been absorbed into Ephraim. See for this K. D. Schunck, *Benjamin*. S. 57-79.

[112] See below, p. 176-178.

'branch' of the whole people, and had no meaning without that whole.[113] At the same time the tribes expressed the inevitable territorial, linguistic and historical differentiation.[114] The tribe was for the Israelite the manner in which the people functioned for him in his region, though he remained aware that the people was more than the tribe. That the contours of the concept 'tribe' remain more vague than those of the clan, is due to the nature of the Israelite tribe. This vagueness is increased by the way the concepts *mišpāḥā* and *šēbeṭ* are used in a fashion which may often strike us as careless.[115]

Excursus 1. South-Arabia.

This paragraph concerning the social structure of the Israelite people is not really finished once the concepts *bēt 'āḇ*, *mišpāḥā* and *šēbeṭ* have been discussed. For all the above was written on the supposition that such a form of organization can be imagined in the case of a people essentially *sedentary* and mainly agrarian, and without explaining such a structure as the residue of a former non-sedentary existence. In by far the greater part of the literature on this subject, such a social structure is always explained from a former different, viz. semi-nomadic way of life. Once that has been done, the next step is usually that the social structure

[113] This brings us, by quite a different way, to practically the same conclusion as drawn by G. A. Danell, *Studies in the Name Israel*, p. 72. After a thorough examination of the histories in the book of Judges, he finds an old and authentic 'strong feeling that the unit, Israel, is nevertheless a living reality.' However, he specifies this feeling no further than by a reference to the hypothesis of the Amphictyony.
[114] We have an instance in the famous '*sibboleth*' incident in Judg. 12:6. Another case of difference in dialect is seen in Judg. 18:3. Yet the role of the tribe with regard to this phenomenon should not be exaggerated, as it is *int. al.* in Hoebel's definition (above, note 98). There are numerous indications that the boundaries of linguistic phenomena – isoglossics – intercross all other boundaries, and that the situation in Palestine differed but little from that in western Arabia in the first centuries of our era, where Rabin has shown that the tribal tie as non-biological sphere answered very poorly indeed to the definition of 'linguistic unit'. 'The real linguistic unit of the bedouin Arab was the *ḥajj*'. Of sedentary people Rabin says: 'Local speech varies from village to village'. Of isoglosses: 'There is no definite proof that the tribe did constitute a linguistic unit. With regard to the larger geographical units, it is often certain that linguistic boundaries ran across them'. C. Rabin, *Ancient West-Arabian*. London 1951, p. 15. For the important differences in dialect between the north and the south at the time of the two monarchies, see D. N. Freedman, The Orthography of the Arad Ostraca. *IEJ* XIX (1969) p. 52-57.
[115] In the earliest version of Judg. 18 the tribe of Dan is called *mišpāḥā*, and so is Judah in 17:7. On the other hand Judg. 20:12 and I Sam. 9:21 speak of the tribes of Benjamin. Because of this and similar phenomena, C. Umbau Wolf, Terminology of Israel's Tribal Organization, *JBL* LXV (1946) p. 46, considers the *mišpāḥā* to be far older than the *šēbeṭ/maṭṭē*. This conclusion does not seem necessary.

of the Arabian Beduin and semi-nomads is made use of as an analogy with ancient Israel.[116] It is therefor necessary to insert this excursus in order to discuss the following two points more thoroughly: 1) is such a tribal organization conceivable and practical for a people living a sedentary life, and 2) is not such a structure an ineluctable pointer towards a nomadic past?

What is now known of South-Arabia, though still far too little, shows us the phenomenon of an agrarian society which is yet tribally organized. Analogies, of course, never have conclusive force, while also in South-Arabia it was not a purely tribal organization, but really concerned smaller units, the clans. Yet a comparison with South-Arabia is permissible and interesting for the following reasons:

Firstly, both in Israel and in South-Arabia we have a purely Semitic culture. Secondly, these two cultures, that of Saba and of ancient Israel, were largely contemporary. The history of Saba is now known to us from *ca.* 800 B.C.E., and it is assumed that the typical South-Arabian culture certainly goes back to 1000 or 1200 B.C.E.[117] Jacqueline Pirenne is practically alone in her far lower dating.[118] Thirdly, South-Arabia and the Levant have always maintained close cultural contact. Particularly in the field of lexicography there are resemblances between southern Arabic

[116] This method is very strongly present in the work of Joh. Pedersen. Yet also R. de Vaux discusses the social organization of Israel under the title of 'Le nomadisme et sa survivance'! Nearly all the studies which have contributed to the social and anthropological history of Israel are given to that fault, particularly the works of A. Causse (*Du groupe ethnique à la communauté religieuse*, Strassbourg 1937) and of S. Nyström (*Beduinentum und Jahwismus*, Lund 1946). In his 'Method in the Study of Early Hebrew History' (*The Bible in Modern Scholarship*, Nashville 1965, p. 25) De Vaux does indeed admit that there was some justification for G. E. Mendenhall's criticism of what he called 'Bedouinism' (The Hebrew Conquest of Palestine, *BA* XXV (1962) p. 66-87), yet he fully maintains a non-sedentary past for Israel. Cf. also the 'Responses' in the same volume by Mendenhall and M. Greenberg. De Vaux's *Histoire ancienne d'Israël* is therefore still totally dependent of the "sedentarization-model" for his reconstruction of Israels most ancient history. Very much to the point are in my opinion the remarks of Fr. Altheim and Ruth Stiehl, *Beduinisierung*. In: *Antike und Universalgeschichte* (Festschrift H. E. Stier). Münster 1972, S. 294-301.

[117] A short historical survey in G. van Beek, South Arabian History and Archaeology, in: *BANE* p. 229-48. Also: H. von Wissmann, Geographische Grundlagen und Frühzeit der Geschichte Südarabiens. *Saeculum* IV (1953) S. 61-114. A. G. Lundin, Die Eponymenliste von Saba. *Oestr. Akk. d. Wiss., Phil. Hist. Kl., Sitzungsberichte* 248, I, Wien 1965, S. 96, posits that the Sabaean state must reach back into the 11th century, because of the fact that the list covers some 800 years.

[118] Jacqueline Pirenne, *Le Royaume Sud-Arabe de Qatabân et sa Datation*. Bibliothèque du Muséon, nr. 48, Louvain 1961.

and the north-western Semitic languages. Many scholars hold that the script was developed from an ancient Canaanite script[119] and indeed, the Old Testament is still aware that the Sabaeans are of northern origin.[120] Fourthly, and that is the principal point in this context, the economic circumstances were almost the same.[121] If one examines the geophysical and economic maps to be found *int. al.* in the work of Von Wissmann,[122] then South-Arabia and the Levant prove to have been the only regions of considerable surface to have an agriculture based on rain-fall. The great irrigation works (dams!) did indeed afterwards much extend the agricultural area in South-Arabia and make it more efficient, but it was not until a second phase that the irrigated plains were made suitable for agriculture and were populated.

On the basis of these points it is possible to indicate both some evident parallels with ancient Israel and some evident differences. The first resemblance, already referred to above, is geophysical. The nuclei of South-Arabian culture lie in naturally wooded areas, *i.e.* at a height with sufficient rainfall to guarantee a good vegetation.[123] In this region an economy of small farmers developed, flocks and donkeys being raised in addition. Local circumstances will have determined which was the

[119] M. Noth, *Welt des Alten Testaments*, 1962⁴ S. 200 and S. Moscati, *A Comparative Grammar of the Semitic Languages*, Wiesbaden 1964, p. 19 are still positive on this point. D. Diringer, *Writing*, London 1962, p. 121-2, is fairly sceptical however. The resemblance of some signs of the yet undeciphered Deir 'Alla script to characters of the South-Arabian alphabet, was at once noticed by many. See for this matter the highly critical, important discussion of the attempts at decipherment by M. Weippert, Archäologischer Jahresbericht, *ZDPV* LXXXII (1966) esp. S. 299-310.

[120] Gen. 10:7; 25:3; Ezek. 38:13; I Chron. 1:33. *Cf.* also F. Hommel, Geschichte Südarabiens im Umriss. *Handbuch der Altarabischen Altertumskunde*, hrgb. v. D. Nielsen; Bd. I Kopenhagen/Leipzig 1927, S. 57-108, esp. S. 65-67.

[121] First mention deserves the pioneering work done by H. von Wissmann in this field: H. von Wissmann und Maria Höfner, Beiträge zur historischen Geographie des vorislamischen Südarabien. *Akk. d. Wiss. u. Litt. in Mainz, Abhandlungen d. Geistes- und Soz. wiss. Kl.* 1952/4. H. von Wissmann, Geographische Grundlagen und Frühzeit der Geschichte Südarabiens. *Saeculum* IV (1953) S. 61-114. H. von Wissmann, Ursprungsherde und Ausbreitungswege von Pflanzen- und Tierzucht und ihre Abhängigkeit von der Klimageschichte. *Erdkunde* XI (1957) S. 81-94 und 175-93. Id., Bauer, Nomade und Stadt im islamischen Orient. In: *Die Welt des Islam und die Gegenwart*, hrgb. v. R. Paret, Stuttgart 1961, S. 22-63. Id., Zur Geschichte und Landeskunde von Alt-Südarabien. *Oester. Akk. d. Wiss., Phil. Hist. Kl., Sitzungsberichte* nr. 246, Wien 1964. Id., *Zur Archäologie und antike Geographie von Südarabien.* Nederlands Hist. Arch. Instituut, nr. XXIV, Istanbul 1968. Very important also is the survey of the literature in the Introduction to A. Salonen, *Agricultura Mesopotamica.* Helsinki 1968, p. 11-36.

[122] *E.g. Saeculum* IV (1953) S. 68, and Zur Geschichte und Landeskunde, S. 64.

[123] For this esp. H. von Wissmann, Ursprungsherde *etc.*, esp. the map on p. 177. Also: Bauer, Nomade und Stadt, esp. p. 28-36.

more important. The development in the Levant was just the same.[124] A second parallel we have also named already: the population spread from the mountain country into the plains. In South-Arabia this process can be followed by the temple inscriptions. All the mother-temples lie in the highland, the daughter-temples in the plains.[125] The same process is known from Palestine. There the ancient towns of the Canaanites usually lie on the edge of the plains, at the foot of the mountains. The highland settlement was of very ancient date, and far more primitive, while the plains were not settled until a later phase.[126] One aspect of the movement from the highland to the plains is formed by what Alt called the sedentarization of the Israelites. At any rate Alt well observed the process itself. Albright's counter-argument that this earlier occupancy of the highland was impossible owing to lack of water, as it only became feasible with the invention of the waterproof lime plaster in the Iron Age, can no longer stand now that this plaster has been found in the Early Bronze Age already![127] A third parallel, and the most important in this context, is that in both cases the pattern of settlement was one of little towns inhabited and dominated by one clan. In South-Arabia, too, the resemblance between clan names and the names of towns or districts (they are mostly called 'counties') is striking. Often such a name may have three meanings: name of a town, of a clan and of a county.[128]

[124] Besides the publications of Von Wissmann, the good synopsis made by J. Henninger, *Über Lebensraum und Lebensformen der Frühsemiten*. Arbeitsgemeinschaft für Forschung des Landes Nordrhein-Westfalen, Geisteswissenschaften Heft 151, Köln/Opladen 1968.

[125] Many examples in Von Wissmann, *int. al. Zur Geschichte und Landeskunde*, S. 271. In southern Arabia the effect of this extension was far more sweeping than in Palestine, for there the southern plains extend into the zone of tropical climate!

[126] That the plains were not lived in until so late a period – the plain of Sharon at a very late time! – was due not only to a environmental reason (malaria) but also to an economic one: the plains were unsuited to the ancient Israelite agriculture which was based upon 'wheat and barley, oil and wine' (II Chron. 2:15). See for this esp. D. Baly, *Geographisches Handbuch zur Bibel*, Neukirchen 1966, S. 61-69.

[127] For Alt's view of the *Landnahme*: Erwägungen über die Landnahme der Israeliten, *KS* I, München 1953, S. 126-75. *Cf.* also M. Weippert, *Die Landnahme der israelitischen Stämme*, S. 14-28. It is significant that no old traditions of *Landnahme* have been transmitted regarding the real nucleus of Israel, the central mountain country and ancient Gilead around Jabbok. For the matter of the waterproof plaster: W. F. Albright, *The Archaeology of Palestine*, London 1956⁴, p. 113. Also: P. W. Lapp, The 1968 Excavations at Tell Taᶜannek. *BASOR* 195 (1969) p. 2-49, esp. p. 33. See also the same author's remarks in *BASOR* 185 (1967) p. 14-15 and 33-34.

[128] For examples see again Von Wissmann, Zur Geschichte und Landeskunde. *E.g.* S. 234: ᶜ*RR*ᵐ = Clan-name, ᶜ*RRT*ᵐ = City-name. The inscription then speaks of 'the tribe of this town' (*o.c.* S. 30¹⁵). Then: *ṢRWḤ* = both clan-name and

The next parallel is this: while the clans come to the fore, the tribes remain vague. Frequently the translation 'tribe' for *bnw* is only to be explained by the subjective choice of the translator, in which it is often quantity that is decisive.[129] The historical process in South-Arabia quite certainly took place in such a manner that the actual political power remained with a few clans, who always had their original land (often with a stronghold!) to fall back upon. Clans rule over tribes.[130] It is plain that the tribes themselves are a later development in South-Arabia. According to Maria Höfner they owe their origin primarily to the formation of religious confederacies between various clans. These confederacies are closely bound up with a highly important aspect of the South-Arabian religion, *viz.* that the deity is the owner of the land. Tribe, territory and god coincide in so far, that the clans of a particular region must conclude a kind of religious community with the temple through the intermediary of the *mukarrib*, to be allowed to till the soil. Here the cult dominates over the political aspect.[131] W. Caskel, on the other hand,

city-name. S. 235: *ḤLḤLN* = name of a city, a clan and a county! Famous clans such as the Hamdamides, Marṭadides, Bataʿides, Garatides *etc.* also give their name to a county. (*o.c.* S. 64).

[129] A. Jamme, *Sabaean Inscriptions from Maḥram Bilqîs*, Baltimore 1962, translates *bnw* + (*ḏ* + name) sometimes as 'descendants of (the tribe of (name))', and sometimes as 'descendants of (the family of (name))'. This is a matter of exegesis. The actual word for tribe is *šʿb(m)*.

[130] Some examples from Jamme (see the previous note) may suffice:

559/1-2 'The people of Garat, ru(lers of the tribe Ḏamrî,) and their tribe Sumḥurâm, (have) dedicated ...'

560/1-3 'Ǧaw)ṯum ... r (and) ʿAslam and their son (ʾAbkari)b of (the clan) ʿA(y)-nawum, people of Gulmaylân ʿArgân, lead(ers of) the tribe Muyaddʿum ...'

562/1-2 '(Suḫ-)mân Yuhaṣbiḥ, descendant of (the clan) Bataʾ, masters of the house Wakilum, rulers of the tribe Sumʿay, third of Ḥumlân ...'

In such cases 'tribes' are often families owning much land, certainly in later times. The tribal name may then be derived from the territory they possess; often too it is simply a place- or clan-name. *E.g.* Naǧran, Raydân; *cf.* W. Caskel, *Ǧamharat an Nasab* II, S. 442, 484. A good illustration is formed by the powerful tribe ḏû-Raydân, once an independent kingdom. The name means: 'those from Raydân'. Raydân stands for the tribal territory. At the same time, however, the territory took its name from the powerful stronghold Raydân of Zafâr with the clan of the same name ruling the territory. J. Rijckmans, *L'Institution Monarchique en Arabie Méridionale avant l'Islam. (Maʿîn et Saba)*. Bibliothèque du Muséon, nr. 28, Leuven 1951, p. 158-162.

[131] Maria Höfner, War der sabäische Mukarrib ein 'Priesterfürst'? *WZKM* LIV (1957) S. 77-85. In Von Wissmann, Zur Geschichte und Landeskunde, S. 276-278 the following example: The realm of SMcY took its name from the god Samaʿ (afterwards superseded by Taʾlab). SMcY was originally the name of the district where the god Samaʿ was venerated, the clan bore the name Bani SMYᵉⁿ, and

remains convinced that the South-Arabian tribes were essentially geographical concepts.[132] Politically, one may say that in a later period the formation of tribes was much stimulated by the kings, in the first place with the intention of obtaining larger administrative districts, but probably also to lessen the power of certain clans. The result, however, was unadulterated feudalism, since large tracts of land were given to particular clans. In Saba, though, the concept 'tribe' remained an administrative term; they spoke of 'Saba and the tribes'. Qataban had a less pyramidal structure, but there too the tribes functioned as administrative units.[133] Very interesting in this context is the Sabaean list of eponyms already referred to, which shows how the function of eponym circulated among the three most powerful clans. The eponym was consecrated to the god, so that the bond between the three clans on which the tribe was founded, had a clear religious and cultic aspect.[134]

The South-Arabian states were never able to break the power of the clans; on the contrary, kingship was based upon it. The consequent feudalism first caused the downfall of the various kingdoms, and afterwards even the loss of all national independence.[135]

In conclusion we may say that under comparable physical and economic circumstances, a comparable social structure grew up in Palestine and in South-Arabia, based upon dwelling-place and blood-relationship. In both areas this is expressed by the concept 'clan'. The example of South-Arabia shows that such a form of organization is very well possible for a sedentary population. The effect of the old South-Arabian structure is still perpetuated in Yemen, where the organization is entirely tribal and a religious leader is really the only acceptable head of the state. Yemen has but one Beduin tribe![136]

Sam'ân was the name of the larger territory. This bond between the god and the people was founded on a covenant.

[132] W. Caskel, *Ǧamharat an-Nasab* II, S. 66. *Cf.* also J. Henninger in his important review of Caskel, in *Anthropos* LXI (1966) S. 852-870, espec. S. 861-862.

[133] N. Rhodokanakis, *Das öffentliche Leben in den alten südarabischen Staaten*, *Handbuch der altarabischen Altertumskunde*, Hrgb. v. D. Nielsen; Band I, Kopenhagen/Leipzig 1927, S. 109-142, espec. S. 117-140.

[134] A. G. Loundine (= Lundin) et J. Ryckmans, Nouvelles données sur la chronologie des rois de Saba et Ḏû-Raydân. *Le Muséon*, LXXVII (1964) p. 407-428. Idem, Die Eponymenliste von Saba. Wien 1965.

[135] H. von Wissmann, Ḥimyar: Ancient History. *Le Muséon*, LXXXVII (1964) p. 429-499.

[136] *I.e.* the Dahm, now the only Yemenite tribe with nomads. The name is a continuation of a tribal federation of antiquity: the Duhma. Von Wissmann, Zur Geschichte und Landeskunde, S. 88. Really the religious aspect dominates the political aspect with all Arab heads of state, whether they are called king, caliph or emir. Such, at least, is the theory.

155

Comparison with South-Arabia has answered the first part of our question by showing that a sedentary culture may well have a tribal organization. Now the second part remains to be answered, whether both in Palestine and South-Arabia this should not, after all, be explained from an earlier phase of their history, when these peoples were indeed nomadic.[137] The answer to such a possible objection is to be found in paragraph 2. It was pointed out there that nomadism and semi-nomadism are comparatively late phenomena and cannot be regarded as the proto-Semitic way of life. In the second millennium nomadism can only really be imagined for hunters and gatherers. Compare also what will have to be said *infra* p. 173-174 about the 'nomads' around Mari. Another clear resemblance with Israel lies in the fact that compared with the clans the concept 'tribe' remains vague and has a mainly geographical meaning. At the same time we observe a striking difference: we cannot find that in South-Arabia the tribes were seen as (fictitious) consanguineous groups, as they were in Israel.[138] This I think due to two factors; firstly the population of Palestine was far more ethnically mixed than that of South-Arabia. Secondly South-Arabia, with its feudal clans of nobility holding strong citadels, at an early date saw the rise of a 'power' apart from 'blood'. In Palestine this 'power' was exercised by the ethnically foreign Canaanite city-states. These prevented particular clans in Palestine gaining too much power, and that again strengthened mutual solidarity of the clans in a particular region.

4. The ethnic unity of the Israelites

This condition of affairs allows us to conclude that the social structure of ancient Israel in no wise *compels* us to presume that an earlier nomadic phase had existed, leaving the tribal system as its relic. On the contrary, the social structure of ancient Israel agrees extremely well with what we know of the political and economic circumstances of the time of the Judges. That the 'tribe' remains so vague, therefor requires a structural and not a historical explanation. The Israelite tribes were regional alliances of essentially independent clans. The real power resided with

[137] This was formerly always maintained for South Arabia also: *e.g.* F. Hommel, who viewed the culture of South Arabia as built on a substratum of nomadism, which he was constantly able to recognize. Geschichte Südarabiens im Umriss, S. 55. In the publications of Von Wissmann mentioned above there is no longer any trace of this!

[138] Indeed, the old genealogists were faced with tremendous problems when trying to fit the South Arabian tribes into a single great genealogical system with the Beduin tribes of North Arabia. See W. Caskel, *Ġamharat an-Nasab* I, S. 19-21.

the clans, or a few of them, but not at tribal level. The tribe was not something superimposed, and it had no head![139] When the elders of some tribe are mentioned, this is to be understood as the representatives of the principal clans and towns, as appears very plainly in I Sam. 30:26-31.

Now Noth did consider it right to ascribe an important part to the tribes as organs of over-all control. He even has a special office attached to the tribe, that of $n\bar{a}\acute{s}\bar{\imath}$'. It is true this office is not political, but cultic. Noth does not translate it as 'prince', for that translation is derived from the deviant use of the term $n\bar{a}\acute{s}\bar{\imath}$' by Ezekiel, who contrasts it with $m\underline{e}l\underline{e}\underline{k}$. Noth regards it as deriving from the expression $n\bar{a}\acute{s}\bar{a}$' $q\bar{o}l$, 'to raise the voice', and translates it as '$Sprecher$'. This 'speaker' is the representative of the tribe, especially at the central sanctuary.[140] It is only P that transmits this tradition, and in ch. II we already noted what Noth thinks of the reliability of P, in discussing Num. 1:5-16.[141] This exegesis of the title $n\bar{a}\acute{s}\bar{\imath}$', and especially the cultic significance attributed to it, is completely untenable. Such has been sufficiently shown by Van der Ploeg and Speiser.[142] The title of $n\bar{a}\acute{s}\bar{\imath}$' may be borne by various distinguished Israelites, and in the vast majority of cases it indicates a fully mundane, political function. It does seem that a certain 'position' was always required. According to Num. 7:2 and Josh 22:14 the $n^e\acute{s}\bar{\imath}$'$\bar{\imath}m$ had to be $r\bar{o}\acute{s}$ of a $b\bar{e}t$ '$\bar{a}\underline{b}$. Noth is right, then, that the translation 'prince' is definitely incorrect. Any person holding a high office in ancient Israel could be called $n\bar{a}\acute{s}\bar{\imath}$'. Since these functionaries were recruited from particular families, the term $n\bar{a}\acute{s}\bar{\imath}$' may be regarded not only as a title, but also as a social (here 'noble') predicate. Van der Ploeg rightly points out that the Semitic languages are usually possessed of a very rich vocabulary, so that it is not permissible to draw too many conclusions from the many synonyms, while in most cases it is not possible exactly to distinguish all concepts one from the other. One has the impression,

[139] The list of names in Num. 1:4-16 undoubtedly contains ancient material, but as we saw in ch. II, it was not transmitted in the original context. $Cf.$ also note 141. Though in itself the expression $n^e\acute{s}\bar{\imath}$'$\bar{e}$ $ma\underline{t}\underline{t}ot$ '$^ab\bar{o}tam$ is unique, it is entirely built up of elements current in P, $cf.$ Num. 1:47; 7:12; 17:21; 26:55; 32:28; 34:18; Josh. 14:1; 21:1. In nearly all cases the formulation varies a little. Therefore I cannot agree with Noth's reasoning that the expression here in 1:16 is so singular that it must have been taken over together with the list of names. ATD VII, $Das\ Vierte\ Buch\ Mose$, S. 20.

[140] M. Noth, $Das\ System\ der\ zwölf\ Stämme$, Exkurs III S. 151-162 und S. 97-98.

[141] Ch. II, p. 84. We saw there that the interpretation of the twelve names as $n^e\acute{s}\bar{\imath}$'$\bar{\imath}m$ is secondary!

[142] J. van der Ploeg, Les chefs du peuple d'Israël et leurs titres. RB LVIII (1950) p. 40-62. Les 'nobles' israélites. OTS IX, Leiden 1951, p. 49-64. Van der Ploeg still assumes that in the Pentateuch $n\bar{a}\acute{s}\bar{\imath}$' has the meaning of 'tribal chief'. E. A. Speiser, Background and Function of the Biblical Nāsī'. CBQ XXV (1963) p. 111-118.

though, that the word *nāśī'* had a rather solemn sound.[143] That P should use this word to indicate chiefs and representatives of tribes, is in itself not at all unusual. We have already seen that it is a social title rather than the name of a political function.[144]

Once again: the Israelite tribes were regional leagues of essentially independent clans. Tribe and people pass one into the other, and both are very difficult to define in general terms. Concepts such as 'race', 'culture', 'language' are far too vague to be really useful.[145] The same applies to the concept 'tribe'.[146] So the question is not only: what exactly

[143] Van der Ploeg, Les chefs du peuple d'Israël et leurs titres. *RB* LVIII (1950) p. 47-50.

[144] In Num. 25:14-15 *nāśī'* is really used as a title of nobility, quite parallel here with *rōš*.

[145] The concept 'tribe' is just as difficult to define and to handle as the concept 'race', Fried, *o.c.* p. 4. All the definitions which started from the concept of '*group*' proved incorrect! In the whole collection of *Essays on the Problem of Tribe* no definition has been attempted any more. The only form which might be defined is the phenomenon of the autonomous tribe. By autonomy political autonomy is meant. Therefore an autonomous unit or tribe is to be understood as a unit which has the right or the power of self-government. Gertrud Dole, Tribe as the autonomous unit. *Essays on the Problem of Tribe*, p. 92-96[4]. If any aggregates of independent groups are regarded as a unit on some other basis than political autonomy, they should possess the following feautures: "a) a linguistic unit; b) a local group; c) a culture unit or culture area; d) a conference (= co-operation in ceremonial activities); e) a coecon (= bound by economic interaction); f) a connubium." Gertrud Dole, p. 95-96.

[146] On p. 22 of Band I of his '*Die Beduinen*', M. von Oppenheim remarks: 'Die Beduinen leben in Stämmen'. Not a word more. It is obviously taken for granted that the concept of tribe is clear to everyone. Yet in that work (as in many others) 'tribe' comprehends extremely divergent entities: great tribal collectives of hundreds of thousands of people, having only a territorial and perhaps a vague juridical meaning, are called tribes just as well as quite tiny sub-tribes which are actual living communities. Moreover the statement is not correct. Von Oppenheim's collaborator E. Bräunlich has clearly shown how with the Beduin the tribal system functions on two levels: a biological (Bräunlich calls it 'somatic') and a historico-juridical level. (E. Bräunlich, Beiträge zur Gesellschaftsordnung der arabischen Beduinenstämme. *Islamica* VI (1934) S. 68-111 und 182-229). In a critical review of Von Oppenheim's work G. Rentz points out that this work, as Wüstenfeld's did before, gives the impression that every Beduin knows the composition and connexions of his tribe! Rentz even gives examples of Beduin in the interior of Saudi Arabia who were quite unable to place themselves in the schemes after the manner of Wüstenfeld and Von Oppenheim. (*Oriens* X (1957) p. 77-89.) For the Beduin, his 'tribe' hardly functions, he lives in his *ḥamūle*, the group of relations. Even the '*ašīre*, the political equivalent of the *ḥamūle*, is something vague and theoretical to him, so what interest will he take in the *ḳabīle*? See for this the aforesaid essay by Bräunlich and the schema in W. Dostal, Die Ṣulubba. *AVK* XI (1956) S. 34. In spite of the fact that the works of Wüstenfeld (F. Wüstenfeld, *Genealogische Tabellen der Arabischen Stämme und Familien*. 2 Bde. Göttingen 1852 und 1853.

is a tribe? but also: what is an *Israelite* tribe? This brings us to a field of many pitfalls, for it is extremely difficult to fit a definition to that which was formed by historical processes, as a people is. We have the famous definition of Herodotus with the criteria of blood, language and religion.[147] No sooner is the political aspect included, however, than the definition breaks down: a state cannot be defined in these terms! When the Athenians appeal to the Spartans, it is on the ground of a 'Hellenic' unity which goes beyond the state. Therefore Meinecke's famous distinction of *Kulturnation* (still defined with practically the same three criteria) and *Staatsnation* is really no more than an adaptation of the definition of Herodotus.[148]

Obviously the concept 'state' cannot serve to delimit peoples who have no state system, or only a weak one. But the general concept 'culture' is not satisfactory in the Semitic world either. It can be applied to some extent in the case of very large groups, such as the Arabs,[149] but it is no use at all for smaller and related groups. And that is the situation we have to deal with if we want to draw a line between the Israelites and the peoples who are their neighbours. The cultural differences were on a very small scale and usually remain outside our field of vision. In so far as we can observe them, one culture seems to merge into the other, so that conditions in larger Israelite centres were hardly different from those in non-Israelite ones. We must point out once more that archaeology has still failed to find definite aspects of material culture that could be specifically Israelite. Even religion, in this case Yahwism, does not help

And: *Die Wohnsitze und Wanderungen der Arabischen Stämme*. AGG, Band XIV, Göttingen 1869) and Von Oppenheim may certainly be called monumental, they have yet introduced a greater schematization and simplification of the problems than is admissible for the Arab world. Moreover, they have insufficiently observed the theoretical and preponderantly juridical character of the tribal systems and tribal genealogies. Meanwhile, these works have had a very considerable influence upon theories held about the social organization of ancient Israel, as at once appears from the bibliography of De Vaux, *Les Institutions de l'Ancien Testament*, part I. Fortunately Von Oppenheim's work was broken off and his collaborators Caskel and Dostal have taken other paths, which have resulted *int.al.* in the aforesaid new 'edition' (Caskel does not yet consider the time ripe for a truly scientific edition!) of the *Ǧamharat un-Nasab*. See further: W. Caskel, Der arabische Stamm vor dem Islam und seine gesellschaftliche und juristische Organisation. *Dalla Tribù allo Stato*, Rome 1962, p. 139-152. W. Montgomery Watt, The Tribal Basis of the Islamic State. *Dalla Tribù allo Stato*, p. 153-161. E. Peters, The Proliferation of Segments in the Lineage of the Bedouin of Cyrenaica. Reprinted in: Louise E. Sweet, *Peoples and Cultures of the Middle East*, vol. I, New York 1970, p. 363-398.
[147] *Histories* VIII, 144.
[148] Fr. Meinecke, *Weltbürgertum und Nationalstaat*. München/Berlin 1922[6], S. 1-22.
[149] *Cf.* for this G. E. von Grunebaum, The Nature of Arab Unity before the Islam. *Arabica* X (1963) p. 5-23.

sufficiently. The Calebites and Kenites, who are almost universally held to have worshipped Yahweh, were for a long time felt to be strangers. It was not until fairly late that they were enrolled in the genealogical system, and that was done upon political grounds.[150] Moreover, we know very little indeed of the Canaanite religions of the earliest Iron Age, or even in fact of the Israelite religion. This also holds good if one lets Yahwism be introduced from without at some particular moment, by the Rachel tribes, the Levites, the 'Moses group' or otherwise. Of the pre-Yahwistic 'religion of the patriarchs' that would then have to be postulated, and which in the period under discussion was certainly still in full vigour, we actually know extremely little![151] Yet it is possible that in the sharing of a cult the religion, whatever it was like, had a unifying inward effect and an outward effect of demarcation. We must of course not overlook that at the level of the clans specific clan cults such as the $zebah$ of I Sam. 20:19 had the same effect.[152] A methodical consideration here is that religion is rather the expression of a particular identity than its foundation. In my opinion it is an essential mistake in the religious explanation of the phenomenon of Israel that the possible role of religion, $c.q.$ the cult, has been overestimated in this context. Naturally no one can deny that a common cult may have a strongly unifying effect, but it should always be remembered that 'religion' is but one aspect of a culture, so that a particular culture and a particular social organization are its necessary presuppositions.[153] It is not the case that 'religion' spontaneously produces these, even if religious movements may sometimes pass into political ones.

[150] Cf. s.v. Kaleb in RGG³ (M. Noth) and H. Heyde, Kain der erste Jahwe-Verehrer. Arb. z. Th. I 23, Stuttgart 1965. Reference here is not so much to the Kenite hypothesis to explain the origin of Yahwism, as to the phenomenon of the Calebites and Kenites who, in spite of worshipping Yahweh, were only really incorporated into Israel at a late date.
[151] There is a very extensive literature regarding the patriarchs and their religion. Cf. B. Gemser, Vragen rondom de patriarchenreligie. Groningen 1958. F. M. Cross, Yahweh and the God of the Patriarchs. HThR LV (1962) p. 225-259. R. de Vaux, Les patriarches hébreux et l'histoire. RB LXXII (1965) p. 5-28. G. Fohrer, Geschichte der israelitischen Religion. Berlin 1969, S. 76-77.
[152] Contrary to what is often assumed, we do indeed know examples of common cults in which the ethnic and cultural differences are not smoothed out, but have a most essential function. For instance, the common initiation ceremonies of Bantu tribes and pygmies in Africa. For this and other such examples, see the already quoted essay by M. H. Fried, On the concepts of 'tribe' and 'tribal society'.
[153] For the function of religion in a culture, see the essay of C. Geertz, Religion as a Cultural System in the volume Anthropological Approaches to the Study of Religion. Ed. by M. Banton, London 1966. Cf. also the article by Th. P. van Baaren, Systematische Religionswissenschaft. NThT XXIV (1969) S. 81-88.

Of little more more use to us is another important element of culture: language. We have seen in ch. I that for a very long time it was customary to assume that after their arrival in Palestine the Israelites gave up practically the whole of their culture – including their language – to adopt that of Canaan.[154] As the close relationship between Hebrew and Canaanite came to be more and more clearly established,[155] such a change of language became a necessary presumption if one wished to uphold the idea that the Israelites came from elsewhere and were not autochthonous in Palestine.[156] Generally speaking, one may say that in recent years there is a growing inclination to assign a place of its own to Hebrew, and to regard it no longer as simply a Canaanite dialect or a 'mixed language' (*Mischsprache*). For it is becoming increasingly plain that Hebrew has preserved some traits which show that it is related to what is at present called 'Amorite' (always in quotation marks, since a corresponding ethnic entity 'Amorites' is difficult to demonstrate).[157]

[154] Actually this rests only on the text Isa. 19:18, which certainly does not state what it is often supposed to say, that the Israelites originally spoke a different language. This is then usually assumed to have been an Aramaic dialect.

[155] For the relationship of Hebrew and the Canaanite dialects, see especially the many studies of W. L. Moran and in particular the survey: The Hebrew Language in its Northwest Semitic Background. *BANE*, New York 1961, p. 54-72. Also: H. Cazelles, L'Hébreu. In: *Linguistica Semitica, Presente e Futuro*. Racc. da G. Levi della Vida. Roma 1961, p. 91-113. See also the same author on 'Amorite': Mari et l'Ancien Testament. *XVth RAI*, Paris 1967, p. 73-90. For this 'Amorite' in a wider context: W. G. Lambert, The Language of Mari. *XVth RAI*, Paris 1967, p. 29-38.

[156] This theory is carried to somewhat absurd lengths by Kl. Koch, Der Tod des Religionsstifters. *KuD* VIII (1962) S. 100-123. A full disquisition upon the supposed change of language in W. Baumgartner, Die hebräische Sprache und ihre Geschichte. *Studien zum Alten Testament und seiner Umwelt*. Leiden 1959, S. 208-239.

[157] A more 'Amoritic' placing of Hebrew, not as just a Canaanite dialect, is defended by O. Rössler, Die Präfixkonjugation Qal der Verba I^{ae} Nûn im Althebräischen und das Problem der sogenannten Tempora. *ZAW* LIV (1962) S. 125-141. Also, and strongly attacking the 'change of language'. A. Jepsen, Kanaanäisch und Hebräisch. *Akten des 25. Orientalistenkongresses*, Moskau 1962, S. 316-321. J. Blau (Some Difficulties in the Reconstruction of 'Proto-Hebrew' and 'Proto-Canaanite'. *In memoriam P. Kahle*. BZAW 103, Berlin 1968, p. 29-43) holds with an independent development of both proto-Canaanite and proto Hebrew. Blau takes far more account than was done formerly of local differentiation and intensive mutual influence of the various dialects. Around the Canaanite city-states in the plains and on the coast, this influence was naturally much stronger than in the interior where the Israelites lived somewhat apart. As a warning against premature reconstructions, Blau points out that the differences between the various dialects were greater when they began, than at the end of their development. Thus the change from á to ó, for instance, proves to have been a process which had not yet reached Ugarit. So also: Kl. Beyer, *Althebräische Grammatik*. Göttingen 1969,

These traits concern particulars of lexicography and formation of personal names. They afforded the material upon which Noth, on the theory that biblical Hebrew became a *Mischsprache* owing to the migration to Canaan, based his famous thesis that the proto-Israelites were proto-Aramaeans.[158] This thesis proved very premature, but it did bring Hebrew into the limelight once more.[159] It would seem best to follow Blau in assuming a separate development of Hebrew and Canaanitic, without insisting upon a separate origin. The geographical dissemination of Canaanites and Israelites, rightly pointed out by Jepsen, well agrees with this view. This distribution is also expressed in place-names. Those of a more 'Amorite' type are mainly found in the central mountain country of Palestine, in typically Israelite regions of old.[160] The two 'languages' cannot be followed far back into the second millennium, just as the origins of Aramaic are also (still) lost there. A linking up with the 'Amoritic' of the Mari letters in particular would be premature. But it must never be forgotten that 'Amoritic' is of West Semitic origin![161] Although then at present the distinctive character of Hebrew is more willingly recognized than formerly, and also its greater age, yet language cannot offer us a reliable criterion to mark off those who speak it as a unit distinct from other groups. In the first place it must once again be pointed out that in the Syro-Palestine area the isoglossic regions have frontiers of their own, which quite definitely do not coincide with the geographical, ethnic or political boundaries known to us. Secondly, dialectical differences among the Israelites prove to be at least as great as the differences with other groups.[162]

S. 11-14. Here special attention is paid to Hebrew as the Israelites' own language. Beyer's reconstruction and argumentation was much criticized, but received strong support of E. Vogt, Zur Geschichte der hebräischen Sprache. *Biblica* LII (1971) S. 72-78. *Cf.* also J. P. Lettinga, *De "Tale Kanaäns"*. Groningen 1971. On the "Amorites" in general: A. Haldar, *Who were the Amorites?* Leiden 1971. M. Liverani, The Amorites. *POTT*, London 1973, p. 100-133.

[158] M. Noth, *Die Ursprünge des alten Israel im Lichte neuer Quellen*. Arbeitsgemeinschaft für Forschung des Landes Nordrhein-Westfalen, Heft 94, Köln/Opladen 1961.
[159] D. O. Edzard, Mari und Aramäer? *ZA* XXII (1964) S. 142-150. *Cf.* also M. Weippert, *Die Landnahme der israëlitischen Stämme*. Göttingen 1967, S. 98.
[160] B. S. J. Isserlin, Place Name Provinces in the Semitic Speaking Ancient Near East. *Proceedings of the Leeds Philosophical Society* VII (1956) p. 83-110. Israelite and Pre-Israelite Place Names in Palestine. *PEQ* LXXXIX (1957) p. 133-145.
[161] In spite of the objections of W. von Soden (Zur Einteilung der semitischen Sprachen, *ZDMG* LVI (1960) S. 177-191), it seems to me methodically correct to side with S. Moscati and not to introduce the distinctions of the first millennium B.C.E. into the Northwest Semitic of the second millennium. This particularly concerns the distinction of 'Canaanite' and 'Aramaic'. (*An Introduction to the Comparative Grammar of the Semitic Languages*. Wiesbaden 1964, p. 7-8).
[162] See also above, note 114.

Since 'blood' is no use at all as a criterion, and we already saw that for larger entities such as 'tribe' and 'people' the concept of blood-relationship is altogether fictitious, the three norms of Herodotus prove unfit for our purpose. Yet it is possible to find two other norms which also follow from that which was summarized above regarding the concepts 'tribe' and 'people'. The terms *'connubium'* and *'forum'* determine these norms. The connubium as a binding or a dividing element in ancient Israel has already been extensively discussed,[163] and also the important role in this matter of the tribes in particular. The importance for the ancient Israelites and for many other Semitic peoples of the rules of connubium can hardly be overestimated.[164] It really will not do to reserve the striving after 'purity of race' to post-exilic times!

The second point requires to be examined a little more in full. By *'forum'* we understand its juridical aspect. Those are fellow tribesmen and fellow-countrymen who accept the same norms. The most concrete evidence of this is seen in the vendetta and the *ius talionis*: the tribe and the people constitute the widest circle within which one may count on solidarity and support. In this sense it may be said that the expression *gᵉḇūl yiśrā'ēl* has a juridical as well as a geographical meaning.[165] He who offends against the sacred tie uniting the group, the real or fictitious blood-relationship, must take to flight.[166] His own act has cut him off from his people. In this respect M. Noth is certainly right when he points out this ethico-juridical significance of the concept Israel.[167] Particularly in the expression *nᵉḇālā bᵉyiśrā'ēl*.[168] It is this recognition of the same norms which determines whether a man belongs to a certain people or not. The concept of *nomos* functioned in a like manner for the ancient Greeks, and research into the nature of Arab unity before the coming of Islam leads to similar results.[169] This concept of nomos is not only juridical

---

[163] See above, p. 146-148

[164] It is needless, perhaps, to remind the reader of the ancient tradition appearing in Num. 25. A cultic or religious explanation of the abhorrence of intercourse with 'strange women' does not seem sufficient. The official nomos given in v. 14-15 of the young couple Phinehas transfixed with his spear show, I think, that they were united in marriage.

[165] *Cf.* for instance I Sam. 27:1.

[166] B. van Oeveren, *De vrijsteden in het Oude Testament*. Kampen 1968.

[167] M. Noth, *Das System*, S. 100-108.

[168] Gen. 34:7; Josh. 7:15; Judg. 20:6; II Sam. 13:12; Jer. 29:23. Of these five passages, four concern sexual transgressions, showing how serious these were felt to be.

[169] A survey of the Greek concept of *nomos* and its development is found in H. Schaefer, *Staatsform und Politik*. Leipzig 1932, S. 144-175. Also: H. Strasburger, Der Einzelne und die Gemeinschaft im Denken der Griechen. *HZ* CLXXVII (1955) S. 227-248. H.Schaefer, Das Problem der griechischen Nationalität (1955). *Pro-*

and ethical, it may also have an esthetic content. Beduin prefer to raid other tribes than sedentary or non-*aṣīl* tribes. This is not only because then the booty is more attractive (camels), but especially because the 'acts of valour' performed only have a meaning before a 'forum' recognizing the same norms. One might say, then, that a people is determined by the limits within which something is accepted, appreciated, admired or disapproved. In this context Von Grunebaum speaks of an admiring, disapproving or censuring 'ever present public'.[170] Hence Meinecke's distinction may be adapted to say with Schaefer that the ancient Israelites, like the ancient Greeks, were rather a *'Gesellschafts-nation'* than a real *'Kulturnation'*.[171]

5. Consequences for the Conquest

Returning now to the question posed at the beginning of this chapter, it would seem an unavoidable hypothesis that Israelite unity was primarily of an ethnic nature, as indeed their own earliest traditions represent it to be. The Israelites formed a people because they were kept together by *connubium*, which presupposes a single social system, and by the recognition of a common *nomos*. We would only give a third place to the factor of history, although of course it naturally played a principal part in the formation of this people. Shared history, especially living together in a particular region as brought about by historical factors, naturally evoked a strong feeling of communal fortune. This was certainly so in a people such as Israel, whose time was mostly passed in passive submission to history, while action of historical importance on their part was rare.[172] Of course further factors such as language and religion increased the sense of solidarity while giving it expression. The next step is to establish at least a probability that Israel already formed an ethnic unity in the time of the Judges, as suggested above.

Since owing to lack of direct data we are entirely dependent on 'Ver-

bleme der Alten Geschichte. Gesammelte Abhandlungen und Vorträge. Göttingen 1963, S. 269-306. And: Politische Ordnung und individuelle Freiheit im Griechentum. *HZ* CLXXXIII (1957) S. 5-22. G. E. von Grunebaum, The Nature of Arab Unity before Islam. *Arabica* X (1963) p. 5-23.

[170] *O.c.* p. 23. Our use of the notion of *forum* here, brings us also quite close to the point of view of Gertrud Dole, *cf.* her contribution in the collection *Essays on the Problem of Tribe*. Seattle/London 1968.

[171] Das Problem der griechischen Nationalität, S. 298.

[172] The great importance of the historical factor was rightly stressed by Noth, *Geschichte Israels*, S. 12-13. His other factors, inhabiting a district together (insofar as this is not a purely historical factor) and the language, we consider far less convincing.

mutungen und Rückschlüsse'[173] for the beginning of Israelite habitation in Palestine, it is highly important that both starting-points and conclusions should be set down in clear terms. Let us once more repeat the conclusions:

1. The unity of the Israelites is of an ethnic nature.
2. The social structure of the Israelites gives no occasion to postulate their having come from a nomadic milieu. Israel's social structure during the so-called time of the Judges was entirely adequate to the economic and political condition of the people at that time.
3. The tribes were fairly vague territorial entities, groups of related clans, and did not have any particular political functions. Nor does this require an historical explanation.

It will be clear that these conclusions, if correct, have some very important consequences for the reconstruction of Israel's earliest history. Although the present study does not aim at a full discussion of the problems around the *Landnahme*, a few points will have to be touched upon. The principal consequence is, I think, that we should take the roots of Israel's history further back than especially Alt and Noth did, and lay most of the scene in Palestine.

The most important result of Alt's research into the territorial history of Palestine was, that he was able to demonstrate that the 'maps' of Palestine one might draw on the basis of the known Israelite settlements at the beginning of the Iron Age (that is *ca.* 1200 B.C.E.) and of the Canaanite cities do not overlap. The Israelites dwelt in the areas between the Canaanite town-states.[174] We know that Alt always explained this historically, for he was searching for a *'Landnahme'* as a *historical* process. But should the explanation not be economic rather than historical? If we suppose that around 1200 B.C.E. the Israelites had a mixed economy: agriculture on a rainfall basis and flock-keeping, then the pattern of their settlement on the map of Palestine is very well explained.[175] Specifically for products such as wine and barley, which we know to have been of great importance in the economy of ancient Israel,

---

[173] M. Weippert, *Die Landnahme*, S. 47.

[174] A. Alt, Die Landnahme der Israeliten in Palästina (1925). *KS* I, München 1953, S. 89-125. Erwägungen über die Landnahme der Israeliten in Palästina (1939). *KS* I, München 1953, S. 126-176. Also the excellent survey in Weippert, *o.c.* S. 14-28.

[175] See especially the extensive argumentation in Baly, *Geographisches Handbuch zur Bibel*, Neukirchen 1966, espec. S. 61-79. Also Y. Aharoni, *The Land of the Bible*, London 1967, p. 13-18. Aharoni justly points out that this economy is already supposed in Jacob's speech to his sons, Gen. 49. *O.c.* p. 176. apart from in Baly, one also finds a general physical geography of Palestine and the Middle East in W. B. Fisher, *The Middle East. A Physical, Social and Regional Geography*. London 1950.

there would hardly be other suitable locations in Palestine than were actually occupied by the Israelites. The same areas will also have offered very good natural pasturage for sheep.[176] If the division of the country between the Canaanite city-states, with their crafts and trades, and the Israelites was based on economic considerations, this also affords a better explanation for the peaceful symbiosis already found by Alt. There was no competition, but two economic sets lived together, neither being self-sufficient.

The pattern of settlement in itself therefore does not compel us to seek an historical explanation. Something else, however, does seem to point in that direction: habitation strikingly increases in these areas in the beginning of the Iron Age, as has been observed particularly in Transjordan and Galilee. Settlements appear in places that were formerly not or barely inhabited permanently.[177]

Without wishing to detract from these archaeological facts, their *historical* interpretation is subject to the following remarks.

1. The phenomena observed rest mainly upon surface exploration. An exception is the work of Aharoni, who carried out a few trial digs. This surface exploration can only yield provisional results. The examples of excavations producing results altogether different from what was expected after a surface exploration, are legion.

2. Nearly all the excavations carried out in Palestine and Syria con-

---

[176] M. Rowton, The Physical Environment and the Problem of the Nomads. *XVe RAI*, Paris 1967, p. 109-122. By the same author also: The Topological Factor in the Ḥapiru Problem. In: *Studies in honor of B. Landsberger*. AS XVI, Chicago 1965, p. 375-387.

[177] For Galilee in the first place Y. Aharoni, *The Settlement of the Israelite Tribes in Upper Galilee*. Jerusalem 1957 (Hebrew). Also by the same author: Galilean Survey: Israelite Settlements and their Pottery. *EI* IV (1956) p. 56-63. Problems of the Israelite Conquest in the Light of Archaeological Discoveries. *Antiquity and Survival* II 2/3 (1957) p. 131-150. *The Land of the Bible*, p. 200-202. Also interesting is the pre-war research of A. Saarisalo, published in *JPOS* IX (1929) and XI (1931). For Transjordan one must name first of all the work of N. Glueck. *Cf.* now his survey in *Archaeology and Old Testament Study*, ed. by D. Winton Thomas, p. 443-445. The steadily increasing information about habitation in the Bronze Age, such as that from Ammān, Deir 'Allā, Jalūl *etc.*, makes quite plain that Glueck's view that in the Middle and Late Bronze Age Transjordan was only inhabited by Beduin (*sic*), is far too simplistic.

The phenomenon of the new settlements is not, though, confined to these areas. *Cf.* for Benjamin, K. D. Schunck, *Benjamin*, S. 21. For the central mountain country: R. Bach, *ZDPV* LIV (1958) S. 41-54. For the Shephelah, A. Saarisalo, Topographical Researches in the Shephelah. *JPOS* XI (1931) p. 98-104. In a survey on p. 103 (in the periodical erroneously: 19) two places are named with Early Iron I ware, where there was no former settlement. This EI I corresponds to what Saarisalo found in Galilee. See further M. Weippert, *Die Landnahme*, S. 130-131.

cerned the *tell* of a sizable town. Attention was paid especially to the promising large old Canaanite city-states.

We have hardly any archaeological knowledge of the countryside! It is worth recalling here that the choice of the Dutch site Deir 'Allā in Jordan was determined by the desire to study the transition from the Bronze to the Iron Age on a little *tell* in the country. That Deir 'Allā proved not to have been a town in the Bronze Age but a very large open sanctuary, was therefore in a sense a miscalculation. What we do know, however, of the countryside in Palestine, which is the hill country, shows that we must take account of a different archaeological situation there: far more stone and wood were used, and the former material especially will have been used and reused, so that the various periods left far fewer traces. Thus real *tells* could not easily develop there, and also the material of the mud-bricks – the clay was usually sun-dried – often eroded together with the humus layer and was washed away.[178]

3. The pottery that appears in these new settlements of around 1200 B.C.E. is certainly much more primitive than that of the Bronze Age, but it is usually forgotten that the process of degeneration of the LBA pottery already set in in the Late Bronze Age itself![179] The important point here is that there is no essential difference between this pottery and that found in the towns, including those towns which remained in Canaanite possession, such as Megiddo.[180] Where infiltration is seen of really new pottery, which cannot be derived from earlier LBA types, this takes place already in the fourteenth century.[181]

[178] See also the words of warning of Miss Kenyon, *AHL*² p. 246!
[179] Miss Kenyon, *AHL*² p. 209.
[180] A type frequently appearing in this context is that with the *collared rim*, cf. W. F. Albright, *Archaeology of Palestine*, p. 118. Weippert rightly characterizes this as 'eine Mode-erscheinung der beginnenden Eisenzeit'. (*Landnahme*, S. 130). Aharoni's reaction: 'Whoever has handled this pottery in excavations or in surveys can hardly doubt its distinctness and difference from the previous wares. Its sudden and almost exclusive appearance among the ruins of the Canaanite cites and at newly-founded settlements, mainly in the hilly regions, is certainly more than a deterioration of Canaanite fashions' (*IEJ* XIX [1969] p. 61) is irrelevant. The essential point is that this pottery also appears in places where Canaanite culture is re-established.
[181] For this, H. J. Franken, *Tell Deir 'Allā, vol. I*, Leiden 1969, p. 122. And M. Dothan, The Excavations at 'Afula. *'Atiqot* I (1955) p. 19-71. A good example of this difficulty is seen in J. L. Kelso's report of the excavations at Bethel. Practically at a breath, we are authoritatively told that the town built up after the destruction at the end of the 13th century was so different from the one before that it simply has to be ascribed to the Israelites, and that the ordinary pottery, the cooking-pot in particular, remained the same! *The Excavation of Bethel*. AASOR XXXIX, Cambridge Mass. 1968, p. 48 and 63.

4. We have already seen that Albright's reasoning with regard to the introduction of the waterproof cistern in this period cannot be maintained.[182] On the other hand the introduction of iron as a comparatively cheap material will have made the mountain country much more accessible. We think of iron picks and ploughs.

5. While the number of usually small settlements in the highlands between the territories of the old Canaanite city-states noticeably increased, a great many of these city-states grew smaller or disappeared. Although it is unlikely that after the decay of their towns the inhabitants went back to the country, there must have been a reverse effect: excess population in the country could no longer be absorbed by the big towns. Here again we must stress the fact that the decay of the large LBA cities began long before the final phase of *ca.* 1250-1200, as clearly appeared from the excavations of Hazor.[183] Now Gordon Childe already pointed out that the large-scale introduction of iron greatly improved conditions of production. One of the consequences was the opening up of new areas for agriculture, and owing to the larger food supply a fairly rapid increase in population.[184]

6. As a final conclusion, we would repeat that the phenomenon in question is far more general than is usually assumed. The reason for that is, once more, that Palestine is the only country of the Levant where we have any archaeological information regarding the highlands. For good measure, let us point out that the phenomenon of the new settlements is also found in the Shephelah, which was certainly not Israelite at this time![185]

Taking account of these six objections, one can only say that there are no convincing archaeological arguments for any large-scale invasion by a new population group at this time.[186] Another matter is that archaeologists are beginning more and more to drop the habit of automatically ascribing changes in pottery styles, or even in pottery techniques,

---

[182] See above. p. 153.

[183] *Cf.* Y. Yadin, The Fifth Season of Excavations at Hazor, 1968-1969. *BA* XXXII (1969) p. 53.

[184] V. Gordon Childe, *What happened in History*. London 1952.

[185] See above, note 177.

[186] That this invasion is usually dated *c.* 1220 is due to a methodically incorrect combination of the most suitable date for the exodus from Egypt and the climax of the wave of destruction that passed over Palestine in this period, culminating in the destruction of Hazor, *c.* 1225 B.C.E. *Cf.* Y. Aharoni, *Land of the Bible*, p. 206-208 and also M. Noth, Hat die Bibel doch recht? *Festschrift für Günther Dehn*, Neukirchen.

to new elements in the population.[187] Naturally new groups came into Palestine in the disturbed times between the Bronze and the Iron Age – we need only think of the Philistines – but the dominant picture suggests rather greatly changed conditions of living for an essentially constant population. The hypothesis of the ethnic unity of the Israelites cannot therefore be supported by the argument that as a group they demonstrably 'came from abroad'.

Now we have the paradoxical situation that Noth will not hear of a primarily ethnic unity, while yet attaching very much importance to the '*Landnahme*' in one form or another. Yahwism and Palestine formed Israel, and in his eyes these there are inseparable. The origins of the Israelites before the Conquest – Noth calls these proto-Israelites – are lost in a common prehistory with other Aramaic peoples such as Ammonites, Moabites, Edomites and the real Syrian little Aramaic states. That, following Alt, this Conquest is viewed as a fairly lengthy process of sedentarization, makes no difference to its essential function: Israel comes into being through and after the Conquest. What counts is, that groups which formerly had hardly anything in common, were now as it were forced into community by the historical conditions they shared in. The hypothesis of the amphictyony is then applied to explain why this 'unity through action' was not lost in times of peace and increasing prosperity.

Although there is a lot of truth in this view of the earliest history, which is supported by judicious use of method, there are two serious objections to it. In the first place, even if one allows a very ample period for the Conquest, the time between that and the period when Israel acts as a unit, be it not yet as a politically organized unit, is very short. Of

---

[187] See also for this the warning words of M. Weippert, *Landnahme*, S. 129-131. Also: W. Y. Adams, Invasion, Diffusion, Evolution? *Antiquity* XLII (1968) p. 194-215. B. G. Trigger, *Beyond History: The Methods of Prehistory*. New York/ London 1968. A warning is also in place here against the manner in which history and archaeology are combined in the work of P. W. Lapp, gifted archaeologist as he was. Cf. his *Biblical Archaeology and History*. Cleveland 1969. With regard to the *Landnahme* problem Lapp maintained his earlier opinion that the archaeological facts allow us to conclude to an entry under Joshua. Cf. also his The Conquest of Palestine in the Light of Archaeology, *Concordia Theological Monthly* XXXVIII (1967) p. 283-301). Lapp's reasoning was also mainly based on the so-called 'Israelite fossil-ware' from Hazor *int. al.*, but we have already seen that this ware was also found in places where the Israelites did not settle. Another argument was taken from Deir 'Allā. The identification of the new-comers after the destruction of the L.B.A. sanctuary as Israelites led by Joshua is entirely an effect of Lapp's imagination. He obviously thought the simplest solution was to attribute this to Joshua. Dr. Franken, however, only speaks of 'semi-nomadic tribes'. Cf. *VT* XIV (1964) p. 418-420, and *Excavations at Deir 'Allā, vol. I*, p. 20-21.

course there was a gradual transition from the period of entry to the time of the Judges, but one cannot stretch this beyond one-and-a-half or two centuries. We must seriously question whether this period, in such troubled times, was long enough for historical circumstances to fashion totally different groups into a single people.[188] In the second place we agree this time with W. F. Albright, when he says in discussing Alt's treatment of the traditions of the patriarchs and the stories of the entry into Palestine: 'I cannot accept his approach to the traditions of the Mosaic period and the Conquest of Canaan, where he atomizes tradition by tying it to local sites, and by giving geography priority over ethnic grouping. In general Alt's work on Moses and Joshua ... suffers from unwillingness to recognize the historical continuity of the Hebrew people ...'[189] Obviously these two points are intimately connected!

This reasoning of Alt and Noth is taken up again by Weippert, though he enters more fully into the Israelites not being autochthonous: 'Die These, dass die israelitische Landnahme wesentlich eine soziale Umwälzung innerhalb der kanaanäischen Gesellschaft der ausgehenden Spätbronzezeit ohne ein statistisch ins Gewicht fallenden Zuwanderung von aussen gewesen sei, übersieht das zu allen Zeiten lebendige Bewusstsein Israels, im Lande Kanaan nicht autochthon zu sein. Dass sich dieses Bewusstsein in den uns vorliegenden Quellen in der Regel in kerygmatischen Formulierungen ausdrückt, ist kein Grund, ihm historische Relevanz abzusprechen. Dies ist um so weniger erlaubt, als das Alte Testament selbst ja noch, wie wir gesehen haben, Andeutungen darüber bewahrt hat, dass die in das Kulturland eintretenden "Israeliten" aus dem Lebenszusammenhang der Steppe kamen und ursprünglich nicht Ackerbauer, sondern Kleinviehzüchter waren.'[190] Weippert's view that the

---

[188] If one places the *Conquest* of the Leah tribes as early as the Amarna period, then one is forced to assume a second *Conquest*, as already proposed by Steuernagel and indeed accepted by Noth. Yet this gives rise to new problems. It would be contrary to the fact that the Rachel tribes were always regarded as the nucleus of Israel, and their region as the core of the land of Israel. Both Steuernagel's idea that Leah tribes formerly lived in the central mountain country, and Noth's attempt to make out Benjamin to be a Leah tribe, have failed. Moreover, one must question whether the function Noth ascribes to the *Conquest* is consonant with its taking place twice.

[189] W. F. Albright in a review of Alt's Kleine Schriften. *JBL* LXXV (1956) p. 172.

[190] Weippert, *o.c.* S. 102-103. Weippert criticizes the essay 'The Hebrew Conquest of Palestine' by G. E. Mendenhall (*BA* XXV [1962] p. 66-87). We shall return to Mendenhall's 'sociological' solution, see below p. 186. In his article Fragen des israelitischen Geschichtsbewusstseins, *VT* XXIII (1973) S. 415-442, Weippert argues that the notion of not being autochtonous, together with the understanding of the country in which they were living as the most important divine gift, are the kernel of Israel's notion of history!

primary object of the traditions of the patriarchs is to provide an ideological foundation for the Israelites' living in Palestine, is absolutely correct.[191] At the same time this means that their not being autochthonous is connected with the patriarchs and not with an entry in the time of Joshua![192] This not being authochthonous, having come from elsewhere, has first of all a juridical function in the Old Testament and only in the second place an aetiological one. With Weippert, however, we must at once postulate that this juridical function, in its indeed often kerygmatic form, does not in itself mean that these traditions have no historical significance. In my opinion the time of the patriarchs does indeed form part of Israel's history, and it is not right to call them 'proto-Israelites' or 'Israelites' in quotation marks.

6. The milieu of the patriarchs

Although, generally speaking, the dates given to the time of the patriarchs cover a period of more than 800 years, *i.e.* from the beginning of the EB - MB period around 2200 B.C.E. until the Amarna time *ca.* 1400 B.C.E.,[193] it seems pretty certain that the setting of the stories of the patriarchs is Syria and Palestine of the Middle and Late Bronze Age.[194]

[191] His criticism of J. Hoftijzer, *Die Verheissungen an die drei Erzväter*, Leiden 1956, is justified insofar as it concerns the way Hoftijzer connects the traditions of the patriarchs with the exodus traditions of Sinai. We do, though, agree with Hoftijzer in believing the traditions of the 'promised land' and the entry to date from a period when things became difficult in the old country.
[192] Deut. 26:5; Josh. 24:2-3. See espec. H. Seebass, *Der Erzvater Israel*. BZAW 98, Berlin 1966.
[193] The various standpoints and the chief archaeological data are well summarized by M. L. Zigmond, Archaeology and the 'Patriarchal Age' of the Old Testament. *Explorations in Cultural Anthropology. Essays in Honor of G. P. Murdoch.* New York 1964, p. 571-598. The whole complex of questions around the patriarchs is at present intimately linked with the way the *linguistic* phenomenon of 'Amorite' is treated in archaeology and history. For this first of all: K. M. Kenyon, *Amorites and Canaanites*. London 1966. Also: C. H. J. de Geus, The Amorites in the Archaeology of Palestine. *Ugarit Forschungen*, vol. III (1971) p. 41-60.
[194] This is at the moment the *communis opinio*. Especially the publications of R. de Vaux have been very influential, *e.g.* his Les patriarches hébreux et l'histoire. *RB* LXXII (1965) p. 5-28. Further the abundant material assembled in his *Histoire ancienne d'Israël*, vol. I, p. 151-273. When, however, Weippert remarks: "Diese Ueberlieferungen aber reflektieren nach allgemeinem Konzenns die Verhältnisse der (Mittel- und) Spätbronzezeit..." (*o.c.* S. 103), this means in fact a choice for a lower date than is found in most works on this period! H. Seebass, *Der Erzvater Israel*, Berlin 1966, places the patriarchs in the second half of the Middle Bronze Age (archaeologically MBA IIb-c). *Cf.* also Kenyon, *AHL²* p. 162-163. Very recently Th. L. Thompson argues for an Iron Age date for the

This date is also best suited to make use of the parallels with the 'Amorite' milieu along the Middle Euphrates. The Middle Bronze Age was a period when Palestine and Syria were much involved together, and one may even say they had the same material culture.[195] In the Late Bronze Age on the other hand the strong Egyptian domination – though interrupted in the Amarna period – and the formation of larger political entities with a consequent cultural differentiation undoubtedly made free traffic and ethnic migration much more difficult.[196] For this reason also I think we should take it as a fact that the Israelites had been living longer in Palestine than was formerly often assumed because of various Conquest theories.

By this we do not of course mean to say there was no eisodus of the exodus group! But this group itself undoubtedly originated largely in Palestine, as the Old Testament indeed explicitly tells us. They rejoined their relations. Unfortunately we still cannot identify this group.[197] The so-called 'desert traditions' tell us nothing of an earlier stage in Israel's history; they can, at least according to Fritz, be entirely explained from the situation in which especially the southern tribes found themselves. For part of these tribes lived in the marginal strip between the desert and the sown.[198]

Noth and Weippert see the unmistakable relationship to the 'Amorites' in this way, that a group of these 'Amorites' moved – back – westward, the precursors of the later Israelites being among them. In our

patriarchal stories. The stories themselves he considers not historical. As his work was written between 1969 and 1971, he did not know my arguments in *UF* III. However, I think that most of his conclusions are in agreement with mine since I also see the "Amorite" milieu of the Genesis narratives as an autochthonous Palestinian development. On the problem of the "historicity" I remain somewhat more positive. Th. L. Thompson, *The Historicity of the Patriarchal Narratives.* BZAW 133, Berlin 1974.

[195] J. van Seters, *The Hyksos.* New Haven/London 1966, p. 9. Miss Kenyon, *AHL*[2] p. 162.

[196] M. Liverani, Implicazzioni sociale nella politica di Abdi-Ashirta di Amurru. *RSO* XL (1965) p. 267-277. G. Buccellati, *Cities and Nations of Ancient Syria.* Roma 1967. W. Helck, Zur staatlichen Organisation Syriens im Beginn der 18. Dynastie. *AfO* XXII (1968/69) S. 27-29.

[197] See above, p. 160.

[198] 'Die Wüstentraditionen sind als Einzelgeschichten im Bereich der Südstämme entstanden und weitergegeben worden. In den einzelnen Ueberlieferungen spiegeln sich die Erfahrungen der Südstämme, die das judäische Gebirge, die Schefela und den Negeb bewohnten. Da sich in den Wüstentraditionen keinen Erinnerungen an die Zeit vor der Landnahme erhalten haben, müssen diese Traditionen hinsichtlich der Wohnsitze und der Geschichte dieser Stämme in der Zeit zwischen Landnahme und Staatenbildung befragt werden'. V. Fritz, *Israel in der Wüste.* Marb. Th. St. VII, Marburg 1970, S. 101.

opinion in Palestine also the not really Canaanite and urbanized part of the population belonged to this 'Amorite' Syro-Palestinian culture of the Middle Bronze Age.[199] It was from this group that Israel developed. That particular persons or clans maintained contact with related groups on the Upper Euphrates is not exceptional in this period. Moreover it is comprehensible when we see that the stories of the patriarchs continue in the same ecological milieu.

The issue has been much confused by the habit of giving the 'Amorite' population of eastern Syria, known to us int.al. from the archives of Mari, the name of *nomads*.[200] True, everyone immediately adds that they mean *semi-nomads*, but they then go on to treat the 'Amorites' as flock-keeping nomads pure and simple. It is the unfortunate result of the deeply rooted habit of seeking the original milieu of the Semites in the desert. When this postulated original milieu was actually uncovered in Mari, the fences were down.[201] We do not of course mean to deny the unmistakable resemblances between the 'Amorite' milieu of the inhabitants of the steppe belts and the hill country of the ancient Near East, of which we have at last obtained a clear picture from the archives of Mari, and the milieu which the earliest traditions of Israel seem to postulate.[202] Our objection is primarily to the one-sided historical interpretation of these resemblances, as if they could only be explained by borrowing or migration! Also to using these resemblances as 'external

---

[199] Just how these people stand to the Amorites named in the Old Testament as one of the pre-Israelite population groups of Palestine is not yet clear. We must draw no premature conclusions here. Two possible theories are brought forward in C. H. J. de Geus, The Amorites in the Archaeology of Palestine. *Ugarit Forschungen*, vol. III (1971) p. 41-60.

[200] *Cf.* the standard work of J. R. Kupper, *Les nomades en Mésopotamie au temps des rois de Mari*. Paris 1957. This period is also treated by Weippert under the title 'Die Nomaden des 2. Jahrtausend'. For relevance to the patriarchs, see esp. R. de Vaux, Les Patriarches Hébreux et les découvertes modernes. Paragraph VII 'Le milieu social' and Par. VIII 'Les coutumes sociales et juridiques'. *RB* LVI (1949) p. 5-36.

[201] These ideas and the presupposition they are founded on were already fully discussed above, p. 125-127.

[202] Of the already very extensive literature in this field I will only mention: H. Cazelles, Mari et l'Ancien Testament. *XVth RAI*, Paris 1967, p. 72-90. A. Malamat, Mari and the Bible. Some Patterns of Tribal Organisation and Institutions *JAOS* LXXXII (1962) p. 143-150. Aspects of Tribal Societies in Mari and Israel. *XVth RAI*, Paris 1967, p. 129-138. M. Noth, Mari and Israel. In: *Geschichte und Altes Testament, Festschrift für A. Alt*. Tübingen 1953, S. 127-153. Remarks on the sixth volume of Mari texts. *JSS* I (1956) p. 322-333. *Die Ursprünge des alten Israel im Lichte neuer Quellen*. Köln/Opladen 1961. W. von Soden, Jahwe, 'Er ist, Er erweist sich'. *WO* III (1966) S. 177-186. Also the survey in M. Weippert, *Die Landnahme der israelitischen Stämme*, S. 102-123.

evidence' and then neglecting to make a thorough historical literary examination of the patriarchal traditions themselves.

Since the milieu of Mari also plays an important part in the argumentation of Weippert, we must briefly describe it.[203] The milieu of the 'Amorites' of Mari is a) not really nomadic and b) their economy is not solely based on flock-keeping.

That the 'Amorites' around Mari, and especially the Jaminites, did indeed possess settled dwelling-places, has now become certain.[204] It simply will not do to play down these data by constantly referring to 'temporary nomad encampments' or 'villages provided by the authorities to hasten sedentarization', although no doubt such forms of habitation also existed. Of course it is quite indisputable that the Jaminite economy was largely based on their great flocks of sheep, which they were always taking to new pastures. There is equally clear evidence, however, that the Jaminites grew barley. The picture thus formed seems to me to be that of shepherds spending a large part of the year 'out with the flocks', while their wives and children and the older people remain at the home base, which is even capable of being defended.[205] In this context it is

[203] R. de Vaux, Les patriarches Hébreux et les découvertes modernes. *RB* LVI (1949) p. 5-36. J. R. Kupper, *Les nomades en Mésopotamie au temps des rois de Mari*. Paris 1957. Le rôle des nomades dans l'histoire de la Mésopotamie. *JESHO* II (1959) p. 113-127. G. Dossin, Les Bédouins dans les textes de Mari. *L'Antica Società Beduina*. Roma 1959, p. 35-52. D. O. Edzard, Altbabylonisch *nawûm*. *ZA* NF XIX (1959) S. 168-173. H. Klengel, Halbnomaden am mittleren Euphrat, *Das Altertum* V (1959) S. 195-205. Zu einigen Problemen des altvorderasiatischen Nomadentums. *ArOr* XX (1962) S. 585-596. Sesshafte und Nomaden in der alten Geschichte Mesopotamiens. *Saeculum* XVII (1966) S. 205-222. Halbnomadischer Bodenbau im Königreich von Mari. *VBVHS*, Berlin 1968, S. 75-82. *Geschichte Syriens im 2. Jahrtausend V.U.Z.* Espec. Teil II, Berlin 1969, S. 11-15. *Zwischen Zelt und Palast*. Leipzig 1972. A. Haldar, *Who were the Amorites?* Leiden 1971. J. T. Luke, Observations on ARMT III: 39. *JCS* XXIV (1971) p. 20-23. M. B. Rowton, The Topological Factor in the Ḫapiru Problem. *Studies in Honor of B. Landsberger*. AS XVI Chicago 1965, p. 375-387. The Physical Environment and the Problem of the Nomads. *XVth RAI*, Paris 1967, p. 39-50. Soziale und Wirtschaftliche Verhältnisse von Mari. *VBVHS*, Berlin 1968, S. 83-90. (*Cf*. also the two publications by Rowton mentioned in note 215). M. Liverani, The Amorites. *POTT*, London 1973, p. 100-133. Th. L. Thompson, The Historicity of the Patriarchal Narratives, Berlin 1974, treats the social, juridical or economic organization of the patriarchs only in relation to the Nuzi-texts.

[204] It is indeed plainly acknowledged by Weippert, who speaks of 'dauerhafte Siedlungen'. The principal evidence is to be found most conveniently in his *Die Landnahme*, S. 116-117.

[205] In spite of Weippert's doubt, *o.c.* S. 115, we draw attention here to D. O. Edzard's remarks in his article on the concept *nawûm*. *Nawûm* and *ālum* are in a way contrasted: *ālum* may indicate any place where the tribe has a permanent or

important to note that the Accadian word for 'tent', *kuštārum*, has not so far appeared in any of the Mari texts![206] The attempt to explain the fairly common word *ālum* as *'ōhel* – tent, can be dismissed out of hand.[207] We have already tried to show that social structure or certain religious conceptions, such as here 'gods of our fathers' who remain anonymous, form no indication to prove that a particular way of living is nomadic or not.[208] Thus the god Martu is indeed the god of the Amurrū, but he is in no wise a typical god of nomads. Nor does the special worship of Sin on the Upper Euphrates prove anything;[209] this god was worshipped by purely agrarian groups. On the other hand the typically 'Amorite' god Dagān is a real god of the grain![210] In my opinion, then, G. E. Mendenhall is not only completely justified in his protest against most 'parallels' with present-day Beduin and their culture, but also in remarking that 'Kupper, *Les nomades en Mésopotamie* has greatly overestimated the amount of true nomadism in the Mari period. Much of the material refers simply to the seasonal transhumance of sheepherding villagers.'[211] Kupper's choice of the word 'nomads' has caused much confusion. Indeed, I think that on this point Weippert goes too far in his controversy with Mendenhall.[212]

temporary settlement; *nawûm* refers to the flock and includes the members of the tribe accompanying it.

[206] This was already pointed out by J. R. Kupper, *Les nomades en Mésopotamie*, p. 14. *Cf.* for *kuštārum* Von Soden *AHW*, Sp. 517 und *MSL* IV 117/119. In the Early Babylonian period there is indeed a place-name Kuštāru in the Middle Euphrates region; we note that it is mentioned in a context of grain-supplies! Rivca Harris, The Archives of the Sin Temple in Khatajah (Tutub). *JCS* IX (1955) esp. p. 39 and 65-66 (26:8).

[207] As M. Weippert rightly does, *o.c.* S. 116[3].

[208] See above, note 93.

[209] H. Klengel suggests that the Moon-god owed his worship especially to the facility of nocturnal orientation, *Saeculum* XVII (1966) S. 215. Yet comparative religion shows worship of the moon to be more at home in an agrarian complex. M. Eliade, *Traité d'histoire des Religions*, Paris 1933, chapitre IV.

[210] W. von Soden points this out in J. Henninger, *Lebensraum und Lebensformen*, S. 54.

[211] The Hebrew Conquest of Palestine. *BA* XXV (1962) p. 69[7].

[212] *O.c.* S. 122. I must also object to Weippert's frequent use of the disparaging remarks made by the Mesopotamian aboriginal and sedentary population about the inhabitants of the steppes, whom they regarded as hardly more than semi-barbarians. This argumentation seems methodically very risky to me: such remarks usually tell us more of the speaker than of those to whom they refer. The sometimes equally disparaging remarks in the book of Genesis regarding the way of life in the towns – if not anachronisms – show that the aversion felt by these two groups was mutual. G. Wallis, Die Stadt in den Ueberlieferungen der Genesis. *ZAW* LXXVIII (1966) S. 133-147.

There are really four geographical zones to be distinguished in Syria and Mesopotamia, in which different geophysical conditions led to the establishment of different economies.

In the first place there is the region of the big rivers and of the oases, where agriculture by irrigation developed. This form of agriculture requires an essentially sedentary population. Most of the large towns also lie in this region.

Secondly, the 250 mm (precipitation) isohyete goes right across the Middle East. Roughly, it runs from Moab, curving out to the right over the Djebel Druze, along the Orontes to the north and then turns, roughly again, along the line Hama, Aleppo, Ḥarrân to the east. In the country west and north of this line a rainfall-based agriculture is possible, and the natural landscape, especially at the higher levels, is much wooded.[213]

Within the semicircle described by the 250 mm isohyete, the 100 mm isohyete runs almost concentrically. The strip of country between the two is at present about 50 km wide in the west, and some 100 to 200 km in the north and east. Where local conditions are favourable, agriculture is still possible in this strip, although as a rule there is only one harvest, in spring. Hence sheep-farming was the economic mainstay here.

The fourth distinct region is formed by the actual desert, which begins where precipitation is less than 100 mm a year.

Although the climate is not likely to have undergone important changes since about 2300 B.C.E., the landscape has altered considerably. Thus the fertile alluvial land in Mesopotamia was lost, mainly through salification. The zone of more than 250 mm precipitation will have been chiefly wooded in antiquity. Increased indications are found that deforestation in his region only started to become serious in the course of the Iron Age.[214] In the steppe zone between the 250 mm and the 100 mm isohyete there must also have been far more vegetation than to-day, while in antiquity this zone may also have been wider than it is now. According to Rowton this steppe must have been covered alternately with wood-land, 'maquis' and lower vegetation.' Such a variegated aspect is usually called a 'park landscape'. Obviously this steppe belt was well provided with game, while offering excellent pasturage and some opportunity for agriculture. Now one must not of course imagine the isohyetes as constituting real frontiers. Within the region of the 250 mm isohyete there were also islands of steppe-like appearance, and within the 100 mm isohyete there were oases and

[213] An exception is the steppe-like enclave of the Lower Jordan and the area around the Dead Sea. There are, though, a few oases here: Jericho, En-Gedi. For lit. see the notes 173, 175, 176, and 203.
[214] The first clear traces of erosion are dated in Anatolia around 500 B.C.E. M. B. Rowton, The Physical Environment and the Problem of the Nomads, p. 111.

local areas with increased or diminished rainfall. The two zones were interlocked. Unfortunately the small amount of precipitation and the quickly activated erosion made the vegetation very vulnerable. Once damaged by man (mainly by over-grazing and as a result of crop rotation) it was unable to re-establish itself. This process must already have been clearly observable in the Bronze Age.

The real 'Amorite' nucleus, the region around Palmyra and the Djebel Bišrī, lies entirely in this belt of steppe. Palestine proper, though, largely falls outside it, except for the Lower Jordan and the Negev. As we saw that no straight line can be drawn between the two zones, we must also take account of the way their economic circumstances gear into each other. Rowton speaks of an economy characterized by dichotomy, by interaction between town and steppes.[215] This dichotomy may take various forms. The two most important are:

a) A plain symbiosis between town and tribe(s), arable land and steppe. This symbiosis usually rests upon compacts and upon the fact that neither of the two economies is really self-sufficient. The economically stronger culture of the town is in a manner balanced by the greater political and military power of the inhabitants of the steppe. In a number of cases, too, the ruling dynasty comes from the 'Amorite' milieu.[216]

b) Another style of life, sometimes combined with the above, is the periodically divided: half the year fully sedentary, while during the other half the men at least are out with the flocks. This second form is the more adapted to the steppe belt; the first is mostly found where there are areas of steppe near large towns.

We see from the foregoing that one may not too hastily identify the milieu of the patriarchs with that of Mari. Those who do so, have special reasons e.g. for placing Abraham in the Negev. Yet places like Beersheba and Hebron also lie just within the 250 mm isohyete![217] After all, the

---

[215] The Physical Environment, p. 117-121. Autonomy and Nomadism in Western Asia. Or NS XLII (1973) p. 247-258. Urban Autonomy in a Nomadic Environment. JNES XXXII (1973) p. 201-215.

[216] The word 'Amorite' really comes from linguistics. We must give credit to Dame K. M. Kenyon for being the first to have established this dichotomy in the Bronze Age culture of Syria and Palestine on a non-linguistic basis, even if her theories require correction on various points. Cf. C. H. J. de Geus, The Amorites in the Archaeology of Palestine. Ugarit Forschungen, vol. III (1971) p. 41-60.

[217] See int.al. the sketch maps in De Vaux, RB LVI (1949) p. 13 and Kupper JESHO II (1959). p. 114. It should be realized that again Mari itself does not lie within the real steppe belt, but in a marginal area between the desert and the river. Probably for the Jaminites and others the kingdom of Mari was mainly a passing-place; their true habitat lay north and south of Mari and east of the river.

traditions regarding Abraham and Jacob speak mainly of contacts with the region around Ḥarrân and the Ḫabur, *i.e.* always within the 250 mm isohyete! Disregarding the mountain country for a moment, one may say that the milieu there on the Upper Euphrates was not essentially different from that of Palestine. In the Bronze Age the mountain country hardly counted yet. In both regions we find the clearly separated, but collaborating economies of the great city states Alalach, Yamḫad and Ḥarrân, with in between large areas where the population lived in small settlements. There also agriculture was a very important means of subsistence, although naturally the great flocks of sheep and goats attracted more attention. Because archaeologists have always fastened on the tells of the big towns, where also the most important textual finds were made, the milieu of the great city-states is much better known than that of the extensive countryside, particularly in the steppe belt.[218] The Mari texts give us for the first time a clear view of the great economic activity that obtained in these regions. Our information regarding the economic and social circumstances of the countryside comes mainly from other texts, found in Nuzi and Arrapḫa, east of the Euphrates.[219] It is especially interesting that the texts from Arrapḫa clearly show the economic and social structure of that region to have been founded on the *dimtu* (literally: tower). These were fortified settlements, often no bigger than a large fortified farmhouse. Such a *dimtu* was inhabited by a single *extended family*. The land was the property of the extended family as such. The *dimtu* was named after the fictive common ancestor. Thus the word *dimtu* may have three different meanings: 'a) fortified dwelling of an extended family commune; b) the extended family commune itself; c) the territory of its possessions, including its buildings and fields in their totality.'[220] Besides purely agrarian *dimātu* there are also communes of weavers, potters etc.

Now this region shows a strong Hurrian influence, and the difference with Palestine must not be underestimated: a state already existed here and also a strongly developing feudalism. On the other hand the *dimātu* behaved with great political and social independence of the state and the king. They undoubtedly represent a pattern of organization and production that had been functioning for a very long time, and over a far

---

[218] Miss Kenyon will always have the distinction of having first attempted the archaeological demonstration of this 'second milieu'. See also note 216.

[219] N. B. Jankowska, Extended Family Commune and Civil Self-Government in Arrapḫa in the Fifteenth-Fourteenth Century B.C. (1957-1960). In: I. M. Diakonoff ed. *Ancient Mesopotamia*, Moscow 1969, p. 235-252. And: Communal Self Government and the King of the State of Arrapḫa. *JESHO* XII (1969) p. 233-282.

[220] N. B. Jankowska, *JESHO* XII (1969) p. 237-238.

wider area than only this region.[221] Moreover, E. A. Speiser has repeatedly shown that the social, juridical and economic circumstances we find depicted in the Nuzi texts also determine the milieu of the tales of the patriarchs.[222]

On the one hand, then, we see the city-states with their monarchic form of political organization, in which the king is the greatest and sometimes even the only landowner. He parcels out the land to others. Trade, handicrafts and the exploitation of extensive estates and demesnes formed the main economic support of these cities.[223] On the other hand there is the countryside with its innumerable little settlements of a mixed economy, agriculture and sheep-farming. There the social and political structure entirely coincided with consanguinity – real or fictitious.[224] Slavery is very rare here and private landownership quite unknown.[225]

In conclusion we may say that the patriarchs, and Jacob/Israel in particular, are best understood if seen in the milieu which was dominant in the countryside of Syria and Palestine in the Middle and Late Bronze Age. That the name of 'Amorite' has been given to this milieu is both a

[221] This was already pointed out by P. Koschaker, Fratriarchat, Hausgemeinschaft und Mutterrecht in Keilschriftrechten (ZA N.F. VII [1933] S. 1-89). Koschaker assumes that there was a similar system in ancient Babylonia! O.c. S. 74. Thus also I. M. Diakonoff, Agrarian Conditions in Middle Assyria. In: I. M. Diakonoff ed., Ancient Mesopotamia, Moscow 1969, p. 204-234.

[222] Of Speiser's many publications in this field I will only mention: New Kirkuk Documents Relating to Family Laws. AASOR X (1928-1929) p 1-74. And: The Hurrian Participation in the Civilization of Mesopotamia, Syria and Palestine (1953). Now in Finkelstein/Greenberg, Oriental and Biblical Studies of A. E. Speiser, Philadelphia 1967, p. 244-269. As against the historical conclusions drawn by Speiser and many others, which are indeed often somewhat premature, it is interesting to note the objections voiced by M. Noth (Der Beitrag der Archäologie zur Geschichte Israels. SVT VII, Leiden 1960, S. 270-271) and R. de Vaux (Method in the Study of Early Hebrew History. The Bible in Modern Scholarship. Nashville 1965, p. 25-26). They both point out that for a long time the Hurrians were found nearly everywhere in Semitic country, so that the texts from Nuzu may only be used as illustrating a milieu of the Late Bronze Age. It is as such that they are intended here. In Palestine also the Hurrian upper layer always rested upon earlier Semitic substrata.

[223] In the Russian volume 'Ancient Mesopotamia. A Socio-Economic History', to which we have several times referred, great stress is laid upon the exploitation of slaves in agriculture which arose under these circumstances.

[224] How these little units functioned politically, is seen in H. Reviv, On Urban Representative Institutions and Self-Government in Syria-Palestine in the Second Half of the Second Millennium B.C. JESHO XII (1969) p. 283-297. Cf. by the same author: The Government of Shechem in the El-Amarna Period and in the Days of Abimelech. IEJ XVI (1966) p. 252-257.

[225] In the state of Arrapḫa these different conditions of landownership also often caused conflicts between the king and chiefs of a dimtu.

linguistic and an ethnical simplification, since it also included Hurrians. There is no necessity at all to explain such a milieu in Palestine by an influx of peoples from the east. Rather the reverse![226] The data from Nuzi or Mari cannot and need not be used in any way to deny the presence in Palestine of the majority of the Israelite tribes during the Late Bronze Age. Zobel's dating of the tribes, *i.e.* for the period when the tribal form of organization was in full function, between 1400 and 1000, is entirely acceptable.[227] Of the time before that, when there must have existed small groups like the *bᵉnē ya'ᵃqoḇ* and the *bᵉnē yiśrā'ēl*, we know hardly anything yet.[228] Perhaps one may imagine the historical development to have been as follows: in the second half of the Middle Bronze Age and in the beginning of the Late Bronze Age a dichotomous economy existed in Palestine also. That is to say, an economy consisting of a give and take between town and country. In this, the country, largely maintained its own ethnic identity. The people there lived mainly from keeping sheep and from fairly primitive agriculture (barley). Socially and politically they were organized in 'extended families' and clans. With the towns in their area they kept up an economically necessary relationship of friendly enmity. We may thus vaguely recognize the *bᵉnē ya'ᵃqob* around Bethel and the *bᵉnē yiśrā'ēl* around Shechem.[229] Clans such as the *bᵉnē 'aḇrāhām* (-*rām*) and the *bᵉnē yiṣḥaq* may have lived around towns such as Hebron and Beersheba. As the cities and city culture decayed in the Late Bronze Age, due in part to the troublous political times, from which the towns suffered more than the country people, the balance of power shifted within the dichotomy. Formerly the two parties were either equal or the balance of power lay with the cities. The latter case held particularly in the plains where the great Canaanite city-states had an entirely dominant position, as shown very clearly in tribal names such as Machir and Issachar.[230] The coming of

[226] C. H. J. de Geus, The Amorites in the Archaeology of Palestine. *Ugarit Forschungen*, vol. III (1971) p. 41-60.
[227] H. J. Zobel, *Stammesspruch und Geschichte*. BZAW 95, Berlin 1965, S. 127.
[228] Although De Pury does seem to have shed some light upon this matter. Genèse XXIV et l'histoire. *RB* LXXVI (1969) p. 1-49. *Cf.* also H. Seebass, *Der Erzvater Israel*. BZAW 98, Berlin 1966. The same conclusions now by A. Lemaire, Asriel, *šr'l*, Israël et l'origine de la conféderation israélite. *VT* XXIII (1973) p. 239-243. See also our Excursus II.
[229] De Pury, *o.c.* p. 39-42. Seebass, *o.c.* S. 21-34. That the name Israel originally belongs near Shechem, was already concluded by Steuernagel from the expression *'ēl 'ᵉlōhē yiśrā'ēl* (Jahwe, der Gott Israels. Eine stil- und religionsgeschichtliche Studie. *Wellhausen-Festschrift*, BZAW 27, Berlin 1914, S. 329-349).
[230] De Pury takes a very 'amphictyonic' view. This forces him to deny the existence of tribes in the Late Bronze Age. Also, he overestimates their true role in the later period. *O.c.* p. 36.

iron finally ended this dichotomy. Through the use of iron, a tremendous expansion of the area of cultivation became possible, and the political result was the rise of the territorial state, which was more than an enlarged city-state.[231] This transition took more than two centuries, the Biblical period of the Judges. In this period the old contrast between town and country practically came to an end in the hill country, where agriculture became more and more important.

The problem of the Conquest finally, is first of all a problem of literary history.[232] Although as such it lies outside the scope of the present study, I would remark that I agree with Mowinckel in an extreme scepticism as to whether the Old Testament really contains an authentic and reliable Conquest tradition.[233] Should one reduce the Conquest to a process of sedentarization, then one does not do justice to the real literary problem.[234]

---

[231] See for this in the first place again V. Gordon Childe, *What happened in History*? Also G. Buccellati, *Cities and Nations of Ancient Syria*. Roma 1967. Unfortunately Buccellati's most interesting and important book is impaired by the fact that the author considers an amphictyony a necessary phase of transition between 'tribe' and 'state'. A secularized, or rather a paganized 'model' of the Israelite amphictyony – which he considers to be completely proved – he then applies to Syria. Something of the same kind is now also to be seen in the article by E. F. Campbell and G. E. Wright, Tribal League Shrines in Amman and Shechem. *BA* XXXII (1969) p. 104 116. The answer in both cases is: a) tribe and state do not form a sequence; that is an evolutionary simplification. And b) this again rests upon the old denial of sedentarization in the hill country and in Transjordan.

[232] This is also the final conclusion of Weippert's examination. *Die Landnahme*, esp. S. 131-139. Compare De Vaux's remarks in the introduction to his *Histoire ancienne d'Israël*. Vol. I, Paris 1971 and Th. L. Thompson, *The Historicity of the Patriarchal Narratives*. Berlin 1974, p. 1-9.

[233] S. Mowinckel, *Tetrateuch, Pentateuch, Hexateuch. Die Berichte über die Landnahme in den drei altisraelitischen Geschichtswerken*. BZAW 90, Berlin 1964. Mowinckel only recognizes a report of Conquest in the stricter sense in Num. 32, concerning the tribes of Transjordan. In an article on Judg. 1, referred to more fully above, I formerly tried to show that the *Conquest* traditions as they seem to be delivered in Josh. 1-12 and Judg. 1, are in fact aetiological. Alt and Noth regraded their intent as 'archaeological and historical', but it seems to me primarily juridical. The traditions from Joshua are called upon to explain why the Israelites have a right to Palestine. That this became urgent around 586 B.C.E. goes without saying. This also explains the important function of these traditions precisely in the Deuteronomist history, to which Judg. 1:1-2:5 is a later addition. C. H. J. de Geus, Richteren 1:1-2:5. *Vox Theologica* XXXVI (1966) p. 32-54.

[234] So Weippert finally concludes, after all, *o.c.* S. 123. It is a pity that while Weippert does realize the importance of the literary historical aspect of his survey, *i.e.* the most specific Old Testamentary aspect, he yet does not work it out sufficiently.

181

7. The 'Apiru

Whenever it is argued that the Israelites cannot be autochthonous in Palestine and did not form an ethnic unity, the 'Apiru turn up. As indeed they also do when the contrary is argued! It is necessary therefore briefly to discuss the problem of the 'Apiru.[235]

In chapter I we saw that the term 'Apiru was for a long time regarded as an appellative indicating a social group.[236] In the last decade there has been a veering of opinion, and various scholars now regard it rather as an ethnic name.[237]

The whole complex of problems around the 'Apiru and their possible relationship to the Israelites hinges on four cardinal questions, each in itself a highly complicated matter:

A. Who were the 'Apiru?
B. How are they related to the Ḫabiru of the Amarna letters?
C. How are the 'Apiru/Ḫabiru related to the Hebrews?
D. How are the Hebrews related to the Israelites?

Ad A. Persons who are called 'Apiru appear in the whole of the Ancient Orient, from Asia Minor to Nuzi and from Mesopotamia right into Egypt. At the Fourth RAI it already became clear that what they have in common is something negative: they are always clearly distinguished from the local population; they do not coincide with one particular social class which is always the same; neither do they have the same status;

---

[235] The rendering in the Egyptian and Ugaritic texts have removed all doubt of this being the correct rendering of the sumerogram SA-GAZ. This West-Semitic word was inadequately rendered as ḫabiru in the Amarna letters, simply because Accadian has no 'ayin. For the interchange of b and p, see the examples in Weippert, *Landnahme* S. 78-81.

[236] First of all J. Bottéro, *Le problème des Ḫabiru à la quatrième rencontre assyriologique internationale*. Paris 1954. In this especially the historical survey on p. V-XXXII. Then M. Greenberg, *The Ḫab/piru*. AOS XXXIX, New Haven 1955. N. A. van Uchelen, *Abraham de Hebreeër*. Assen 1964. W. Helck, Die Bedrohung Palästinas durch Einwandernde Gruppen am Ende der 18. und am Anfang der 19. Dynastie. *VT* XVIII (1968) S. 472-480. The 'standard article' for Old Testament students was for a long time: M. Noth, Erwägungen zur Hebräerfrage. *Festschrift O. Procksch*, Leipzig 1934, S. 99-113.

[237] Thus principally A. Pohl, Einige Gedanken zur Ḫabiru-Frage. *WZKM* LIV (1957) S. 157-161. Miss M. G. Kline, The ḪA-BI-ru, kin or foe of Israel. *Westminster Theol. Journal* XIX (1956) p. 1-24; 170-184 and XX (1957) p. 46-70. H. Schmökel, Geschichte des alten Vorderasiens. *Hb. d. Orientalistik*, Leiden 1957. Also R. de Vaux, Le problème des Ḫapiru après quinze années. *JNES* XXVII (1968) p. 221-228. And K. Koch, Die Hebräer vom Auszug aus Ägypten bis zum Grossreich Davids. *VT* XIX (1969) S. 37-81.

also they do not exercise the same callings.[238] In spite of the arguments of Pohl, De Vaux and Koch, we still think a social explanation best fits the greater part of the texts.[239] The term 'outlaw' chosen by Weippert seems serviceable to render the intention. That there could yet be fairly large groups of these people has become far more comprehensible since the remarks of Rowton.[240] Yet De Vaux is perfectly right in saying that the opposition of *appellativum* and *gentilicium* may not be forced: gentilicia often develop into appellatives and vice versa. Often the number is the criterion, or the extent to which they are incorporated in the receiving community. It is not fortuitous that in Egypt, where they were mostly pressed into forced labour and did not really form part of the community, their name was always written with the determinative for 'peoples'. I think myself that the hypothesis of B. Landsberger is very interesting: he regards the 'Apiru as a substratum of the original population, come down from the mountains.[241] That such groups also become social groups and that their name may become an appellative, is a very familiar phenomenon.

Ad B. In the Amarna period the Ḥabiru form a source of great unrest in Palestine and Syria. That Ḥabiru equals 'Apiru is linguistically pretty well established now.[242]
The great complication in the Amarna period is formed by the phenomenon that the term Habiru is also applied to the indigenous population. There are even repeated complaints in the Amarna correspondence about persons, rulers even, who 'have become Ḥabiru'.[243] In this period the 'Apiru are useful as mercenaries, or even as a refuge – Idrimi of Alalaḥ! – but the majority of the texts are decidedly disparaging. In the real

---

[238] Bottéro, *o.c.* p. 187-198. De Vaux, Le problème des Ḥapiru, p. 225.
[239] This is now also the opinion of J. Bottéro in his very useful survey of the existing texts which mention the Ḥabiru, *s.v.* Ḥabiru in *RLA* (1972) and further of H. Cazelles, The Hebrews. *POTT*, London 1973, p. 1-28. De Vaux considers 'Apiru an ethnic appellation of the same order as Amorites, *Sutū*, Aramaeans *etc.* While this is correct, it is also a problem with these appellations whether they are ethnic or social, certainly with regard to the first two.
[240] M. B. Rowton, The Topological Factor in the Ḥapiru Problem. *Studies in Honor of B. Landsberger*, AS 16, Chicago 1965, p. 375-387.
[241] *Cf.* Landsberger's remarks in Bottéro, *o.c.* sp. S. 160. In that case the word 'Apiru would not need to be West-Semitic at all, but might come from the language of such a substratum.
[242] See above, note 235. We are completely convinced by Weippert's reasoning, which also fully answers the objections of R. Borger, *ZDPV* LXXIV (1958) S. 121-132, with regard to the interchange of p and b. So also J. Bottéro in *RLA*.
[243] *Cf.* for this the popular yet instructive essay by E. F. Campbell, The Amarna Letters and the Amarna Period. *BA* XXIII (1960) p. 2-22.

Amarna correspondence the term often simply means 'traitor', 'rebel'. Although in the Amarna period there are certainly still indications of invasion by foreign groups[244], the great majority of the 'Apiru is autochthonous. To speak, with Mendenhall, of social revolt, is going too far.[245] That the phenomenon is connected with the transition to the political and economic situation of the Iron Age, seems fairly plain. The concept 'Apiru seems to have been extended in the Amarna period to something it did not cover before.

Ad C. This is the most knotty problem. A connexion between Ḥabiru and Hebrews has been as fiercely defended as attacked.[246] An important step forward is the insight nowadays that linguistically it is at least possible to identify the two.[247] Yet it must be realized that a possibility is far from being a proof![248] The great question now is: who are the Hebrews in the Old Testament? As long as these were also regarded as a social category, there was not so much of a problem. On this matter, however, opinion has definitely changed. In the article by R. Borger mentioned before, Borger denies any direct connexion, because 'Hebrews' appears in the Old Testament as an ethnic name, whereas the meaning of Ḥabiru in the Amarna letters is clearly appellative.[249] He also advances linguistic arguments for this, but these were sufficiently countered by Weippert, as we have seen. Yet Weippert also accepts the idea that 'iḇrī in the Old Testament functions primarily as an ethnic name. Koch's article of 1969 fully supports the argumentation of Borger: 'iḇrīm is an ethnic name, 'apiru an appellative.[250] I think Weippert has found the right way out here. He points out that in the earlier texts the term 'Hebrew' appears in a juridical context and there may still have

---

[244] The usual reference is to the fragment of the so-called second stela of Sethos I, which was found in Beth-Shan. In this, however, there is only mention of "Apiru of the mountains of the jrd(n)'. If this is the Jordan, the reference might be to Transjordan. K. Galling, *TGI¹*, Tübingen 1950, S. 30.

[245] The Hebrew Conquest of Palestine, p. 73-76. And: The *'Apiru* Movements in the Late Bronze Age. *The Tenth Generation*. Baltimore 1973, p. 122-141.

[246] The principal opponent of a connection is at present Miss Kline. But up to now Landsberger's arguments in J. Bottéro, *Le problème des Ḥabiru*, are still authoritative for many scholars.

[247] *Cf.* for this first of all once more the philological acuteness of Weippert. The interchanges of h/' and b/p we discussed above. Since adjectives of the *fa'il* class often incline to segolation, one can easily imagine the following development: 'apiru > 'apr + nisbe-ending-ay > 'a/ipray > 'iḇrī. Weippert, *o.c.* S. 76-84.

[248] Thus K. Koch, Die Hebräer, S. 37.

[249] *ZDPV* LXXIV (1958) S. 121-132.

[250] Koch, *o.c.* S. 39.

an appellative or social meaning.[251] For the rest, as an ethnic name the word makes a very archaic impression, when we see for instance how in Gen. 14 *hā-'ibrī* is contrasted with *hā-'emōrī*.[252] The notorious texts from the first book of Samuel, I Sam. 4:6, 9; 13:3, 19; 14:11, 21; and 29:3 perhaps show how the old appellative meaning still took effect in a time when the word was really only still in use as an ethnic name.[253]

Taking as a starting-point the identity of the word Hebrews with the 'Apiru/Ḫabiru of the Amarna period – incapable of proof though it is – we must then conclude that within the Old Testament tradition the word changed from an appellative into an ethnic name. When used appellatively, 'Hebrew' has something of its older meaning of '*outlaw*' and does not carry the wider sense it had in Amarna times.

Ad D. There remains the problem of the relation between 'Hebrews' and 'Israelites'. Apart from the development of an ethnic meaning of the term *'ibrī* within the Old Testament, we must emphasize that the phenomenon of the 'Apiru/Ḫabiru/Hebrews is of far greater extent than only the appearance of the earliest Israelites. If there was a direct connexion, then it can only have been that the Israelites once formed part of the far larger group of the 'Apiru. This is also the view of K. Koch, who regards both 'Hebrews' and "'Apiru' entirely as ethnic terms, and following De Vaux considers the Hebrews to have been a people scattered over a lage part of Western Asia.[254] That this people was so scattered is still reflected, Koch finds, in the genealogy of Eber, Gen. 10:21-32. The people of Israel is merely the political form of a part of the far larger Hebrew collective, and may be compared to *e.g.* Moab or Edom. David would have aspired to unite all the former Hebrew peoples

---

[251] Weippert, *o.c.* S. 84-89. The juridico-social context, in which *'ibrī* closely approaches terms such as *gēr* and *tōšāb*, was also pointed out by J. Levy, Origin and Signification of the Biblical Term 'Hebrew'. *HUCA* XXVIII (1957) p. 1-14. S Yeivin, The Origin and Disappearance of the Khab/piru. *Acts of the 25th World Congress of Orientalists*, Moscow 1962, p. 439 111. *Cf* also W. von Soden, Muškēnum und die Mawālī des frühen Islam. *ZA* NF XXII (1964) s. 133-142.

[252] Weippert, *o.c.* S. 101.

[253] Weippert, *o.c.* S. 88-90.

[254] We already saw that Koch excluded the Ḫabiru of the Amarna period. As we know, Koch also sees a difference between the proto-Israelites (Yahwists) and the proto-Aramaeans, the bearers of the patriarchal traditions. Der Tod des Religionstifters, S. 107-113. The proto-Aramaeans, now, largely coincide with the Hebrews. The relationship between Hebrews and Yahwism Koch leaves undecided: 'Unklar sind die religiösen Verhältnisse. Sind alle Hebräer bereits Jahwä-Verehrer? Findet sich also ein Jahwä-Kult auch jenerseits der Grenzen Israels? Jedenfalls wird ein Anschluss an Israel die Anerkennung der Jahwä-Verehrung eingeschlossen haben'. Die Hebräer, S. 49.

into one state, of which he wore the crown.[255] Koch finally takes up Böhl's famous old definition: 'Alle Israeliten sind Hebräer, aber nicht alle Hebräer sind Israeliten.'[256] It is interesting that Koch, whose thought clung to the ethnic principle, suggests that the form of a political and religious amphictyony was typical of the Hebrew peoples.[257] In spite of the fascination of Koch's fine and logical argumentation, we are not convinced. Firstly, we agree with Weippert in still considering an appellative meaning more probable than an ethnic one for the ancient 'Apiru. Secondly, we do in contrast see a connexion with the Ḥabiru of the Amarna letters, through the indication of a social category.

Exactly the reverse of Koch's idea is proposed by G. E. Mendenhall.[258] Mendenhall's point of departure is a social indication, and he sees the people of Israel originating as a result of a social revolt of the Late Bronze Age 'serfs' against their feudal lords. Contrary to Weippert, we think Mendenhall has a proper appreciation of the economic and social aspects and consequences of the turbulent transition from the Bronze Age to the Iron Age. His protest against 'Beduinism' and the accepted theories of entry is also fully justified. After a long time, Mendenhall is the first again to reckon with the possibility of the great majority of the 'proto-Israelites' having been autochthonous 'Palestinians'. That his general conclusion, however, entirely fails to convince us, is due in the first place to the way Mendenhall simplifies the various problems.[259] Then also we see the roots of Israel stretching back much further, and certainly accept an ethnic distinction between the later Canaanites and the Israelites. Moreover, the picture of a nation and a state being formed as a result of social revolt, class war and a movement of mass conversion, seems altogether too idealistic and romantic![260]

Let us return for a moment to the article by Koch. He denies all

---

[255] Koch, Die Hebräer, S. 78-81.

[256] Fr. Böhl, *Kanaanäer und Hebräer*. Leipzig 1911, S. 67. *Cf.* also on S. 73: 'Hebräer ist die Bezeichnung einer ganzen Völkergruppe, zu der neben anderen auch die Israelstämme gehören'.

[257] Die Hebräer, S. 73-78. *Cf.* also Der Tod des Religionsstifters, S. 110.

[258] G. E. Mendenhall, The Hebrew Conquest of Palestine. *BA* XXV (1962) p. 66-87.

[259] Weippert very justly points out that the habit in Anglo-Saxon countries of saying 'Hebrews' instead of 'Israelites' has greatly favoured such simplifications and misunderstandings. Weippert, *o.c.* S. 67[3].

[260] In the case of Mendenhall we may once again speak of the 'primacy of religion' in reconstructing the earliest history of Israel. No instance of a nation originating from a religious movement has ever come to our knowledge. Mendenhall here seems entirely to lose sight of the actual function of religion in a culture. Of course religious movements can take a political turn or may, as religious movements, become a political factor. Yet surely that is something very different from determining the origin of a nation!

connexion between the Ḥabiru and the ʿApiru, even with those ʿApiru who turn up in Egypt in Ramesside times. Yet he does accept these latter ʿApiru as Hebrews: those Hebrews who were afterwards to become Israel, the Leah tribes.[261] It is very interesting to note how here again the dogma of the (semi-) nomadic way of life of the proto-Israelites has its effect. The Ḥabiru of the Amarna period are hardly ever nomads or intrusive groups, *therefore* they cannot be identical with the Hebrews according to Koch, Weippert and Campbell and many others.[262] Yet this argument loses its force if one takes account of the Israelites having been autochthonous far longer, as (part of) the 'Amorite' inhabitants of Palestine in the Middle and Late Bronze Age. If we regard 'Ḥabiru' as having been an appellative[263] in this period, we can surely draw a line over the Ḥabiru of the Amarna period to the Hebrews of the Old Testament. In a juridical context and in the special context of the Amarna letters the word *ʿibrī/ʿapiru* can have an appellative function quite unconnected with the ethnic group to which the person(s) so designated belong(s). That is why, under certain circumstances, both Israelites and non-Israelites may be designated in this way. The fact that the word 'Hebrew' is afterwards used in an ethnic sense in the Old Testament, assimilates this word to the other *gentilicia* in the Old Testament which are still a mystery to us.[264] Here again we finally come to a literary problem!

Excursus 2. The name Israel.

It may be supposed a matter of general knowledge that proper names of the type *yqtl*-ND or *(y)qtlanum* belong to the so-called 'Amorite' names, and that especially among the earlier Israelites such names are frequent. This phenomenon, indeed, we consider one of the most im-

[261] Koch, Die Hebräer, S. 67.
[262] Koch, *o.c.* S. 69. Weippert, *o.c.* S. 66-67: 'Ist Mendenhalls soziologisch begründete Gleichung richtig, brauchen wir uns um die Frage, ob die "Israeliten" vor der Landnahme in Palästine "Nomaden" oder "Halbnomaden" gewesen sind, nicht mehr zu bekümmern. Sie wäre dazu negativ entschieden; denn die "ḫab/piru" waren nach dem übereinstimmenden Zeugnis sämtlicher Texte, in denen sie vorkommen, keine Bevölkungsgruppe "nomadischen" oder "halbnomadischen" Charakters.' Campbell, The Amarna Letters and the Amarna Period. *BA* XXIII (1960) p. 15: 'If this view has anything to commend it, then it can be added that the ʿApiru are not a foreign element in the land, coming from outside, but an indigenous element, and therefore *not* the Israelites coming from the desert.'
[263] Often with the political implication of treason, *scil.* to the Egyptian authority.
[264] For this *int.al.* J. C. L. Gibson, Observations on some important ethnic terms in the Pentateuch. *JNES* XX (1961) p. 217-238. C. H. J. de Geus, The Amorites in the Archaeology of Palestine. *Ugarit Forschungen*, vol. III (1971) p. 41-60. Also the articles in the handbooks.

portant indications that also the earliest Israelites formed part of the 'Amorite' milieu. In form, the name Israel belongs to the former of these two types. Since the present study is devoted to Israel in its earliest period, a few philological notes on the name Israel are appended here. The name itself affords no indication whether it was originally borne by a person, a group, a town or a district. Many other names, though, are in the same case. Its etymology is still not fully understood. The explanation given in the Old Testament in Gen. 32 is clearly secondary. Usually the name is regarded as a sentence composed of a verb in the imperfect tense and a subject. Names of this type are very common in the world of the western Semites and in South Arabic. M. Noth even considers them characteristic of a 'protoaramäischer Schicht'.[265] Such names may equally well be names of persons, tribes or places. Yet there have always been scholars who regarded the first member of the name *yiśrā'ēl* not as a verb but as a noun. Flavius Josephus was already one of these (Antiquit. I, 20): ὁ ἀντιστας.[266] *Cf.* Luther's 'ein Gotteskempffer'. The great difficulty is that precisely in the case of weak verbs it is extremely hard to make out whether we are dealing with a form of the imperfect or with a noun formed from the stem of the verb by means of a yōd as prefix.[267] This way of forming nouns is very ancient. Yet a solution in this direction has less probability, since this formation has always remain infrequent in most of the Semitic languages, Arabic excepted. In Hebrew it is even rare.[268] Thus no purely philological argument can be given why *yiśrā* cannot be a noun. There remains always the possibility that the *y* is a prothetic element.[269] On the other hand, the view that we have to do with a verbal form is supported by the fact that the name Israel appears in a literary context in which names of the type imperf. +'ēl are very numerous. This points to an origin of the name in an area where this type of name may even be called characteristic of the language – see above – whereas nouns formed with a yōd are scarce.[270] While it thus seems reason-

[265] M. Noth, *Die Israelitischen Personennamen im Rahmen der gemeinsemitischen Namengebung*. Stuttgart 1928, S. 43 *seq.*
[266] In *ZAW* XXXIV (1914) S. 1-15, Ed. Sachsse gives a survey of all the etymologies suggested until that date. Here all particulars may be found. *Cf.* also note 275 and 276.
[267] H. B. Huffmon, *Amorite Personal Names in the Mari Texts*. Baltimore 1965, p. 63. There is indeed some difference of opinion regarding various names beginning with *ya* + weak stem, see *e.g. s.v. yśr* on p. 216.
[268] J. Barth, *Die Nominalbildung in den semitischen Sprachen*. Leipzig 1889, S. 225 *seq.*
[269] N. Walker, Israel. *VT* IV (1954) p. 434.
[270] Noth, Personennamen, S. 27 *seq.* und 207 *seq. Idem* Mari und Israel, *Alt-Festschrift*, Tübingen 1953, S. 127-153. *Idem* Remarks on the sixth volume of Mari texts. *JSS* I (1956) p. 322-333.

188

able to take the name as an imperfect $+$'ēl, three problems remain. Firstly, in names of this type the theophorous element is always subject and never object, except occasionally with verbs meaning to glorify or praise. Secondly, in a derivation from śrh as suggested in Gen. 32:29, the long ā after the rēš is difficult to explain. Thirdly, a root śrh is practically a *hapax legomenon*. The only other locus is Hos. 12:4 and possibly also vs. 5, and here again the context contains references to the stories of Jacob.[271] The translation 'to fight' is always defended by a comparison with the Arabic śrj^{III} = to fight.

As to the first difficulty, that 'ēl must perforce be subject, there is hardly any difference of opinion.[272] Meyer's solution, to regard the name as a nominal sentence and translate: 'He who fights is El', has found no adherents.[273] The name is clearly recognizable as belonging to the class of verbal sentences, consisting of a verbal form and a theophorous element. It belongs to the oldest form of this type, in which the verb is in the imperfect tense.[274] With regard to the second and the third point matters are more complicated. Surely a normal derivation from śrh would give yiśri'ēl or yiśre'ēl? The different vocalization has always been a strong argument for distrusting the traditional derivation from a root śrh, which is otherwise unknown. Ed. Sachsse, who has made a thorough study of the name Israel,[275] therefore concludes that the name has not been transmitted to us in the Old Testament in its original form. On the basis of ancient transcriptions from non-Biblical sources, particularly the stela of Merenptah, an inscription of Shalmaneser II, and an analysis of his own of Hosea 12:4-5, Sachsse concludes that the original pronunciation must have been j^{e}šar-'ēl, that is from the verb yšr 'to be sincere'. The change from ś to š is to be explained by the difference in dialect between Judah and the Northern realm, cf. Judg. 12:6. This derivation from yšr is very old, it is already found with Hieronymus.[276]

[271] In v. 5 many would read wayyiśar instead of wayyāśar (< śwr or śrr). Cf. int.al. Koehler-Baumgartner's Lexicon s.v. śrh. On the other hand H. W. Wolff in his commentary (*Hosea* BKAT 1965², S. 267, 274) retains MT. He then reads 'ēl instead of 'ēl. W. Rudolph though, *Hosea* KAT XIII, 1, 1966, does follow the derivation from śwr. In this he is followed now by L. Ruppert, Herkunft und Bedeutung der Jakob-Traditionen bei Hosea. *Biblica* LII (1971) S. 488-504.
[272] Eb. Nestle, *Die israelitischen Eigennamen*, Haarlem 1876. Nestle's view that names of the type imperf. + divine name express a wish, was strongly defended by G. Buchanan Gray, *Hebrew Proper Names*. London 1896.
[273] *Die Israeliten und ihre Nachbarstämme*, S. 252.
[274] See note 270.
[275] Ed. Sachsse, Die Etymologie und älteste Aussprache des Namens yiśrā'ēl. *ZAW* XXXIV (1914), S. 1-15. Also: Der Ursprung des Namens Israel. *ZS* IV (1926) S. 63-69.
[276] '*Vir videns Deum sed melius rectus Domini*'. Here Hieronymus depends on Philo in

It is indeed most tempting, in view of expressions such as *sēfẹr hayyāšār*
and *yᵉšūrūn*, which is clearly used as a parallel of *yiśrā'ēl*.[277] Sachsse
translates: 'El ist *yāšār* gewesen'.

This solution of Sachsse is followed by a rather violent reaction on the
part of W. Caspari.[278] He energetically defends the idea that the traditional form *yiśrā'ēl* is the original one, and translates: 'Gott kämpft'.
He supposes the long ā to represent an earlier form.[279] The name would
then probably be an abbreviation of *jiśrā-'ēl-šadday* or something of the
kind. Sachsse's exchange of *ś* and *š* is linguistically impermissible. That
the Old Testament should play upon the word *yiśrā'ēl* and the root *yšr*
is natural, and it is done deliberately. This tells us nothing of the origin
and etymology of the name Israel. M. Noth takes, in principle, the side of
Caspari:[280] any alteration of the transmitted form of the name must be
rejected, certainly if made on the authority of non-Israelite sources.
These most certainly do not carry the authority Sachsse attributes to
them. 'Jede Veränderung der überlieferten Aussprache ist abzulehnen,
da der Name niemals, wie so mancher andere, nur noch in der literarischen
Tradition sein Dasein gefristet hat und da den Gefahren der Textverderb-
nis ausgesetzt gewesen ist, sondern stets in lebendigem Gebrauch war, die
massoretische Vokalisation also auch keinerfalls, wie vielleicht gelegent-
lich bei anderen Namen, späte Kombination ist, sondern auf uralter
Überlieferung beruht.'[281] Noth explains the ā by pointing to the familiar
phenomenon that in Hebrew forms of the groups *lāmẹd-hē* and *lāmẹd-'ālef*
interchange rather easily. Noth thinks of a root *śr'*, afterwards lost, with

two respects, for Philo's famous etymology *'īš* + *'ēl* + *rā'ā*, which was the etymology officially accepted by the Church during the whole of the Middle Ages, provided
the *videns*. Moreover Hieronymus states that his *melius rectus Domini* also comes
from Philo. Exact references and other ancient etymologies are to be found in
Sachsse's Die Etymologie   S. 2 *seq.* There is also an extensive survey in G. A.
Danell, *Studies in the Name Israel in the Old Testament*. Upsala 1946.

[277] Thus Sachsse was by no means the first to suggest the derivation from *yšr*.
In modern times it is given *int.al.* by Renan, *Histoire du peuple d'Israël* I, p. 106,
and defended by W. Bacher, *Yᵉšūrūn. ZAW* V (1885) S. 161 *seq.* Down to the present
time this derivation from *yšr* has many supporters. Bacher explained Jeshurun,
the upright, as a poetical and artificial name for Israel, on the analogy of Zebulun
and in contrast with Jacob, though it hardly seems applicable to Deut. 32:15.
Cf. Noth, *Personennamen*, S. 10. Wallis *s.v.* Jesurun in *BHH*.

[278] W. Caspari, Sprachliche und religionsgeschichtliche Bedeutung des Namens
Israel. *ZS* III (1924), S. 194-212.

[279] Thus already P. de Lagarde, *Uebersicht über die im Aramäischen, Arabischen
und Hebräischen übliche Bildung der Nomina*, S. 131 *seq.* An original 'Futur'
yiśray is posited, pronounced as *yiśrā*. Exactly the same is found in the ancient
name *Ismael*.

[280] *Die Israelitischen Personennamen*, S. 207 *seq.*

[281] *O.c.* S. 207.

the meaning 'to rule', and points to a word such as *miśrā* 'domination' and the proper name *śerāyā*.[282] Since most names of this type express a wish, Noth translates: 'Gott möge herrschen'.

A complete list of all etymologies proposed in the past may be found in the aforenamed works of Sachsse and Danell. Two should still be mentioned, though. First of all that of Albright, since it has been very little regarded.[283] Albright starts from a common Semitic root *śr*, referring to the Ethiopian *śrj* 'to heal', and the Arabic *naśara*. The Hebrew equivalent would then have been *yśr*. Albright explains the ā by pointing out that there are other cases of *śewa'* before a laryngeal becoming an ā. He supposes the development to have been: *yaśir'ēl* > *yiśir'ēl* > *yiśr'ēl* > *yiśrā'ēl*, and translates: 'God heals'. Unfortunately, Albright is forced to seek evidence in the LXX, *e.g. bil'am → Βαλααμ*. Yet Sachsse has made it clear, in this instance strongly supported by Noth, that 1) the LXX occasionally interjects an additional α, *e.g. yiṣḥaq → Ισαακ* and 2) that we know far too little of the vocalization of the LXX to derive any arguments from it.[284] In the second place we must mention the derivation of M. Naor, who again takes *yiśrā'ēl || yiśrā'ēl* as his starting-point, and derives the name from *'śr*, in which he sees the name of the ancient Semitic god Athar.[285] This derivation is important because it is taken over by Danell. Yet we cannot accept it, because its point of departure is not the traditional form of the name. Of course no one would deny that the Old Testament knows many instances where *ś* and *š* were interchanged. Or that in Judg. 12:6 is suggested that both phonemes were pronounced as *š* in Ephraim. But the conclusion that the Masoretic differentiation between *ś* and *š* is completely to be explained as influence from the Aramaic, is at least premature.[286] Therefore I am not convinced

[282] Noth, *o.c.* S. 191. These names and the noun *mśrh* are mentioned in Koehler-Baumgartner's Lexicon under II *śrh*. *Cf.* also H. Bauer-P. Leander, *Historische Grammatik*, S. 406 *seq.* Huffmon *o.c.* points out the same phenomenon in Mari. *Cf.* the name Išme-Dagan in Mari (Assur) and Išma-Dagan in Palestine (Hazor), *o.c.* p. 303.
[283] W. F. Albright, The Names 'Israel' and 'Judah'. *JBL* XLVI (1927) p. 151-185.
[284] Sachsse, Ursprung des Namens Israel, S. 65. Noth, *Personennamen*, S. 208 note 3. For the possibility of reconstructing the Hebrew on the basis of the ancient transliterations, see first of all the works of A. Sperber, Hebrew Based upon Biblical Passages in Parallel Transmission. *HUCA* XIV (1939) p. 153-249. And: *A Historical Grammar of Biblical Hebrew*. Leiden 1966, espec. p. 227-229. *Cf.* R. Meyer, *A. Sperbers neueste Studien über das masoretische Hebräisch*. Leiden 1962. Also G. Janssens, Enkele Problemen der Hebreeuwse grammatika in het licht van Origenes' transcripties. *Handelingen van het XXIIe Vlaams Filologencongres* 1957, blz. 95-99.
[285] M. Naor, *y'qb* und *yśr'l*, ZAW XLIX (1931), S. 317-321.
[286] As is done by Klaus Beyer in his *Althebräische Grammatik*, S. 12[1] and strongly supported by E. Vogt in *Biblica* LII (1971) S. 72-78.

by the recent arguments of Wächter[287] or Lemaire[288]. It is not permissible to conclude almost automatically from the fact that in many West-Semitic languages no difference is made in *writing* between *ś* and *š*, that this difference was also completely lost in the pronunciation. In this connexion the well-known Phoenician exception is significant: '*sr* // Hebrew '*śr* (ten).[289] One has to assume with Friedrich that in the case of this undoubtedly much used word a more ancient pronunciation found expression in writing. Following Caspari and Noth I base myself on the assumption that surely in a case as with the name of Israel, the ancient pronunciation is accurately handed down. Puns with the root *yśr* were of course obvious in Northern Israel since the *ś* was pronounced there as *š*![290] The existence and possible meaning of a root *śrh* was recently dealt with by Coote.[291]

Therefore it still seems best to follow the solution of Noth. As to the long ā one has to bear in mind that already Lagarde suggested here the possibility of an ancient form, possibly some optative, or even an emphatic element, rather than from a root *śr'*. On the one hand the latter requires to be postulated, and on the other ancient names such as *yaḫne'ēl* and *yirpe'ēl* show that a difference between *lāmęd-hē* and *lāmęd-'alęf* verbs need not show in the vocalization. All the same, the great advantage of Noth's explanation is that it does not force the text and remains the simplest.

That personal names as *yśr-il* from Mesopotamia (Accad-period!) and Ugarit are true parallels to the biblical name *yiśrā'ēl* remains unproven.[292] To conclude I want to mention the suggestion put forward by Yeivin: *yiśrā'ēl* = *yaśśōr'ēl* "Supreme is El".[293]

---

[287] L. Wächter, Israel und Jeschurun. In: *"Schalom". Studien zur Glaube und Geschichte Israels.* Festschrift A. Jepsen, Hrgb. v. K. H. Bernhardt, Stuttgart 1971, S. 58-64.
[288] A. Lemaire, Asriel, *śr'l*, Israël et l'origine de la conféderation israélite. *VT* XXIII (1973) p. 239-243.
[289] J. Friedrich, *Phoenizisch-Punische Grammatik*. Rome 1970, S. 18. The same warning is given by C. H. Gordon, *Ugaritic Textbook*. Rome 1967, p. 28-29.
[290] Th. L. Thompson, *The Historicity of the Patriarchal Narratives*, p. 40-44 seems also to have a preference for an original *śin*, but he does not make a definite choice.
[291] R. Coote, The Meaning of the Name Israel. *HThR* LXV (1972) p. 137-142.
[292] V. Scheil, Cylindres et Légendes inédits, I Le cylindre d'Išre-il. *RA* XIII (1916) p. 5-25. Ch. Virolleaud, Nouvelles tablettes alphabétiques de Ras-Shamra. *Comptes Rendus Ac. d. Inscr. et Belles Lettres*, 1956, p. 65. Cf. Thompson, *o.c.* p. 40-44.
[293] S. Yeivin, The Age of the Patriarchs. *RSO* XXXVIII (1961) p. 301.

CHAPTER IV

THE AMPHICTYONIC INSTITUTIONS

1. The concept 'Amphictyony'

One of the reasons why after the publication of 'Das System der Zwölf Stämme' continually more institutions of ancient Israel were ascribed to the amphictyony, is that Noth was in a sense the victim of a misconception. He imagined that the word 'amphictyony' might be used as a *terminus technicus* and so transferred to situations elsewhere. This misconception is stressed by F. R. Wüst in a study about the amphictyony.[1] By 'the amphictyony' the classical authors always mean Delphi. Strabo is the first to call other possible associations, such as that of Calauria, 'a kind of amphictyony'. In a way, then, the use of this word as a technical term goes back to him.[2] Wüst points out that both the use and the spelling of the word 'amphictyony' indicate that it was in origin a *proper name*. Probably there was at first a tribe called by this name, which was forcibly dispersed. Only then did it give its name, its structure and its cult to a supertribal organization, based upon the great authority of the old tribal sanctuary. The date tradition gives for the founding of this first sanctuary, about 1520 B.C.E., Wüst thinks perfectly suitable. The founding of 'the' amphictyony, some centuries later, Wüst too sees against the background of the Dorian invasions. The original tribe were probably Ionians. Interesting is Wüst's conclusion that the notion of twelve was deeply rooted in Ionian thought, so that the ancient cult of the tribe in all probability already had twelve hieromnemons. The origin of this set of twelve has therefore nothing to do with the supertribal aspect. It was necessary for the cult.[3]

Greece and Italy have seen a great many associations in the style of an amphictyony. That is, associations resembling *the* amphictyony, and in some cases consciously inspired by it. To use the *name* 'amphictyony'

---

[1] F. R. Wüst, Amphiktyonie, Eidgenossenschaft, Symmachie. *Historia* III (1954/1955) S. 129-153.
[2] *O.c.* S. 130. The translation 'neigbouring peoples' is not permissible either. According to Wüst it is based upon the younger, secondary spelling 'amphiktiony'.
[3] *O.c.* S. 137.

as *terminus technicus* for a certain form of supertribal religious organization is going much too far.[4] It is noteworthy that the older amphictyonies, for instance those of Onchestos and Calauria with sanctuaries of Poseidon, and also that at Pylae with its Demeter sanctuary of Anthela, go back to earlier groups of the population (and their cults). That the centre of importance was moved from Anthela to Delphi and from Demeter to Apollo is undoubtedly connected with the coming of the Dorians.[5] The Italic-Etruscan 'amphictyonies' display a slightly more 'political structure' than the Greek ones, for one thing because they regulated relations with other groups.[6] M. Weippert would therefore rather use these 'amphictyonies' for an analogue.[7] Yet the only data we have about these associations are really fairly young, while in their historic form the partners were always cities, and not tribes or ethnic groups.[8]

Another point must be kept in mind if one would make comparisons with the 'amphictyonies' of the classical world. The true function of such associations did not lie in the ethnic or cultic field, although these aspects naturally played an important part. There was always a certain

---

[4] *O.c.* S. 140-142. *Cf.* Noth, *Das System*, S. 46: 'Die älteste griechische Geschichte kennt Stammverbände, deren Gruppierung ebenfalls die Zwölf- oder Sechszahl zugrunde liegt und die die griechische Ueberlieferung, weil diese Verbände ein als Stätte eines gemeinsamen Kultes dienendes Heiligtum als lokal festliegendes Zentrum besassen, unter dem Namen "Amphiktyonien", Vereinigungen der "Umwohnenden", kennt.'

[5] For the Greek 'amphictyonies' see, besides Wüst's above-mentioned essay: H. Bürgel, *Die Pylaeisch-Delphische Amphiktyonie.* München 1877. F. Cauer, *sub voce 'amphiktyonia'. Paulys Real-Encyclopädie der Classischen Altertumswissenschaft*, Hrgb. v. G. Wissowa, Bd. I, Stuttgart 1894, Sp. 1904-1935. V. Ehrenberg, *Der Staat der Griechen.* Bd. I, Der hellenische Staat. Leipzig 1957. W. S. Ferguson, The Delian Amphictyony. *CR* XV (1901) p. 38-40. G. Forrest, The First Sacred War. *BCH* LXXX (1956) p. 33-52. J. P. Harland, The Calaurian Amphictyony. *AJA* XXIX (1925) p. 160-171. Anneliese Manzmann, *s.v. 'amphiktyonia'* in: *Der kleine Pauly* I, Stuttgart 1964, Sp. 311-313. E. Szanto, Die griechischen Phylen. *Sitzungsberichte der Philosophisch-Historischen Classe der kaiserlichen Akademie der Wissenschaften*, Band CXLIV, Abh. V, Wien 1902.

[6] Concerning the Italic 'amphictyonies': A. Alföldi, *Early Rome and the Latins.* Ann Arbor 1964. Ida Calabi, *Ricerche sui rapporti fra le poleis.* Firenze 1953. M. Pallottino, *The Etruscans.* Pelican Books A 310, London 1956. Emeline Richardson, *The Etruscans.* Chicago 1964. A. Rosenberg, *Der Staat der alten Italiker.* Berlin 1913.

[7] Weippert, *Die Landnahme der israelitischen Stämme*, S. 46[2]. Now Weippert no longer considers the term 'amphictyony' *'sachgemäss'* for ancient Israel. Abraham der Hebräer? *Biblica* LII (1971) S. 425[2].

[8] Although the associates are cities, the texts always speak of 'the twelve peoples'. It is still uncertain whether the word *populus* is of Etruscan or Indo-Germanic origin. $Me\chi l(um)$, which often appears in this context, may according to Pallottino mean 'nation' or 'league'. *O.c.* p. 131-135.

tension in Greece between politics and the geographical situation. The independent city states were always inclined towards expansion at the expense of others, yet at the same time their own independence was the core of all policy, strongly supported by geographical conditions. A 'political' means of balancing these forces was formed by the 'amphictyonies', (sea) leagues, *etc.* The partners joined in the association against a possible or actual enemy from without, but their first object was to be safe from one another. One might call such a league the cultic confirmation of a political equilibrium.[9]

After the above, it will not seem strange that it is almost impossible to arrive at a definition covering all the 'amphictyonies'. As we shall here discuss the institutions of a possible Israelite amphictyony, we shall start with Wüst's definition: '... ein sakrales Verband ... bei dem eine bestimmte Zahl von Stämmen oder Staaten Mitglieder sind und durch Vertreter eine Organisation bilden, die sakrale Aufgaben durchführen und überwachen'.[10] We see at once that on several points this definition is more vague than that of Noth. The number of twelve is by no means essential. As remarked above, the number of members does not affect the principle. Nor need there be one central sanctuary; what is essential, is a *central cult.* These might often coincide, as in the case of the *fanum Voltumnae* in Etruria, but sometimes they did not. Why, even the most famous amphictyony had two centres: Delphi and Anthela! For our subject this means that even if Israel cannot be shown to have possessed a central sanctuary in the time of the Judges, this would not automatically disallow an analogy with the classical 'amphictyonies'. Undoubtedly, though, the single central sanctuary is essential to Noth. He desires to see the unity and the cult of Ancient Israel expressed as concretely as possible.[11] For Noth the central sanctuary is certainly the most important institution of the amphictyony.

2. The Central Sanctuary

Considering the above, we must now put two questions: are there indications of a central sanctuary in the time of the Judges, and/or are there indications of a central (= communal) cult?

---

[9] V. Ehrenberg, *Aspects of the Ancient World*. Oxford 1946, esp. Ch. II, The Greek Country and the Greek State. J. A. O. Larsen, Federation for Peace in Ancient Greece. *CP* XXXIX (1944) p. 145-162. T. T. B. Ryder, *Koine-Eirene, General Peace and Local Independence in Ancient Greece.* London 1965. *Cf.* also the essay by Wüst.
[10] Wüst, *o.c.* S. 140.
[11] See above, p. 41.

The possibility of a central sanctuary in ancient Israel has been studied by A. Besters[12] and W. H. Irwin.[13] They both come to a more or less negative conclusion. Besters finds that there is no question of a central sanctuary in Judg. 19-21. The references to the ark and to Bethel (hence also to their combination!) are secondary. Therefore the original story contained no mention of a central sanctuary. That much Noth had seen himself. His argument is based on the whole event with 'Israel' as its 'hero', so that it must have been transmitted by 'Israel'. The story requires as it were an amphictyony to relate it.[14] Besters is also of opinion that the glossator who afterwards inserted Bethel and the ark, did so because he missed the central sanctuary with which he was acquainted.

Irwin makes three main points:
1) The structure of the Israelite league of tribes was differently directed from that of the classical amphictyonies. The centre was not formed by a common cult, but by a common history.
2) The traditions regarding the ancient sanctuaries are difficult to arrange in a linear chronology; moreover, there were essential differences between the various sanctuaries.
3) The general religious sitation in the time of the Judges was not favourable to the existence of a central sanctuary.
Point 2 undoubtedly contains the principal and strongest argument against the existence of a central sanctuary.

In the closing paragraph of chapter I some critics of the amphictyony hypothesis were quoted, who pointed out that it is practically impossible to find a sanctuary in ancient Israel of such pre-eminent importance that it might be called a central sanctuary. This applies to Shechem, Gilgal, Bethel, Mizpah, Shiloh or any other candidate. Though undoubtedly correct, this remark does not do full justice to Noth's standpoint that the true central sanctuary consisted of the ark alone, and was not located at one sanctuary during the whole period of the Judges. He considers that various sanctuaries played this part in succession, while the ark was lodged there.[15] It proves impossible, however, thus to place them in a linear chronology, beginning with Shechem and ending with Shiloh.

---

[12] A. Besters, Le sanctuaire central dans Jud. XIX-XXI. *EThL* (1965) p. 20-42. I was unable to obtain the original Belgian doctoral dissertation. See also A. D. H. Mayes, Israel in the pre-monarchy period. *VT* XXIII (1973) p. 151-170.
[13] W. H. Irwin, Le sanctuaire central israélite avant l'établissement de la monarchie. *RB* LXXII (1965) p. 161-185.
[14] Noth, *Das System*, S. 166-170.
[15] *Das System*, S. 94-95.

That was Irwin's main conclusion.[16] Indeed, it would seem a highly improbable course of events within a period of barely two centuries! At present, then, our conclusion remains: a) no sanctuaries are to be found whose authority was for a time so great that they might be regarded as a central sanctuary or could have functioned as such; b) even if it is clear that the standing of certain sanctuaries varied at different times, there was always more than one sanctuary held in particular esteem at the same time; c) it is not possible to show that the ark was always present in the most important place(s) of cult (for instance in Shechem[17] or Mizpah). On the other hand it is nowhere evident that the sanctuary where the ark finally came to rest held a central position (Shiloh).

Before leaving the matter of the central sanctuary to inquire after a central cult in connexion with the ark, there is one more question regarding the central sanctuary. One might indeed wonder whether such a sanctuary must not be postulated in order to understand the later centralization of the cult in Deuteronomy. That was always the opinion of Von Rad, and many agreed with him.[18] It must be objected first of all that this would be reversing the matter. The postulating of an amphictyonic central sanctuary ended a long discussion as to whether Deuteronomy did or did not require a single sanctuary, and if so which it was. One cannot now go back and say that such a sanctuary must be supposed because of Deuteronomy.[19] Secondly, the foundation of Deuteronomy's motive is clearly theological and not historical. Deuteronomy is concerned to keep Yahwism pure, which can only be done with a single sanctuary and a single cult.[20] In the third place, the demand in Deuteronomy that the cult shall be centralized and exclusive is clearly formulated as something new.[21]

Now if a central sanctuary cannot be found, how is it with a possible central cult? Was there for instance a special festival in Israel celebrating

[16] Irwin, o.c. p. 171-178. An attempt at constructing such a sequence was made by J. Dus, Ein richterzeitliches Stierbildheiligtum zu Bethel? Die Aufeinanderfolge der früh-israelitischen Zentralkultstätten. ZAW LXXVII (1965) S. 268-286.

[17] Mention of the ark at Shechem rests upon an admixture of Gilgal traditions and is a later Deuteronomist addition. E. Nielsen, Shechem, p. 74-80.

[18] G. von Rad, Deuteronomiumstudien. FRLANT 58, Göttingen 1948². Von Rad's view in this matter transpires in all his later publications. Cf. also A. R. Hulst, Het karakter van den cultus in Deuteronomium. Wageningen 1938.

[19] One need only see the summaries of the discussion in Hulst and in E. W. Nicholson, Deuteronomy and Tradition. Oxford 1967.

[20] Here I will only mention three authors who reject this thesis of Von Rad, although otherwise quite accepting the amphictyony hypothesis. They are: A. R. Hulst, o.c. p. 33-34. R. E. Clements, God and Temple. Oxford 1965, p. 93. E. W. Nicholson, o.c. p. 57 and 120-121.

[21] As remarked by W. H. Irwin, o.c. p. 169.

the national bond and re-affirming it, and did the ark play a central part there? One naturally thinks of a festival renewing the Covenant, as many imagine one at Shechem. Irwin points out that to have a real central function such a festival must comply with three conditions: 1) the ark must be present; 2) it should celebrate the renewal of the Covenant; 3) the twelve tribes or their representatives must participate. Irwin says there are two places where we may reasonably presume that a festival was held for the renewal of the Covenant: Shechem and Gilgal.[22] At the former it was very probably combined with an autumn festival (Feast of Tabernacles – New Year festival), but except for a late addition the ark is never mentioned at Shechem;[23] the latter had a spring festival (the Passover). The ark is mentioned at Gilgal, and so are the twelve tribes. Gilgal would therefore comply with all requirements, were it not that the Old Testament very explicitly connects a festival renewing the Covenant with Shechem.[24]

It seems to me that Irwin hits the nail on the head in pointing to I Sam. 7:15-17. There we are told that Samuel travelled round every

[22] With regard to Gilgal, then, Irwin mainly agrees with H. J. Kraus, Gilgal. Ein Beitrag zur Kultusgeschichte Israels. *VT* I (1951) S. 181-199. So do J. Alberto Soggin, Gilgal, Passah und Landnahme. *SVT* XV, Leiden 1966, S. 265-277 and F. Langlamet, *Gilgal et les récits de la traversée du Jourdain*. Paris 1969. A good survey of all these problems is given by A. R. Hulst, Der Jordan in den alttestamentlichen Ueberlieferungen. *OTS* XIV, Leiden 1965, S. 162-188. Kraus is not usually followed in his opinion that the crossing of the Jordan (also that of the Red Sea) was represented in the cult and 'acted'. This reasoning is based on Gilgal *not* being identical with the cult site in or near Shechem, as Sellin thought it was (E. Sellin, *Gilgal. Ein Beitrag zur Geschichte der Einwanderung Israels in Palästina*. Leipzig 1917). In my opinion also the literary data do not tend towards the conclusion drawn by Sellin. On the other hand, in the southern part of the Jordan plain every square metre of ground has been vainly searched for possible remains of Gilgal (H. J. Franken, Tell es-Sultan and Old Testament Jericho. *OTS* XIV, p. 200). We must still seriously reckon with the possibility that Gilgal was the cult site at some town of a different name. Another view is that of G. Schmitt, *Der Landtag von Sichem*, Stuttgart 1964, S. 82[5], that there were two Gilgals: one at Samaria and one at Jericho. The interpretation of Josh. 24 always remains a difficulty. The present text certainly shows traces of considerable Deuteronomist revision. It is sometimes assumed that the tradition is based on some historical event. But what event? Was it the introduction of Yahwism? (Seebass, *Der Erzvater Israel*, S. 90). A league between Ephraim and Manasseh, the Ephraimites bringing in Yahwism? (Nielsen, *Shechem*, p. 128-133). New cultic laws given to an Israel already in existence? (G. Schmitt, *Der Landtag*, S. 80-94). Or a combination of the thesis of Sellin-Noth with a new cultic code, *i.e.* the introduction of the Book of the Covenant? (J. L'Hour, L'Alliance de Sichem, p. 26 and 350-368).
[23] See above, note 17.
[24] The objection felt by Irwin, that chronologically Gilgal comes before Shechem in the book of Joshua, I cannot look upon as very serious.

year to three well-known sanctuaries in Benjamin and Ephraim: Bethel, Mizpah and Gilgal, to judge the people there.[25] There is every reason to suppose that these three sanctuaries corresponded to the three 'high feasts' of ancient Israel. Each sanctuary had its own special great festival. As there were many more temples or sanctuaries in the rest of Israel at this time, it is to be presumed there were more of such 'triads'. In any case one may *not* deduce from Exod. 23:14-19 that the Israelite was called upon to go up three times a year to one and the same central sanctuary. No doubt a number of famous sanctuaries, such as those on Mount Gerizim and Mount Tabor, at Gilgal, Bethel or Beersheba, will have attracted great numbers of pilgrims every year. Pilgrimages of this kind were often combined with more worldly objects, such as a fair.

Finally I would mention Irwin's reasoning that if a central sanctuary or a central cult existed,[26] it is highly peculiar that it is never referred to in any of the cultic prescripts of ancient Israel, not even in Exod. 23:14-19! The whole book of the Covenant, the *Sitz im Leben* of which, should be according to Noth the amphictyony, contains no single mention of a central sanctuary or a central cult.[27] Noth's arguments to explain the absence of these data for the historical fact of the amphictyony might be accepted,[28] but they are definitely not valid with regard to the cult, which the Old Testament rates so highly.

One thing more in reference to Irwin's very sound essay, concerning the point of criticism I have named in number 1. Irwin opines that Israel was not held together by a cult, but by past history. Not a common cult, but a common history![29] I think chapter III will have shown how entirely I subscribe to this. Even if one accepts Noth's view that their history functioned in the cult, 'history' being taken in the sense of the whole set of historically determined factors, the fact remains that the history is primary and the cult secondary.[30] Indeed, there is no saying whether the cult was the only place where history functioned and was transmitted. One thinks equally of the *bēt 'āb* where not only the old ethos, but also the old traditions may have been handed on.

Finally, there is the question of the ark. Is it conceivable that in the

[25] Irwin, *o.c.* p. 182.

[26] Irwin does not distinguish between the two.

[27] The only support Noth himself finds, is the rule about the *nāśî'* in Exod. 22:27. We have seen in the previous chapter that there was no office of *nāśî'*. The word is a title and does not indicate a function.

[28] *Das System*, S. 64.

[29] Irwin, *o.c.* p. 166.

[30] Most recent studies of Joshua 24 also come to this conclusion. I quote G. Schmitt: 'Der Jahwebund, von dem wir wissen, begründet nicht die Einheit des Volkes als eines Bundespartners, er setzt sie voraus'. *o.c.* S. 90.

time of the Judges the ark was the real central sanctuary in a postulated cult of the twelve tribes? This question could only be answered if we had some kind of certainty as to the function of this ark. A recent study by H. A. Brongers shows only too clearly how little we can be certain of regarding the ark.[31] One thing we know is, that in ancient times the ark had no authority of its own, but was destined to contain or transport something. According to Deuteronomy that something was the Tablets of the Law. Was it originally a depiction or a symbol of Yahweh? The appearance of the ark always seems to have given rise to a strong sense of divine proximity.[32] The conception that the ark was originally instrumental in giving oracles, or served as repository of oracular implements is a mere variant of this, as implying the presence of the divine will.[33]

Remembering now that the ark was of old intimately connected with Yahweh,[34] which was not the case of the ancient sanctuaries in the country, one might argue as Noth did that it was the presence of the ark which guaranteed a 'Yahwist' celebration of an actually older cult. In that case the ark would have had to be continually travelling between the various sanctuaries, and might then with justice be termed a mobile sanctuary. A first objection to this is, that owing to lack of data such a reconstruction must remain speculative, while the ark is not named in

[31] H. A. Brongers, Einige Aspekte der gegenwärtige Lage der Ladeforschung. *NThT* XXV (1971) S. 6-27. This survey also gives most recent literature. Afterwards there also appeared J. Gutmann, The History of the Ark. *ZAW* LXXXIII (1971) p. 22-30.

[32] This is one of the few aspects of the ark that all are agreed upon! *Cf.* Brongers, *o.c.* S. 24-25 with the literature cited there, and J. Gutmann, *o.c.* p. 24. According to G. von Rad, Zelt und Lade, *GSAT*, S. 112, the view that the ark was nothing but a repository and means of transport for the tables of the law, was a typical new idea in Deuteronomy. Yet it need not really conflict – as a kind of de-mythologization – with the conception of the ark as 'symbol of the presence of God'. T. E. Fretheim, The Ark in Deuteronomy. *CBQ* XXX (1968) p. 6-7. This different approach to the ark by Deuteronomy does make it impossible, though, to look upon it as going back to earlier amphictyonic traditions.

[33] Brongers, *o.c.* S. 26-27.

[34] The passages where instead of *'arōn yhwh* the expression *'arōn (hā) 'ęlōhīm* is used do not admit of the conclusion that the latter is older than the former, or that a different god than Yahweh was meant. Considering also the close link between the ark and the Levites – see below – I think we cannot accept the opinion of G. Fohrer (*Geschichte der israelitischen Religion*, S. 100-101), who ascribes a pre-Yahwistic and extra-Palestinian past to the ark as the tribal sanctum of Ephraim. Actually, F. Horst already did so too in his review of Noth's *Das System* (*ThBl* XII (1933) Sp. 107); this is the only point where he seriously criticizes Noth's thesis. Horst is followed by R. Smend, *Jahwekrieg und Stämmebund*. S. 70.

connexion with such an important cult as that of Shechem. The chief objection, however, is that in the Old Testament the ark is nearly always closely associated with the Levites, whereas in chapter II we have seen that the rise of the Levites as the particular servants of Yahweh was not unopposed. In the time of the Judges this process was still far from completion. If the ark was already connected with the Levites in the time of the Judges, it is altogether improbable that it already had a generally recognized central function then.

Now this theory stands or falls with the supposition that the priesthood of Eli and his sons was already Levitical. Yet for this only two arguments can be advanced: 1) the Egyptian names appearing in the Levite genealogies and given to the sons of Eli; 2) if indeed Zadok was originally not a Levite, as is often suggested, than the claim of the Jerusalem priesthood to a Levitical origin would rest entirely upon a later fiction, if Eli's descendant Abiathar was not a Levite either. Surely this is highly improbable.[35]

If this supposition is right, it would explain the increasing authority of the Levites: they had the ark! That David brought the ark to Jerusalem resulted from the very close tie between his clan, Ephrath, and the Levites. The earliest information about the Levites connects them with Jerusalem. Kiriath-jearim and Bethlehem are closely linked in the Judean genealogies[36] and the names of those who cared for the ark in Kiriath-jearim – Abinadab and Eleazar[37] – appear both in the Levite genealogies and in that of David.[38] The close tie that always subsisted between the Davidic dynasty and the Levites need not be insisted on here.

Altogether we may say in conclusion that it is improbable that Israel in the time of the Judges had a central sanctuary or a central cult. A further examination in the next two sections of political structures in the time of the Judges will make it still more evident how improbable such a central institution is.[39]

---

[35] In this I choose for Cody, *Old Testament Priesthood*, p. 69-72, against A. H. J. Gunneweg, *Leviten und Priester*, S. 112-114.

[36] 1 Chr. 2:50 derives both families from Caleb!

[37] For these interesting connexions I depend upon the fascinating article by J. Blenkinsopp, Kiriath-Jearim and the Ark. *JBL* LXXXVIII (1969) p. 143-156. Abinadab and Eleazar were sons of Aaron, Exod. 6:23.

[38] David's brother was called Abinadab, I. Sam. 17:13.

[39] Both Irwin, *o.c.* p. 171-182, and H. M. Orlinsky (The Tribal System of Israel) already used the 'religious situation in the time of the Judges' as an argument against a central sanctuary.

3. The Sacred War

That a certain aggressiveness belongs to the essence of Yahwism has long been realized. Many have therefore sought the origins of Israel in the encampment of a group of followers of Moses pursuing some religious end by force of arms.[40] This old idea was consciously revived by G. von Rad.[41] He reasons on *formgeschichtlich* lines that the literary elements and expressions referring to the sacred war, together constitute a kind of liturgy.[42] The recurrent formulas are indication of a concrete *Sitz im Leben*, and that is the standing institution of the 'sacred war'.

Von Rad then inquires in what period of Israel's history such an institution can have existed. Since the time of the *Einwanderung* and the *Landnahme* was not a period of large-scale warfare, at most of incidental armed encounters, and as before that there was no Yahwist Israel, the early time of the Judges is left as *terminus a quo*. And since the Kings soon began to wage secular and imperialist wars, the time of Saul way well be regarded as *terminus ad quem*! This would mean that the sacred wars were waged at the time when Israel had just appeared upon the scene in the form of an amphictyony. The sacred war was one of the consequences of the amphictyony, said Von Rad, thus also assigning a political role to the amphictyony.[43] The many separate tribal wars that were also

---

[40] The most well-known example is J. Wellhausen, as we saw in Ch. I. Let us quote once more his famous pronouncement (quoted by Von Rad on S. 14): 'Das Kriegslager, die Wiege der Nation, es war auch das älteste Heiligtum. Da war Israel, und da war Jahwe.' *Abriss*, S. 10. The concept 'sacred war', a term borrowed from Islam, took shape after the famous work of F. Schwally, *Semitische Kriegsaltertümer*. Bd. I, Der heilige Krieg im alten Israel. Leipzig 1901. Weber's men's societies of military trend we already discussed in ch. I. A good survey of how the O.T. depicts Yahweh as a warrior is given by H. Frederiksson, *Jahwe als Krieger. Studien zum alttestamentlichen Gottesbild*. Lund 1945.

[41] G. von Rad, *Der heilige Krieg im alten Israel*. AThANT, Zürich 1951.

[42] Von Rad distinguishes the following items:

a. The participants are summoned by blowing the trumpet,
b. Those summoned are called 'people of Yahweh',
c. They must observe strict taboos,
d. Sacrifices are made and oracles consulted,
e. It is proclaimed that 'Yahweh has delivered your enemies into your hands',
f. Yahweh himself goes before the army,
g. The people must not fear, but believe,
h. The enemy is already losing courage,
i. War cries usher in the actual fighting,
j. Panic among the enemies,
k. Termination with the formula: 'Return to your tents, O Israel!'

[43] 'In diesem Ereignis (the battle of Deborah) haben sich die Stämme als "Israel", d.h. als eine von Jahwe geführte und geschützte Einheit erlebt. Genauer: Sie haben überraschend erfahren, dass die kultische Bindung an Jahwe auch weit-

carried on were not sacred wars. The latter were always defensive, directed against the 'enemies of Yahweh'. The war against the Benjamites in Judg. 19-21 may not be taken as a sacred war either. A sacred war was always led by a *mōšīaʿ*, a 'saviour'.[44]

Thus the institution of the sacred war had but a comparatively short existence, yet it deeply influenced Israel's concept of God. Particularly the firm faith that Yahweh would forcefully protect his property always persisted in Israel.[45] Israel did not fight for Yahwism, but Yahweh fought for Israel!

The connexion between the sacred war and the amphictyony is actually only indirect with Von Rad. His arguments are: a) the date in the period of the Judges; b) Noth's hypothesis that in this peroid 'Israel' was the name of the amphictyony; c) the analogy with the Greek amphictyonies, which also waged 'sacred wars'.[46] This linkage is attacked by R. Smend.[47] He does, however, explicitly accept both the amphictyony and the war of Yahweh.[48] Only he is concerned to dissociate the two and really, again like Wellhausen, to show that especially the wars of Yahweh were constitutive for Israel.[49] Against the linking of the amphictyony with the wars of Yahweh, Smend makes the following points:

1. If, as posited by Von Rad, the song of Deborah is the earliest authentic source for the amphictyonic holy war, then the refusal of some tribes to take part would have been judged very differently. Not as indifference, but as a violation of the covenant!
2. Never were all twelve tribes concerned in any war of Yahweh.
3. The Old Testament contains definite rulings in its information about

reichende Konsequenzen auf politischem Gebiet hatte. Damals begann Israel ein Volk zu werden.' *O.c.* S. 20.

[44] *O.c.* S. 27[44]. See for this our next paragraph about the Judges.

[45] Frederiksson, too, had already pointed this out (see note 40). In Israel's conception of God he derives, *int.al.*, the following elements from Yahweh's image as a warrior: a) his lively, active nature; b) the possibility of strict monotheism; c) the extra stress upon characteristics such as power and sanctity; d) special emotional traits are more accentuated, such as safety, justice.

[46] The ideality of these 'sacred wars' is often overestimated: 'The Sacred War was fought for Delphi, but it was "for the possession of" not "for the sake of". G. Forrest, The First Sacred War. *BCH* LXXX (1956) p. 33-52.

[47] R. Smend jr., *Jahwekrieg und Stämmebund. Erwägungen zur ältesten Geschichte Israels.* FRLANT 84, Göttingen 1963.

[48] Smend modifies Noth's amphictyony hypothesis chiefly with regard to the central sanctuary. He regards the ark as the original sanctum of the Joseph tribes. The ark belongs neither to the war of Yahweh, nor to the amphictyony.

[49] Also Smend says: 'Aber weil Jahwe da ist, ist in irgendeinem Sinne auch Israel da' and 'Der Krieg Jahwes kommt zwar nicht vom Nationalen her, er führt aber auf das Nationale hin.' *O.c.* S. 30; *cf.* also S. 97.

the wars of Yahweh. The expression *milḥāmōt yahwę* is even used. On the other hand no name has been delivered to us for the amphictyony, and rules concerning it are totally absent. This need not mean that there was no amphictyony, but it is certainly an argument against connecting the two institutions.

4. The amphictyony was directed by special officials, the 'Judges'. The wars of Yahweh were commanded by charismatic 'Saviours'.[50] Office and charisma are mutually exclusive here.

The amphictyony and the war of Yahweh were in no way related in their beginnings. Comparisons with the classical or Islamic holy wars will hardly hold good. According to Smend the amphictyony went back to the tribes of Leah. The tribes of Rachel were the bearers of the fierce Yahwism, and brought in the wars of Yahweh. The two themes were united in the Yahweh amphictyony as the common property of all the tribes, but no organic connexion was established between them.

Whatever opinion one may hold regarding the 'wars of Yahweh', Smend has certainly shown that they had nothing to do with the amphictyony. This is all the more convincing, since he himself was an adherent of the amphictyony hypothesis! The concept of the Israelite Holy War as depicted by Von Rad, is the result of the study of the Old Testament in isolation of the study of the cultures of the ancient Near East *in toto*. The notion of the Holy War belongs to the ideology of many Near Eastern cultures.[51]

4. *The Judge of Israel*

In the eyes of Martin Noth the office of the 'Judge of Israel' was the most important and in fact the only office of 'Israel'.[52] Here 'Israel' is again taken in the sense of the name of the ancient Israelite amphictyony. The life of this amphictyony did not primarily make itself felt in and at the cult at the central sanctuary. Nor was it the possession of such a central cult that in the first place distinguished this 'Israel'. The special thing about 'Israel' was, that it was subject to divine law. These divine laws were transmitted in the central cult and proclaimed anew every so many years. This was then followed by a solemn renewal of the

---

[50] See for this distinction the following paragraph.
[51] Once again this has been shown by Manfred Weippert, "Heiliger Krieg" in Israel und Assyrien. Kritische Bemerkungen zu Gerhard von Rads Konzept des "Heiligen Krieges im alten Israel". *ZAW* LXXXIV (1972) S. 460-493. So also A. D. H. Mayes, Israel in the premonarchy period. *VT* XXIII (1973) p. 151-170.
[52] M. Noth, Das Amt des 'Richters Israels'. *Bertholet-Festschrift*, Tübingen 1950, S. 404-417. See also ch. I, p. 42.

covenant. That was the heart and the primary function of the Israelite amphictyony![53] It was the task of the Judge of Israel to guard this divine law and proclaim it periodically, according to Noth. Although typical of the amphictyony, and thus belonging mainly to the time of the Judges, the office must have continued to exist for some time under the Kings, as appears from its mention in Micah 4:14 and Deut. 17:9. Noth only regards the so-called 'lesser' Judges as the true Judges, that is officials of the amphictyony. The fact that we have such a good chronology of them may be explained by the assumption that dating went by their years of office. This again goes to show how weighty that office was. The Judge in this office was therefore concerned with the law and the cult, and not with political or military matters!

That, in short, is the office as Noth saw it. Such an office, however, has never existed.[54] We will sum up our criticism in the following points:
1. Following A. Alt and others, Noth has always understood *špṭ* as a juridical term. It is now evident, however, especially since we know so many Ugaritic texts, that this translation is far too one-sided. *Špṭ* means both to 'rule' and to 'judge'. In the Ancient East these were two aspects of the same thing. This means that we may not see the task of the *šōfēṭ* as confined to the juridical field, and thereby it is no longer possible to draw a strict line between the 'lesser' Judges as bearing an amphictyonic office, and the 'greater' Judges as political leaders and military 'saviours'.[55]
2. Apart from the Judges in the book of Judges, we find that the word *šōfēṭ* chiefly appears in combination with the word *śar*. Examining this further, *šōfeṭîm* and *śārîm* prove to be the terms used to indicate the principal men in power in the little cities of the pre-monarchial period, terms that long continued in use. We have seen in the previous chapter how the social and political organization of ancient Israel rested on two supports: actual or fictitious blood-relationship on the

[53] Noth, Das Amt des 'Richters Israels', S. 414 u. *GI*⁹, S. 97
[54] My view as to the function of the Judges is given at greater length in: C. H. J. de Geus, De richteren van Israël. *NThT* XX (1965/66) p. 81-100. Further relevant literature is also mentioned there. A modification of Noth's views, without any essential change, is found in K. D. Schunck, Die Richter Israels und ihr Amt. *SVT* XV, Leiden 1966, S. 252-262. See also the remarks already made in ch. III, par. 3 about 'Family, Clan, Tribe' as to the social and political structure of ancient Israel. Further R. de Vaux, *Histoire ancienne d'Israël*, vol. II, p. 67-86.
[55] For the meaning of *špṭ* cf. W. Richter, Zu den 'Richtern Israels'. *ZAW* LXXVII (1965) S. 40-72, espec. S. 58-70. Also *DISO* p. 316 s.v. *špṭ*ᴵᴵ. The distinction between 'Judges' and 'Saviours' is chiefly based upon O. Grether, Die Bezeichnung 'Richter' für die charismatische Helden der vorstaatlichen Zeit. *ZAW* LVII (1939) S. 110-122.

one hand, the city on the other. In the case of the most eminent families the two might coincide. Actual power was in the hands of a council of 'elders', and the most prominent among these may be called šōfēṭ and/or śar.[56] In this light, the following hypothesis was formulated: 'The Judge was first of all a municipal official, a ruler whose authority rested upon the power of the council of elders. The office was not hereditary, and the appointment was not always made. In later times the title of šōfēṭ, like śar, remained in use for the municipal governors appointed by the King.'[57]

3. The background of the Judges in the book of Judges and also of someone like Samuel agrees very well with this description. They were all Israelites belonging to the well-to-do class of free landowners. For most of them we can find a clear link with some particular city. Their activity as 'Judge' is focused on two points: the city in which they lived and were buried (where they probably also held residence), and their work as 'Judge' of 'Israel'. The latter we must take in the sense that they were indeed men whose importance in the cultural, political, military or juridical field far transcended the limits of their own city. Gideon is a good example. His father Joash is the typical picture of a real śar in a little city of ancient Israel, but his son became a national figure. He became this by a deed that was originally only locally important, but whose wider import soon penetrated to the Israelites. The next step was taken in the historical traditions, in that the memories of these figures of olden times were set in a lineal chronology, while their importance was extended to the whole of Israel.[58]

The difference between the 'greater' and the 'lesser' Judges is only, that in the case of the 'greater' ones we can still see more or less what was the basis of their national importance. It is quite likely that at first more extensive traditions were also related about the 'lesser' Judges. It is significant that Jephthah appears in both lists.[59]

4. Dus is therefore quite justified in speaking of Israel's 'suffetes',[60] though we must generally imagine the work and the importance of these suffetes on a far smaller scale than in the case of the famous

[56] Exod. 2:41; Isa. 3:2-4; Hos. 7:7; Mic. 7:3; Zeph. 3:3; Job 9:24; 12:17. From Exod. 18:21 and Hos. 13:10 it is evident that the activity of a śar can be expressed with the root špṭ.

[57] De Geus, o.c. p. 90.

[58] O.c. p. 96-100.

[59] That Judg. 12:7 should form part of the list Judg. 10:1-5 plus 12:7-15 was always stressed by Noth himself also, Ueb. Stud. S. 48, and Amt des 'Richter Israels', S. 406.

[60] J. Dus, Die Sufeten Israels. ArOr XXXI (1965) S. 444-469. De Geus, o.c. p. 98-99.

suffetes of Carthage or the dikasts of Tyre. This system of a 'republican' form of government in the small towns and city-states was essentially the same over the whole region of Canaanite culture in the Iron Age.[61] Since, however, these suffetes will have seen their first task in furthering the interests of their own city, the number of them who attained national stature naturally remained small. So the Deuteronomist History (Dtr) is quite right to say that the intervals between the periods of such national figures were quite as typical of this time as their rule, and also that 'every man did what was right in his own eyes.' Thus the Judges were the forerunners, both for good and ill, of the territorial state.

5. Nābī' and Mazkīr

In chapters II and III we have already had to speak of some institutions, and even of an 'office', ascribed to the amphictyony.[62] 'Amphictyonic' law and the 'amphictyonic' ethos were discussed at length in chapter III. We concluded that it was quite unnecessary to call upon the amphictyony hypothesis in order to explain ancient Israelite law. Law and ethos are seen to follow from the social structure of ancient Israel (at that time still largely tribal), and from the existing political and economic circumstances.

We also saw that the naśī' was not an Israelite hieromnemoon. Nāśī' is not the name of function at all, it is a title that indicates a certain position.

This only leaves two other attempts, formulated by Kraus and Reventlow, to reconstruct an amphictyonic office. Both are intimately bound up with the law. Another instance of the extreme importance for the amphictyony hypothesis of especially Alt's views regarding ancient Israelite law and the way it functioned!

H. J. Kraus tried to find back an old amphictyonic office of 'prophet'.[63] He begins with the Israelite offices as enumerated in Deut. 16:18-18:22 and then reasons just as Noth does in his Amt des Richters. Deut. 17:9 speaks of the judge, 17:12 of the priest, 17:14-20 of the king, then in

---

[61] In practice, the political organization was an aristocracy. In the course of the early Iron Age this replaced the feudal monarchy remaining from the Bronze Age. In most cases the aristocracy was again succeeded by territorial monarchies. A. Alt, Die Staatenbildung der Israeliten in Palästina. KS II, S. 25. For discussion of these matters see G. Buccellati, Cities and Nations of Ancient Syria. Roma 1967, and supra, ch. III, 3.

[62] Again mainly in III, par. 3.

[63] H. J. Kraus, Die prophetische Verkündigung des Rechts in Israel. Theol. Stud. Heft 51, Zollikon 1957.

18: 15-18 it is *the* prophet according to Kraus. He supposes the 'central' and 'official' aspects to be mainly concentrated in the office of 'Judge', while that of *the* prophet covers rather the prophetic and charismatic work. Kraus points out that it was not only the Judges, but especially Moses and the Levites[64] who were charged with the prophetic proclamation of the law. Like Noth, Kraus imagines this central prophetic office still to have functioned for a long time in Israel, especially in the Northern Kingdom.

Naturally this whole construction stands or falls with the amphictyony hypothesis and with the view of Deuteronomy that is based upon it. This theory of Kraus was not very successful, mainly owing to the mechanical way he handles his assumptions. All the same, Kraus did indeed signalize a flaw in that Alt and Noth fail to do justice to the prophetic aspect of ancient Israel.

H. Reventlow drew attention to the office of *mazkīr*, that had such an important role during the monarchy.[65] He brings forward the forensic meaning of *zkr*, and especially the expression *mazkīr ʿāwōn. Hizkīr* means 'to proclaim'. Reventlow wonders whether the received opinion that the *mazkīr* was the King's herald[66] does not conflict with Israel's theonomy. The King was himself subject to the divine law, so the guarding of that law cannot have been the charge of a royal officer. Divine law belongs to the sphere of the amphictyony. Thus Reventlow comes to describe the office of *mazkīr* as that of *Generalstaatsanwalt*, whose chief task is the 'Anklageerhebung'. The inclusion of this office in a list of royal functionaries is a mark of honour and says nothing as to its content. For that matter, priests are also included in the list![67]

This theory of Reventlow was soon entirely disposed of. First in the field was H. J. Boecker,[68] who points out that *zkr* does indeed function in forensic language, but that its meaning is by no means confined to 'accusing'. He explains Reventlow's objections to the view that this office derives from Egypt as simply stemming from a collision between the

---

[64] Kraus draws attention to the role of Moses as mediator when the laws are given on Mount Sinai, and to that of the Levites in Deut. 27:14-26; 33:10.
[65] H. Graf Reventlow, Das Amt des Mazkir. Zur Rechtsstruktur des öffentlichen Lebens in Israel. *ThZBs* XV (1959) S. 161-175.
[66] Already so presented by J. Begrich, Sōfēr and Mazkīr. *ZAW* 58 (1940/41) S. 1-30. Begrich had explained the function as borrowed by the Israelites from Egypt. The administration of the early monarchy was set up very much after the model of Egypt. Begrich was followed in this by De Vaux, Les Institutions de l'Ancien Testament I, p. 202-203.
[67] Reventlow even suggests the possibility that *śar* also was originally an amphictyonic title! *O.c.* S. 174[28].
[68] H. J. Boecker, Erwägungen zum Amt des Mazkir. *ThZBs* XVII (1961) S. 212-216.

cherished idea an of amphictyonic Israel under divine law and the conception of a new kingship directed towards the *Umwelt*.

The root *zkr* was treated at still greater length by W. Schottroff.[69] He points out that *hizkīr* means 'to announce', 'to proclaim' with a personal object: 'to announce someone', 'to name somebody'. *Hizkīr ʿāwōn* is 'to make known (hidden) guilt'. The office of *mazkīr* is still best explained as the Israelite parallel to the Egyptian court herald.

The same confirmation of Begrich's standpoint we now find again, with a new detailed argumentation, in Mettinger's fine work on the high-ranking officials in the early monarchy.[70] An amphictyonic office is out of the question! Even more: Mettinger's work clearly shows that the administration of the monarchy does not at any point require to be explained as going back to old amphictyonic or even tribal forms of organization. What can be shown is that in a few cases it falls back upon the earlier structure of the (Canaanite) city-states.[71]

The development is from city to state, *not* from tribe to state! A state is only formed when the tribe is given up. The developments in Israel are conformable to the general remarks made on this matter in chapter III, which are based on conclusions from situations elsewhere.

---

[69] W. Schottroff, *'Gedenken' im Alten Orient und im Alten Testament*. WMANT 15, Neukirchen 1964, espec. S. 253-270. *Cf.* also P. A. H. de Boer, *Gedenken und Gedächtnis in der Welt des Alten Testaments*. Stuttgart 1962.

[70] T. N. D. Mettinger, *Solomonic State Officials*. Lund 1971. Espec. p. 52-62.

[71] An ancient Canaanite office is 'overseer of the statute-labour'. The 'friend of the king' is seen in the Amarna letters and in Gen. 26:26 in Gerar. When he appointed his 'district governors', Solomon fell back upon old Canaanite families.

SUMMARY
OF THE CONCLUSIONS

We will here recapitulate the most important conclusions. The sequence in which they occur in this book is kept as much as possible.

1. We hope to have shown how old the amphictyony hypothesis already is. Martin Noth gave it its final form and most consistent formulation, together with a traditio-historical argumentation.

2. For every reconstruction of the earliest history of Israel the presuppositions in the fields of sociology, economy, politics and the chosen literary methods are of equally fundamental importance. Most authors, however, neglect those first aspects. One is apt to be more interested in the religious aspects of the life of the Hebrews than in the profane. In most cases a process of sedentarization is seen as the *impetus* that led to the historical developments, as a result of which the Hebrew people afterwards came into existence. Since Ed. Meyer's work, this process of sedentarization has been used as a socio-economic "model" to explain the historical developments.

3. The places in the Old Testament where a Joseph-tribe is mentioned are all rather young. They date from the time of the monarchy and "Joseph" always stands in a certain antithesis to "Judah". The older texts always speak of Ephraim and Manasseh.

4. The tribe of the priests, Levi, was included in the tribe system later. A system of twelve essentially equal tribes, including a secular Levi-tribe, never existed. It is not necessary for the correct understanding of the texts about Levi, to postulate a former secular tribe of Levi.

5. The tribe-system of the type "A", with Joseph and Levi, is therefore younger than that of type "B", which in the place of these two tribes still has Ephraim and Manasseh. Moreover, "A" is not a real system of *tribes*, but a genealogical system: a list of eponyms. It came into existence as a result of the desire for restoration of the Davidic imperium, after 722 B.C.E.

The older system "B", however, is in reality a summing up of geographical entities. This system "B" was created at the beginning of the monarchy to provide a feeling of cohesion for groups that until then had lived independent of each other. In the case of Gilead and Gad an increasing inclination was shown to use genealogical instead of geographical terms.

6. The number of twelve most probably originated in a cult, as for instance in Gilgal. Along with other numbers, as "ten" or "seven" it functions as a schematic expression of the total. Twelve in this context simply means: "all".

7. The generally accepted view that all Semitic peoples have known a former stage of their history, in which they lived as nomads or semi-nomads, proved in most cases to be incorrect. More recent investigations suggest for the oldest Semites a sedentary and a mainly agricultural milieu. The epicentre of their spreading out over the ancient Near East is no longer sought in the desert areas.

8. The social structure of the ancient Hebrews consisted of the elements "extended family" – "clan" – "tribe/people". The extended family or *bēt 'āḇ* was an exogamous unit, the clan an endogamous unit.

9. In the unilateral, unilinear kinship system of the Hebrews, the clan – *mišpāḥā* – was the most important unit. This system was based on the communal ownership of the land.

10. The unity of the Israelites was primarily ethnic. It was based on the ideas of *connubium* and *forum*. The Israelites formed what was called a *Gesellschaftsnation* (society-nation).

11. The social structure of the Hebrews gives therefore in itself no reason to postulate an origin in a nomadic or semi-nomadic milieu. This social structure was in the premonarchic period fully adequate for the political and the economic situation of that stage in history. The example of South Arabia demonstrates that such a form of of organization is fully conceivable with a sedentary and agricultural people.

12. The political organization also found its centre in the clan and in the town. The tribes were geographical entities, groupings of related clans, with but few functions of their own. This vagueness is a characteristic of the notion of "tribe".

13. A Conquest of Canaan as a clear break in the historical development of early Israel, is improbable for social and economic reasons. Archaeologically, no Conquest can be demonstrated.

14. The awareness of the Hebrews of not being autochthonous and the juridical claims on the country, are primarily connected with the patriarchs in the Old Testament.

15. The traditions of the patriarchs presuppose a milieu of the later Bronze Age, but not necessarily outside Palestine. We must start to reckon with the fact that the Hebrews have lived much longer in the land than is generally accepted. There is much to be said in favour of the supposition that the earliest Hebrews were the "Amoritic" population of the central highlands.

16. It is not possible to identify with sufficient certainty the group(s) that was (were) the bearer(s) of the Exodus and Sinai traditions. The Desert traditions came from the sphere of life of the southern tribes.

17. One should not use the term "amphictyony" as a technical term for a special kind of bond between tribes. Although Noth only spoke of a *religious* confederation, in the scholarly discussion the amphictyony nevertheless gradually accumulated traits of an incipient *political* institute. But if the term "amphictyony" is not to be used as a technical term, it is also not an intermediate stage between tribe and state. On the contrary, the development went from *city* to state! It appeared impossible to demonstrate the existence of any amphictyonic office or institution.

18. It was not possible to show the existence of a central shrine or a central cult.

19. The "Wars of Yahweh" did not originate from an amphictyony. The notion of the Holy War is to be considered as a theological and literary motive.

20. The Judges were essentially urban administrators, who, because of their specific deeds gained national importance. A real difference between the "greater" and the "lesser" Judges, did not exist.

BIBLIOGRAPHY

ADAMS, W. Y. Invasion, Diffusion, Evolution? *Antiquity* XLII (1968) p. 194-215.
AHARONI, Y. The land of ᶜAmqi. *IEJ* III (1953) p. 153-161.
— Galilean Survey: Israelite Settlements and their Pottery. *EI* IV (1956) p. 56-63.
— *The Settlement of the Israelite Tribes in Upper Galilee.* (Hitnāḥālūt šibṭē yiśrā'ēl bāgālīl hā'ẹlyōn). Jerusalem 1957.
— Problems of the Israelite Conquest in the Light of Archaeological Discoveries. *Antiquity and Survival* II 2/3, Den Haag 1957, p. 131-150.
— The Province-List of Judah. *VT* IX (1959) p. 225-226.
— The Northern Boundary of Judah. *PEQ* XC (1958) p. 27-31.
— *The Land of the Bible. A Historical Geography.* London 1966.
— Anaharoth. *JNES* XXVI (1967) p. 212-216.
— Arad: Its Inscriptions and Temple. *BA* XXXI (1968) p. 2-32.
— New Aspects of the Israelite Occupation in the North. In: *Near Eastern Archaeology in the Twentieth Century. Essays in Honor of N. Glueck.* Ed. by J. A. Sanders, New York 1970, p. 254-267.
AHLSTRÖM, G. W. Oral and Written Transmission: Some Considerations. *HThR* LIX (1966) p. 69-83.
— Solomon, The Chosen One. *History of Religions* VIII (1968) p. 93-110.
ALBRIGHT, W. F. The administrative Divisions of Israel and Judah. *JPOS* V (1925) p. 17-54.
— The names "Israel" and "Judah", with an Excursus on the etymology of tôdâh and tôrâh. *JBL* XLVI (1927) p. 151-185.
— *The Archaeology of Palestine and the Bible.* New York/Chicago 1932.
— The Kyle Memorial Excavation at Bethel. *BASOR* 56 (1934) p. 2-15.
— Further Light on the History of Israel from Lachish and Megiddo. *BASOR* 68 (1937) p. 22-26.
— Archaeology and the date of the Hebrew Conquest of Palestine. *BASOR* 58 (1935) p. 10-18.
— The Song of Deborah in the Light of Archaeology. *BASOR* 62 (1936) p. 26-31.
— The Israelite Conquest of Canaan in the Light of Archaeology. *BASOR* 74 (1939) p. 11-23.
— The Babylonian Matter in the Predeuteronomic Primeval History. *JBL* LVIII (1939) p. 91-103.
— *The Excavation of Tell Beit Mirsim.* Vol. III The Iron Age. AASOR XXI-XXII, New Haven 1941-1943.
— Two little understood Amarna Letters from the Middle Jordan Valley. *BASOR* 89 (1943) p. 7-18.

213

— An Archaic Hebrew Proverb in an Amarna Letter from Central Palestine. *BASOR* 89 (1943) p. 29-32.
— A Prince of Taanach in the Fifteenth Century B.C. *BASOR* 94 (1944) p. 12-27.
— *The Archaeology of Palestine.* Pelican A 199. London 1949[1].
— *Archaeology and the Religion of Israel.* Baltimore 1953[3].
— Northeast-Mediterranean Dark Ages and the Early Iron Age Art of Syria. In: *The Aegaean and the Near East. Studies presented to Hetty Goldman.* Ed. Weinberg. New York 1956, p. 144-164.
— Albrecht Alt†. *JBL* LXXV (1956) p. 169-173.
— *From the Stone Age to Christianity.* New York, Anchor pocket, 1957[2].
— Jethro, Hobab and Reuèl in early Hebrew tradition. *CBQ* XXV (1963) p. 1-11.
— *The Biblical Period. From Abraham to Ezra. A Historical Survey.* Harper Torch-edition, New York 1963.
— *Archaeology, Historical Analogy and Early Biblical Tradition.* Baton Rouge 1966.
— *Jahweh and the Gods of Canaan.* London 1968.
ALFÖLDI, A. *Early Rome and the Latins.* Ann Arbor 1964.
ALFRINK, B. J. L'Expression n'sf 'l l'myw. *OTS* V (1948) p. 118-131.
— *Josue, uit de grondtekst vertaald en uitgelegd.* BOT III, 1. Roermond-Maaseik 1952.
ALT, A. Israels Gaue unter Salomo. (1913) *KS* II, München 1953, p. 76-90.
— Judas Gaue unter Josia. (1925) *KS* II, München 1953, p. 276-288.
— Jerusalems Aufstieg. (1925) *KS* III, München 1959, p. 243-258.
— Die Landnahme der Israeliten in Palästina. (1925). *KS* I, München 1953, p. 89-126.
— *s.v.* "Israeliten". *Reallexikon der Vorgeschichte* hrsg. v. Max Ebert, VI, p. 70-71. Berlin 1926.
— Zur Geschichte von Beth-Sean; 1500-1000 v. Chr. (1926) *KS* I, München 1953, p. 246-256.
— Eine galiläische Ortsliste in Jos. 19. *ZAW* XLV (1927) p. 59-80.
— Das System der Stammesgrenzen im Buche Josua. (1927) *KS* I, München 1953 p. 192-202.
— *s.v.* "Israel", politische Geschichte. *Die Religion in Geschichte und Gegenwart*[2], hrsg. v. H. Gunkel und L. Zscharnack. III. Band, Tübingen 1929, p. 437-442.
— Der Gott der Väter. (1929). *KS* I, München 1953, p. 1-78.
— Die Staatenbildung der Israeliten in Palästina. (1930). *KS* II, München 1959, p. 1-66.
— Beiträge zur historischen Geografie und Topografie des Negeb. (1931-1938). *KS* III, München 1959, p. 382-473.
— Die Ursprünge des israelitischen Rechts. (1934). *KS* I, München 1953, p. 278-332.
— Zur Talionsformel. (1934). *KS* I, München 1953, p. 333-340.
— Zur Geschichte der Grenze zwischen Judäa und Samaria. *PJ* XXXI (1935) p. 94-111.
— Josua. (1936). *KS* I, München 1953, p. 176-192.
— Galiläische Probleme. (1937-1940). *KS* II, München 1959, p. 363-436.
— Die Wallfahrt von Sichem nach Bethel. (1938). *KS* I, München 1953, p. 79-88.
— Erwägungen über die Landnahme der Israeliten in Palästina. (1939). *KS* I, München 1953, p. 126-176.
— Emiter und Moabiter. (1940). *KS* I, München 1953, p. 203-216.
— Ägyptische Tempel in Palästina und die Landnahme der Philister. (1944). *KS* I, München 1953, p. 216-231.

— Megiddo im Übergang von kanaänischen zum israelitischen Zeitalter. (1944). *KS* I, München 1953, p. 256-274.

— Neue Berichte über Feldzüge von Pharaonen des neuen Reiches nach Palästina. *ZDPV* LXX (1954) p. 33-75.

— *s.v.* "Israel", 1 Geschichte (rev. by R. Bach). *RGG*³, III. Band, Tübingen 1959, p. 936-942.

— Bemerkungen zu den Verwaltungs- und Rechtsurkunden von Ugarit und Alalach. *WO* II:1 (1954) p. 7-18, *WO* II:3 (1956) p. 234-244, *WO* II:4 (1957) p. 338-343, *WO* III:1/2 (1964) p. 3-18.

ALTHEIM, FR., STIEHL, RUTH. Beduinisierung. In: *Antike und Universalgeschichte*. Festschrift für H. E. Stier. Münster 1972, p. 294-301.

AMIRAN, D. H. K. The Pattern of Settlement in Palestine. *IEJ* III (1953) p. 65-78, 192-209, 250-260.

AMIRAN, D. H. K. (ed.) *Land Use in Semi-Arid Mediterranean Climates*. Arid Zone Researches XXVI. Unesco, Paris 1964.

AMIRAN, RUTH. Palestine, Syria and Cyprus in the MB 1 Period. *EI* V (1958) p. 25-31.

ANDERSEN, F. I. The socio-juridical background of the Naboth Incident. *JBL* LXXXV (1966) p. 46-58.

— Israelite Kinship Terminology and Social Structure. *The Bible Translator* XX (1969) p. 29-39.

— Note on Genesis 30:8. *JBL* LXXXVIII (1969) p. 200.

ANDERSON, G. W. Israel: Amphictyony: 'Am; Ḳāhāl; 'Ēḏâh. In: *Translating and Understanding the Old Testament*. Essays in Honor of H. G. May. Nashville 1970, p. 135-151.

AP-THOMAS, D. R. The Phoenicians. *POTT*, London 1973, p. 259-286.

ARO, J. Gemeinsemitische Ackerbauterminologie. *ZDMG* CXIII (1963) p. 471-480.

ASHKENAZI, T. *Tribus semi-nomades de la Palestine du Nord*. Paris 1938.

— La tribu arabe: ses éléments. *Anthropos* XLI-XLIV (1946/49) p. 657-672.

AUERBACH, E. Untersuchungen zum Richterbuch, I und II. *ZAW* XLVIII (1930) p. 286-295 en LI (1933) p. 47-51.

— *Wüste und gelobtes Land*, I en II. Berlin 1936.

— *Mozes*. Amsterdam 1953.

— Das Zehngebot–Allgemeine Gesetzes-Form in der Bibel. *VT* XVI (1966) p. 255-276.

AUERBACH, M., SMOLAR, L. Aaron, Jeroboam and the Golden Calves. *JBL* LXXXVI (1967) p. 129-141.

BAAREN, TH. P. VAN. Systematische Religionswissensschaft. *NThT* XXIV (1969-1970) p. 81-88.

BACH, R. Zur Siedlungsgeschichte des Talkessels von Samaria. *ZDPV* LIV (1958) p. 41-54.

BACHER, W. yᵉšūrūn. *ZAW* V (1885) p. 161-163.

BÄCHLI, O. Zur Aufnahme von Fremden in die altisraelitische Kultgemeinde. In: *Wort-Gebot-Glaube*. Festschrift W. Eichrodt. AThANT LIX, Zürich 1970, p. 21-26.

— Nachtrag zum Thema Amphiktyonie. *ThZBs* XXVIII, 1972, p. 356.

— Rev. art of Martin Noth's "Aufsätze zur biblischen Landes – und Altertumskunde". *Kirchblatt f.d. Ref. Schweiz* CXXVIII, 1972, p. 162-164, 179-181.

— Von der Liste zur Beschreibung. Beobachtungen und Erwägungen zu Jos. 13-19. *ZDPV* LXXXIX, (1973) p. 1-14.

BAENTSCH, B. *Altorientalischer und israelitischer Monotheismus*. Tübingen 1906.

BAILLEY, L. R. Israelite 'El Šadday and Amorite Bêl Šadê. *JBL* (1968) p. 434-438.
BALSCHEIT, B. *Alter und Aufkommen des Monotheismus in der israelitischen Religion.* BZAW 69, Berlin 1938.
BALTZER, K. *Das Bundesformular.* Neukirchen 1960.
BALY, D. Geographisches Handbuch zur Bibel. Neukirchen 1966.
BARDTKE, H. Samuel und Saul. Gedanken zur Entstehung des Königtums in Israel. *BiOr* XXV (1968) p. 289-302.
BARNES, W. E. A Note on the Meaning of y'qb ('lhy y'qb) in the Psalter. *JThSt* (1937) p. 405-410.
BARTH, CHR. Zur Bedeutung der Wüstentradition. *SVT* XV, Leiden 1966, p. 14-23.
BARTH, F. Father's brother's daughter marriage in Kurdistan. *Southwestern Journal of Anthropology* X (1954) p. 164-171.
BARTH, J. *Die Nominalbildung in den semitischen Sprachen.* Leipzig 1889.
BARLETT, J. R. The Edomite Kinglist of Genesis 36, 31-39 and 1 Chron 1, 43-50. *JThSt* XVI (1965) p. 301-314.
— The use of the word rōš as a title in the Old Testament. *VT* XIX (1969) p. 1-10.
— The Historical Reference of Numbers XXI, 27-30. *PEQ* CI (1969) p. 94-100.
— The Moabites and Edomites. *POTT*, London 1973, 229-258.
BATTEN, L. W. A Crisis in the History of Israel. *JBL* XLIX (1930) p. 55-60.
BAUER, H., LEANDER, P. *Historische Grammatik der hebräischen Sprache.* Halle 1922. Reprint Hildesheim 1965.
BAUMGARTNER, W. Die hebräische Sprache und ihre Geschichte. In: *Studien zum Alten Testament und seiner Umwelt.* Leiden 1959, p. 208-239.
BEEK, M. A. Das Problem des aramäischen Stammvaters (Deut. XXVI, 5). *OTS* VIII, Leiden 1950, p. 193-213.
— *Wegen en Voetsporen van het Oude Testament.* Delft 1954[2].
— Der Dornbush als Wohnsitz Gottes (Deut. XXXIII, 16). *OTS* XIV (1965) p. 155-162.
— Josua und Retterideal. In: *Near Eastern Studies in Honor of W. F. Albright,* ed. by H. Goedicke, Baltimore 1971, p. 35-42.
BEEK, G. VAN. South Arabian History and Archaeology. *BANE* ,New York 1961, p. 229-248.
BEER, G. *Mose und sein Werk.* Giessen 1902.
— *Welches war die älteste Religion Israels?* Ein Vortrag. Giessen 1927.
BEGRICH, J. Sōfēr und Mazkīr. Ein Beitrag zur inneren Geschichte des davidisch-salomonischen Grossreiches und des Königreiches Juda. *ZAW* LVIII (1940/41) p. 1-30.
BELTZ, W. *Die Kaleb-Traditionen.* Budapest/Berlin 1966.
BEN-GRAVIÊL, M. Y. Das nomadische Ideal in der Bibel. *Stimm. der Zeit.* CLXXI (1962-1963) p. 253-263.
BEN-SHAMMAI, M. H. Bethlehem Efrata. Soziologische Gesichtspunkte zum Buch Ruth. *Beth Miqra'* XII (1966/67) p. 28-78.
BEN-ZVI, I. Tribus d'Israël en Arabie. *Le Muséon* LXXIV (1961) p. 143-190.
BENTZEN, AA. *Die josianische Reform und ihre Voraussetzungen.* Kopenhagen 1926.
BERGMAN, A. The Israelite Occupation of Eastern Palestine in the Light of Territorial History. *JAOS* LIV (1934) p. 169 sq.
— The Israelite tribe of Half-Manasse. *JPOS* XVI (1936) p. 224-254.
BERNHARDT, K. H. Nomadentum und Ackerbaukultur in der frühstaatlichen Zeit Israels. *VBVHS*, Berlin 1968, p. 31-40.

216

BERQUE, J. Nomades and Nomadism in the Arid Zone. Introduction. *ISSJ* XI (1959) p. 481-498.

BERTHOLET, A. *Die Stellung der Israeliten und der Juden zu den Fremden.* Freiburg/ Leipzig 1896.

BESTERS, A. Le sanctuaire central dans Jud. XIX-XXI. *EThL* XLI (1965) p. 20-42.

— "Israël" et "Fils d'Israël" dans les livres historiques (Genèse – II Rois). *RB* LXXIV (1967) p. 5-24.

— L'expression "Fils d'Israël" en Ex., I-XIV. Un nouveau critère pour la distinction des sources. *RB* LXXIV (1967) p. 321-355.

BEYER, KL. *Althebräische Grammatik,* Göttingen 1969.

BEYERLIN, W. *Herkunft und Geschichte der ältesten Sinai Traditionen.* Tübingen 1961.

— Geschichte und heilsgeschichtliche Traditionsbildung im Alten Testament. *VT* XIII (1963) p. 1-26.

BIN GORION, M. J. *Sinai und Garizim. Forschungen zum Hexateuch auf Grund rabbinischen Quellen.* Nachgelassene Schrifte hrsg. v. R. und E. Bin Gorion. Berlin 1926.

BLAU, J. Some Difficulties in the Reconstruction of "Proto-Hebrew" and "Proto-Canaanite". *In memoriam Paul Kahle.* BZAW 103, Berlijn 1968, p. 29-43.

BLENKINSOPP, J. Kiriath-Jearim and the Ark. *JBL* LXXXVIII (1969) p. 143-156.

BOECKER, H. J. Erwägungen zum Amt des Mazkir. *ThZBs* XVII (1961) p. 212-216.

— Anmerkungen zur Adaption im Alten Testament. *ZAW* LXXXVI, 1974, p. 86-89.

BOEHMER, I. "Dieses Volk". *JBL* XLV (1926) p. 131-148.

BOER, P. A. H. DE. Genesis XXXII 23-33. *NThT* I (1947) p. 149-163.

Gedenken und Gedächtnis in der Welt des Alten Testaments. Stuttgart 1962.

BÖHL, F. M. TH. *Die Sprache der Amarnabriefe.* Leipziger Semitistische Studien. Band V, 2, 1909.

— *Kanaanäer und Hebräer.* BWAT 9, Leipzig 1911.

— *Kanaän vóór den intocht der Israëlieten, volgens Egyptische en Babylonische bronnen.* Groningen 1913.

— *Het Tijdperk der aartsvaders.* Groningen 1925.

—- *Palestina in het Licht van de Jongste Opgravingen en Onderzoekingen.* Amsterdam 1931.

BOLAND, B. J. Het beloofde Land. *Theologie en Praktijk* XXVII (1967/68) p. 185-203.

Bönhoff, L. Die Wanderung Israels in der Wüste mit besonderer Berücksichtigung der Frage "Wo lag der Sinai?" *ThStKr* LXXX (1907) p. 150 217.

BORGER, R. Das Problem der 'apiru ('Habiru'). *ZDPV* LXXIV (1958) p. 121-132.

BOTTÉRO, J. *Le problème des Habiru à la quatrième rencontre assyriologique internationale.* Cahiers de la Société Asiatique XII. Paris 1954.

BRÄUNLICH, E. Beiträge zur Gesellschaftsordnung der arabischen Beduinenstämme. *Islamica* VI (1934) p. 68-111. 182-229.

BREKELMANS, C. H. W. *De Herem in het Oude Testament.* Nijmegen 1959.

— Het "historisch Credo" van Israël. *TTh* III (1963) p. 1-11.

BRENTJES, B. *Die Haustierwerdung im Orient.* Wittenberg 1965.

BRENTJES, B. Zum Verhältnis von Dorf und Stadt in Altvorderasien. *Wiss. Zeitschrift Univ. Halle.* XVII (1968) G., H. 6, p. 9-41.

— Grundeigentum, Staat und Klassengesellschaft im Alten Orient. *EAZ* IX (1968) p. 245-266.

BRIGGS, E. G. *A Critical and Exegetical Commentary on the Book of Psalms*. Edinburgh, 1925 and 1927.
BRIGHT, J. *Early Israel in Recent History Writing*. Studies in Biblical Theology 19 London 1956.
— *A History of Israel*. London 1960.
BRINKER, R. *The Influence of Sanctuaries in Early Israel*. Manchester 1946.
BRINKMAN, J. A. *A Political History of Post-Kassite Babylonia 1158-722 B.C.* Analecta Orientalia 43, Roma 1968.
BROADBENT, MOLLY. *Studies in Greek Genealogy*. Leiden 1968.
BRONGERS, H. A. Die Zehnzahl in der Bibel und in ihrer Umwelt. In: *Studia Biblica et Semitica Th. C. Vriezen Dedicata*. Wageningen 1966, p. 30-45.
— *I Koningen*. De Prediking van het Oude Testament. Nijkerk 1967.
— Einige Aspekte der gegenwärtigen Lage der Lade-Forschung. *NThT* XXV (1971) p. 6-27.
BRONGERS, H. A. en WOUDE, A. S. V.D. Wat is de betekenis van 'Ābnāyîm in Exodus 1 : 16? *NThT* XX (1965/1966) p. 241-254.
BUBER, M. *Königtum Gottes*. Heidelberg 1956³.
BUCCELLATI, G. The Enthronement of the King and the Capital City. *Studies presented to A. Leo Oppenheim*, Chicago 1964, p. 54-61.
— *The Amorites of the Ur III Period*. Naples 1966.
— *Cities and Nations of Ancient Syria*. Studi Semitici 26, Roma 1967.
BUDDE, K. Richter und Josua. *ZAW VII* (1887) p. 93-167.
— Das nomadische Ideal im alten Testament. *PrJ* Band 85 (1896) p. 57-79.
BUHL, MARIE-LOUISE and HOLM-NIELSEN, S. *Shiloh. The Danish Excavations at Tall Sailūn, Palestine, in 1926, 1929, 1932 and 1963. The Pre-Hellenistic Remains*. Copenhagen 1969.
BÜRGEL, H. *Die Pylaeisch-Delphische Amphiktyonie*. München 1877.
BURNEY, C. F. *Israel's settlement in Canaan*. (= Schweich Lectures 1917) London 1921³.
CALABI, IDA. *Ricerche sui rapporti fra le poleis*. Firenze 1953.
CALLAWAY, J. A. The Emerging Role of Biblical Archaeology. *Review and Expositor* LXIII (1966) p. 199-209.
CAMPBELL, E. F. The Amarna Letters and the Amarna Period. *BA* XXIII (1960) p. 2-22.
CAMPBELL, E. F. and WRIGHT, G. E. Tribal League Shrines in Amman and Shechem. *BA* XXXII (1969) p. 104-116.
CAPELL, A. *Studies in Socio-Linguistics*. Janua Linguarum Nr. XLVI, Den Haag 1966.
CAQUOT, A. Ahiyya de Silo et Jéroboam 1er. *Semitica* XI (1961) p. 17-28.
CARDASCIA, G. Adoption Matrimoniale et Lévirat dans le Droight d'Ugarit. *RA* LXIV (1970) p. 119-126.
CARROLL, R. P. Psalm LXXVIII: vestiges of a tribal polemic. *VT* XXI (1971) p. 133-150.
CASKEL, W. Zur Beduinisierung Arabiens. *ZDMG* CIII (1953) p. 28*-38*.
— Der Arabische Stamm vor dem Islam und sein Gesellschaftliche und Juristische Organisation. In: *Dalla Tribù allo Stato*. Acc. Naz. dei Lincei CCCLIX, Roma 1962, p. 139-152.
— *Ǧamharat an-Nasab. Das Genealogische Werk des Hišam ibn Muhammad al-Kalbī* 2 Bdn., Leiden 1966.
CASPARI, W. Tochter-Ortschaften im A.T. *ZAW* XXXIX (1921) p. 174-180.

— *Die Gottesgemeinde vom Sinaj und das nachmalige Volk Israel.* Beiträge z. Förd. christl. Theol. 27, 1 Gütersloh 1922.
— Sprachliche und religionsgeschichtliche Bedeutung des Namens Israel. *ZS* 111 (1924) p. 194-212.
— *Die Samuelisbücher.* KAT VII, Leipzig 1926.
— Heimat und soziale Wirkung des alttestamentlichen Bundesbuchs. *ZDMG* VIII (1929) p. 97-120.
— Der Name Jaqob in israelitischer Zeit. *Festschrift G. Jacob.* Leipzig 1932, p. 24-40.
CAUER, F. *s.v.* "Amfiktyonia" in *Paulys Real-Encyclopädie der Classischen Altertums-wissenschaft.* Hrgb. von G. Wissowa, Band 1, Stuttgart 1894, col. 1904-1935.
CAUSSE, A. *Du groupe ethnique à la communauté religieuse.* Straatsburg 1937.
CAZELLES, H. Hébreu, Ubru et Ḫapiru. *Syria* XXXV (1958) p. 198-217.
— a.o. *Moïse, l'homme de l'Alliance.* Paris 1955.
— L'Hébreu. *Linguistica Semitica, Presente e Futuro. Racc. d. G. Levi della Vida.* Roma 1961, p. 91-113.
— Argob biblique, Ugarit et les mouvements hurrites. *Studi sull'Oriente e la Biblia offerti al. P. Giovanni Rinaldi,* Genova 1967, p. 21-27.
— Mari et l'Ancien Testament. *XVth RAI,* Paris 1967, p. 73-90.
— Positions actuelles sur le Pentateuque. *EThL* XLIV (1968) p. 55-78.
— Les Origines du Décalogue. *EI* IX (1969) p. 14-19.
— The Hebrews. *POTT,* London 1973, p. 1-28.
CHABOT, L. Les douze tribus d'Israël ont-elles envahi la Palestine? *Bull. Renan* C (1963) p. 2-4.
CHAMBERLAYNE, J. H. Kinship relationships among the early Hebrews. *Numen* X (1963) p. 153-167.
CHELHOD, J. *Introduction à la sociologie de l'Islam.* Paris 1958.
CHIERA, E. and SPEISER, E. A. *A New Factor in the History of the Ancient Near East.* AASOR VI (1926) p. 75-92.
CORDON CHILDE, V. *What happened in history.* London 1952.
CHILDS, B. S. A Study of the Formula 'Until this Day'. *JBL* LXXXII (1963) p. 279-292.
CLARKE, D. L. *Analytical Archaeology.* London 1968.
CLEMENTS, R. E. *God and Temple.* Oxford 1965.
— Baal-Berith of Shechem. *JSS* XIII (1968) p. 21-32.
COATS, G. W. The traditio-historical character of the Reed Sea motif. *VT* XVII (1967) p. 253-265.
— Moses in Midian. *JBL* XCII, (1973) p. 3-10.
CODY, AE. *A History of Old Testament Priesthood.* Analecta Biblica 35, Roma 1969.
COON, C. S. The Nomads. In: *Social Forces in the Middle East.* ed. by S. N. Fisher. Ithaca 1955, p. 23-42.
COOTE, R. The meaning of the name Israel. *HThR* LXV (1972) p. 137-142.
COPPENS, J. La bénédiction de Jacob. Son cadre historique à la lumière des paralelles ougaritiques. *SVT* IV, Leiden 1957, p. 97-115.
CORNELIUS, FR. *Geistesgeschichte der Frühzeit.* Leiden, without date.
CORNILL, C. H. *Geschichte des Volkes Israel.* 1898.
MOORE CROSS, F. Epigraphic Notes on Hebrew Documents of the Eight-Sixth Centuries B.C.: 1. A New Reading of a Place Name in the Samaria Ostraca. *BASOR* 163 (1961) p. 12-14.
— Yahweh and the God of the Patriarchs. *HThR* LV (1962) p. 225-259.

— The Divine Warrior in Israel's Early Cult. In: A. Altmann ed., *Biblical Motifs*. Cambridge Mass. 1966.

MOORE CROSS, F., FREEDMAN, D. N. The Blessing of Moses. *JBL* LXVII (1948) p. 191-210.

MOORE CROSS, F., WRIGHT, G. E. The Boundary and Province Lists of the Kingdom of Judah. *JBL* LXXV (1956) p. 202-226.

BRIGGS CURTIS, J. "East is East...". *JBL* LXXX (1961) p. 355-363.

— Some suggestions concerning the history of the tribe of Reuben. *JBL* XXXIII (1965) p. 247-250.

DALMAN, G. Der Gilgal der Bibel und die Steinkreise Palästinas. *PJ* XV (1919) p. 5-27.

DANELIUS, EVA. The Boundary of Ephraim and Manasseh in the Western Plain. *PEQ* LXXXIX (1957) p. 55-67; *PEQ* XC (1958) p. 32-44; p. 122-144.

DANELL, G. A. *Studies in the Name Israel in the Old Testament*. Upsala 1946.

DAVIES, G. H. The Ark of the Covenant. *ASThI* V (1966-'67) p. 30-48.

DEBUS, J. *Die Sünde Jerobeams*. FRLANT 93, Göttingen 1967.

DELITZSCH, F. *Die Grosse Täuschung. Kritische Betrachtungen zu den alttestamentlichen Berichten über Israels Eindringen in Kanaan, die Gottesoffenbarung vom Sinai und die Wirksamkeit der Propheten.* (2 Tle.) Stuttgart/Berlin 1921.

DERENBOURG, H. Les noms de personnes dans l'Ancien Testament et dans les inscriptions Himyarites. *REJ* 1 (1880) p. 56-61.

DEVER, W. G. Archaeological Methods and Results: a Review of Two Recent Publications. *Or* XL (1971) p. 459-471.

DHORME, P. Les Ḫabiru et les Hébreux. *JPOS* IV (1924) p. 162-168.

DHORME, ED. La Question des Ḫabiri. *RHR* LIX (1938) p. 170-187.

— *Récueil Eduard Dhorme*. Paris 1951.

DIAKONOFF, I. M. Agrarian Conditions in Middle Assyria. In: I. M. Diakonoff ed., *Ancient Mesopotamia*. Moscow 1969, p. 204-234.

— Socio-Economic Classes in Babylonia and the Babylonian Concept of Social Stratification. In: *Gesellschaftsklassen im Alten Zweistromland und in den angrenzenden Gebieten*. (XVIIIth RAI), BAW, Phil. Hist. Kl. NF 75, München 1972, p. 41-52.

DIEPOLD, P. *Israel's Land*. BWANT NF 15, Stuttgart 1972.

DIJK, H. J. VAN. *Ezekiel's Prophecy on Tyre (Ez. 26.11-28, 19). A New Approach*. Biblica et Orientalia 20, Roma 1968.

DIRINGER, D. *Writing*. Ancient Peoples and Places, London 1962.

DOLE, E. GERTRUD. Tribe as the autonomous Unit. In: *Essays on the problem of tribe*. AES, Seattle/London 1968, p. 83-100.

DONNER, H. Adoption oder Legitimation? Erwägungen zur Adoption im Alten Testament auf dem Hintergrund der altorientalischen Rechte. *OrAnt* VIII (1969) p. 87-119.

DOSSIN, G. Les Bédouins dans les textes de Mari. In: F. Gabrieli ed., *L'Antica Società Beduina*. Roma 1959, p. 35-52.

DOSTAL, W. Die Ṣulubba und ihre Bedeutung für die Kulturgeschichte Arabiens. *AVK* XI (1956) p. 15-42.

— The Evolution of Bedouin Life. In: *L'Antica Società Beduina*, racc. da F. Gabrieli. Studi Semitica 2, Roma 1959, p. 11-34.

— *Die Beduinen in Südarabien. Eine ethnologische Studie zur Entwicklung der Kamelhirtenkultur in Arabien*. Wiener Beiträge zur Kulturgeschichte und Linguistik, Bd XVI. Wien 1967.

DOTHAN, M. The Excavations at 'Afula. *'Atiqot* I (1955) p. 19-71.

DUNCAN, J. G. *Digging up Biblical History*, vols. I and II. London 1930.

— *New Light on Hebrew Origins*. London 1936.

DUPONT-SOMMER, A. Sur les débuts de l'histoire araméenne. *SVT* 1, Leiden 1953, p. 40-50.

DUS, J. Das Sesshaft werden der nachmaligen Israeliten im Land Kanaan. *Comm. Viet.* VI (1963) p. 263-275.

— Bethel und Mispa in Jdc. 19-21 und Jdc. 10-12. *OrAnt* III (1964) p. 227-243.

— Die Thron- und Bundeslade. *ThZBs* XX (1964) p. 241-251.

— Die Sufeten Israels. *ArOr* XXXI (1963) p. 444-469.

— Ein richterzeiliches Stierbildheiligtum zu Bethel? Die Aufeinanderfolge der frühisraelitischen Zentralkultstätten. *ZAW* LXXII (1965) p. 268-286.

DUSSAUD, R. *La Pénétration des Arabes en Syrie avant l'islam*. Inst. Français d'Arch. de Beyrouth, LIX, Paris 1955.

— *Les origines Cananéennes du sacrifice Israélite*. Paris 1921.

DYSON-HUDSON, N. The Study of Nomads. In: *Perspectives on Nomadism*. Ed. by W. Irons and N. Dyson-Hudson. Leiden 1972, p. 2-29.

DYSON-HUDSON, RADA. Pastoralism: Self Image and Behavioral Reality. In: *Perspectives on Nomadism*. Ed. by W. Irons and N. Dyson-Hudson. Leiden 1972, p. 30-47.

EDELKOORT, A. H. *Uittocht en Intocht*. Utrecht 1924.

EDZARD, D. O. *Die "zweite Zwischenzeit" Babyloniens*. Wiesbaden 1957.

— Altbabylonisch *nawûm*. *ZA* NF XIX (1959) p. 168-173.

— Mari und Aramäer? *ZA* NF 22 (56.) (1964) p. 142-150.

EERDMANS, B. D. De Kenieten en het Jahwisme. *Theologisch Tijdschrift* XLI (1907) p. 492-507.

— *Alttestamentliche Studien, II. Die Vorgeschichte Israels*. Giessen 1908.

— *The Covenant at Mount Sinai. Viewed in the Light of Antique Thought*. Leiden 1939.

— *The Religion of Israel*. Leiden 1947².

EHRENBERG, V. *Aspects of the Ancient World*. Oxford 1946.

— *Der Staat der Griechen. Bd I, Der hellenische Staat*. Leipzig 1957.

EHRICH, R. W. ed., *Chronologies in Old World Archaeology*. Chicago 1965².

EISING, H. *Formgeschichtliche Untersuchung zur Jakoberzählung der Genesis*. Emsdetten 1940.

EISSFELDT, O. *Hexateuch-Synopse*. Leipzig 1922. Reprint Darmstadt 1962.

— Stammessage und Novelle in den Geschichten von Jakob und von seinen Söhnen. In: *"Eucharisterion", Gunkel-Festschrift, Band I*. Göttingen 1923, p. 56-77.

— *Die Quellen des Richterbuches*. Leipzig 1925.

— Der Geschichtliche Hintergrund der Erzählung von Gibeas Schandtat (Richter 19-21). In: *Festschrift G. Beer*. Stuttgart 1935, p. 19-40.

— Die Komposition der Bileam-Erzählung. Eine Nachprüfung von Rudolphs Beitrag zur Hexateuchkritik. *ZAW* LVII (1959) p. 212-241.

— Israel und seine Geschichte. *ThLZ* LXXVI (1951) p. 335-340.

— Psalm 80. In: *Geschichte und Altes Testament. Albrecht Alt zum 70. Geburtstag dargebracht*. Tübingen 1953, p. 65-78.

— Die Eroberung Palästinas durch Altisrael. *WO* II:2 (1955) p. 158-171.

— Silo und Jerusalem. *SVT* IV, Leiden 1957, p. 138-148.

— Das Lied Moses Deuteronomium 32[1-43] und das Lehrgedicht Asaphs Psalm 78 samt einer Analyse der Umgebung der Mose-Liedes. *Berichte über die Verhand-*

lungen der sächsischen Akademie der Wissenschaften zu Leipzig. Phil.-Hist. Klasse 104, 5. Berlin 1958/59.
— Sinai-Erzählung und Bileam-Sprüche. *HUCA* XXXII (1961) p. 179-190.
— Ein Psalm aus Nord-Israel, Micha 7:7-20. *ZDMG* CXII (1962) p. 259-268.
— Jakobs Begegnung mit El und Moses Begegnung mit Jahwe. *OLZ* LVIII (1963) p. 325-331.
— "Gut Glück!" in semitischer Namengebung. *JBL* LXXXII (1963) p. 195-200.
— Psalm 80 und Psalm 89. *WO* III(1964-1966) p. 27-31.
— Jakob-Lea und Jakob-Rachel. In: *Gottes Wort und Gottes Land, Herzberg-Festschrift*, Göttingen 1965, p. 50-55.
— The Hebrew Kingdom. *CAH*[2] *vol. II chapter 34*, Cambridge 1965.
— Israels Führer in der Zeit vom Auszug aus Ägypten bis zur Landnahme. In: *Studia Biblica et Semitica Th. C. Vriezen Dedicata*, Wageningen 1966, p. 62-71.
— Die Lade Jahwes in Geschichtserzählung, Sage und Lied. *Das Altertum* XIV (1968) p. 131-145.
— Der kanaanäische El als Geber der den israelitischen Erzvätern geltenden Nachkommenschaft- und Landbesitz-Verheissungen. *Wiss. Z. Univ. Halle* XVII (1968) H 2/3, p. 45-53.
— Protektorat der Midianiter über ihre Nachbarn im letzten Viertel des 2. Jahrtausends v. Chr. *JBL* LXXXVII (1968) p. 383-393.
— Die Psalmen als Geschichtsquelle. In: *Near Eastern Studies in Honor of W. F. Albright*, ed. by H. Goedicke, Baltimore 1971, p. 97-112.
ELLIGER, K. Die Grenze zwischen Ephraim und Manasse. *ZDPV* LIII (1930) p. 265-309.
— Josua in Judäa. *PJ* XXX (1934) p. 47-71.
— Die Nordgrenze des Reiches Davids. *PJ* XXXII (1936) p. 34-73.
— Thappuah. *PJ* XXXIII (1937) p. 7-21.
— Neues über die Grenze zwischen Ephraim und Manasse. *JPOS* XVIII (1938) p. 7-17.
— Der Jakobskampf am Jabbok, Gen. 32, 33ff. als hermeneutisches Problem. *ZThK* XLVIII (1951) p. 1-32.
— Das Gesetz Leviticus 18. *ZAW* LXVII (1955) p. 1-25.
ENGBERT, R. M. Historical Analysis of Archaeological Evidence: Megiddo and the Song of Deborah. With postscript by W. F. Albright. *BASOR* 78 (1940) p. 4-9.
ERBT, W. *Die Hebräer; Kanaan im Zeitalter der hebräischen Wanderung und hebräischer Staatengründungen*. Leipzig 1906.
EVANS, D. G. Rehoboam's Advisers at Shechem, and Political Institutions in Israel and Sumer. *JNES* XXV (1966) p. 273-279.
EWALD, H. *Einleitung in die Geschichte des Volkes Israel. Band I*. Göttingen 1864[3].
FALKENSTEIN, A. La Cité-Temple Sumérienne. *Cahiers d'Histoire Mondiale I*. (1953-1954), p. 784-814.
FEIST, S. Die Etymologie des Namens *yiśrā'ēl*. *MGWJ* 73 (1929) p. 317-320.
FELDMAN, SH. Biblical Motives and Sources. *JNES* XXII (1963) p. 73-103.
FERGUSON, W. S. The Delian Amphictyony. *CR* XV (1901) p. 38-40.
FINLEY, M. I. Archaeology and History. *Daedalus* (1971) p. 168-186.
FISHER, L. R. The Temple Quarter. *JSS* VIII (1963) p. 34-41.
FISHER, W. B. *The Middle East. A Physical, Social and Regional Geography*. London 1950.
FOHRER, G. *Überlieferung und Geschichte des Exodus. Eine Analyse von Ex 1-15*. BZAW 91. Berlin 1964.

222

— Das sogenannte apodiktisch formulierte Recht und der Dekalog. *KuD* XI (1965) p. 49-75.

— Altes Testament – "Amphiktyonie" und "Bund"? *ThLZ* XCI (1966) 1, p. 801-816 II, p. 893-904.

— Die Sprüche Obadjas. In: *Studia Biblica et Semitica Th. C. Vriezen Dedicata.* Wageningen 1966, p. 81-93.

— Israels Haltung gegenüber den Kanaanäern und anderen Völkern. *JSS* XIII (1968) p. 64-75.

— *Geschichte der israelitischen Religion.* Berlin 1969.

— Zur Einwirkung der gesellschaftlichen Struktur Israels auf seine Religion. In: *Near Eastern Studies in Honor of W. F. Albright,* ed. by H. Goedicke, Baltimore 1971, p. 169-186.

DARYLL FORDE, C. *Habitat, Economy and Society. A Geographical Introduction to Ethnology.* London/New York 1961¹².

FORREST, G. The First Sacred War. *BCH* LXXX (1956) p. 33-52.

FORTES, M. The Structure of Unilineal Descent Groups. *The American Anthropologist* LV (1953) p. 17-41.

FRANKEN, H. J. Tell es-Sultan and Old Testament Jericho. *OTS* XIV, Leiden 1965, p. 189-200.

— *Excavations et Tell Deir 'Allā. Part I, A Stratigraphical and Analytical Study of the Early Iron Age Pottery.* Documenta et Monumenta Orientis Antiqui LXX, Leiden 1969.

FRANKENA, R. The vassal-treaties of Esarhaddon and the dating of Deuteronomy. *OTS* XIV, Leiden 1965, p. 122-155.

— Rev. of: M. J. Mulder, "Kanaänitische Goden in het Oude Testament". *ThLZ* XCIII (1968) p. 335-336.

FREEDMAN, D. N. The Orthography of the Arad Ostraca. *IEJ* XIX (1969) p. 52-57.

FREDRIKSSON, H. *Jahwe als Krieger. Studien zum alttestamentlichen Gottesbild.* Lund 1945.

FRETHEIM, T. E. Psalm 132: A Form-Critical Study. *JBL* LXXXVI (1967) p. 289-300.

— The Priestly Document: anti-temple? *VT* XVIII (1968) p. 313-329.

— The Ark in Deuteronomy. *CBQ* XXX (1968) p. 1-14.

FRIED, M. H. On the concepts of "tribe" and "tribal society". In: *Essays on the problem of tribe.* AES, Seattle/London 1968, p. 3-20.

FRITZ, V. Die sogenannte Liste der besiegten Könige in Josua 12. *ZDPV* LXXXV (1969) p. 136-161.

— *Israel in der Wüste. Traditionsgeschichtliche Untersuchung der Wüstenüberlieferung der Jahwisten.* MarThS VII, Marburg 1970.

GALL, A. VON. *Altisraelitische Kultstätten.* BZAW 3, Giessen 1898.

GALLING, K. *Die Erwählungstraditionen Israëls.* BZAW 48, Giessen 1928.

— *Die israelitische Staatsverfassung in ihrer Vorderorientalischen Umwelt.* AO XXVIII 3/4, Leipzig 1929.

— Rev. of: M. Noth, Das System der zwölf Stämme Israels. *DLZ* LII (1931) p. 433-440.

— Bethel und Gilgal. *ZDPV* LXVI (1943) p. 140-155; *ZDPV* LXVII (1944) p. 21-43.

— Erwägungen zum Stelenheiligtum von Hazor. *ZDPV* LXXV (1959) p. 1-13.

— *Textbuch zur Geschichte Israels.* Tübingen 1968².

GARELLI, P. *Le Proche-Orient Asiatique. Des origines aux invasions des peuples de la mer.* La Nouvelle Clio 2, Paris 1969.

GARSTANG, J. The Walls of Jericho. *PEQ* 1931, p. 186-196.
— *The Foundations of Bible History. Joshua, Judges.* New York 1931.
GARSTANG, J. and GARSTANG, J. B. E. *The Story of Jericho.* London 1948.
GEERTZ, C. Religion as a Cultural System. In: *Anthropological Approaches to the Study of Religion.* Ed. by M. Banton, London 1966, p. 1-46.
GELB, I. J. The Early History of the West Semitic Peoples. *JCS* XV (1961) p. 27-48.
— Approaches to the Study of Ancient Society. *JAOS* LXXXVII (1967) p. 1-8.
GELSTON, A. The Wars of Israel: The Lord is a Man of War, Exod 15, 3. *SJTh* XVII (1964) p. 325-331.
GEMOLL, M. *Israeliten und Hyksos. Der historische Kern der Sage vom Aufenthalte Israëls in Ägypten.* Leipzig 1913.
GEMSER, B. Apologetiek en Opgrawingswetenskap. *Universiteit Pretoria Wetenskaplike Blad* I (1937) p. 31-43.
— *Vragen rondom de patriarchenreligie.* Groningen 1958.
GERHARDT, W. The Hebrew/Israelite Wheather-Deity. *Numen* XIII (1966) p. 128-143.
GERSTENBERGER, E. *Wesen und Herkunft des "Apodiktischen Rechts".* WMANT 20, Neukirchen 1965.
GESE, H. Bemerkungen zur Sinaitradition. *ZAW* LXXIX (1967) p. 137-155.
— *Der Verfassungsentwurf des Ezechiel (Kap. 40-48) traditionsgeschichtlich untersucht.* BHTh 25, Tübingen 1957.
GEUS, C. H. J. DE. De Richteren van Israël. *NThT* XX(1965) p. 81-100.
— Richteren 1:1-2:5. *Vox Theologica* XXXVI (1966) p. 32-54.
— The Amorites in the Archaeology of Palestine. *UF* III (1972) p. 41-60.
GHIRSHMAN, R. Invasions des nomades sur le Plateau Iranien aux premiers siècles du 1er millénaire avant J.C. In: *Dark Ages and Nomads c. 1000 B.C.* Published by the Ned. Arch. Instituut, Istanbul 1964, p. 3-8.
GIBSON, J. C. L. Life and Society at Mari and in Old Israel. *Transactions of the Glasgow University Oriental Society.* Volume XVIII, Leiden 1961, p. 15-29.
— Observations on some important ethnic terms in the Pentateuch. *JNES* XX (1961) p. 217-238.
GIESEBRECHT, FR. *Die Geschichtlichkeit des Sinaïbundes.* Königsberg 1900.
GILLISCHEWSKI, EVA. Der Ausdruck 'am hā'āreṣ im AT. *ZAW* XL (1922) p. 137-143.
GIVEON, R. "The cities of our God" (II Sam 10:12) *JBL* LXXXIII (1964) p. 415-416.
— Toponymes ouest-asiatiques à Soleb. *VT* XIV (1964) p. 239-255.
GIVEON, R. Two Egyptian documents concerning Bashan from the time of Ramses II. *RSO* XL (1965) p. 177-195.
— The Shosu of Egyptian Sources and the Exodus. *Proceedings of the Fourth World Congress of Jewish Studies.* Volume I, Jerusalem 1967, p. 193-197.
GLUECK, N. Explorations in Eastern Palestine and the Negeb. *BASOR* 55 (1934) p. 3-22.
— Three Israelite Towns in the Jordan Valley: Zarethan, Succoth, Zaphon. *BASOR* 90 (1943) p. 1-24.
— Some Ancient Towns in the Plains of Moab. *BASOR* 91 (1943) p. 7-27.
GOFF, BEATRICE L. The Lost Jahwistic Account of the Conquest of Canaan. *JBL* LIII (1934) p. 241-250.
GOITEIN, S. D. *Juifs et Arabes.* Paris 1957.
GOLKA, F. Zur Erforschung der Aetiologien im Alten Testament. *VT* XX (1970) p. 90-98.

GOOD, E. M. The "Blessing" on Judah, Gen. 49, 8-12. *JBL* LXXXII (1963) p. 427-432.

— Hosea 5:8-6:6: an alternative to Alt. *JBL* LXXXV (1966) p. 273-286.

GORDON, C. H. Fratriarchy in the Old Testament. *JBL* LIV (1935) 223-231.

— Hebrew Origins in the Light of Recent Discovery. In: *Biblical and Other Studies edited by Alexander Altmann*. Cambridge, Mass. 1963, p. 3-15.

GÖRG, M. *Das Zelt der Begegnung. Untersuchung zur Getalt der sakralen Zelttraditionen Altisraels*. BBB 27, Bonn 1967.

GRADMAN, R. *Die Steppen des Morgenlandes in ihrer Bedeutung für die Geschichte der menslichen Gesittung*. Geogr. Abh. 3. Reihe: 6, Stuttgart 1934.

BUCHANAN GRAY, G. *Studies in Hebrew Proper Names*. London 1896.

GRAY, J. Feudalism in Ugarit and Early Israel. *ZAW* LXIV (1952) p. 49-55.

— *The Legacy of Canaan*. SVT V, Leiden 1957.

GRESSMANN, H. *Palästinas Erdgeruch in der israelitischen Religion*. Kultur und Leben, Band 8. Berlin 1909.

— Sage und Geschichte in den Patriarchenerzählungen. *ZAW* XXX (1910) p. 1-35.

— *Mose und seine Zeit. Ein Kommentar zu den Mose-Sagen*. FRLANT N.F. I, Göttingen 1913.

— *Die Anfänge Israels. Von 2. Mose bis Richter und Ruth*. SAT 1, 2, Göttingen 1914 (1922²).

— Ursprung und Entwicklung der Joseph-Sage. In: *"Eucharisterion" Gunkel-Festschrift*, Bd I, Göttingen 1923, p. 1-55.

GRETHER, O. Die Bezeichnung "Richter" für die charismatische Helden der vorstaatlichen Zeit. *ZAW* LVII (1939) p. 110-122.

GRØNBAEK, J. H. Benjamin und Juda. *VT* XV (1965) p. 421-436.

GRØNBAEK, J. H. Juda und Amalek. Überlieferungsgeschichtliche Erwägungen zu Exodus 17-8-16. *Studia Theologica* XVIII (1964) p. 26-35.

GROEN, J. J. Historical and Genetic Studies on the Twelve Tribes of Israel and their Relation to the Present Ethnic Composition of the Jewish People. *JQR* LVIII (1967) p. 1-13.

GROOT, JOH. DE. *De Palestijnse achtergrond van den Pentateuch*. Groningen 1928.

— *Jozua. Tekst en Uitleg*. Groningen/'s-Gravenhage 1931.

GRUNEBAUM, G. E. VON. The Nature of Arab Unity before Islam. *Arabica* X (1963) p. 5-23.

GUNKEL, H. *Genesis übersetzt und erklärt*. HK I, 1 (hrsg. v. W. Nowack) Göttingen 1902², 1922⁵.

— Jakob. *PrJ* Band CLXXVI (1919) p. 339-362.

GUNNEWEG, A. H. J. Mose in Midian. *ZThK* LXI (1964) p. 1-9.

— Über den Sitz im Leben der sog. Stammessprüche. *ZAW* LXXVI (1964) p. 245-254.

— *Leviten und Priester. Hauptlinien der Traditionsbildung und Geschichte des israelitisch-jüdischen Kultpersonals*. FRLANT 89, Göttingen 1965.

GUREWICZ, S. B. The Bearing of Judges 1-11 5 on the Authorship of the Book of Judges. *Austr. Bibl. Rev.* VII (1959) p. 37-40.

GUSTAVS, A. Der Gott Ḥabiru. *ZAW* XL (1922) p. 313-314.

— Was heisst ilani Ḥabiri? *ZAW* XLIV (1926) p. 23-38.

— Die Personennamen in den Tontafeln von Tell Ta'annek. *ZDPV* L (1927) p. 1-18.

GUTHE, H. *Geschichte des Volkes Israel*. Tübingen 1914³.

GUTMANN, J. The History of the Ark. *ZAW* LXXXIII (1971) p. 22-30.

HABEL, N. C. *Yahweh versus Baal. A Conflict of Religion Cultures*. New York 1964.

HALDAR, A. *The Notion of the Desert in Sumero-Accadian and West-Semitic Religion.* Uppsala Universitets Årsskrift 1950: 3, Uppsala/Leipzig 1950.
— *Who were the Amorites?* Leiden 1971.
HALLEVY, R. The Canaanite Period: A Culture Clash. *Tarbiz* XXXV (1965-1966) p. 95-102.
HALLO, W. W. A Sumerian Amphictyony. *JCS* XIV (1960) p. 88-114.
— Antediluvian Cities. *JCS* XXIII (1970) p. 57-67.
HANČAR, F. Zur Frage der Herdentier–Erstdomestikation. *Saeculum* X (1959) p. 21-37.
HARAN, M. The Religion of the Patriarchs. An Attempt at a Synthesis. *ASThI* IV (1965) p. 30-56.
— Studies in the Account of the Levitical Cities. *JBL* LXXX (1961) p. 45-54, 156-165.
— Zebaḥ hayyamîm. *VT* XIX (1969) p. 11-22, 372-373.
HARLAND, J. P. The Calaurian Amphictyony. *AJA* XXIX (1925) p. 160-171.
HARRIS, RIVCA. The Archive of the Sin Temple in Khafajah (Tutub) *JCS* IX (1955) p. 31-69.
HAUER, CHR. E. Does I Sam. 9:1-11:15 reflect the Extension of Saul's Dominions? *JBL* LXXXVI (1967) p. 306-311.
— The Shape of Saulide Strategy. *CBQ* XXXI (1969) p. 153-167.
HAUPT, P. Lea und Rahel. *ZAW* XXIX (1909) p. 281-287.
HELAISSI, A. S. The Bedouins and Tribal Life in Saudi Arabia. *ISSJ* XI (1959) p. p. 532-538.
HELCK, W. *Die Beziehungen Ägyptens zu Vorderasien im 3. und 2. Jahrtausend v. Chr.* Wiesbaden 1962.
— Zur staatlichen Organisation Syriens im Beginn der 18. Dynastie. *AfO* XXII (1968/1969) p. 27-29.
— Die Bedrohung Palästinas durch Einwandernde Gruppen am Ende der 18. und am Anfang der 19. Dynastie. *VT* XVIII (1968) p. 472-480.
HELEWA, J. L'Institution de la guerre sainte au désert à la lumière de l'alliance mosaïque. *Ephem. Carm.* XIV (1963) p. 3-63.
HEMPEL, J. Westliche Kultureinflüsse auf das älteste Palästina. *PJ* XXIII (1927) p. 52-92.
HENNINGER, J. *Die Familie bei den heutigen Beduinen Arabiens und seiner Randgebiete. Ein Beitrag zur Frage der Ursprünglichen Familienform der Semiten.* Internationales Archiv für Ethnographie, Band XLII, Leiden 1943.
— La société bédouine ancienne. In: *F. Gabrieli, L'Antica Società Beduina.* Roma 1959, p. 69-94.
— Altarabische Genealogie. (rev. of W. Caskel: Ğamharat an-Nasab. Das genealogische Werk des Hišām ibn Muḥammad Al-Kalbī). *Anthropos* LXI (1966) p. 852-870.
— Zum Erstgeborenenrecht bei den Semiten. *Festschrift für W. Caskel, hrgb. v. E. Gräf.* Leiden 1968, p. 162-183.
— *Über Lebensraum und Lebensformen der Frühsemiten.* Arbeitsgemeinschaft für Forschung des Landes Nordrhein-Westfalen, Geisteswissenschaften Heft 151. Köln/Opladen 1968.
HENREY, K. H. Land Tenure in the Old Testament. *PEQ* LXXXVI (1954) p. 5-15.
HENTSCHKE, R. Erwägungen zur israelitischen Rechtsgeschichte. *Theol. Viat.* X (1965/66) p. 108-133.

HEPPENSTAL, E. The Law and the Covenant at Sinai. *Andrews Univ. Sem. Studies* II (1965) p. 18-26.

HERRMANN, S. Das Werden Israels. *ThLZ* LXXXVII (1962) p. 561-574.

— Israel in Ägypten. *ZÄS* XCI (1964) p. 63-79.

— Neuere Arbeiten zur Geschichte Israels. *ThLZ* LXXXIX (1964) p. 813-825.

— Der alttestamentliche Gottesname. *EvTh* XXVI (1966) p. 281-293.

— Der Name JHW³c in den Inschriften von Soleb. *Proceedings of the Fourth World Congress of Jewish Studies*, Volume 1. Jerusalem 1967, p. 123-217.

— Geschichte Israels, Möglichkeiten und Grenzen ihrer Darstellung. *ThLZ* XCIV (1969) p. 641-650.

— Autonome Entwicklungen in den Königreichen Israel und Juda. *SVT* (1969) p. 139-159.

— *Geschichte Israels in alttestamentlicher Zeit.* München 1973.

— Rev. art. of R. de Vaux. Histoire ancienne d'Israel. *VT* XXIII (1973) p. 117-126.

HERRMANN, W. Issakar. *Forsch. und Fortschr.* XXXVII (1963) p. 21-26.

— Aštart. *MIOr* XV (1969) p. 6-55.

HERTZBERG, H. W. Die kleinen Richter. *ThLZ* LXXIX (1954) p. 285-290.

— Rev. of M. Noths, Das System der Zwölf Stämme Israels. *OLZ* XXXI (1931) p. 853-855.

— *Die Bücher Josua, Richter, Ruth.* Das Alte Testament Deutsch, 9. Göttingen 1959².

HERZOG, R. *Sesshaftwerden von Nomaden.* Forschungsberichte des Landes Nordrhein-Westfalen. Nr. 1238. Westdeutscher Verlag. Köln/Opladen 1963.

HESSE, F. Amos 5:4-6, 14f. *ZAW* LXVIII (1956) p. 1-17.

HEYDE, H. *Kain, der erste Jahwe-Verehrer. Die Ursprüngliche Bedeutung der Sage von Kain und ihre Auswirkungen in Israel.* ArTh 1, 23, Stuttgart 1965.

HILLER, D. R. Paḥad Yiṣḥāq. *JBL* XCI (1972) p. 90-92.

HOEBEL, E. A. *Anthropology: The Study of Man.* New York 1972⁴.

HÖFNER, MARIA. War der sabäische Mukarrib ein "Priesterfürst"? *WZKM* LIV (1957) p. 77-85.

— Die Beduinen in den vorislamischen arabischen Inschriften. In: *F. Gabrieli ed., L'Antica Società Beduina.* Roma 1959, p. 53-68.

HOFTIJZER, J. *Die Verheissungen an die drei Erzväter.* Leiden 1956.

— Enige opmerkingen rond het Israëlitische 12-stammensysteem. *NThT* (1959/60) p. 241-264.

— Absalom and Tamar: a Case of Fratriarchy? In: *"Schrift en Uitleg", Feestbundel voor W. H. Gipsen.* Kampen 1970, p. 55-61.

— David and the Tekoite Woman. *VT* XX (1970) 419-444.

HÖLSCHER, G. *Geschichtsschreibung im Israel. Untersuchungen zum Jahwisten und Elohisten.* SHVL, Lund 1952.

HOLZINGER, H. *Das Buch Josua.* KHAT VI. Leipzig/Tübingen 1901.

HOMMEL, F. Geschichte Südarabiens im Umriss. *Handbuch der altarabischen Altertumskunde, Hrgb. v. D. D. Nielsen;* Bd. 1, Kopenhagen/Leipzig 1927, p. 57-108.

HORST, F. Die zwölf Stämme Israels. Rev. of: M. Noth, Das System der Zwölf Stämme Israels. *ThBL* XII (1933) p. 104-117.

HOUTSMA, M. TH. Die Ghuzenstämme. *WZKM* II (1888) p. 219-233.

HUFFMON, H. B. The Exodus, Sinai and the Credo. *CBQ* XXVII (1965) p. 101-113.

— *Amorite Personal Names in the Mari Texts.* Baltimore 1965.

— Yahweh and Mari. In: *Near Eastern Studies in Honor of W. F. Albright,* ed. by H. Goedicke, Baltimore 1971, p. 283-290.

HULST, A. R. *Het karakter van den cultus in Deuteronomium.* Wageningen 1938.
— Der Name "Israel" im Deuteronomium. *OTS* IX, Leiden 1951, p. 65-106.
— *Wat betekent de naam Israël in het Oude Testament*? 's-Gravenhage 1962.
— Der Jordan in den alttestamentlichen Überlieferungen. *OTS* XIV (1965) p. 162-189.
HYATT, J. PH. Was Yahweh originally a creator deity? *JBL* LXXXVI (1967) p. 369-377.
— Was there an Ancient Historical Credo in Israel and an Independent Sinai Tradition. In: *"Translating and Understanding the Old Testament". Essays in Honor of H. G. May.* Nashville/New York 1970, p. 152-170.
HYMES, D. Linguistic problems in defining the concept of "tribe". In: *Essays in the problem of tribe.* AES, Seattle/London 1968, p. 23-48.
INGRAMS, W. H. *A Report of the Social, Economic and Political Conditions of the Hadhramaut.* London 1936.
IRWIN, H. c.s.b. Le sanctuaire central israélite avant l'établissement de la monarchie. *RB* LXXII (1965) p. 161-185.
IRWIN, W. A. Qrî'ê ha-'edhah (Num I 16). *AJSL* LVII (1940) p. 95-97.
Ishida, T. The Leaders of the Tribal Leagues "Israel" in the Pre-Monarchic Period. *RB* LXXX (1973) p. 514-530.
ISSERLIN, B. S. J. Ancient Forests in Palestine: Some Archaeological Implications. *PEQ* LXXXVII (1955) p. 87-89.
— Place Name Provinces in the Semitic-Speaking Ancient Near East. *Proceedings of the Leeds Philosophical Society* VII (1956) p. 83-110.
— Hurrian and Old Anatolian Place Names in the Semitic World: Some Tentative Suggestions. *PEQ* LXXXVIII (1956) p. 141-145.
— Israelite and Pre-Israelite Place Names in Palestine. *PEQ* LXXXIX (1957) p. 133-145.
IVANOV, V. V. L'organization sociale des tribus Indo-Européennes d'après les données linguistiques. *Cahiers d'Histoire Mondiale* V (1959) p. 789-800.
JACK, J. W. The Israel-Stele of Merenptah. *ET* XXXVI (1924/25) p. 40-44.
JACOBSEN, TH. Early Political Development in Mesopotamia. *ZA* LII, NF XVIII (1957) p. 91-141.
JACOBSON, D. *The Social Background of the O.T.* Cincinnati 1942.
JAKOBSON, V. A. The Social Structure of the Neo-Assyrian Empire. (1965) In: *I. M. Diakonoff ed., Ancient Mesopotamia.* Moscow 1969, p. 277-295.
JAMME, A. Sabaean Inscriptions from Maḥram Bilqîs (Mârib). Baltimore 1962.
JAMPEL, S. Die neuesten Aufstellungen über Moses und sein Werk. *MGWJ* NF XVII (1909) p. 641-657.
JANKOWSKA, N. B. Some Problems of the Economy of the Assyrian Empire. (1947) In: *I. M. Diakonoff ed., Ancient Mesopotamia.* Moscow 1969, p. 253-276.
— Extended Family Commune and Civil Self-Government in Arrapḫa in the Fifteenth-Fourteenth Century B.C. (1957-1960). In: *I. M. Diakonoff ed., Ancient Mesopotamia.* Moscow 1969, p. 235-252.
— Communal Self-Government and the King of the State of Arrapḫa. *JESHO* XII (1969) p. 233-282.
JANSSENS, G. Enkele problemen der Hebreeuwse grammatika in het licht van Origenes' transcripties. *Handelingen van het XXIIe Vlaams Filologencongres 1957,* p. 95-99.
JASPER, F. N. Early Israelite traditions and the psalter. *VT* XVII (1967) p. 50-60.
JAUSSEN, A. *Coutumes des Arabes au pays de Moab.* Paris 1908.

JAWAD, A. J. *The advent of the Era of Townships in Northern Mesopotamia*. Leiden 1965.

JENNI, E. Historisch-topographische Untersuchungen zur Grenze zwischen Ephraim und Manasse. *ZDPV* LXXIV (1958) p. 35-40.

JENSEN, P. *Das Gilgamesch-Epos in der Weltliteratur*. Strassburg 1906.

— *Moses, Jesus, Paulus. Drei Sagenvarianten des babylonischen Gottmenschen Gilgamesch*. Frankfurt 1909.

JEPSEN, A. *Die Quellen des Königsbuches*. Halle 1956².

— Kanaanäisch und Hebräisch. *Akten des 25. Orientalistenkongresses*. Moscow 1962, p. 316-321.

JETTMAR, K. Die Entstehung der Reiternomaden. *Saeculum* XVII (1966) p. 1-11.

JIRKU, A. *Die Wanderungen der Hebräer im 3. und 2. Jahrtausend v. Chr*. AO 24:2, Leipzig 1934.

— Götter Ḫabiru oder Götter der Ḫabiru? *ZAW* XLIV (1926) p. 237-242.

JOHNSON, D. L. *The Nature of Nomadism: A Comparative Study of Pastoral Migrations in Southwestern Asia and Northern Africa*. University of Chicago, Dept. of Geography, Research Papers Nr. 118. Chicago 1969.

JOHNSON, M. D. *The Purpose of the Biblical Genealogies*. Cambridge 1969.

JOHNSTONE, W. Old Testament Technical Expressions in Property Holding. *Ugaritica* VI (1969) p. 308-317.

JUNKER, H. Die Entstehungszeit des Ps 78 und des Deuteronomiums. *Biblica* XXXIV (1953) p. 487-500.

KAHN, J. G. Did Philo know Hebrew? The Testimony of the "Etymologies". *Tarbiz* XXIV (1965) p. 337-345.

KALLAI-KLEINMANN, Z. The townlists of Judah, Simeon, Benjamin and Dan. *VT* VIII (1958) p. 134-160.

— *The Tribes of Israel. A Study in the historical geography of the Bible*. Jerusalem 1967.

KAISER, D. Stammesgeschichtliche Hintergründe der Josephsgeschichte. *VT* X (1960) p. 1-15.

KASSIS, HANNA E. Gath and the structure of the "Philistine" society. *JBL* LXXXIV (1965) p. 259-272.

KAUFMANN, Y. *The Biblical Account of the Conquest of Palestine*. Jerusalem 1953.

— Traditions Concerning Early Israelite History in Canaan. *Scripta Hierosalymitana* VIII (1961) p. 303-334.

KELLERMANN, D. *Die Priesterschrift von Numeri 1:1-10:10 literar-kritisch und traditionsgeschichtlich untersucht*. BZAW 120, Berlin 1970.

KELSO, J. L. *The Excavation of Bethel*. AASOR XXXIX, Cambridge Mass. 1968.

KENYON, K. M. *Archaeology in the Holy Land*. London 1965².

— *Amorites and Canaanites*. London 1966.

KILIAN, R. *Die vorpriesterlichen Abrahamsüberlieferungen literarkritisch und traditionsgeschichtlich untersucht*. BBB 24, Bonn 1966.

KINGSBURY, E. C. The Theophany 'Topos' and the Mountain of God. *JBL* LXXXVI (1967) p. 205-210.

— He set Ephraim before Manasseh. *HUCA* XXXVIII (1967) p. 129-136.

KITCHEN, K. A. Some new light on the Asiatic Wars of Ramesses II. *JEA* L (1964) p. 47-71.

— Historical Method and Early Hebrew Tradition. *Tyndale Bulletin* XVII (1966) p. 63-96.

KITTEL, R. *Geschichte des Volkes Israel*, Band I, Gotha 1923⁶, Band II, Gotha 1925⁷.

KJAER, H. The Excavation of Shiloh 1929. *JPOS* X (1930) p. 87-178.
KLENGEL, H. Halbnomaden am mittleren Euphrat. Das *Altertum* V (1959) p. 195-205.
— Zu den šībūtum in altbabylonischer Zeit. *Or* NS XXIX (1960) p. 357-375.
— Zu einigen Problemen des altvorderasiatischen Nomadentums. *ArOr* XXX (1962) p. 585-596.
— Die Rolle der "Ältesten" (Lúmeš Šu-Gi) im Kleinasien der Hethiterzeit. *ZA* NF XXIII (1965) p. 223-237.
— Sesshafte und Nomaden in der alten Geschichte Mesopotamiens. *Saeculum* XVII (1966) p. 205-222.
— Halbnomadischer Bodenbau im Königreich von Mari. *VBVHS*, Berlin 1968, p. 75-82.
— *Geschichte Syriens im 2. Jahrtausend v.u.Z.*, *Teil I* Berlin 1965, *Teil II* Berlin 1969, *Teil III* Berlin 1970.
— *Zwischen Zelt und Palast*. Leipzig 1972.
KLÍMA, J. La via sociale et économique à Mari. *XVeRAI*, Paris 1967, p. 39-50.
— Soziale und wirtschaftliche Verhältnisse von Mari. *VBVHS*, Berlin 1968, p.. 83-90.
KLINE, M. G. The Ḫa-Bi-rum, kin or foe of Israel. *Westminster Theological Journal* XIX (1956) p. 1-24, 170-184; *Westminster Theological Journal* XX (1957) p. 46-70.
KLOSTERMANN, AUG. *Geschichte des Volkes Israel*. München 1896.
— *Der Pentateuch. Neue Folge*. Leipzig 1907.
KNIERIM, R. *Die Hauptbegriffe für Sünde im Alten Testament*. Gütersloh 1965.
KOCH, KL. Der Tod des Religionsstifters. Erwägungen über das Verhältnis Israels zur Geschichte der altorientalische Religionen Gerh. Gloege zum 24-12-1961 gewidmet. *KuD* VIII (1962) p. 100-123.
— *Was ist Formgeschichte? Neue Wege der Bibelexegese*. Neukirchen 1964.
— Die Hebräer vom Auszug aus Ägypten bis zum Grossreich Davids. *VT* XIX (1969) p. 37-81.
KÖHLER, L. *Der Hebräische Mensch*. Tübingen 1953.
KONING, J. DE. *Studiën over de El-Amarnabrieven en het Oude Testament inzonderheid uit historisch oogpunt*. Delft 1940.
KOSCHAKER, P. Fratriarchat, Hausgemeinschaft und Mutterrecht in Keilschriftrechten. *ZA* NF VII (1933) p. 1-89.
KRADER, L. The Ecology of Nomadic Pastoralism. *ISSJ* XL (1959) p. 499-510.
KRAELING, E. G. The Origin of the Name "Hebrews". *AJSL* LVIII (1941) p. 237-253.
KRAUS, F. R. Le Rôle des Temples depuis la Troisième Dynastie d'Ur jusqu'à la Première Dynastie de Babylone. *Cahiers d'Histoire Mondiale* I (1953-1954) p. 518-545.
— *Könige, die in Zelten wohnten*. Betrachtungen über den Kern der Assyrischen Königsliste. Med. d. Kon. Med. Akkad. v. Wet. afd. Letterkunde, NR 28, 2. Amsterdam 1965.
KRAUS, H. J. *Geschichte der historisch-kritischen Erforschung des Alten Testaments. Von der Reformation bis zur Gegenwart*. Neukirchen 1956.
— Gilgal. Ein Beitrag zur Kultusgeschichte Israels. *VT* I (1951) p. 181-199.
— *Die prophetische Verkündigung des Rechts in Israel*. Theol. Stud. Heft 51, Zollikon 1957.
KREBS, W. "... und sie haben Stiere gelähmt" Gen. 39:6. *ZAW* LXXVIII (1966) p. 359-361.

KRISTENSEN, W. B. *De ark van Jahwe.* Kon. Ned. Akk. van Wetenschappen, Amsterdam 1933.

KUENEN, A. Critische bijdragen tot de geschiedenis van den Israëlietischen Godsdienst. Deel VI, De stamvaders van het Israëlietische Volk. *ThT* V (1871) p. 255-312.

KUPPER, J. R. *Les nomades en Mesopotamie au temps des rois de Mari.* Paris 1957.
— Le rôle des nomades dans l'histoire de la Mésopotamie. *JESHO* II (1959) p. 113-127.

KUSCHKE, A. Historisch-topographische Beiträge zum Buche Josua. In: *Gottes Wort und Gottes Land, Hertzberg-Festschrift,* Göttingen 1965, p. 90-109.

LABUSCHAGNE, C. J. *The Incomparability of Yahweh in the Old Testament.* Leiden 1966.

LACK, R. Les Origines de 'Elyôn. Le Très-Haut dans la tradition culturelle d'Israël. *CBQ* XXIV (1962) p. 44-64.

LAGARDE, P. DE. Übersicht über die im Aramäischen, Arabischen und Hebräischen übliche Bildung der Nomina. *Abh. der Königlichen Ges. d. Wiss. zu Göttingen, Hist.-Phil. Kl.* XXXV. Band (1888) p. 131f. (Register im XXXVIII. Band (1889))

LAMBERT, W. G. The language of Mari. *XVe RAI,* Paris 1967, p. 29-39.

DARELL LANCE, H. Gezer in the Land and in History. *BA* XXX (1967) p. 34-47.

LANGLAMET, F. *Gilgal et les récits de la traversée du Jourdain.* Cahiers de la Revue Biblique XI, Paris 1969.
— Israël et "l'habitant du pays". *RB* LXXVI (1969) p. 321-350, 481-507.
— Jos., III-IV et l'Hexateuque. *RB* LXXIX (1972) p. 7-38.

LAPP, P. W. Tel el-Fûl. *BA* XXVIII (1965) p. 1-10.
— *The Dhahr Mirzbâneh Tombs.* ASOR, New Haven/Jerusalem 1966.
— The Conquest of Palestine in the Light of Archaeology. *Concordia Theological Monthly.* XXXVIII (1967) p. 283-301.
— The 1968 Excavations at Tell Ta'annek. *BASOR* 195 (1969) p. 2-49.
— *Biblical Archaeology and History.* Cleveland 1969.

LARSEN, J. A. O. Federation for Peace in Ancient Greece. *CP* XXXIX (1944) p. 145-162.

LECERF, J. Note sur la famille dans le monde arabe et islamique. *Arabica* III (1956) p. 31-60.

LEMAIRE, A. Asriel, šr'l, Israel et l'origine de la conféderation israélite. *VT* XXIII (1973) p. 239-243.

LEHMANN-HAUPT, C. F. *Israel. Seine Entwicklung im Rahmen der Weltgeschichte.* Tübingen 1911.

LEHMING, S. Zur Überlieferungsgeschichte von Gen. 34. *ZAW* LXX (1958) p. 228-250.
— Die Erzählung von den Geburt der Jakobsöhne. *VT* XIII (1963) p. 74-81.

LEIBOVITCH, J. Le problème des Hyksos et celui de l'Exode. *IEJ* III (1953) p. 99-112.

LEVI, M. A. *Political Power in the Ancient World.* London 1965.

LEWIS, H. S. Typology and Progress in Political Evolution. In: *Essays on the problem of tribe.* AES Seattle/London 1968, p. 101-110.

LEWIS, I. M. *A Pastoral Democracy. A Study of Pastoralism and Politics among the Northern Somali of the Horn of Africa.* London 1961.

LEWY, HILDEGARD. Šubat-Šumaš and Tuttul. *Or* NS 27 (1958) p. 1-18.

LEWY, J. Ḫabiru and Hebrews. *HUCA* XIV (1939) p. 587-623 en XV (1940) p. 47-58.

— Origin and Signification of the Biblical Term "Hebrew". *HUCA* XXVIII (1957) p. 1-14.
LÉVY, J. PH. Les Ventes dans la Bible. In: *Mélanges Philippe Meylan.* Lausanne 1963, vol. II, p. 157-167.
L'HOUR, J. L'Alliance de Sichem. *RB* LXIX (1962) p. 5-36, 161-184, 350-368.
LIERE, W. J. VAN. Capitals and Citadels of Bronze-Iron Age Syria in their Relationship to Land and Water. *AAS* XIII (1963) p. 109-122.
LIPÍNSKI, E. 'Anaq - Kiryat 'Arba'-Hébron et ses sanctuaires tribaux. *VT* XXIV (1974) p. 41-55.
LIVER, J. The Literary History of Joshua IX. *JSS* VIII (1963) p. 227-243.
— The Book of the Acts of Solomon. Biblica XLVIII (1967) p. 75-101.
LIVERANI, M. Il fuoriscitismo in Siria nella tarda eta del bronzo. *Rivista Storica Italiana* LXXVII (1965) p. 315-336.
— Implicazioni sociale nella politica di Abdi-Ashirta di Amurru. *RSO* LX (1965) p. 267-277.
— The Amorites. *POTT*, London 1973, p. 100-133.
LODS, A. *Israel, des origines au milieu du VIIIe siècle.* L'évolution de l'humanité, vol. XXVII, Paris 1930.
LOEWENSTAMM, S. E. Rueben and Judah in the Joseph-cycle. *Proceedings of the Fourth World Congres of Jewish Studies.* Volume I, Jerusalem 1967, p. 257ff.
LONG, B. O. *The Problem of Etiological Narrative in the Old Testament.* BZAW 108. Berlin 1968.
LOON, M. N. VAN. The Oriental Institute Excavations at Mureybit, Syria. Preliminary Report on the 1965 Campaign. *JNES* XXVII (1968) p. 265-282.
LOUNDINE (= LUNDIN) A. G. et RYCKMANS, J. Nouvelles données sur la chronologie des rois de Saba et Dū-Raydān. *Le Muséon* LXXVII (1964) p. 407-428.
LUCKENBILL, D. D. On Israel's Origins. *AJTh* XXII (1918) p. 24-53.
LUNDIN, A. G. Die Eponymenliste von Saba. *Oestr. Ak. Wiss., Phil.-Hist. Klasse, Sitzungsberichte* 248, 1, Wien 1965.
LUTHER, B. Die Israelitischen Stämme. *ZAW* XXI (1901) p. 1-77.
LURJE, M. *Studien zur Geschichte der wirtschaftlichen und sozialen Verhältnisse im Israelitisch-Jüdischen Reiche.* BZAW 45, Giessen 1927.
MAAG, V. Malkût Jhwh. *SVT* VII, Leiden 1960, p. 129-153.
— Der Hirte Israels. *SThU* XXVIII (1958) p. 2-28.
— Sichembund und Vätergötter. *SVT XVI, "Hebräische Wortforschung",* Leiden 1967, p. 205-218.
MAASS, F. Hazor und das Problem der Landnahme. *BZAW* 77, Berlin 1961², p. 105-118.
MACALISTER, R. A. S. *A Century of Excavation in Palestine.* London 1925.
McADAMS, R. *The Evolution of Urban Society.* London 1966.
— Agriculture and Urban Life in Early South-Western Asia. *Science* CXXXVI (1962) Nr. 3511, p. 109-122.
McFAYDEN, F. Telescoped History. *ET* XXXVI (1924/25) p. 103-110.
McKENZIE, D. A. Judicial Procedure at the Town Gate. *VT* XIV (1964) p. 100-105.
— The Judge of Israel. *VT* XVII (1967) p. 118-122.
McKENZIE, J. L. The City and Israelite Religion. *CBQ* XXV (1963) p. 60-70.
— Jacob at Peniël: Gn 32, 24-32. *CBQ* XXV (1963) p. 70-77.
— *The World of the Judges.* Englewood Cliffs, N. J. (Prentice Hall) 1966.
MACLAURIN, E. C. B. *The Hebrew Theocracy in the tenth to the sixth centuries B.C. An Analysis of the Books of Judges, Samuel and Kings.* Sidney 1959.

MAIER, J. *Das altisraëlitische Ladeheiligtum.* BZAW 93, Berlin 1965.
MAISLER, B. Die Landschaft Bašan im 2. Vorchr. Jahrtausend. *JPOS* IX (1929) p. 80-87.
— *Untersuchungen zur alten Geschichte und Ethnografie Syriens und Palästinas,* 1. Giessen 1920.
— Das vordavidische Jerusalem. *JPOS* X (1930) p. 181-191.
— Canaan on the Threshold of the Age of the Patriarchs. *EI* III (1954) p. 18-31. Further publications under the name B. Mazar.
MALAMAT, A. Cushan Rishataïm and the decline of the Near East around 1200 B.C. *JNES* XIII (1954) p. 231-242.
— Campaigns of Amenhotep II and Thutmose IV to Canaan. *Scripta Hierosalymitana* VII (1961) p. 218-231.
— Mari and the Bible. Some patterns of tribal organisation and institutions. *JAOS* LXXXII (1962) p. 143-150.
— The Ban in Mari and in the Bible *.Die Ou-Testamentiese Werkgemeenskap in Suid-Afrika,* 1966, p. 40-49.
— Aspects of Tribal Societies in Mari and Israel. *XVth RAI,* Paris 1967, p. 129-138.
— King Lists of the Old Babylonian Period and Biblical Genealogies. *JAOS* LXXXVIII (1968) p. 163-173.
— Western Asia Minor in the Time of the "Sea Peoples". *Yediot XXX* (1966) p. 195-208.
— Organs of Statecraft in the Israelite Monarchy. *The Biblical Archaeologist Reader.* Vol. III, New York 1970, p. 163-198.
— The Danite Migration and the Pan-Israelite Exodus-Conquest: A Biblical Narrative Pattern, *Biblica* LI (1970) p. 1-16.
— *The World History of the Jewish People.* Vol III, Chapter II "The Egyptian Decline in Canaan and the Sea-Peoples", and VII "The Period of the Judges" Jerusalem/London 1971.
— Rev. art of R. de Vaux "Histoire ancienne d'Israël". *RB* LXXX (1973) p. 82-92.
— The Aramaeans. *POTT,* London 1973, p. 134-155.
MALLON, A. Les Hyksos et les Hébreux. *JPOS* V (1925) p. 85-91.
— *Les Hébreux et Égypte.* Roma 1920.
MANNZMANN, ANNELIESE. "Amphiktuonia", *Der Kleine Pauly,* 1; Stuttgart 1964, p. 311-313.
MARGULIS, B. Gen, XLIX 10/Deut. XXXIII 2-3. *VT* XIX (1969) p. 202-210.
MARX, EM. *Bedouin of the Negev.* Manchester 1967.
MATTHEWS, C. D. Bedouin life in contemporary Arabia. *RSO* XXXV (1960) p. 31-62.
MAYER, R. Der Gottesname Jahwe im Licht der neuesten Forschung. *BZ* II (1958) p. 26-53.
MAYES, A. D. H. Israel in the pre-monarchy period. *VT* XXIII (1973) p. 151-170.
— The historical context of the battle against Sisera. *VT* XIX (1969) p. 353-361.
MAXWELL MILLER, J. The Elisha cycle and the accounts of the Omride wars. *JBL* LXXXV (1966) p. 441-455.
MAZAR, B. The Sanctuary of Arad and the family of Hobab the Kenite. *EI* VII (1964) p. 1-5 (Hebr.); *JNES* XXIV (1965) p. 297-303.
— The Historical Background of the Book of Genesis. *JNES* XXVIII (1969) p. 73-83.
— The Philistines and the Rise of Israel and Tyre. *The Israel Academy of Sciences and Humanities 1. 7.* Jerusalem 1967.

MEEK, TH. J. *Hebrew Origins.* New York/London 1936.
— The Israelite Conquest of Ephraim. *BASOR* 61 (1936) p. 17-19.
— Moses and the Levites. *AJSL* LVI (1939) 113-120.
MEINHOLD, J. Review of: M. Noth: System der zwölf Stämme Israels. *ThLZ* LVI (1931) p. 411-414.
MENDENHALL, G. E. The Census Lists of Numbers 1 and 26. *JBL* LXXVII (1958) p. 52-67.
— The Hebrew Conquest of Palestine. *BA* XXV (1962) p. 66-87.
— Early Israel as the Kingdom of Yahweh: Thesis and Methods.
   In: *The Tenth Generation, the Origins of the Biblical Tradition.* Baltimore 1973, p. 1-31.
— The 'Apiru Movements in the Late Bronze Age. In: *The Tenth Generation, the Origins of the Biblical Tradition.* Baltimore 1973, p. 122-141.
— Tribe and State in the Ancient World: The Nature of the Biblical Community.
   In: *The Tenth Generation, the Origins of the Biblical Tradition.* Baltimore 1973, p. 174-197.
MENES, A. *Die vorexilischen Gesetze Israels im Zusammenhang seiner kulturgeschichtlichen Entwicklung. Vorarbeiten zur Geschichte Israels, 1.* BZAW 50, Giessen 1928.
MERENDINO, R. P. *Das Deuteronomische Gesetz.* BBB 31, Bonn 1969.
MERWE, B. J. VAN DER. Joseph as successor of Jacob. In: *Studia Biblica et Semitica Th. C. Vriezen Dedicata.* Wageningen 1966, p. 221-232.
MERX, P. *Die Bücher Moses und Josua.* (Religionsgeschichtliche Volksbücher II, 3) Tübingen 1907.
METTINGER, T. N. D. *Solomonic State Officials. A Study of the Civil Government Officials of the Israelite Monarchy.* Coniectanea Biblica, OTS V, Lund 1971.
MEYER, Ed. Kritik der Berichte über die Eroberung Palästinas. *ZAW* I (1881) p. 117-146.
— Der Stamm Jakob und die Entstehung der israelitischen Stämme. *ZAW* VI (1886) p. 1-17.
— *Die Israeliten und ihre Nachbarstämme. Alttestamentliche Untersuchungen.* Mit Beiträge von B. Luther. Halle 1906, reprint Darmstadt 1967.
— *Geschichte des Altertums, I* Stuttgart-Berlin 1907²; *I:2* Stuttgart-Berlin 1909²; *II:2* Stuttgart-Berlin 1931², Hrgb. v. H. E. Stier.
MEYER, R. Sperbers neueste Studien über das masoretische Hebräisch. *VT* XI (1961) p. 475-486.
MILLER, P. D. jr. El the Warrior. *HThR* LX (1967) p. 411-431.
MITTMANN, S. *Beiträge zur Siedlungs- und Territorialgeschichte des nördlichen Ostjordanlandes.* ADPV II, Wiesbaden 1970.
MÖHLENBRINK, K. Die levitischen Überlieferungen des Alten Testaments. *ZAW* LII (1934) p. 184-231.
— Die Landnahmesagen des Buches Josua. *ZAW* LVI (1938) p. 238-268.
— Sauls Ammoniterfeldzug und Samuels Beitrag zum Königtum des Sauls. *ZAW* LVIII (1940/41) p. 57-70.
MONTEIL, V. *Les Tribus du Fârs et la sédentarisation des nomades.* Den Haag 1966.
MONTGOMMERY WATT, W. The Tribal basis of the islamic State. In: *Dalla tribú allo Stato.* Acc. Naz. dei Lincei CCCLIX:54, Roma 1962, p. 153-161.
MORAN, W. L. The Hebrew Language in its Northwest Semitic Background. In: *The Bible and the Ancient Near East.* New York 1961, p. 45-72.
MORENZ, S. Joseph in Ägypten *ThLZ* LXXXIV (1959) p. 401-416.
MORGENSTERN, J. Beena-Marriage (matriarchat) in ancient Israel and its historical

234

implications. *ZAW* XLVII (1929) p. 91-110 en *ZAW* XLIX (1931) p. 46-59.

— *Rites of Birth, Marriage, Death and Kindred Occasions among the Semites.* Cincinnati/Chicago 1966.

MOSCATI, S. La questione delle antiche divinità semitiche. In: *S. Moscati, ed., L'Antiche Divinità Semitiche,* Studi Semitici I, Roma 1958, p. 1-11.

— The "Aramaean Aḫlamu". *JSS* IV (1959) p. 303-308.

— *Die altsemitische Kulturen.* Stuttgart 1961.

— Dalla tribù allo stato nel vicino oriente antico. In: *Dalla Tribù allo Stato.* Acc. Naz. dei Lincei CCCLIX: 54, Roma 1962, p. 55-65.

— *An Introduction to the Comparative Grammar of the Semitic Languages.* Wiesbaden 1964.

MOWINCKEL, S. *Le Décalogue.* Études d'histoire et de philosophie religieuses, no. 16, Paris 1927.

— Der Ursprung der Bil'āmsage. *ZAW* XLVIII (1930) p. 233-271.

— *Zur Frage nach dokumentarischen Quellen in Josua 13-19.* Avh. det Norske videnskaps-Akademi. Oslo 1946.

— Die Gründung von Hebron. *Donum Natalicum H.S. Nyberg Oblatum.* Uppsala 1954, p. 185-194.

— Rahelstämme und Leastämme. *BZAW* 77, Berlin 1961², p. 129-151.

— Israelite Historiography. *ASTI* II (1963) p. 4-27.

— *Erwägungen zur Pentateuch Quellenfrage.* Oslo 1964.

— *Tetrateuch, Pentateuch, Hexateuch. Die Berichte über die Landnahme in den drei altisraelitische Geschichtswerken.* BZAW 90, Berlin 1964.

— *Israels opphav og eldeste historie.* Oslo 1967.

MÜHLMANN, W. E. *Staatsbildung und Amphiktyonien in Polynesien.* Stuttgart 1938.

MUILENBURG, J. The Birth of Benjamin. *JBL* LXXV (1956) p. 194-201.

MÜLLER, H. P. Der Aufbau des Deboraliedes. *VT* XVI (1966) p. 446-460.

MÜLLER, W. M *Asien und Europa nach altägyptischen Denkmälern.* Leipzig 1893.

MURPHY, R. F. and KASDAN, L. The Structure of Parallel Cousin Marriage. *The American Anthropologist* LXI (1959) p. 17-29.

MURTONEN, A. The Semitic Sibilants. *JSS* XI (1966) p. 135-151.

NADEL, S. F. *The Foundations of Social Anthropology.* London 1963⁴.

NAOR, M. ya'aqob und yiśrā'ēl. *ZAW* XLIX (1931) p. 317-321.

NESTLE, E. *Die Israelitischen Eigennamen nach ihrer religionsgeschichtlichen Bedeutung* Haarlem 1876.

NEUBAUER, K. W. Erwägungen zur Amos 5:4-15. *ZAW* LXXVIII (1966) p. 292-316.

NEUFELD, E. The Emergence of a Royal-Urban Society in Ancient Israel *HUCA* XXXI (1960) p. 31-53.

NICHOLSON, E. S. *Deuteronomy and Tradition.* Oxford 1967.

NIEBUHR, C. *Geschichte des Ebräischen Zeitalters,* Band I. Berlin 1894.

NIELSEN, E. *"Shechem". A traditio-historical investigation.* Copenhagen 1959².

— Some Reflections on the History of the Ark. *SVT* VII, Leiden 1960, p. 61-70.

— The Levites in Ancient Israel. *ASTI* III (1964) p. 16-27.

NÖLDEKE, TH. *Über die Amelekiter und einige andere Nachbarvölker der Israeliten.* 1864.

NORTH, R. Caleb. *Biblia e Oriente* VIII (1966) p. 167-171.

— The Hivites. *Biblica* LIV (1973) p. 43-62.

NOTH, M. Gemeinsemitische Erscheinungen in der israelitischen Namengebung. *ZDMG* NF VI (1927) p. 1-45.

— Das Krongut der israelitischen Könige und seine Verwaltung. *ZDPV* L (1927) p. 211-244.
— *Die israelitischen Personennamen im Rahmen der gemeinsemitischen Namengebung.* BWANT 3:10, Stuttgart 1928.
— *Das System der zwölf Stämme Israels.* BWANT 4:1, Stuttgart 1930, (reprint Darmstadt 1966).
— Der Beiträge der samarischen Ostraka zur Lösung topographischer Fragen. *PJ* XXVII (1932) p. 54-67.
— Die fünf Könige in der Höhle von Makkeda. *PJ* XXXIII (1933) p. 22-36.
— Das Reich von Hamath als Grenznachbar des Reiches Israel. *PJ* XXXIII (1933) p. 36-52.
— Die Ansiedlung des Stammes Juda auf dem Boden Palästinas. *PJ* XXX (1934) p. 31-47.
— Erwägungen zur Hebräerfrage. In: *Festschrift O. Procksch*, Leipzig 1934, p. 99-113.
— Bethel und Ai. *PJ* XXXI (1935) p. 7-29.
— Zur historischen Geografie Südjudäas. *JPOS* XV (1935) p. 35-50.
— Studien zu den historisch-geographischen Dokumenten des Josuabuches. *ZDPV* LVIII (1935) p. 185-255.
— Grundsätzliches zur geschichtlichen Deutung archäologische Befunde auf dem Boden Palästinas. *PJ* XXXIV (1938) p. 7-22.
— Der Wahlfahrtsweg zum Sinai (4. Mose 33). *PJ* XXXVI (1940) p. 5-29.
— Die Gesetze im Pentateuch (1940). *GSAT*, München 1960², p. 9-142.
— Numeri 21 als Glied der Hexateucherzählung. *ZAW* LVIII (1940/41) p. 162-189.
— Beiträge zur Geschichte des Ostjordanlandes, I. Das Land Gilead als Siedlungsgebiet israelitischer Sippen. *PJ* XXXVII (1941) p. 50-102.
— Die syrisch-palästinische Bevölkerung des II. Jahrhunderts. *ZDPV* LXV (1942) p. 9-67.
— Israelitische Stämme zwischen Ammon und Moab. *ZAW* LX (1944) p. 11-56.
— Zum Ursprung der phönikischen Küstenstädte. *WO* I (1947-1952) p. 21-28.
— *Überlieferungsgeschichte des Pentateuch.* Stuttgart 1948.
— Beiträge zur Geschichte des Ostjordanlandes III. Die Nachbarn der israelitischen Stämme im Ostjordanlande. *ZDPV* LXVIII (1949) p. 1-50.
— Das Amt des "Richters Israels". In: *Bertholet Festschrift*, Tübingen 1950, p. 404-418.
— Überlieferungsgeschichtliches zur zweiten Hälfte des Josuabuches. In: *Alttestamentliche Studien Fr. Nötsche zum 60. Geburtstage.* BBB I, Bonn 1950, p. 152-167.
— Jerusalem und die Israelitische Tradition (1950). *GSAT* München 1960², p. 172-180.
— Mari und Israel. Eine Personennamenstudie. In: *"Geschichte und Altes Testament". Festschrift A. Alt.* Tübingen 1953, p. 127-153.
— Remarks on the Sixth volume of Mari Texts. *JSS* I (1956) p. 322-333.
— *Geschichte Israels.* Göttingen 1956³.
— Hat die Bibel doch recht? In: *Festschrift für Günther Dehn*, Neukirchen 1957, p. 7-22.
— *Überlieferungsgeschichtliche Studien.* Tübingen 1957².
— Gilead und Gad. *ZDPV* LXXV (1959) p. 14-73.
— *Die Ursprünge des alten Israel im Lichte neuer Quellen.* Arbeitsgemeinschaft für Forschung des Landes Nordrhein-Westfalen, Band 6, Heft 94, Keulen 1961.

236

— *Exodus, das zweite Buch Moses übersetzt und erklärt*. ATD 5, Göttingen 1961².
— *s.v.* Stämme Israels. *RGG³* VI, Tübingen 1962, p. 325-326.
— *Die Welt des Alten Testaments*. Berlin 1962⁴.
— *Numeri, das vierte Buch Moses übersetzt und erklärt*. ATD 7. Göttingen 1966.
NÜBEL, H. U. *Davids Aufstieg in der Frühe israelitische Geschichtsschreibung.* Bonn 1959.
NYBERG, H. S. Studien zum Religionskampf im Alten Testament. *ARW* XXV (1938) p. 329-387.
NYSTRÖM, S. *Beduinentum und Jahwismus*. Lund 1946.
OBBINK, G. TH. Het Exodus-Vraagstuk. I *ThT* XLIII (1909) p. 238-258; II *ThT* XLIV (1910) p. 127-161.
O'DOHERTY, FA. The Literary Problem of Judges I₁-III₃. *CBQ* XVIII (1956) p. 1-7.
OESTERLEY, W. O. E. and ROBINSON, TH. H. *A History of Israel, Vol I and II.* Oxford 1932.
OLMO LETE, G. DEL. La conquesta de Jericó y la legenda ygaritica de KRT. *Sefarad* XXV (1965) p. 3-15.
OLMSTEAD, A. T. E. *History of Palestine and Syria to the Macedonian Conquest.* New York/London 1931.
OPPENHEIM, A. L. A New Look at the Structure of Mesopotamian Society. *JESHO* X (1967) p. 1-16.
OPPENHEIM, M. VON. *Die Beduinen*. 3 Bde. Leipzig/Wiesbaden 1939-1952.
ORELLI, K. VON. *s.v.* "Israel", biblische Geschichte. *Realencyklopädie für protestantische Theologie und Kirche*, hrsg. v. A. Hauck, IX. Band, Leipzig 1901, p. 458-483.
ORLINSKY, H. M. *Ancient Israel.* Cornell University Press, Ithaca/New York 1954.
— The tribal system of Israel and related groups in the period of the judges. *OrAnt* I (1962) p. 11-20.
OSSWALD, EVA. *Das Bild des Mose in der kritischen alttestamentlichen Wissenschaft seit Julius Wellhausen.* Berlin 1962.
OTTOSSON, M. *Gilead, Tradition and History.* Coniectanea Biblica, OTS III, Lund 1969.
OTZEN, B. *Studien über Deuterosacharja.* Copenhagen 1964.
PALLOPPINO, M. *The Etruscans.* Pelican A 310, London 1956.
PATAI, R. *Sex and Family in the Bible and in the Middle East.* New York 1959.
PEDERSEN, JOHS. *Israel. Its Life and Culture.* Vol. I and II. London/Copenhagen 1926.
PETERS, E. The Proliferation of Segments in the Lineage of the Bedouin of Cyrenaica. Reprinted in: *Louise E. Sweet, Peoples and Cultures of the Middle East*, vol. I, New York 1970, p. 363-398.
PHILLIPS, A. *Ancient Israel's Criminal Law.* Oxford 1970.
— Some aspects of family law in pre-exilic Israel. *VT* XXIII (1973) p. 349-361.
PHILLIPS, E. D. New Light on the Ancient History of the Eurasian Steppe. *AJA* LXI (1957) p. 269-280.
— The Scythian domination in Western Asia: its record in history, scripture and archeaeology. *World Archaeology* IV (1972) p. 129-138.
PIRENNE, JACQUELINE. *Le Royaume Sud-Arabe de Qatabân et sa Datation.* Bibliothèque du Muséon 48, Leuven 1961.
PLOEG, J. VAN DER. Les chefs du peuple d'Israël et leurs titres. *RB* LVII (1950) p. 40-62.
— Les "nobles" israélites. *OTS* IX, Leiden 1951, p. 49-64.

POHL, A. Einige Gedanken zur Ḫabiru-Frage. *WZKM* LIV (1957) p. 157-161.

PORTER, J. R. *The Extended Family in the Old Testament.* Occasional Papers in Social and Economic Administration. Edutext Publications. London 1967.

— Pre-Islamic Arabic Historical Traditions and the Early Historical Narratives of the Old Testament. *JBL* LXXXVII (1968) p. 17-27.

POUCHA, P. Bodenbauern und Nomaden im alten Mittel- und Zentralasien. *VBVHS*, Berlin 1968, p. 121-126.

POWIS SMITH, J. M. Some Problems in the Early History of Hebrew Religion. *AJSL* XXXII (1916) p. 81-97.

PRITCHARD, J. B. Archaeology and the Future of Biblical Studies: Cultures and History. In: *The Bible in Modern Scholarship.* Ed. by J. Ph. Hyatt, New York 1965, p. 313-325.

PROCKSCH, O. *Das Nordhebräische Sagenbuch: Die Elohimquelle.* Leipzig 1906.

— Fürst und Priester bei Hesekiel. *ZAW* LVIII (1940/41) p. 99-133.

PURY, A. DE. Genèse XXXIV et l'histoire. *RB* LXXVI (1969) p. 1-49.

RABE, V. W. The Identity of the Priestly Tabernacle. *JNES* XXV (1966) p. 132-134.

RABIN, C. *Ancient West-Arabian. A Study of the Dialects of the Western Highlands of Arabia in the Sixth and Seventh Centuries A.D.* London 1951.

RAD, G. VON. *Das formgeschichtliche Problem des Hexateuch.* BWANT IV:26, Stuttgart 1926.

— *Das Gottesvolk im Deuteronomium.* BWANT 3:11, Stuttgart 1929.

— Zelt und Lade. (1931) *GSAT*, München 1958, p. 109-129.

— Das Reich Israel und die Philister. *PJ* XXIX (1933) p. 30-42.

— *s.v.* Israel, A: Israel, Juda und Hebräer im AT. *ThWNT* III, Stuttgart 1938, p. 356-360.

— Verheissenes Land und Jahwes Land im Hexateuch. *ZDPV* LXVI (1943) p. 191-205.

— Der Anfang der Geschichtsschreibung im alten Israel. (1944) *GSAT*, München 1958, p. 148-149.

— *Deuteronomiumstudien.* FRLANT 58, Göttingen 1948[2].

— *Der Heilige Krieg im alten Israel.* AThANT, Zürich 1951.

— Josephsgeschichte und ältere Chokma. *SVT* I, Leiden 1953, p. 120-127.

— *Theologie des Alten Testaments. Bd. I, Die Theologie der geschichtlichen Überlieferungen Israels.* München 1961[3].

— *Das fünfte Buch Mose. Deuteronomium.* ATD 8, Göttingen 1964.

RAFEL, D. Bemerkungen zu den Eigennamen und Genealogien im Buche Numeri. *Bet Miqra',* XI (1966) p. 87-90.

RAHTJEN, B. D. Philistine and Hebrew Amphiktyonies. *JNES* XXIV (1965) p. 100-104.

RAINEY, A. F. The System of Land Grants at Ugarit in its Wider Near Eastern Setting. *Proceedings of the Fourth World Congres of Jewish Studies, Vol. I,* Jerusalem 1967, p. 187-191.

REIFENBERG, A. *The Struggle between the Desert and the Sown; Rise and Fall of Agriculture in the Levant.* Jerusalem 1957.

RENAN, E. *Histoire du Peuple d'Israël I.* Paris 1887[2], 1919[18].

RENDTORFF, R. Zur Lage von Jaser. *ZDPV* LXXVI (1960) p. 124-135.

— El, Ba'al und Jahwe. Erwägungen zum Verhältnis von kanaanäischer und israelitischer Religion. *ZAW* LXXVIII (1966) p. 277-292.

— *Studien zur Geschichte des Opfers im Alten Israel.* WMANT 24, Neukirchen 1967.

RENGER, J. *Marat ilim:* Exogamie bei den semitischen nomaden des 2. Jahrtausends. *AFO* XXIV (1973) p. 103-108

RENTZ, G. Notes on Oppenheim's Die Beduinen. *Oriens* X (1957) p. 77-89.

REVIV, H. The Government of Shechem in the El-Amarna Period and in the Days of Abimelech. *IEJ* XVI (1966) p. 252-258.

— On Urban Representative Institutions and Self-Government in Syria-Palestine in the Second Half of the Second Millennium B.C. *JESHO* XII (1969) p. 283-297.

REVIV, M. Regarding the History of the Territory of Shechem in the El-Amarna Period. *Tarbiz* XXXIII (1963) p. 1-7.

GRAF REVENTLOW, H. Das Amt des Mazkir. Zur Rechtsstruktur des öffentlichen Lebens in Israel. *ThZBs* XV (1959) p. 161-175.

RHODOKANAKIS, N. *Bodemwirtschaft im Alten Südarabien.* Wien 1916.

— Das öffentliche Leben in den alten südarabischen Staaten. *Handbuch der Altarabischen Altertumskunde. Hrgb. von D. Nielsen; Band I,* Copenhagen/Leipzig 1927, p. 109-142.

RICHARDSON, EMELINE. *The Etruscans.* Chicago 1964.

RICHTER, W. *Traditionsgeschichtliche Untersuchungen zum Richterbuch.* BBB 18, Bonn 1963.

— *Die Bearbeitungen des "Retterbuches" in der deuteronomistische Epoche.* BBB 21, Bonn 1964.

— Zu den "Richtern Israels". *ZAW* LXXVIII (1965) p. 40-72.

Die Nāgīd-Formel. Ein Beitrag zur Erhellung des nāgīd-Problems. *BZ* NF IX (1965) p. 71-84.

— Die Überlieferung um Jephtah. Ri. 10, 17-12, 6. *Biblica* XLVII (1966) p. 485-556.

RIEDEL, W. Die Reihenfolge der Sprüche im Segen Mosis Deut. 33. *ZAW* XX (1900) p. 315 218.

ROBERTS, J. J. M. The Davidic Origin of the Zion Tradition *JBL* XCII (1973) p. 329-344.

ROBINSON, TH. H. The Origin of the Tribe of Judah. "Amicitiae Corolla", 1933, p. 265-275.

ROSENBERG, A. *Der Staat der alten Italiker. Untersuchungen über die ursprüngliche Verfassung der Latiner Osker und Etrusker.* Berlin 1913.

ROSS, J. F. Gezer in the Tell el-Amarna Letters. *BA* XXX (1967) p. 62-71.

ROSS, J. P. Yahweh Seba'ot in Samuel and Psalms. *VT* XVII (1967) p. 76-93.

RÖSSLER, E. *Jahwe und die Götter im Pentateuch und im Deuteronomistischen Geschichtswerk.* Bonn 1966.

RÖSSLER, O. Die Präfixkonjugation Qal der Verba 1ae Nûn im Althebräischen und das Problem der sogenannten Tempora. *ZAW* LXXIV (1962) p. 125-141.

ROSSUM, J. VAN. *De praedeuteronomistische bestanddelen van het boek der Richters.* Winterswijk 1966.

— Wanneer is Silo verwoest? *NThT* XXIV (1970) p. 321-332.

ROST, L. Die Bezeichnungen für Land und Volk im Alten Testament. In: *Festschrift O. Procksch,* Leipzig 1934, p. 125-149.

— Israel bei den Profeten. BWANT 4:19. Stuttgart 1937.

— Weidewechsel und altisraelitischer Festkalender. *ZDPV* LXVI (1943) p. 205-216.

— Zur Vorgeschichte der Kultusreform des Josia. *VT* XIX (1969) p. 113-120.

ROWLEY, H. H. Israel's sojourn in Egypt. *BJRL* XXII (1938) p. 243-290.

— The Exodus and the Settlement in Canaan. *BASOR* 85 (1942) p. 27-31.

— From Joseph to Joshua. Biblical traditions in the light of Archaeology. The Schweich Lectures of the British Academy 1948, London 1964².

ROWTON, M. B. The Problem of the Exodus. PEQ LXXXV (1953) p. 46-60.

— The Topological Factor in the Ḫapiru Problem. Studies in Honor of B. Landsberger, AS 16. Chicago 1965, p. 375-387.

— The Physical Environment and the Problem of the Nomads. XVth RAI, Paris 1967, p. 109-122.

— The Role of the Watercourses in the Growth of Mesopotamian Civilization. "Lišān mithurti" Festschrift W. Frhr von Soden, AOAT 1, Neukirchen 1969, p. 307-316.

— Autonomy and Nomadism in Western Asia. Or NS LXII (1973) p. 247-258.

— Urban Autonomy in a Nomadic Environment. JNES XXXII (1973) p. 201-215.

RUDOLPH, W. Der "Elohist" von Exodus bis Josua. BZAW 68. Berlin 1938.

— Chronikbücher. HAT I₂₁, Tübingen 1955.

— Hosea. KAT XIII, 1, Gütersloh 1966.

RUPPERT, L. Die Josephserzählung der Genesis. Ein Beitrag zur Theologie der Pentateuchquellen. München 1965.

— Herkunft und Bedeutung der Jakob-Traditionen bei Hosea. Biblica LII (1971) p. 488-504.

RIJCKMANS, J. L'Institution Monarchique en Arabie Méridionale avant l'Islam (Maᶜin et Saba). Bibl. du Muséon 28, Leuven 1951.

— L'Apparition du cheval en Arabie ancienne. JEOL XVII (1963) p. 211-226.

RYDER, T. T. B. Koine-Eirene. General Peace and Local Independence in Ancient Greece. London 1965.

SAARISALO, A. Topographical Researches in the Shephela. JPOS XI (1931) p. 98-104.

SACHSSE, ED. Die Bedeutung des Namens Israel. Eine quellenkritische Untersuchung. diss. Bonn 1910.

— Die Etymologie und älteste Aussprache des Namens yiśrā'ēl. ZAW XXXIV (1914) p. 1-15.

— Die Bedeutung des Namens Israel. Eine geographisch-geschichtliche Untersuchung. Gütersloh 1922.

— Der Ursprung des Namens Israel. ZS IV (1926) p. 63-69.

SALO, V. Joseph, Sohn der Färse. BZ CII (1968) p. 94-95.

SALONEN, A. Agricultura Mesopotamica. Helsinki 1968.

SASSON, J. M. A Sketch of North Syrian Economic Relations in the Middle Bronze Age. JESHO IX (1966) p. 161-181.

— The Military Establishments at Mari. Studia Pohl 3, Roma 1969.

SAUER, G. s.v. Sippe, BHH III, Göttingen 1966, p. 1808-1809.

— Bemerkungen zu 1965 edierten ugaritischen Texten. ZDMG 116 (1966) p. 235-241.

— Die chronologischen Angaben in den Büchern Deut. bis 2. Kön. ThZBs XXIV (1968) p. 1-15.

SÄVE-SÖDERBERG, T. The Navy of the Eighteenth Egyptian Dynasty. Uppsala Univ. Årsskrift 1946:6.

SAYCE, A. H. The Early History of the Hebrews. London 1897.

— Early Israel and the surrounding nations. London 1899.

SCHAEFER, H. Staatsform und Politik. Untersuchungen zur Griechischen Geschichte des 6. und 5. Jahrhunderts. Leipzig 1932.

— Politische Ordnung und individuelle Freiheit im Griechentum. HZ CLXXXIII (1957) p. 5-22.

— Das Problem der griechischen Nationalität. *Probleme der Alten Geschichte, gesammelte Abhandlungen und Vorträge.* Göttingen 1963, p. 269-306.

SCHAEFFER, H. *Hebrew Tribal Economy and the Jubilee as illustrated in Semitic and Indo-European Village Communities.* Leipzig 1922.

SCHAUENBURG, K. *Die Kameliden im Altertum.* Bonner Jahrbücher 155/6 (1955/6) und 162 (1962).

SCHEIL, V. Cylindres et Légendes Inédites, I Le cylindre d'išre-il. *RA* (1916) p. 5-25.

— *Kodex Hammurapi.* MDP 4 (Paris 1902) p. 11-162 + pl. 3-15.

SCHILDENBERGER, J. Psalm 78(77) und die Pentateuchquellen. In: *"Lex tua veritas" Festschrift Junker.* Trier 1961, p. 231-256.

SCHLAURI, I. Wolfgang Richters Beitrag zur Redaktionsgeschichte des Richterbuches. *Biblica* LIV (1973) p. 367-403.

SCHMID, H. Der Stand der Moseforschung. *Judaica* XXI (1965) p. 194-221.

— Gottesbild, Gottesschau und Theophanie. *Judaica* XXIII (1967) p. 241-254.

— *Mose. Überlieferung und Geschichte.* BZAW, Berlin 1968.

SCHMID, R. Meerwunder- und Landnahmetradition. *ThZBs* XXI (1965) p. 260-268.

SCHMIDTKE, FR. *Die Einwanderung Israels in Kanaan.* Breslau 1933.

SCHMITT, G. *Der Landtag von Sichem.* Stuttgart 1964.

— *Du sollst keinen Frieden schliessen mit den Bewohnern des Landes.* BWANT 91, Stuttgart 1970.

SCHMÖKEL, H. Die theophoren Personennamen Babyloniens und Assyriens. *JEOL* XIX (1967) p. 468-491.

SCHNEIDER, H. *Die Entwicklung der Jahureligion und der Mosesagen in Israel und Juda.* Leipziger Semitistische Studien, Band V, 1, 1909.

SCHNEIDER. N. Aram und Aramäer in der Ur-III Zeit. *Biblica* XXX (1949) p. 109-111.

SCHOTTROFF, W. *Gedenken im Alten Orient und im Alten Testament. Die Wurzel Zakar im semitischen Sprachkreis.* WMANT XV, Neukirchen 1964.

— *Der altisraelitische Fluchspruch.* WMANT XXX, Neukirchen 1969.

SCHULZ, H. *Das Todesrecht im Alten Testament. Studien zur Rechtsform der Mot-Jumat-Sätze.* BZAW 114, Berlin 1969.

SCHUNCK, K. D. Ephron und Ephraim. *VT* XI (1961) p. 188-200.

— Erwägungen zur Geschichte und Bedeutung von Mahanaim. *ZDMG* CXIII (1963) p. 34-40.

— *Benjamin.* BZAW 86, Berlin 1963.

— Die Richter Israels und ihr Amt. *SVT* XV, Leiden 1966, p. 252-262.

— Zentralheiligtum, Grenzheiligtum und 'Höhenheiligtum' in Israel. *Numen* XVIII (1971) p. 132-140.

— Juda und Jerusalem in vor- und frühisraelitischer Zeit. In: *"Schalom". Studien zur Glaube und Geschichte Israels. Festschrift A. Jepsen.* Hrgb. v. K. H. Bernhardt, Stuttgart 1971, p. 50-57.

SCHWALLY, F. *Semitische Kriegsaltertümer. Bd. I, Der heilige Krieg im alten Israel.* Leipzig 1901.

SCHWARZENBACH, A. W. *Die geografische Terminologie im Hebräischen des Alten Testamentes.* Leiden 1954.

SEEBASS, H. *Mose und Aaron, Sinai und Gottesberg.* Bonn 1962.

— *Der Erzvater Israel und die Einführung der Jahveverehrung in Kanaan.* BZAW 98, Berlin 1966.

— Zur Königserhebung Jerobeams I. *VT* XVII (1967) p. 325-333.

— Die Verwerfung Jerobeams I. und Salomos durch die Prophetie das Ahia von Silo. *WO* IV (1967/68) p. 163-182.

241

SEESEMANN, O. *Die Ältesten im Alten Testament.* Phil. Diss., Leipzig 1895.
SEGAL, J. B. *The Hebrew Passover. From the Earliest Times to A.D. 70.* London 1963.
SEGERT, ST. Surviving of Canaanite Elements in Israelite Religion. In: *Studi sull' Oriente e la Biblia offerti al P. Giovanni Rinaldi.* Genova 1967, p. 155-161.
SELLIN, E. *Gilgal. Ein Beitrag zur Geschichte der Einwanderung Israels in Palästina.* Leipzig 1917.
— *Wie wurde Sichem eine israelitische Stadt?* Leipzig/Erlangen 1922.
— *Geschichte des israelitisch-jüdischen Volkes. Band I.* Leipzig 1924.
— Das Deboralied. *Festschrift O. Procksch,* Leipzig 1934, p. 149-166.
SELMS, A. VAN. The Southern Kingdom in Hosea. Studies in the Books of Hosea and Amos. *Papers read at the 7th and 8th meetings of Die O.T. Werkgemeenskap in Suid-Afrika,* 1964-1965; Potchefstroom 1966, p. 100-111.
— Isaac in Amos. *Papers read at the 7th and 8th meeting of Die O.T. Werkgemeenskap in Suid-Afrika,* 1964-1965; Potchefstroom 1966, p. 157-166.
SETERS, J. VAN. *The Hyksos. A new Investigation.* New Haven/London 1966.
— The Problem of Childlessness in Near Eastern Law and the Patriarchs of Israel. *JBL* LXXXVII (1968) p. 401-408.
— The Conquest of Sihon's Kingdom: A Literary Examination. *JBL* XCL (1972) p. 182-197.
SETHE, K. Die Wissenschaftliche Bedeutung der Petrieschen Sinaifunde und die angebliche Moseszeugnisse. *ZDMG* NF V (1926) p. 24-54.
SIERKSMA, F. Religie en politiek leiderschap. *NThT* X (1955/56) p. 208-236.
SIMONS, J. *Opgravingen in Palestina.* Bijbelse Monographieën, Roermond-Maaseik 1936.
— "Landnahme" en "Landesausbau" in de Israëlitische Traditie. *Bijdragen Ned. Jezuïten* IV (1941) p. 201-223.
— The Structure and Interpretation of Josh. XVI-XVII. In: *"Orientalia Neerlandica", A volume of Oriental Studies.* Leiden 1948, p. 190-215.
— Two Notes on the Problem of the Pentapolis. *OTS* V (1948) p. 92-117.
SIMPSON, C. A. *The Early Traditions of Israel. A Critical Analysis of the Pre-deuteronomic Narrative of the Hexateuch.* Oxford 1948.
— *The Composition of the Book of Judges.* Oxford 1957.
SINCLAIR, L. A. An Archaeological Study of Gibeah. *BA* XXVII (1964) p. 52-64.
SKEHAN, P. W. Joab's Census: How Far North? (2 Sm 24,6). *CBQ* XXXI (1969) p. 42-49.
SMEND, R. *Lehrbuch der alttestamentlichen Religionsgeschichte.* Freiburg und Leipzig 1893.
R. SMEND JR. *Das Mosebild von Heinrich Ewald bis Martin Noth.* Beiträge zum Geschichte der biblischen Exegese, 3. Tübingen 1959.
— *Jahwekrieg und Stämmebund.* FRLANT 34, Göttingen 1963.
— Gehörte Juda zum vorstaatlichen Israel? *Proceedings of the Fourth World Congress of Jewish Studies, Vol. I,* Jerusalem 1967, p. 57-62.
— *Elemente alttestamentlichen Geschichtsdenkens.* Theol. Stud. Heft 95, Zürich 1968.
— Zur Frage der altisraelitischen Amphiktyonie. *EvTh* XXXI (1971) p. 623-630.
SMITH, H. P. *The Books of Samuel.* ICC. Edinburgh 1912.
SNAITH, N. H. The daughters of Zelophehad. *VT* XVI (1966) p. 124-127.
— The Advent of Monotheism in Israel. *Annual of the Leeds Oriental Socieity* V (1963-1965) p. 100-113.
SODEN, W. VON. Zur Einteilung der Semitischen Sprachen. *WZKM* LVI (1960) p. 177-191.

— Muškēnum und die Mawālī des frühen Islam. *ZA* NF XXII (56) (1964) p. 133-142.

— Jahwe, "Er ist, Er erweist sich". *WO* III (1966) p. 177-186.

SOGGIN, J. A. Kultätiologische Sagen und Katechese im Hetaxteuch. *VT* X (1960) p. 341-347.

— Die Geburt Benjamins, Genesis XXXV 16-20(21). *VT* XI (1961) p. 432-440.

— La conquista israelitica della Palestina nei sec. XIII e XII e la scoperte archeologiche. *Protes.* XVII (1962) p. 194-208.

— *When the Judges Ruled.* New York 1965.

— Il regno di Ešba'al, figlio di Saul. *RSO* XL (1965) p. 89-106.

— Der offiziell geförderte Synkretismus in Israel während des 10. Jahrhunderts. *ZAW* LXXVIII (1966) p. 179-204.

— Gilgal, Passah und Landnahme. Eine neue Untersuchung des kultischen Zusammenhangs der Kap. III-VI des Josuabuches. *SVT* XV, Leiden 1966, p. 263-278.

— Bemerkungen zur alttestamentlichen Topografie Sichems. *ZDPV* LXXXII (1967) p. 183-199.

— *Das Königtum in Israel.* BZAW 104, Berlin 1967.

SPEISER, E. A. Ethnic Movements in the Near East in the Second Millenium B.C. *AASOR* XIII, Cambridge, Mass. 1931-1932, p. 13-54.

— The Hurrian Participation in the Civilization of Mesopotamia, Syria and Palestine. (1953) *Finkelstein/Greenberg, Oriental and Biblical Studies of E. A. Speiser*, Philadelphia 1967, p. 244-269.

— The Muškēnum. *Or* NS XXVIII (1958) p. 19-28.

— 'People' and 'Nation' of Israel. *JBL* (1960) p. 157-163.

— Background and function to the Biblical Nāsī'. *CBQ* XXV (1963) p. 111-118.

SPERBER, A. Hebrew Based upon Greek and Latin Transliterations. *HUCA* XII/XIII (1937/38) p. 103-274.

— Hebrew Based upon Biblical Passages in Parallel Transmission. *HUCA* XIV (1939) p. 153-249.

— *A Historical Grammar of Biblical Hebrew.* Leiden 1966.

SPIEGELBERG, W. Die erste Erwähnung Israels in einem aegyptischen Texte. *Sitzungsberichte des Berliner Akademie der Wissenschaflen*, Jahrgang 1896, p. 593-398.

SPINNER, S. *Herkunft, Entstehung und antike Umwelt des hebräischen Volkes.* Vienna 1933.

SPOONER, B. The Status of Nomadism as a Cultural Phenomenon in the Middle East. In: *Perspectives on Nomadism.* Ed. by W. Irons and D. Dyson-Hudson. Leiden 1972, p. 122-131.

STADE, B. Nachwort zu Meyer's "Kritik der Berichte über die Eroberung Palästinas". *ZAW* I (1881) p. 146-150.

— Zur Entstehungsgeschichte des vordeuteronomistischen Richterbuches. *ZAW* I (1881) p. 339-343.

— *Geschichte des Volkes Israel.* Band I, Berlin 1887.

— Beiträge zur Pentateuchkritik I, Das Kainszeichen. *ZAW* XIV (1894) p. 250-318.

— Die Entstehung des Volkes Israel. Giessen 1897. In: *Ausgewählte akademische Reden und Abhandlungen*, Giessen 1907², p. 97-121.

STADELMANN, R. Die Abwehr der Seevölker unter Ramses III. *Saeculum* XIX (1968) p. 156-171.

STAERK, W. *Studien zur Religions- und Sprachgeschichte des alten Testaments.* Berlin 1899.

STAMM, J. J. Zum Ursprung des Namens der Ammoniter. *ArOr* XVII (1949) p. 379-382.

243

DUDLEY STAMP, L. *A History of Land Use in Arid Regions*. Arid Zone Research XVII, Unesco, Paris 1961.

STARCKY, J. Le nom Divin El. *ArOr* XVII (1949) p. 383-386.

— Review of: S. Moscati a.o., Le Antiche Divinità Semitiche. Studi Semitici 2, Roma 1959. *RB* LXVII (1960) p. 269-276.

STAVE, E. *Israels Histor a*, Stockholm 1916.

STECK, O. H. *Überlieferung und Zeitgeschichte in den Elia-Erzählungen*. WMANT 26, Neukirchen 1968.

STEIN, L. *Die Schammar-Gerba. Beduinen im Übergang vom Nomadismus zur Sesshaftigkeit*. Berlin 1967.

STEINDORF, G. Israel in einer altägyptischen Inschrift. *ZAW* XVI (1896) p. 330-334.

STEINER, G. Die aḫḫijawa-Frage heute. *Saeculum* XV (1964) p. 365-392.

STEUERNAGEL, C. *Die Einwanderung der israelitischen Stämme in Kanaan*. Berlin 1901.

— *Jahwe, der Gott Israels. Eine stil- und religionsgeschichtliche Studie*. BZAW 27, Giessen 1914, p. 329-349.

— Jahwe und die Vätergötter. *Festschrift G. Beer*, Stuttgart 1935, p. 62-71.

STRANGE, J. The inheritance of Dan. *Studia Theologica (Scandinavia)* XX (1966) p. 120-139.

STRASBURGER, H. Der Einzelne und die Gemeinschaft im Denken der Griechen. *HZ* CLXXVII (1955) p. 227-248.

STRAUSS, H. *Untersuchungen zu den Überlieferungen der Vorexilischen Leviten.* diss. Bonn 1960.

STROETE, G. TE. *Exodus uit de grondtekst vertaald en uitgelegd*. BOT 1, 2, Roermond/ Maaseik 1966.

STUDER, G. Der Ringkampf Jakobs. *JpTh* (1875) p. 536ff.

SULZBERGER, M. The Polity of the Ancient Hebrews. *JQR* NS III (1912) p. 1-81.

SWEET, LOUISE E. Camel Pastoralism in North Arabia and the Minimal Camping Unit. In: *Man, Culture and Animals. The Role of Animals in Human Ecological Adjustments*. Ed. by A. Leeds and A. P. Vayda. Washington 1965, p. 129-152.

SZANTO, E. Die griechischen Phylen. *Sitzungsberichte der Philosophisch-Historischen Classe der kaiserlichen Akademie der Wissenschaften, Band CXLIV, Abh. V.* Wien 1902.

TALMON, S. The Town Lists of Simeon. *IEJ* XV (1965) p. 235-242.

— The Judaean 'Am Ha'areṣ in Historical Perspective. *Proceedings of the Fourth World Congres of Jewish Studies, Vol. I*, Jerusalem 1967, p. 71-76.

TÄUBLER, E. *Biblische Studien: Die Epoche der Richter*. Hrgb. v. H. J. Zobel. Tübingen 1958.

THOMPSON, TH. L. *The Historicity of the Patriarchal Narratives. The Quest for the Historical Abraham*. BZAW 133, Berlin 1974.

THUREAU-DANGIN, F. Nouvelles Lettres d'El-Amarna. *RA* XIX (1922) p. 91-100.

TOURNAY, R. Le nom du "Buisson Ardent". *VT* VII (1957) p. 410-413.

TRIGGER, B. G. *Beyond History: The Methods of Prehistory*. New York/Chicago 1968.

TUNYOGI, A. C. The Book of the Conquest. *JBL* LXXXIV (1965) p. 374-380.

UCHELEN, N. A. VAN. *Abraham de Hebreeër*. Assen 1964.

— De Filistijnen in het Oude Testament. *NThT* XX (1965/1966) p. 339-353.

UMHAU WOLF, C. Terminology of Israel's Tribal Organization. *JBL* LXV (1946) p. 45-50.

— Traces of Primitive Democracy in Ancient Israel. *JNES* VI (1947) p. 98-108.

UPHIL, E. P. Pithom and Raamses: Their Location and Significance. *JNES* XVII (1968) p. 291-316 en XVIII (1969) p. 15-39.

VAUX, R. DE. *Les Institutions de l'Ancien Testament. Vol I* Paris 1961², *Vol. II* Paris 1967².

— La Palestine et la Transjordanie au IIe millénaire et les origines israélites. *ZAW* LVI (1938) p. 225-238.

— Les Patriarches Hébreux et: Les découvertes modernes, VII: Le milieu social et VIII: Les coutumes sociales et juridiques. *RB* LVI (1949) p. 5-36.

— "Lévites" minéens et Lévites israélites. In: *Lex tua veritas". Festschrift für H. Junker.* Trier 1961, p. 265-273.

— Les patriarches hébreux et l'histoire. *RB* LXXII (1965) p. 5-28.

— Method in the study of Early Hebrew History. With responses by G. E. Mendenhall and M. Greenberg. In: *The Bible in Modern Scholarship. Ed. by J. Ph. Hyatt.* New York 1965, p. 15-43.

— Le problème des Ḥapiru. *JNES* XXVII (1968) p. 221-228.

— Le Pays de Canaan. *JAOS* LXXXVIII (1968) p. 23-30.

— Sur l'origine Kénite ou Madianite du Jahwisme. *EI* IX (1969) p. 28*-32*.

— The Settlement of the Israelites in Southern Palestine and the Origins of the Tribe of Judah. In: *Translating and Understanding the Old Testament, Essays in Honor of H. G. May.* Nashville 1970, p. 108-134.

— Le thèse de l'"Amphictyonie Israélite". *HThR* LXIV (1971) p. 415-436.

— *Histoire ancienne d'Israël. Vol. I* Paris 1971, *Vol. II* Paris 1973.

VINCENT, L. H., GARSTANG, J. The Chronology of Jericho. *PEQ* (1931) p. 104-107.

VINK, J. G. The Date ond Origin of the Priestly Code in the Old Testament. *OTS* XV, Leiden 1969, p. 1-144.

VIROLLEAUD, CH. Nouvelles tablettes alphabétiques de Ras-Shamra. *Académie des Inscriptions et Belles-Lettres. Comptes Rendu des séances de l'année 1956,* Paris 1956, p. 60-67.

VOEGELIN, E. *Rasse und Staat.* Tübingen 1933.

— *Order and History, Part I. Israel and Revelation.* Louisiana State University Press 1956.

VOGT, E. Zur Geschichte der hebräischen Sprache. *Biblica* LII (1971) p. 72-78.

VOLBORN, W. Der Richter Israels. In: *Sammlung und Sendung. Eine Festgabe für H. Rendtorff,* Berlin 1958, p. 21-31.

VÖLTER, D. *Aegypten und die Bibel.* Leiden 1903.

VOLZ, P. *Mose. Ein Beitrag zur Untersuchung über die Ursprünge der israelitischen Religion.* Tübingen 1907.

— *Mose und sein Werk.* Tübingen 1932.

VRIES, S. J. DE. The Origin of the Murmuring Tradition. *JBL* LXXXVII (1968) p. 51-58.

VRIEZEN, TH. C. La tradition de Jacob dans Osée XII. *OTS* I (1942) p. 64-78.

— Hoofdlijnen der theologie van het Oude Testament. Wageningen 1966³.

— Exodusstudien, Exodus 1. *VT* XVII (1967) p. 334-353.

VYHMEISTER, W. The History of Heshbon from Literary Sources. *Andrews University Seminary Studies* VI (1968) p. 158-177.

WÄCHTER, L. Israel und Jeschurun. In: *Schalom". Studien zur Glaube und Geschichte Israels. Festschrift A. Jepsen.* Hrgb. v. K. H. Bernhardt, Stuttgart 1971, p. 58-64.

WAGNER, M. Beiträge zur Aramaeismenfrage im Alttestamentlichen Hebräisch. *SVT* XVI, *"Hebräische Wortforschung".* Leiden 1967, p. 355-371.

WALKER, N. "Israel". *VT* IV (1954) p. 434.
WALLIS, G. Eine Parallele zu Richter 19:20ff und 1 Sam. 11:5ff aus dem Briefarchiv von Mari. *ZAW* LXIV (1952) p. 57-61.
— Thaanath-Silo. *ZDPV* LXXVII (1961) p. 38-45.
— Die Anfänge des Königtums in Israel. *Wiss. Zeitschr. d. M. Luther Universität Halle-Wittenberg; Sprachwiss. Klasse* XII (1963) p. 239-248.
— a.o. Die Geschichte der Jacobtradition. *Wissenschaftliche Zeitschr. der M. Luther Universität Halle-Wittenberg. Sprachwiss. Klasse* XIII (1964) p. 427-440.
— Die Stadt in den Überlieferungen der Genesis. *ZAW* LXXVIII (1966) p. 133-147.
— Die Tradition von den drei Ahnvätern. *ZAW* LXXXI (1969) p. 18-40.
— Die Sesshaftwerdung Alt-Israels und das Gottesdienstverständnis der Jahwisten im Lichte der elohistischen Kritik. *ZAW* LXXXI (1971) p. 1-15.
— *Geschichte und Überlieferung. Gedanken über alttestamentliche Darstellungen der Frühgeschichte und der Anfänge seines Königtums.* Berlin 1968.
WATERMAN, L. Jacob the Forgotten supplanter. *AJSL* LV (1938) p. 25-44.
WATZINGER, C. Zur Chronologie der Schichten von Jericho. *ZDMG* NF V (1926) p. 131-136.
WEBER, M. *Gesammelte Aufsätze zur Religionssoziologie. Band III, Das antike Judentum.* Tübingen 1923².
WEIHL, R. L'Installation des israélites en Palestine et la légende des patriarches. *RHR* LXXXVII/LXXXVIII (1922/23) p. 1-40, 69-120.
— La légende des patriarches et l'histoire. *RES* (1937) p. 145-206.
WEINBERG, J. P. Das beit 'ābōt im 6.-4. Jh. v.u.Z. *VT* XXIII (1973) p. 400-414.
WEINFELD, M. The period of the conquest and of the judges as seen by the earlier and the later sources. *VT* XVII (1967) p. 93-114.
WEINGREEN, J. Saul and the Ḫabirū. *Proceedings of the Fourth World Congres of Jewish Studies. Vol. I,* Jerusalem 1967, p. 63-67.
WEINHEIMER, H. Hebräer und Israëliten. *ZAW* XXIX (1909) p. 275-280.
— Die Einwanderung der Hebräer und der Israeliten in Kanaan. *ZDMG* LXVI (1912) p. 365-389.
— Zu Genesis Kap. 2 und Kap. 4. *ZAW* XXXII (1912) p. 33-41.
WEIPPERT, HELGA. Das geographische System der Stämme Israels. *VT* XXIII (1973) p. 76-89.
WEIPPERT, M. Erwägungen zur Etymologie des Gottesnamens 'El Šaddaj. *ZDMG* CXI (1962) p. 42-62.
— Archäologischer Jahresbericht. *ZDPV* LXXII (1966) p. 274-330.
— *Die Landnahme der israelitischen Stämme in der neueren wissenschaftlichen Diskussion.* FRLANT 92, Göttingen 1967.
— Abraham der Hebräer? Bemerkungen zu W. F. Albrights Deutung der Väter Israels. *Biblica* LII (1971) p. 407-432.
— "Heiliger Krieg" in Israel und Assyrien. Kritische Anmerkungen zu Gerhard von Rads Konzept des "Heiligen Krieges im alten Israel". *ZAW* LXXXIV (1972) p. 460-493.
— Fragen des israelitischen Geschichtsbewustseins. *VT* XXIII (1973), p. 415-442.
WEISBERG, D. S. *Guild Structure and Political Allegiance in Early Achaemenid Mesopotamia.* New Haven/London 1967.
WEISER, A. Das Deboralied. *ZAW* LXXI (1959) p. 67-97.
— *"Samuel". Seine geschichtliche Aufgabe und religiöse Bedeutung.* FRLANT 81, Göttingen 1962.
— Die Legitimation des Königs David. *VT* XVI (1966) p. 325-354.

Wellhausen, J. *Geschichte Israels, 1*. Berlin 1878 (N.B. = *Prolegomena!*).
— *Prolegomena zur Geschichte Israels*. Berlin 1905⁶, Reprint 1927.
— s.v. "Israel". *Encyclopaedia Brittanica*. 1881.
— *Abriss der Geschichte Israels und Juda's*. (Skizzen und Vorarbeiten, I. 1. Heft p. 3-102). Berlin 1884.
— *Israelitische und Jüdische Geschichte*. Berlin 1894.
— *Das arabische Reich und sein Sturz*. Berlin 1960².
Welter, P. Naboths Weinberg. *EvTh* XXXIII (1973) p. 18-29.
Wette, W. M. L. de *Lehrbuch der historisch-kritischen Einleitung in die kanonischen und apokryphischen Bücher des Alten Testaments*. Berlin 1833⁴, 1845⁶.
Wheeler Robinson, H. *The History of Israel*. London 1949⁵.
Whybray, R. N. The Joseph story and pentateuchal criticism. *VT* XVIII (1968) p. 522-528.
Widengren, G. Rev. art of: S. Moscati ed., *L'Antiche Divinità Semitiche. JSS* V (1960) p. 397-410.
Wiener, H. The Conquest Narratives. *JPOS* IX (1929) p. 1-26.
Wildeboer, G. *Het Oude Testament van historisch standpunt toegelicht*. Groningen 1908.
Williamson, R. W. *The social and political Systems of Central Polynesia*. 3 vols. Cambridge 1924.
Willis, J. T. An Anti-Elide Narrative Tradition from a prophetic Circle at the Ramah Sanctuary. *JBL* XC (1971) p. 288-308.
Wilms, F. E. Das jahwistische Bundesbuch in Ex 34. *BZ* XVI (1972) p. 24-53.
Winckler, H. *Geschichte Israels in Einzeldarstellungen*. I, Leipzig 1895; II, Leipzig 1900.
Winnett, F. V. The Arabian Genealogies in the Book of Genesis. *"Translating and Understanding the Old Testament", Essays in Honor of H. G. May*. Nashville 1970, p. 171-196.
Wissmann, H. von. Geographische Grundlagen und Frühzeit der Geschichte Südarabien. *Saeculum* IV (1953) p. 61-114.
— Ursprungsherde und Ausbreitungswege von Pflanzen- und Tierzucht und ihre Abhängigkeit von der Klimageschichte. *Erdkunde* XI (1957) p. 81-94, 175-193.
— Bauer, Nomade und Stadt im islamischen Orient. *Die Welt des Islam und die Gegenwart*. Hrgb. v. R. Paret. Stuttgart 1961, p. 22-63.
— Zur Geschichte und Landeskunde von Alt-Südarabien. *Oesterreichische Akademie der Wissenschaften, Phil.-Hist. Klasse, Sitzungsberichte Nr. 246*, Wien 1964.
— Himyar, Ancient History. *Le Muséon*, LXXVII (1964) p. 429-499.
— Zur Archäologie und antike Geographie von Südarabien. Uitgaven van het Nederlands Historisch-Archeologisch Instituut te Istanbul, nr. XXIV, Istanbul 1968.
Wissmann, H. von und Höfner, Maria Beiträge zur historischen Geographie des vorislamischen Südarabien. *Akkademie der Wissenschaften und Literatur in Mainz. Abhandlungen des Geistes- und Sozialwissenschaftlichen Klasse* 1952/4.
Wittvogel, K. A. *Oriental Despotism. A Comparative Study of Total Power*. New Haven 1967⁷.
Woude, A. S. van der. *Uittocht en Sinaï*. Nijkerk 1960.
Woudstra, M. H. *The Ark of the Covenant from Conquest to Kingship*. Philadelphia 1965.
Wright, G. E. Iron: The Date of its introduction into common use in Palestine. *AJA* XLIII (1939) p. 458-463.

WRIGHT, G. E. Remarks on the Period of the Judges and Early Monarchy. *JBL* LX (1941) p. 27-42.
— The Literary and Historical Problem of Joshua 10 and Judges 1. *JNES* V (1946) p. 105-114.
— The Levites in Deuteronomy. *VT* IV (1954) p. 325-330.
— *Biblical Archaeology.* Philadelphia and London 1957.
— Archaeology and Old Testament Studies. *JBL* LXXVII (1958) p. 39-51.
— The Archaeology of Palestine. *The Bible and the Ancient Near East, Essays in honor of W. F. Albright.* New York 1961, p. 73-112.
— The Provinces of Solomon. (1 Kings 4:7-19). *EI* VIII (1967) p. 58*-68*.
WRIGHT, H. T. *The Administration of Rural Production in an Early Mesopotamian Town.* Papers of the Museum of Anthropology, Univ. of Michigan, No. 38, Ann Arbor 1969.
WÜRTHWEIN, E. *Der 'amm ha'areṣ im Alten Testament.* BWANT 4:17, Stuttgart 1936.
WÜST, F. R. Amphiktyonie, Eidgenossenschaft, Symmachie. *Historia* III (1954/55) p. 129-153.
WÜSTENFELD, F. *Genealogische Tabellen der arabischen Stämme und Familien.* Register. 2 Bde. Göttingen 1852 und 1853.
— *Die Wohnsitze und Wanderungen der Arabischen Stämme.* Abhandlungen der kön. Gesellschaft der Wiss. zu Göttingen, Band XIV, Göttingen 1869.
YADIN, Y. The Fourfold Division of Judah. *BASOR* 163 (1961) p. 6-12.
— The Fifth Season of Excavations at Hazor, 1968-1969. *BA* XXXII (1969) p. 50-71.
YEIVIN, S. The Israelite Settlement in Galilee and the wars with Jabin of Hazor. *Mélanges Bibliques en l'honneur de A. Robert.* Paris 1956, p. 95-104.
— The Origin and Disappearance of the Khab/piru. *Acts of the 25th World Congress of Orientalists.* Moscow 1962, p. 439-441.
— The Age of the Patriarchs. *RSO* XXXVIII (1963) p. 277-302.
ZEIST, W. VAN. *Oecologische aspecten van de neolithische revolutie.* Groningen 1969.
ZIGMOND, M. L. Archaeology and the "Patriarchal Age" of the Old Testament. *Explorations in Cultural Anthropology, Essays in Honour of G. P. Murdock, ed. by W. H. Goodenough.* New York 1964, p. 571-598.
ZIMMERLI, W. *Geschichte und Tradition von Beersheba im alten Testament.* Göttingen 1932.
— Israel im Buche Ezechiel. *VT* VIII (1958) p. 75-90.
— *Ezechiel.* BK XIII, Neukirchen 1969.
ZOBEL, H. J. *Stammesspruch und Geschichte.* BZAW 95, Berlin 1965.
— Die Stammessprüche des Mose-Segens. *Klio* XLVI (1965) p. 83-92.
— Ursprung und Verwurzelung des Erwählungsglaubens Israels. *ThLZ* XCIII (1968) p. 1-11.

INDICES

Names and Subjects

Biblical Citations